The Integration of Language and Society

EXPLORATIONS IN LINGUISTIC TYPOLOGY

GENERAL EDITORS: Alexandra Y. Aikhenvald and R. M. W. Dixon
Centre for Indigenous Health Equity Research, Central Queensland University

This series focuses on aspects of language that are of current theoretical interest and for which there has not previously or recently been any full-scale cross-linguistic study. Its books are for typologists, fieldworkers, and theory developers, and designed for use in advanced seminars and courses.

PUBLISHED

1 Adjective Classes
edited by R. M. W. Dixon and Alexandra Y. Aikhenvald

2 Serial Verb Constructions
edited by Alexandra Y. Aikhenvald and R. M. W. Dixon

3 Complementation
edited by R. M. W. Dixon and Alexandra Y. Aikhenvald

4 Grammars in Contact
edited by Alexandra Y. Aikhenvald and R. M. W. Dixon

5 The Semantics of Clause Linking
edited by R. M. W. Dixon and Alexandra Y. Aikhenvald

6 Possession and Ownership
edited by Alexandra Y. Aikhenvald and R. M. W. Dixon

7 The Grammar of Knowledge
edited by Alexandra Y. Aikhenvald and R. M. W. Dixon

8 Commands
edited by Alexandra Y. Aikhenvald and R. M. W. Dixon

9 Genders and Classifiers
edited by Alexandra Y. Aikhenvald and Elena I. Mihas

10 Phonological Word and Grammatical Word
edited by Alexandra Y. Aikhenvald, R. M. W. Dixon,
and Nathan M. White

11 The Integration of Language and Society
edited by Alexandra Y. Aikhenvald, R. M. W. Dixon,
and Nerida Jarkey

PUBLISHED IN ASSOCIATION WITH THE SERIES
Areal Diffusion and Genetic Inheritance
Problems in Comparative Linguistics
edited by Alexandra Y. Aikhenvald and R. M. W. Dixon

The Integration of Language and Society

A Cross-Linguistic Typology

Edited by

ALEXANDRA Y. AIKHENVALD,
R. M. W. DIXON, AND NERIDA JARKEY

OXFORD
UNIVERSITY PRESS

OXFORD
UNIVERSITY PRESS

Great Clarendon Street, Oxford, OX2 6DP,
United Kingdom

Oxford University Press is a department of the University of Oxford.
It furthers the University's objective of excellence in research, scholarship,
and education by publishing worldwide. Oxford is a registered trade mark of
Oxford University Press in the UK and in certain other countries

First Edition published in 2021

Impression: 1

Published in the United States of America by Oxford University Press
198 Madison Avenue, New York, NY 10016, United States of America

British Library Cataloguing in Publication Data
Data available

Library of Congress Control Number: 2021939024

ISBN 978–0–19–284592–4

DOI: 10.1093/oso/9780192845924.001.0001

Printed and bound in the UK by
TJ Books Limited

Contents

Preface

Each language bears an imprint of the society that speaks it—speakers' relationships to each other, their beliefs and ways of viewing the world, and other facets of their social environment, alongside speakers' habitat, subsistence, and physical environment. A grammar of each language will relate to—and be integrated with—the meanings and the choices which reflect societal practices. Integration of language and society is what this endeavour is about.

The volume starts with a typological introduction summarizing the main issues relevant to the integration of language and society, with special focus on grammatical phenomena. These include honorific forms, genders and classifiers, possession, evidentiality, comparative constructions, and demonstrative systems. The introduction is followed by revised versions of papers presented at the International Workshop 'The Integration of Language and Society' organized by the editors and held at the Language and Culture Research Centre, James Cook University, 21–23 August 2019 (based on the Australian Research Council Discovery Project, 'The Integration of Language of Society', with the editors as Chief Investigators and Anne Storch and Maarten Mous as Partner Investigators). An earlier version of Chapter 1 was circulated to the contributors, with a list of issues to be addressed, so as to ensure that the studies of individual languages within this volume were cast in terms of a common set of parameters. This is the eleventh monograph in the series *Explorations in Linguistic Typology*, devoted to volumes from International Workshops organized by the former Language and Culture Research Centre and its predecessor.

The Workshop and subsequent discussions between the editors and the authors were intellectually stimulating, with cross-fertilization of ideas, new synergies, and scholarly debate. Each author has undertaken intensive fieldwork and has firsthand in-depth knowledge of the language(s) they discuss in their chapter, in addition to experience of working on linguistic typology, historical and comparative linguistics, and language contact and areal diffusion. The analysis is uniformly cast in terms of basic linguistic theory—the cumulative typological framework which provides the foundation for sound empirically-based descriptive and analytic works. We avoid formalisms (which provide restatements rather than explanations, and come and go with such frequency that any statement made in terms of them is likely to soon become inaccessible).

It is our hope that this volume will contribute to creating a consolidated conceptual and analytic framework, for further work on how grammar reflects the world around us and the features of the societies in which we live. Our aim is to outline, and explain, the parameters of such integration, opening further perspectives on how languages work and why they are the way they are.

We are grateful to all the participants in the Workshop and colleagues who took part in the discussion, providing feedback on presentations, particularly Firew Girma Worku, and Rosita Henry. Many thanks to Felix Ameka for his fascinating oral contribution. We owe a special debt of gratitude to David Ellis, for helping us organize the Workshop in a most efficient manner. Brigitta Flick's and Jolene Overall's support and editorial assistance in preparing the volume were invaluable.

The Workshop was made possible through the Australian Research Council Discovery Project 'The integration of language and society' (to Aikhenvald, Dixon, and Jarkey). We gratefully acknowledge financial assistance from the Division of Research and Innovation at James Cook University, and wish to express our appreciation to Professor Andrew Krockenberger for opening the Workshop and his personal support for linguistics.

Last but not least, we would like to extend our thanks to Julia Steer and Victoria Sunter at Oxford University Press, for their efficiency and ongoing support.

Notes on the contributors

ALEXANDRA Y. AIKHENVALD is Adjunct Professor at the Centre for Indigenous Health and Equity Research at Central Queensland University, Australian Laureate Fellow, and Foundation Director of the Language and Culture Research Centre at James Cook University. She is a major authority on languages of the Arawak family, from northern Amazonia, and has written grammars of *Bare* (1995) and *Warekena* (1998), plus *A grammar of Tariana, from Northwest Amazonia* (CUP, 2003), and *The Manambu language of East Sepik, Papua New Guinea* (OUP, 2008) in addition to essays on various typological and areal topics. She is the editor of *The Oxford handbook of evidentiality* (OUP, 2018) and co-editor, with R. M. W. Dixon, of *The Cambridge handbook of linguistic typology* (CUP, 2017). Her other major publications include *Classifiers: A typology of noun categorization devices* (OUP, 2000), *Evidentiality* (OUP, 2004), *Imperatives and commands* (OUP, 2010), *Languages of the Amazon* (OUP, 2012), *The art of grammar* (OUP, 2014), *How gender shapes the world* (OUP, 2016), *Serial verbs* (OUP, 2018), and *A guide to genders and classifiers* (OUP, forthcoming). *Address*: CQ University, 42-52 Abbott Street & Shields Street, Cairns, N Qld 4870, a.y.aikhenvald@live.com, nyamamayratakw@gmail.com, a.aikhenvald@cqu.edu.au

LUCA CIUCCI is Postdoctoral Research Fellow at the Language and Culture Research Centre at James Cook University. In 2007, he began his research on the Zamucoan languages (Ayoreo, Chamacoco, and †Old Zamuco). During his PhD years, he discovered the earliest grammar of Ecuadorian Quechua, published in 2011. In 2013, he completed his PhD at *Scuola Normale Superiore* in Pisa. His monograph *Inflectional morphology in the Zamucoan languages* (CEADUC, 2016) is considered the most detailed morphological description of a small language cluster from South America. His research activities include the grammatical description of Ayoreo and Chamacoco, the reconstruction of Proto-Zamucoan, and the analysis of the historical data available for †Old Zamuco. In 2017, he began documenting Chiquitano (also known as Bésɨro), an isolate. He is particularly interested in language contact between Chiquitano and the surrounding languages (such as Zamucoan), and in the comparison between the different Chiquitano varieties spoken nowadays plus the historical documents available on this language. *Address*: Language and Culture Research Centre, James Cook University, PO Box 6811, Cairns, N Qld 4780, Australia; *e-mail*: luca.ciucci@jcu.edu.au

R. M. W. DIXON is Adjunct Professor at the Centre for Indigenous Health and Equity Research at Central Queensland University Foundation Deputy Director of the Language and Culture Research Centre at James Cook University. He has published grammars of a number of Australian languages (including Dyirbal and Yidiñ), in addition to *Edible gender, mother-in-law style, and other grammatical wonders* (OUP, 2015, paperback 2020), *A grammar of Boumaa Fijian* (University of Chicago Press, 1988), *The Jarawara language of southern Amazonia* (OUP, 2004, paperback 2011), *A semantic approach to English grammar* (OUP, 2005), *Making new words: Morphological derivation in English* (OUP, 2014), and *The unmasking of English dictionaries* (Cambridge University Press, 2018). His works on typological theory include *Where have all the adjectives gone? And other essays in semantics and syntax* (Mouton, 1982), and *Ergativity* (Cambridge University Press, 1994). *The rise and fall of languages* (Cambridge University Press, 1997) expounded a punctuated equilibrium model for language development; this is the basis for his detailed case study *Australian languages: Their nature and development* (Cambridge University Press, 2002). He is also the author of the three seminal volume work *Basic linguistic theory* (OUP, 2010–12) and of an academic autobiography *I am a linguist* (Brill, 2011). His controversial study *Are some languages better than others?* was published by OUP in 2016 (paperback 2018). His *Australia's original languages: An introduction*, a volume aimed at the general public, was published by Allen and Unwin (Sydney) in 2019. *Address*: CQ University, 42-52 Abbott Street & Shields Street, Cairns, N Qld 4870, Australia; *e-mail*: r.m.w.dixon@outlook.com

NERIDA JARKEY is Honorary Associate Professor in Japanese Studies at the University of Sydney. She has a particular interest in the semantics of grammar, with a focus on transitivity and on multi-verb constructions in Japanese and White Hmong. She is the author of *Serial verbs in White Hmong* (Brill's Studies in Language, Cognition and Culture, 2015). Nerida also investigates how speakers use grammatical elements not only to convey propositional and interpersonal meanings but also to construct socio-cultural meanings and identities. *Address*: School of Languages and Cultures (A18), University of Sydney, NSW, 2006, Australia; *e-mail*: nerida.jarkey@sydney.edu.au

MAARTEN MOUS is Professor of African Linguistics at Leiden University. His main interests are the description of Cushitic and Bantu languages, and language contact. His publications include *A grammar of Iraqw* and *The making of a mixed language: The case of Maʾa/Mbugu*. He has done fieldwork and published on various aspects of Iraqw, Alagwa, Konso, Yaaku (all Cushitic), Maʾa/Mbugu, Mbugwe, Chathu (Pare), Nen (all Bantu), and Seereer (Atlantic). *Address*: Leiden University Centre for Linguistics, PO Box 9515, 2300 RA Leiden, the Netherlands; *e-mail*: m.mous@hum.leidenuniv.nl

DINEKE SCHOKKIN is a Lecturer in Linguistics at the University of Canterbury, Christchurch. She received her PhD in 2014 from James Cook University. Her thesis, titled *A grammar of Paluai: The language of Baluan Island, Papua New Guinea*, was published in 2020 with De Gruyter Mouton. Between 2014 and 2019, she worked on the Papuan language Idi, spoken in southern Papua New Guinea, as a research fellow in the ARC Laureate project *The Wellsprings of Linguistic Diversity*, based at the Australian National University. Her main research interests include the ways in which methodologies from fields such as quantitative sociolinguistics can contribute to grammatical descriptions, and conversely, how understudied languages and socio-cultural contexts can advance theoretical knowledge in these fields. She is also interested in the relation between different types of multilingualism and contact-induced grammatical change, and in New Guinea as a linguistic area more generally. *Address*: Department of Linguistics, University of Canterbury, Private Bag 4800, Christchurch 8041, New Zealand; *email*: dineke.schokkin@canterbury.ac.nz

ANNE STORCH is Professor of African Linguistics at the University of Cologne. Her principal research has been on the various languages of Nigeria (including Jukun and Maaka), on the Atlantic language region, and on Western Nilotic (Southern Sudan and Uganda). Her work combines contributions on cultural and social contexts of languages, the semiotics of linguistic practices, epistemes and ontologies of colonial linguistics, as well as linguistic description. She has contributed to the analysis of registers and choices, language as social practice, ways of speaking and complex repertoires. Presently, she is interested in epistemic language, metalinguistics, noise and silence, as well as language use in settings of inequality, such as tourism. Her publications include *Secret manipulations* (Oxford University Press, New York 2011), *A Grammar of Luwo* (John Benjamins, Amsterdam 2014), and several other volumes. She has worked on language and ruination in East African tourism with Angelika Mietzner (*Language and tourism in East Africa*, Channel View Publications, Bristol 2021), on linguistics and its silences in a neocolonial world with Ingo H. Warnke (*Sansibarzone*, De Gruyter, Bielefeld 2020), and on the language of sex and transgression with Nico Nassenstein (*Metasex*, John

Benjamins, Amsterdam 2020). In 2017, she received the prestigious Leibniz Award, for excellence in linguistics. *Address*: Institut für Afrikanistik, Universität zu Köln, Meister-Ekkehart Str-7, D-50923 Cologne, Germany; *e-mail*: a.storch@uni-koeln.de

PEMA WANGDI is a PhD student at the Language and Culture Research Centre, James Cook University. He is working on a comprehensive grammar of Brokpa, a transhumant language of Bhutan. He received a Graduate Diploma and MA in Linguistics from Australian National University in 2003 and 2005 respectively. He worked for Dzongkha Development a Commission (National Language Commission of Bhutan), producing bilingual dictionaries in Dzongkha and English. He carried out parts-of-speech tagging and morphological segmentation in Dzongkha, used for writing dictionaries and developing Dzongkha Natural Language Processing systems. He has taught International Baccalaureate courses in language and literature at Institut Le Rosey, Switzerland, from 2009 to 2013. His research interests include studying indigenous languages and culture and their interconnection. *Address*: Language and Culture Research Centre, James Cook University, PO Box 6811, Cairns, N Qld 4780, Australia; *e-mail*: permondi@gmail.com

STEPHEN WATTERS earned a PhD in linguistics from Rice University in 2018. His doctoral research resulted in a grammar of spoken Dzongkha with a focus on interactive conversational data as the corpus of study. He has had various research and lectureship positions in connection with his work in the Himalayas where he has spent a large portion of his life. He currently serves as Research Director for SIL International, a role that entails, broadly speaking, investigating the relationship between language and human flourishing. He is a Scholar in the Pike Center for Integrative Scholarship, Visiting Scholar at the Institute for Studies of Religion, Baylor University, and has an adjunct research position with the Language and Culture Research Centre, James Cook University. He has broad interests in the communities of the Himalayas, including grammatical descriptions, and studies in the intersection of language and human flourishing. *Address*: Institute for Studies of Religion, Baylor University, One Bear Place #97236, Waco, TX 76798; *e-mail*: steve_watters@sil.org

KATARZYNA (KASIA) IZABELA WOJTYLAK is currently an Assistant Professor at the University of Warsaw. Her PhD dissertation entitled 'Grammar of Muri' (2017, published with Brill 2020) stems from her immense fieldwork in Colombian Amazon between 2010 and 2017. In her work, Kasia focuses on languages of the Caquetá-Putumayo River Basin, including Witotoan and Boran languages. She is also interested in research into zone of highest concentrations of biodiversity, and linguistic and cultural diversity. Kasia's main interests include language documentation, anthropological linguistics, typology, and language contact. *Address*: Center for Research and Practice in Cultural Continuity, Faculty of 'Artes liberales', University of Warsaw, Dobra 72, 00-312 Warsaw, Poland; *e-mail*: katarzyna.wojtylak@jcu. edu.au; k.wojtylak@al.edu.pl

Abbreviations

♀	female speech
♂	male speech
1	1st person
2	2nd person
3	3rd person
A	transitive subject
ABL	ablative
ABS	absolutive
ACC	accusative
ADV	adverb, adverbializer (Chapter 2)
AF	argument form
AFF	affix
AHON	addressee honorific
ALL	allative
ANIM	animate
ANT	anterior
ANTIPASS	antipassive
APPLIC	applicative
APPR	apprehensive
ART	article
ATTRIB	attributive
AUG	augmentative
AUX	auxiliary
BGND	background
CAUS	causative
CL	classifier
CL:ABSTR	classifier for abstract entities
CL.POSS	close possession
COLL	collective
COLLOQ	colloquial
COMP	complementizer
COMPAR	comparative
COMPL	completive
CON	construct
COND	conditional
COP	copula

CORE	core case (flags S, A, and O)
CSEC	consecutive
DAT	dative
DECL	declarative
DEF	definite
DEM	demonstrative
DEM.ANIM	animate deminstrative
DEM.INAN	inanimate demonstrative
DEP	dependent
DESID	desiderative
DIM	diminutive
DIR	directional
DIST	distal
DIST. POSS	distant possession
DISTR	distributive
DM	discourse marker
DR	derivational
du, DU	dual
DUR	durative
EGO	egophoric
EGR	egressive
EMPH	emphasis
EPSTM	epistemic
ERG	ergative
EXC	exclusive
EXIST	existential (copula)
EXO	exophoric
EXPEC	expectative
FEM, F, f	feminine
FOC	focus
fs	female speaker
FUT	future
GEN	genitive
GEN.ADJ	generic adjective
GERUND	gerund (no abbreviation)
GF	generic form
HITH	hither
HON	honorific
HUM	humble; humilific
IF	indeterminate form
IMP	imperative
IMPER	imperfect
IMPERS	impersonal

IMPERV	imperfective
INAN	inanimate
INC	inclusive
INCH	inchoative
INDEF	indefinite
INFIN	infinitive
INST	instrumental
INT	intentional
INT	intermediate
INTENS	intensifier
INTER	interrogative
INTR	intransitive, intransitive verbalizer (Chapter 5)
INV	inverse
LINK	linker
LOC	locative
LOC.NOM	locative nominalization
M/F	epicene
MASC, M, m	masculine
MOD	modal
MS	male speaker
NCL	noun class
NCL ANIM	animate noun class
NEG	negation
NEUT, N, n	neuter
nf, NF	nonfeminine
NOM	nominative
NOM.FUT	nominal future
NOM.PAST	nominal past
NOMPRT	nominal particle
NOMZ	nominalizer
NP	noun phrase
NPAST	non-past
nsg, NSG	non-singular
NUM.CL	numeral classifier
O	transitive object
OBJ	object, object case
P	plural gender
PART	particle
PAST	past (no abbreviation)
PAUS	pausal form
PCLF	possessive classifier
PEJ	pejorative
PERV	perfective

PF	predicative form
pl, PL	plural
PN	pronoun
POL	polite
POSS	possessive
POSTP	postposition
PRED	predicative
PRES	present
PRES.NONVIS	present nonvisual
PRES.VIS	present visual
PRES.VIS.INTER	present visual interrogative
PROG	progressive
PROX	proximal
PURP	purposive
Q	question particle
QUOT	quotative
R	possessor
REAL	realis
REC	recent
REC.P.ASSUM	recent past assumed
REC.P.NONVIS	recent past non-visual
REC.P.VIS	recent past visual
REC. P.VIS.INTER	recent past visual interrogative
RECIP	reciprocal
REDUP	reduplicated
REF	referential
REFL	reflexive
REL	relative, relativizer
REM	remote
REM.P.ASSUM	remote past assumed
REC.P.NONVIS	recent past non-visual
REM.P.NONVIS	remote past nonvisual
REM.P.REP	remote past reported
REM.P.VIS	remote past visual
REP	reported
RESP	respectful
RETR	retrospective
RMSPT	remote past
S	intransitive subject
S/A.TOP	topical subject
S$_a$	'active' S, marked like A
SEQ	sequential
SEQ:SS	sequential same subject

sg, SG	singular
S$_o$	'stative' S, marked like O
STAT	stative
SUB	subjunctive
SUPL	suppletive
TAM	tense-aspect-mood
THEM	thematic marker
TITLE	title (no abbreviation)
TOP	topic
TOP.ADV	topic advancing voice
TOP.NON.A/S	topical non-subject case
TR	transitive
V	verb
VERT	vertical
VIS	visual

1

The integration of language and society

A cross-linguistic perspective

Alexandra Y. Aikhenvald, R. M. W. Dixon, and Nerida Jarkey

1 The integration of language and society: Theoretical framework

There are several approaches to how language can be studied. One prevalent view is that language is a cognitive mechanism, whose nature can be uncovered through deductive hypotheses concerning various structural features. Other approaches link language to the world within which it is used. Some linguists espouse a relativism, in either of two directions.

A strong version of the Sapir-Whorf hypothesis suggests that the grammatical and lexical structure of a language determines the way in which its speakers view the world around them, their conceptualizations and categorizations. Approaching matters from the opposite direction, an alternative view is that it is the world which is 'the given', with the nature of the reality in which a language is spoken determining its grammatical categories and lexical contrasts.[1]

We pursue a different agenda:

- **Starting point.** Language is a facet of human behaviour. It only has meaning and significance with respect to the society in which it is used. Language and society are mutually cross-defining as each reflects the other. In Dixon's (2014a: 46) words, 'language is a vital cultural tool... Its structure reflects the speakers' life-style, social organisation, way of viewing the world, and also their environment'.

---

[1] For overviews of Sapir-Whorf and varied approaches to the linguistic relativity hypothesis see Lucy (1992a,b, 1996), Enfield (2000), Bickel (2000), Brown (1976), Boroditsky (2003), additional critique in Deutscher (2010), Carroll (1963), Salzmann (2004), and papers in Gumperz and Levinson (1996), Mathiot (1979), to name but a few.

Alexandra Y. Aikhenvald, R. M. W. Dixon, and Nerida Jarkey, *The integration of language and society: A cross-linguistic perspective*. In: *The Integration of Language and Society: A Cross-Linguistic Typology*. Edited by: Alexandra Y. Aikhenvald, R. M. W. Dixon, and Nerida Jarkey, Oxford University Press. © Alexandra Y. Aikhenvald, R. M. W. Dixon, and Nerida Jarkey 2021. DOI: 10.1093/oso/9780192845924.003.0001

- **Initial observations.**
  (a) There are some pervasive similarities of social behaviour and ways of living across every group of people around the world.
  (b) All languages share certain recurrent grammatical and semantic characteristics (word classes, commands and questions, possession, negation, distinct verbs for perception, among others).

- **The challenge.** There are also
  (i) significant social and life-style differences between different groups; and
  (ii) differences in many particular features of language structure.

What makes a language the way it is? A combination of factors are at play.

Firstly, each language has a genetic history. In each language, certain features and forms are inherited from the ancestral proto-language; others may have been lost. Having a shared ancestor may explain why related languages develop in similar ways, along the lines of Sapir's 'parallelism in drift' (1921: 171–2).

Secondly, contact between speakers of adjacent languages may result in sharing forms, categories, and ways of saying things. A language may be partly shaped by speakers' interaction with their neighbours. And some categories and concepts are more prone to being spread through contact than others.

Thirdly, a language is likely to bear an imprint of its speakers' habitat and physical environment, their relationships to one another, and their beliefs and ways of viewing the world, as integral components of their social environment. These factors are the primary matter of concern within this volume. We focus on the mutual co-dependence between the grammar of a language and the non-linguistic parameters of the society where it is spoken.

We begin with a hypothesis.

HYPOTHESIS. Language and society are closely integrated and mutually supportive (rather than one being dependent on the other). An unusual (non-universal) facet of a language may relate to a specific trait of social organization, or life-style, etc., evidenced among the society of language users.

Our AIMS are:

I.   On the basis of detailed individual studies, to put forward inductive generalizations concerning recurrent correlations underlying the congruence, or mutual integration, of language and society, and to identify dependencies between the established correlations.

II. To put forward predictions concerning
   (i) which linguistic features are likely to be associated with a given assemblage of societal values, and also which cultural and societal characteristics are likely to co-occur with particular linguistic elements:[2]
   (ii) how these linguistic features may change if the society changes.

The recurrent correlations between the language and societal practices will help explain

(a) the patterns of language change which accompany societal changes, and
(b) the ways in which contact between societies may affect the languages spoken by their members. In this way, we expect the correlations to have a predictive power.

We now turn to the empirical basis for our endeavour.

2 The empirical basis: Grammar versus lexicon

Meaning in language is essentially coded through two independent but interlocking parts—grammar and lexicon. Grammar involves sets of systems with limited choices—tenses, aspects, cases, genders, and so on. A closed grammatical system imposes restricted options on the speaker. If a language has two grammatical genders—say, feminine and masculine—all entities have to be categorized as one or the other. This is in contrast to lexicon where the choices are potentially open: any language will have a large set of words referring to males, females, and perhaps other natural and social genders (see Aikhenvald 2015a: 4–5, 2016: 3–5, Dixon 2010a: 47–54, 2016: 77, for further discussion). The third component of language is phonology, dealing with the

---

[2] In using the term 'culture' we recognize the potential pitfalls of attempting to make generalizations about norms of social behaviour, or shared beliefs, values, and practices in any human society. Rather, we agree with Enfield (2004a: 17) that cultural generalizations can be thought of as 'descriptions of ideas about social identities, and about what is collectively assumed to be "normal" – or, more precisely, what is assumed to be assumed to be normal'. In this sense, the notion of culture is anchored in shared symbolism, rather than in the actual beliefs, values, and practices of all those who identify as members of a particular group. Furthermore, along with Anne Storch (Chapter 11), we recognize that the 'mooring' provided by this shared notion of normality is far from a stable one, and that 'the fragility and precariousness of the camp and resting place' is a norm itself, though often unrecognized.

ways in which lexical and grammatical means are realized in communication. This has a tangential role in relation to our current investigation (see §4).

In the words of Boas (1938: 132–3), grammar 'determines those aspects of each experience that *must* be expressed…To give an example: while for us definiteness, number, and time are obligatory aspects, we find in another language location near the speaker or somewhere else, source of information—whether seen, heard, or inferred—as obligatory aspects'. And, consequently, 'the form of our grammar compels us to select a few traits of the thought we wish to express and suppresses many other aspects which the speaker has in mind' (Boas 1942: 182).[3]

Our main question is: Which of these limited linguistic features interact with societal traits and conventions, and how—if at all—can one be framed by the other? That is, how are the categories and distinctions made within the limited resources of the grammatical system integrated with the society of those who speak it?

In considering the relationship between language and society, the potentially open-ended resource of the lexicon is the more common, and more obvious, focus of attention. The lexicon of each language will indeed bear an imprint of the habitual activities and the beliefs of its speakers. Cattle-herding groups in East Africa are well-known for their elaborate categorization of different kinds of cattle based on their distinctive colours. As Evans-Pritchard (1940: 41) put it, 'linguistic profusion in particular departments of life is one of the signs by which one quickly judges the direction and strength of a people's interest'…as can be seen in the 'volume and variety of the Nuer cattle vocabulary'. Similarly, the Mursi, a Surmic-speaking group of south-western Ethiopia, have no colour terms other than those which correspond to the terms used for the various colours of their cattle (Turton 1980). A community with weaving as a traditional activity will have numerous specific terms for warp, weft, ribbing, twill, selvage, and the like.

The character of any society correlates with the specificities of its non-basic vocabulary. When, in Indigenous Australia, anyone came to another group's campsite, they would stop just outside, waiting to be invited in. So, in Dyirbal, for instance, there is an appropriate verb *yilga-l* 'almost come to a place, but not quite reach it'.

---

[3] This is reminiscent of Slobin's reformulation of a similar principle as 'thinking for speaking', whereby 'even within a single language grammar provides a set of options for schematising experience for the purposes of verbal expression. Any utterance is multiply determined by what I have seen or experienced, my communicative purpose in telling you about it, and the distinctions that are embodied in my grammar' (Slobin 1996: 75).

A large community whose members are trained to compete and vie for superiority, be it in sports, head-hunting, or any social activities, would be expected to have an array of lexemes for 'compete', 'win', or 'lose'. As Dixon (2008: 814) put it, 'small tribes with an egalitarian social system and item-for-item trade do not generally indulge in competition; they often lack words for "compete", "win", "lose" and "beat" (as in a game)'. In Dixon's (2016: 93) words, 'in the traditional culture of Dyirbal speakers, from North Queensland, and of the Jarawara, from southern Amazonia [...], there was no factor of competitiveness. The vocabularies include no words which could render "compete", "win", "lose", "victory", or "victor"'. The same applies to Yalaku, spoken by just over 300 people in the hilly area off the Sepik river in Papua New Guinea (Aikhenvald 2018c).

Such gaps in the lexicon may have consequences for the grammar. Many languages have dedicated comparative constructions, such as *Mary is bigger than Jean*. Languages spoken within small tribal societies with no institutionalized ideas of competition and hardly any lexemes meaning 'win' or 'lose (in a competition)' often have few if any such comparative constructions in their grammar. Instead, speakers will just juxtapose opposite statements, saying *Mary is big, Jean is small*.

Erstwhile egalitarian groups with no tradition of competing inevitably come in contact with larger societies, where 'winning', 'losing', and competition are a key to success. To render the notion of 'win', or 'surpass'—part and parcel of the mainstream Papua New Guinea society—the Yalaku now employ the loan verb *winim* 'surpass, get ahead of someone', from Tok Pisin, the lingua franca of the country. The concept, alien to the Yalaku previously, is now expressed with a foreign term. This is what we find in a number of other essentially egalitarian societies with no fixed hierarchical relations. In contrast, the existence of traditional competitive practices among the Brokpa of Bhutan correlates with the presence of special comparative and superlative constructions (§3 of Chapter 4). A more complex situation has been documented for the Chamacoco and the Ayoreo (§7 of Chapter 8).

It would, of course, be dangerous and simplistic to expect a one-to-one correlation between the idea of competitiveness and the presence of a comparative construction in a language. Or between the traditional lack of strict societal hierarchy and avoidance of direct commands, accompanied by the absence of a specialized imperative form. As for most linguistic generalizations, we expect to uncover tendencies rather than strict rules. Such tendencies may be indicative of current trends. Or they may be indicative of the attitudes and societal practices of the past. As Ameka (2004: 11) notes, 'from an ethnosyntactic point of view, today's grammatical constructions may reflect cultural preoccupations of yesterday'. Investigating the integration of language and society may contribute to a historical study of both, and of the ways in which modern developments may affect language use.[4]

Throughout this volume, we take account of the features of lexicon, inasmuch as they are reflected in the grammar and relevant to it. Beyond these, we will not dwell on the immense and potentially limitless body of lexical correlates of societal structures and practices.[5]

Correlations between individual linguistic categories, cultural values, and social parameters have been the focus of a large body of work. Relevant studies include Enfield's analysis of 'ethnosyntax', which begins (2004a: 3):

'Encoded in the semantics of grammar we find cultural values and ideas, we find clues about social structures which speakers maintain, we find evidence, both historically and otherwise, of the social organisation of speech communities'.[6]

---

[4] The present framework does not claim the necessary presence of any universal causal relationship between the obligatory character of any grammatical feature, and a societal and cultural trait which may be associated with this. Difficulties in proving mutual co-dependence between grammatical phenomena and cultural or cognitive traits have been specifically addressed by Lucy (1996). The size of the phonemic inventory was suggested as a correlate of community's isolation and its size (Trudgill 2004). Community size, degree of contact or isolation, and denseness or looseness of social networks have been claimed to influence the degree of 'complexity' of languages spoken (Trudgill 2009, 2011). In view of the difficulty in defining the universally applicable scale of 'complexity' at every level of linguistic structure, we refrain from addressing this tangled issue. Unjustified ideas have been expressed about how linguistic minorities—whose languages differ from the mainstream European lects—may have a different mentality which would explain 'why' their languages are so different from what a speaker of English would expect. One finds assertions about the 'passive' nature of ergative languages (more on those in Dixon 1994: 214–5), or a suggestion that people who live in damp areas tend to 'select sounds requiring minimal lip opening' (Brosnahan 1961: 19; further examples in Aikhenvald 2004: 356–7, 2000: 345, and Lucy 1996: 48). We eschew such questionable attempts, and will make no further mention of these.

[5] Wierzbicka (1997 and later work) has attempted to describe different cultures in terms of what she calls 'key concepts' and 'cultural scripts'. This approach differs significantly from the one taken here. Wierzbicka attempts to identify words and concepts that capture elements of the essence of a culture, and in which difference from other cultures can be seen to reside (see also Aitchison 1999 and Bulygina and Shmelev 1997). We seek to identify, in a systematic way, points of integration between the grammar of languages and the societies in which they are spoken. These integration points do, indeed, provide significant insights into important aspects of each society concerned, but none of them are proposed as a 'key' to understanding any one of those societies as a whole.

[6] Grammatical features and their social and cultural correlates were discussed by Bickel (1999, 2001) with regard to deixis (with Burenhult 2008 adding a further topographic dimension); by Trudgill (2011) with regard to the presence of unusual or exotic features; by Heine (1997) with regard to possession, comparison, and spatial orientation; by Ameka (2004), for triadic communication and logophoric practices, by Bauman and Briggs (1990) for poetic genres, and by Enfield (2014) for the evolution of meaning.

The main point of the present endeavour is the 'integration' approach. We aim at systematically investigating the associations and mutual dependencies of specific facets of language with particular traits of society—that is, the ways in which they are integrated together.

Grammatical features which recur in all languages we know of can be considered universal, and presumably necessary, components of human language (see Dixon 2016: 47–73, for a summary). Every language will have a way of expressing negation or possession, saying who did what to whom, and what has what properties. In every language one can make a statement, ask a question, or issue a command or a request. Just some languages have several ways of expressing commands depending on who the speaker is or who they are addressing—something that will reflect social organization and social hierarchies. The non-universal means of expressing seemingly universal concepts alert us to the potential focal points of how language and society fit together. We now turn to the linguistic parameters which are demonstrably sensitive to societal traits.

3 Linguistic parameters demonstrably sensitive to societal traits

Five groups of linguistic parameters and corresponding categories show strong correlations and integration with non-linguistic societal traits. These are as follows:

1. Reference classification: The composition and use of genders and classifiers—§3.1
2. Types of possession—§3.2
3. Directing and addressing—§3.3
4. Information source, transmission of information, and interaction patterns—§3.4
5. Special speech styles—§3.5.

The focal clusters of the following non-linguistic traits can be shown to be integrated with these linguistic features:

A. Relations within a community, social hierarchies, and kinship categorization
B. Social constraints (taboo and avoidance)
C. Principles of interaction, and attitudes to information and its sources
D. Beliefs, religion, spirits, and dreams

E. Means of subsistence and physical environment
F. Language awareness, language engineering, and sensitivity to societal changes.

Parameters A–D are interrelated, and may be hard to disentangle. Parameter E may stand apart from all these. In a similar vein, parameter F may be separate from all of A–E.

Speakers may be aware of how a particular category correlates with their society and practices, and be prepared to talk about it and explain the social underpinnings of a linguistic feature, in the form of metalinguistic discourse. Grammatical categories and meanings can be amenable to conscious language engineering, so as to adjust them to what speakers, or those in positions of power over them, perceive, and impose, as societal requirements.

Grammatical categories which show a degree of integration with the society and the uses of these categories may change if the social conditions change. Thus, if the traditional societal practices fall into disuse, the linguistic category may no longer remain in place, or may undergo obsolescence and be gradually forgotten (some of the issues of 'disintegration' between language and society are addressed in §4 of Chapter 6, for the Tariana, and in §4 of Chapter 7, for the Murui, both from north-west Amazonia). These points, subsumed under F, are different from A–E: they allow us to test a correlation between a linguistic feature and a societal practice (or a feature of the physical environment) in historical perspective (and even at a shallow time depth spanning two or three generations).

Demonstrable associations between linguistic features and non-linguistic parameters will be referred to as 'integration points'. We now turn to illustrations of these.

3.1 Reference classification: composition and use of genders and classifiers

Reference classification relates to gender, noun classes, and classifiers of various kinds. We distinguish numeral classifiers, noun classifiers, verbal classifiers, locative, and deictic classifiers (following the typological parameters in Aikhenvald 2000 and 2017). Genders and classifiers are known to mirror social attitudes and hierarchies, social organization, physical environment, and means of subsistence (a critical overview and references are in Aikhenvald

2000, 2016, 2017; see also Denny 1979, Bradley 2001, and Bisang 2017, among others, and Aikhenvald 2021 on the semantic functions of classifiers with specific meanings). They also reflect language awareness, and can be prone to language engineering and reflect social changes.

A. Relations within a community, social hierarchies, and kinship categorization. The composition of a gender or of a noun class may reflect kinship categorization and social hierarchies. Sets of specific classifiers in Korean and many South-east Asian languages (Adams 1989, 1992; Lee 2014) reflect kinship relationships. So do noun classifiers for humans in Jacaltec and a few other Mayan languages (Craig 1986: 266–7; Aikhenvald 2000: 284–5, 342–3). In Setswana (Bantu), all human beings and many names of peoples belong to the 'human' noun class (termed 1/2 in the Bantuist tradition). Ethnonyms which refer to groups perceived as inferior—such as the Chinese or the Bushmen— belong to Class 5/6 which comprises substances, such as dirt or clay, and also abstract nouns (including foreign institutions: Anderson and Janson 1997: 34–5; Joseph Tsonope, p.c.).

Specialized noun classifiers are used for respected relatives and humans of higher status (e.g. monks) in many Austroasiatic languages, including Vietnamese (see Adams 1989: 59–61). Fulfulde, a West Atlantic language, has a special noun class for cattle and the sun (Breedveld 1995). Manipulation of noun classes is a major means of expressing honorific and humiliative meanings in Ichibemba, a Bantu language (Lüpke and Storch 2013: 99–101).

B. Social constraints (taboo and avoidance). Genders, noun classifiers, and classifiers of most types reflect social constraints. Gender choice may reflect power relations within a society. Manambu has two genders—masculine and feminine. Any non-human can be assigned to either gender, with masculine objects perceived as being longer, bigger, and more socially important than feminine ones. A traditional story will be referred to as masculine, and a less important tale as feminine (see also Ciucci 2019, and §3 of Chapter 8, on how societal roles and relationships correlate with gender choice in Ayoreo and reflect the roles of personified non-humans). The expression of respect in stratified societies across the African continent correlates with noun class choice (see Storch 2013b: 100–1 and Irvine 1998: 54–5, for Ichibemba and others). The social status of women among the Tariana of north-west Amazonia is reflected in the gender switch (whereby a respected woman can be referred to with masculine gender) (see §4.2 of Chapter 6). Within Zamucoan society, the equality of social genders correlates with the presence of parallel gender forms for men and for women (§8 of Chapter 8).

C. Principles of interaction, and attitudes to information and its sources. Social constraints may impact interaction between people, the ways in which they talk, and manipulate noun classification to reflect their status. Wolof, a West Atlantic language, has a complex system of noun classes, only in part based on semantic principles. Verbal fluency, correctness, and elaboration are associated with low social rank. Using a wrong noun class on purpose is associated with high rank of the speaker: only respectable elders consistently make such deliberate errors (Irvine 1978: 41–3, 1990: 143).

D. Beliefs, religion, spirits, and dreams. A network of beliefs and legends may motivate the way in which objects of the real world are mapped into the system of reference classification. In Dyirbal, an Australian language, birds are believed to embody the spirits of deceased women and thus are placed in feminine gender. In Tamil, gods and demons are assigned to the class of rational beings, alongside humans (Asher 1985: 136). Among the Manambu, blood is associated with matrilineal inheritance, and this could be a motivation for its assignment to the feminine gender. The system of classifiers in Murui reflect the people's belief system (§3.1 of Chapter 7).

E. Means of subsistence and physical environment. Large systems of classifiers often contain terms which reflect the ways in which people live. River-dwelling peoples, such as the Tariana, the Baniwa, and the Murui of north-west Amazonia, have special classifiers for canoes, and for numerous types of waterways. Specific classifiers reflect agricultural practices and other means of subsistence among the Murui and the Tariana (see §4.3 of Chapter 6 and §3.1 of Chapter 7). Numeral classifiers in Nivkh, a Paleo-Siberian isolate, reflect traditional arrangements of fish on skewers (Gruzdeva 2004). In many languages from northern Australia, there is one gender (exclusively or predominantly) for edible plants; others have a noun classifier with a similar meaning (Dixon 2015)—highlighting the importance of edible plants for the hunter-gatherer populations.

In a similar vein, Craig (1986: 287) points out that the system of noun classifiers 'encompasses all aspects of traditional Jacaltec life'. There is a specific classifier *ixim* for 'corn', *tx'al* for 'thread', and *tx'añ* for 'twine'. The classifiers are 'few enough to isolate very selectively certain objects of the Jacaltec culture (corn but not beans, weaving but not carpentry)'.

A special type of reference classification device concerns classifiers employed just in possessive constructions, to categorize the possessee. Having a special classifier of this type for 'domestic animal, pet' is a linguistic corollary of animal husbandry and domestication. This is what we find in Yuman and in Uto-Aztecan languages, and a few languages in South America, including Zamucoan in Bolivia and Paraguay and Mataguayan in Argentina (Langacker 1977; Aikhenvald 2013: 25; Ciucci and Bertinetto 2019). Maká, a Mataguayan language from Argentina, has a possessive classifier for cultivated plants (Messineo 2011: 202). This reflects the fact that the Maká have agricultural practices.

F. Role in language awareness, language engineering, and sensitivity to societal changes. Speakers of languages with genders are often aware of their meanings, and are prepared to discuss them. The Manambu point out that dividing the world into 'female' and 'male' is a salient feature of their language. Larger objects are masculine, and smaller ones are feminine. Many of the Manambu people have studied overseas, and have been to London. We had numerous discussions—initiated by Joel Yuakalu, a man with a degree from Sheffield University—about whether Buckingham Palace is 'big enough' to be considered masculine. Everyone agreed that Big Ben belongs to the masculine gender—based on its size and on its significance.

In many European languages, including English, the masculine gender form, such as *he*, or a noun, such as *man*, are—or used to be—an unmarked choice. In recent times, this usage has come under fire: the generic *he* and the generic *man* are seen as a way of subsuming women under 'men', making them invisible and insignificant (see Aikhenvald 2016: 195–9, and also Lakoff 1973, 1975, Pauwels 1998, Cheshire 2008, to name a few). And why should our Lord be a 'he', reproducing the out-dated male dominance? A gradual increase in linguistic awareness brought about a call for change. In November 1971, women-students at Harvard Divinity School openly called for a ban on the use of 'man' and masculine pronouns to refer to God and to people in general. This proposal to 'recast part of the grammar of the English language' provoked a famous letter to the Harvard University periodical, *The Harvard Crimson*, dated 16 November 1971. The letter was signed by many luminaries of linguistics—including Calvert Watkins, Jay Jasanoff, Sandra Chung, and Einar Haugen. The linguists pleaded that the language be left as it is, asserting the masculine to be the unmarked choice, 'and hence is used as a neutral or unspecified term'. Notwithstanding the plea, this part of the grammar of English is being recast. This change is an example of relatively recent and relatively rapid integration of the societal principles of gender equality into the language.

Similarly, semantic extensions of noun classes can be manipulated by language planners. In Setswana, a Bantu language with a large set of noun classes, it is now considered incorrect to refer to ethnic minorities, such as the Chinese or the Bushmen, using noun class 5/6 (which includes inanimates); all humans have to be referred to with the 'human' class 1/2 (Anderson and Janson 1997: 34–5; Joseph Tsonope, p.c.).

The choice of numeral classifiers in Maonan, a Tai-Kadai language spoken in China, reflects the gradually changing place of women within the society. Like a number of languages of South-east Asia, women used to be counted with the classifier $t\jmath^2$, which also subsumes animals and children. In contrast, respected women were typically counted using the human classifier $\text{?}ai^1$ (NUM.CL:HUMAN). At present, all women who have a professional status are referred to with the human classifier (Lu 2012: 83–4, 101–2, 119–21).

Numeral classifiers can be further amenable to language engineering. Following an order of King Mongkut issued in 1854 with regard to classifiers in Thai, 'noble' animals such as elephants and horses should be counted without any classifier; the classifier *tua* could only be used for animals of a 'lower' status (Juntanamalaga 1988).

Obsolescence of a societal practice may correlate with a loss of a meaning or a form within a system of reference classification. Cahuilla (Uto-Aztecan: Seiler 1977: 306) had a special possessive classifier for 'moiety animals'. In the early days, Cahuilla society was divided into two moieties, one associated with the Coyote, and the other with the Wildcat. The two moieties were in an exogamous relationship. The obsolescence of the moiety system led to the loss of the appropriate classifiers. In Minangkabau, from Sumatera in Indonesia (Marnita 1996: 163–5), drastic reduction in the system of numeral classifiers goes together with a narrowing of the spheres in which the language is used, under the pressure of Indonesian, the national language. The increase in use of loan measure terms (metre, litre, and kilogram) contributed to the loss of traditional mensural classifiers. Young people appear to be unfamiliar with some culture specific classifiers, e.g. *sumpik* 'blowing bamboo weapon', simply because they do not use the object.

The radical reduction of the numeral classifier system in the obsolescent Nivkh language, of the Sakhalin peninsula, is another case in point. Fishing used to be the main activity of the Nivkh. Numerous specific sortal and mensural classifiers referring to this means of subsistence—collected by Krejnovich and Panfilov in the 1930s—included classifiers for 'fishnet strips', 'fishnets for fishing hunchback and Siberian salmon', 'poles for fish-spears', and 'special twigs with smelt strung on them' (Gruzdeva 2004: 325). Nowadays, even fluent speakers do not remember—and cannot even recognize—any of those forms.

The principles of gender choice can be affected by cultural obsolescence. Schmidt (1985: 156–7) describes a series of changes in Young People's Dyirbal. Mythological association as a basis for gender membership is lost. As noted, in traditional times birds were believed to be spirits of dead human females, and consequently assigned to Gender II, 'feminine'. With the loss of this belief, speakers of Young People's Dyirbal treat birds as members of the 'animate' Gender 1. The loss of the gender switch (from feminine to masculine) among the Tariana (§4.2 of Chapter 6) may be indicative of a change in the status of women within the Vaupés River Basin society.

3.2 Types of possession

Division of nouns into possession classes and the meanings of possessive classifiers (mentioned in §3.1, as part of reference categorization) reflect features of the societies where the languages are spoken. Distinctive ways of marking special relations often reflect 'the foundations of bio-socio-cultural kin relations which are being given special treatment in the grammar of possession' (Ameka 2013: 235).

A. Relations within a community, social hierarchies, and kinship categorization. Kinship terms typically form a special subclass of inalienably, or obligatorily, possessed nouns (see Aikhenvald 2013; Dixon 2010b). The ways in which different groups of relatives are assigned to different possession classes may depend on their status in the society. Maternal relatives in Hone and other Jukunoid-speaking groups in Nigeria are accorded privileged position, and the corresponding terms are always inalienably possessed (Storch 2013a).

The form of a possessive marker may reflect community relations, and attitudes to the nature of ownership. Among the Murui-Muina of Colombian Amazonia, important possessions—such as 'garden', 'law', 'forest', 'river', and 'language'—cannot be 'owned' by an individual. As shown in example (4) in Chapter 7 (this volume), the elders always stress the importance of 'talking in collective terms'—as a consequence, it is infelicitous to say 'my garden', 'my river', or 'my language'. Table 2 in Chapter 7 shows that the 'possessor' for these entities has to be plural, reflecting the Murui 'aversion' against individualism (these issues are discussed in §3.2 of Chapter 7, alongside special archaic possessive marking of important kinship relations and possessions in Witotoan languages). This is reminiscent of the 'centrality of togetherness' among the Iraqw of Tanzania, reflected in the lexicon and the grammar, including the possessive verb whose meaning is 'be with, be together' (§3 of Chapter 10). A preferred plural possessor reflects the collective ownership of important emblems, such as 'language'. In Chamacoco, the term *ahwoso* 'words' is normally used with plural possessor to refer to 'language' (Luca Ciucci, p.c.). Language is an emblem of cultural identity for the Tariana (and other peoples of the Vaupés River Basin area: see §2 of Chapter 6). One always refers to the language one identifies with as 'our language' (*wa-yarupe*, literally, our thing), underscoring the collective sense of belonging to a language group which defines a person.

The use of possessive markers may reflect attitudes, and histories. Idi, a member of the Pahoturi River language family in Southern New Guinea, distinguishes between two sets of possessive markers—those expressing 'close' and those expressing 'distant' possessive relations (see §4.4 of Chapter 9). Markers of 'close' possession are used with kin terms (especially close consanguineal kin) and with other notions expressing close links between the possessor and the possessee (along the lines of Aikhenvald 2013: 19). Markers of 'distant' possession reflect a more 'distant' relationship (for instance, a bird someone just shot, rather than a bird one owns). One's own language is referred to with a marker of 'close' possession. Possession marking can be manipulated to reflect speaker's attitudes and histories. A speaker used a distant possessive to refer to the Idi language, to which his group had shifted in the recent past. Idi is his main language at present; however, the use of the distant possessive form reflects the speaker's awareness of the historical language shift (which had occurred before he was born) (§9 of Chapter 9).

The practice of referring to one's consanguineal relatives with a plural possessive marker ('our mother, our father, our brother', etc.) in Khinalug, a Nakh-Daghestanian language, is rooted in the predominance of large families with many children. To refer to close relatives as 'my' (mother, father, etc.) is considered impolite (Rind-Pawlowski 2019).

Special relations may be reflected in exceptional possession patterns. Kinship terms in Paluai, an Oceanic language from the Manus province in Papua New Guinea, are directly—or inalienably—possessed, in agreement with a general Oceanic pattern (Schokkin 2014: 81–2; Schokkin and Otto 2017: 239). The term for 'in-law', *polam*, is an exception: it is treated as alienably, or indirectly, possessed. So is the term for 'cross-cousin', *pwai* (that is, the child of a parent's opposite sex sibling: mother's brother's child, or father's sister's child). The status of cross-cousins and in-laws in the traditional Paluai society points towards an explanation for this exceptional behaviour. One is in a taboo relationship with the *polam* 'in-law relative', and needs to treat them with special respect. The social distance between the ego and the in-law (and a cross-cousin) iconically correlates with linguistically longer and more elaborate expression of alienable possession (following the principles of iconicity outlined by Haiman 1983). In agreement with the rules of Paluai kinship, cross-cousins do not belong to the ego's lineage, and thus are less close to the speaker than other relations. This is reflected in the way possession is expressed.

One consanguineal kinship term, *pên* 'daughter', is also treated as alienably possessed in Paluai. Once again, societal practices offer a possible reason. Marriage in Paluai operates on an exogamous principle, and so daughters usually marry someone who does not belong to their own clan; their children will belong to their husband's clan. Hence the treatment of 'daughter'—a potential outsider not intrinsically connected to the speaker's clan—as alienably possessed. This is closely linked to B.

B. Social constraints (taboo and avoidance). In Jukun, male sexual organs and body effluvia are taboo and cannot be used in possessive constructions (Storch 2013a: 213). In Martuthunira, an Australian language, a special suppletive form of the first-person singular pronoun *jurti* is used to code close kinship relationships and also special relations between men established through male initiation (Dench 2013: 140).

Relations within a community, further social hierarchies, and constraints are reflected in possessive classifiers in Pohnpean. The honorific register is used by common people to address a member of the nobility and by the nobility to talk between themselves. The humiliative register is used by socially inferior people to talk to the chiefs. There is also a common register, unmarked for politeness (more on this in Keating 1997, 1998). The distinction between registers is reflected in a large system of possessive classifiers. Two 'common register' classifiers, *kene* 'edible' and *nime* 'drinkable', correspond to three in the honorific speech: *koanoat* 'possession of food/drink by paramount chief', *pwenieu* 'possession of food/drink by paramount chieftainess', and *sahk* 'possession of food/drink by secondary chief'. In contrast, the humiliative register uses just one classifier, *ah tungoal*.

C. Principles of interaction, and attitudes to information and its sources. Principles of interaction between different kinds of relations may correlate with the assignment of the kinship terms to possession classes (shown under A and B above). We have found no demonstrable correlations of marking possession with attitudes to information.

D. Beliefs, religion, spirits, and dreams. Possessive classifiers in Pohnpean correlate with traditional beliefs and kinship hierarchies (linking this with parameter A above). The notion of *mana* refers to 'the sacred and dangerous power which flows from the deities through the chiefs to the people'. *Mana* is believed to flow 'matrilineally to descendants within chiefly clans'. As a result, the 'belief that *mana* extends to possessions makes possessive constructions a meaningful category' in distinguishing honorific, status-lowering, and common speech registers (Keating 1997: 249). As a sign of salience of the maternal line, the language has specific classifiers for maternal rather than for paternal relatives (Keating 1997: 253). Beliefs, attitudes, and traditional associations explain the structure of possessive classifiers. The honorific general classifier, *sapwellime*, is composed of *sapwe* 'land' and *lime* 'hand, arm'. This can be explained by a strong cultural link between high status and land ownership, especially for chiefs (Keating 1997: 263). In contrast, the all-purpose possessive classifier in humiliative speech, *tungoal*, means 'food, eating and this correlates with the link between low status and food, or nourishment as the product of the land' (Keating 1997: 264).

Possessive (or relational) classifiers in Oceanic languages reflect culture-specific ways of handling the Possessee which can only be understood within the peoples' belief system. Fijian dialects of Eastern Viti Levu have a classifier for an object which the Possessor contributes 'as a customary obligation—a mat or pig for presentation at a feast, a house being built for a chief, or a spade to be used in a communal garden project' (Geraghty 2000: 246). This same marker (*loga-/laga-*) is also used as a classifier for totems in part of northeast Viti Levu—reflecting the belief system and the totemic organization of the world.

In Zamucoan languages, animals, plants, and fruits cannot be directly possessed, correlating with speakers' traditional attitudes to consumable goods and natural resources. On the other hand, in Ayoreo, one of Zamucoan languages, the newly introduced resource of money is considered the property of an individual and takes possessive inflection directly, unlike traditonal consumable goods—see §6 of Chapter 8.

E. Means of subsistence and physical environment. The meanings of possessive classifiers tend to reflect the means of subsistence, physical environment, and traditional occupations. Travel by watercraft is essential for the Mussau-Emira, speakers of an Oceanic language from Papua New Guinea who live on a group of islands. The language has a special possessive classifier for 'canoes, watercrafts', their means of transport. The presence of a possessive marker for domestic animals correlates with the practice of animal husbandry (Brownie and Brownie 2007: 71–86) (and see E in §3.1). Means of subsistence and salient features of physical environment are reflected in the systems of classifiers used in multiple contexts (including possessive constructions: §4.3 of Chapter 6 and §3.1 of Chapter 7).

In Dakota, a Siouan language, 'natural objects like land, water, animals including the dog but excepting the horse cannot take the possessive pronoun, because under aboriginal conditions they could not be exclusive property of anyone' (Boas and Deloria 1941: 128; cf. Aikhenvald 2013: 16). We find similar restrictions in numerous languages of South America, including the Arawak-speaking Waujá and Baniwa of Içana of Brazil and the Nanti of Peru. What happens when these peoples are confronted with different, Western-based notions of ownership? This takes us to F.

F. Role in language awareness, language engineering, and sensitivity to societal changes. Expression and conceptualization of possession, and possessability, may change as societies undergo transformations. Traditionally, land was not considered 'ownable' among the Nanti, an Arawak-speaking minority in Peru (Michael 2013: 165). As a result of encounters with Western concepts of land ownership—through contact with the closely related Matsigenka, who are much more exposed to the Western influence—the Nanti started talking about land ownership. The word for 'land' is now used in a possessive construction: one can now say *no-gipatsi-te* (1sg-land-POSS) 'my (alienable) land'. Alexandra Aikhenvald observed a similar change among the Arawak-speaking Baniwa of Içana in north-west Brazil: as a result of recent changes and ongoing issues to do with ownership rights for traditional lands, the noun *hipe* 'land' (cognate to Nanti *-gipa-* 'land') can now be used in possessive constructions (as alienably possessed).

A similar example comes from Dakota, a Siouan language (Boas and Deloria 1941: 128). Traditionally, animals were not possessable, just like 'land'. But 'at present the cattle on large ranches are considered as property and not as food. Therefore they are expressed as separable property by the prefix *t'a'-*. The relatively new practice of having cattle on a ranch as property has affected possessive marking in the language. The prefix *t'a'-*, a marker of alienable possession, has been extended in its usage' (see also Aikhenvald 2019: 22).

We saw under A within this section that, for the Murui, culturally important items could not be conceptualized as owned by an individual. A garden, a law, a river, or coca could only be 'ours', and not 'mine' (see Table 4 and §3.2 of Chapter 7). Now that the Murui people are gradually being drawn into the

Colombian market economy, the patterns of ownership are changing. The ways of talking follow suit. Many young Murui own their gardens individually—and freely refer to them as 'mine'. The elders voice their disapproval, commenting that the younger generation 'have lost their way of life'. Speakers are aware of the ongoing change in ownership patterns and of the corresponding changes in their linguistic expression.[7]

3.3 Directing and addressing

Directing and addressing can be expressed through the choice of pronouns, or commands and directive speech acts.

A. Relations within a community, social hierarchies, and kinship categorization. In many European languages, contrasting forms of second person pronouns (e.g. *tu* and *vous* in French) depend on social relationships (see, for instance, Braun 1988, Clyne et al. 2006). In Fijian, a single person may be addressed with second person dual, paucal, or plural pronoun. The second person dual pronoun is used for a single person belonging to one set of in-law relatives (mother-in-law, father-in-law, son-in-law, daughter-in-law) and the second person paucal pronoun is used to the other set (an actual or classificatory brother-in-law or sister-in-law of the opposite sex). Second person plural pronoun is reserved for addressing a village chief (Dixon 2012: 444). The hierarchy of kinship relations is reflected in the use and structure of address forms in Iraqw (§5 of Chapter 10).

Along similar lines, plural form for the addressee in commands in Luwo expresses a deferential attitude, as this 'symbolically heightens the agency and role of the addressee and thereby helps to soften an otherwise irrevocable command' (Storch 2014: 143; further examples are in Aikhenvald 2010: 212–18). At the same time, 'greeting rituals and ritualistic communication forms are not marked in a salient way for social hierarchy', as 'Luwo communities are characterized by low-key hierarchical differentiation' (Storch 2014: 251).

In Japanese, commands are couched in a different manner according to the social status of speaker and of addressee (a comprehensive analysis and references are in Jarkey 2017; see also Chapter 2 of this volume for a general perspective on Japanese). The choice of honorific speech level in commands in Korean is determined by the relative status of the speaker with regard to the

---

[7] We have not encountered any clear examples of the impact of language engineering on linguistic expression of possession.

addressee (Sohn 1994: 9–10). The choice between regular, polite, and impolite imperative in Maale, an Omotic language from Ethiopia, also depends on the status and age of speaker and addressee (Azeb Amha 2001: 126). Honorific systems as part of social deixis are a salient feature of Tibeto-Burman languages of Bhutan—these are discussed throughout Chapter 3, for Dzongkha, and in §5 of Chapter 4, for Brokpa.

Similarly, commands among the Ilongot of the Philippines are used in line with 'age- and sex-linked social rank' (Rosaldo 1982: 204). The use of direct imperative or of another form to express commands and injunctions in Arapaho correlate with age and kinship relations (Cowell 2007; and also see Mihas 2017 for the role of a person's status in the choice of an imperative form among the Ashaninka Satipo).

The absence of dedicated imperative forms in a language may reflect the original societal conventions and organization. Traditional Dyirbal, spoken in a society where 'life was regulated by common consent', had 'no clearly defined speech act of command' (Dixon 2017: 128). Forms with potential meaning were used to phrase suggestions and injunctions. A combination of particle plus verbal suffix was used to 'provide advice about some negative happening which might eventuate' (p. 142). These could, at a pinch, be translated into English as positive and negative imperatives. But such labels would not fully bring out the genius of the language as used by a small, egalitarian, and consensus-based group where commands used not to be part of traditional social practices.

B. Social constraints (taboo and avoidance). Kinship-based avoidance relationships are a prominent feature of many Australian languages. Yankunytjatjara (Goddard 1983: 306–7) has a strict avoidance relationship between a man and his parents-in-law. This imposes restrictions on the use of an imperative. A mother-in-law's or father-in-law's requests for food cannot be addressed directly to the son-in-law, but have to be done through an intermediary. Even the intermediary's speech cannot contain a direct command (or an imperative form of the verb). A request has to be relayed using the quotative particle *kunyu* without any reference to a request. In-law avoidance relations are the basis for the special language style, Jalnguy, used among the Dyirbal people of North Queensland and their neighbours (the topic of Chapter 5 of this volume). Avoidance and respect used to be expressed through choices made in the lexicon (more on these in §3.5).[8]

Among the Manambu, an initiated man could, traditionally, only be commanded by someone of the same level of initiation (or above).

---

[8] Contrary to Agha (2007: 321), neither Dyirbal, nor Guugu Yimidhirr, nor any other Australian languages, used titles or special forms of second person pronouns.

C. Principles of interaction, and attitudes to information and its sources. Principles of interaction and societal conventions may help explain gaps in paradigms and exceptional grammatical behaviour in vocative forms. Affinal relatives among the Trio, a North Carib-speaking group of Brazil and Suriname, do not talk to each other directly, as part of an avoidance register. This correlates with a gap in the paradigm of vocative forms—typically used in direct address: there are no such forms for father-in-law, mother-in-law, son-in-law, and daughter-in-law (Carlin 2004: 140). As Rivière (1969: 198) put it, 'that affines do not talk to each other is logically portrayed in the absence of direct address forms for affines'.

Obligatory marking of information source in grammar, or evidentiality, may correlate with the cultural requirement to be precise. We return to this in §3.4. A few languages with obligatory marking of information source have it not just in statements, but also in commands. A most typical evidential in this context is a reported evidential (Aikhenvald 2010: 138–44, 2017: 19–20).

D. Beliefs, religion, spirits, and dreams. Deities can be addressed in unusual ways, e.g. in Russian, God is usually spoken to with the familiar second person singular pronoun (Aikhenvald 2010: 232, and Maiden and Robustelli 2007: 463 on how some speakers of Italian address God). Speakers of Arapaho, an Algonquian language, use the indirect imperative in their prayers to God, as they 'seem reluctant to "order" God' directly (Cowell 2007: 47). Among the Ashaninka Satipo, special address forms reflect the indigenous classification of spirits and powers attributed to them (Mihas 2017: 102).

E. Means of subsistence and physical environment. Special directives and imperative forms may reflect life-style and means of subsistence. Zargulla, an Omotic language from Ethiopia, is rich in special directive forms addressed to domestic animals. This feature—shared with other Omotic languages, including Maale and Wolaitta—fits in well with the cultural focus on animal herding in this society, and the variety of cattle and domestic animals traditionally bred (Azeb Amha 2013). In contrast, the Matses from Peru, for whom hunting is the major activity, have special directives only for hunted animals and hunting dogs (Aikhenvald 2010: 318–20). We have so far found no examples of how directives may correlate with physical environment.

F. Role in language awareness, language engineering, and sensitivity to societal changes. Speakers are generally aware of the correlations between the ways of addressing and directing and relations within the community; they will provide explanations to researchers as to how politeness forms are to be used: see, for instance, explanations given by the Ilongot to Rosaldo (1982), or by the Arapaho to Cowell (2007).

A social change may accompany the frequency of use and the ways of framing a command. Traditional Lakota, a Siouan language, had a number of imperative particles used by men, or by women (see Boas and Deloria 1941; Ullrich 2008: 764–5; Trechter 1995: 189). Nowadays 'the speaker who most often uses a command form is a woman, correcting the delivery style of her husband as she interrupts his explanation [...] to tell him to speak in Lakota or to clarify his explanations'. This new role of a woman as a language keeper— and an authority in matters traditional—has enhanced the frequency of commands in women's speech, and the way the commands are phrased.

The use of imperatives and other means of framing commands appears to be susceptible to the impact of language contact and concomitant social changes. In many European languages, systems of address and imperatives reflect new social hierarchies and the demise of older ones, as a consequence of the 'democratization' of language (see, for instance, Braun 1988, Clyne et al. 2006, Coates 2003: 33–4, and Burke and Burridge 2021). The development of honorifics, and their change over time, in Japanese—which subsume address terms and the framing of directive speech acts—has its roots in social factors. These include an elaborate social hierarchy surrounding the imperial court (already established by the Heian period: 794–1195), with the growing salience of ingroup/outgroup relations associated with practices of social control in feudal times (the Tokugawa period: 1603–1868) and the subsequent modernization and urbanization (the Meiji period: 1868–1912 and beyond)— see §5 of Chapter 2. The importance of ingroup/outgroup relations in the use of honorifics in Japanese sets it apart from the principles behind their use in Korean: the main criterion there is difference in age, including the paramount importance of showing respect for one's parents and grandparents within the family—see §4 of Chapter 2 (and references there). In each instance, speakers show a high degree of language awareness, as they are able to comment on the principles of choice for the appropriate forms and are usually happy to discuss them.

3.4 Information source, transmission of information, and interaction patterns

Grammatical marking of information source, or grammatical evidentiality, shows demonstrable correlations with a number of societal features. So do conventionalized modes of interaction within communities. The parameters under A–D are intertwined.

A. Relations within a community, social hierarchies, and kinship categorization. In numerous West African communities, in some types of interaction, one tends not to communicate information directly to the addressee. Instead, this is done through an intermediary, or a spokesperson. The societies in the Sahel region are stratified; the 'nobles' are not allowed to speak in public, using bards or griots as their spokespersons. In the societies along the coast, 'respect' for the king or the chief requires the use of his spokesperson in communicating with the public (Ameka 2004: 6; Irvine 1990). If A wishes to tell something to B, they are likely to use C, an intermediary: A will tell C who in turn tells B, rather than A speaking directly to B. The presence of triadic communication patterns in West African languages correlates with the presence of logophoric markers: special pronominal forms that ensure the avoidance of ambiguity of an anaphoric pronoun, thus preventing confusion between A, B, and C. This cultural practice of triadic communication may involve one intermediary, or a chain of intermediaries. Or there can be a social class or a caste of griots, specialized as speech intermediaries (Ameka 2004: 13–5 offers examples and references).

Within the West African context, the presence of logophoric marking can be seen to 'reflect a preoccupation with channelling information through intermediaries, and therefore constitute 'an instance of the grammatical elaboration of a cultural theme' (Ameka 2004: 25), and 'an instantiation of a cultural preoccupation in grammar' (Ameka 2017: 533).

Kinship relations may play a role in the choice of evidentials. Nonvisual evidentials are used to refer to one's own internal states (including fever, sadness, and happiness). They may be extended to talking about the internal states of close family members. This is one of the means of distinguishing nuclear family from extended classificatory kin among the Tariana of northwest Amazonia (§§5.2–3 of Chapter 6). Similarly, an egophoric marker—whose main meaning is privileged access to information by the speaker—can be extended to cover members of the speaker's family (see Sun 2018: 55–6, for such 'upgraded access' to personal knowledge in Taku, a Tibetic language).

The choice of preferred information source marker, in languages with evidentiality as part of grammar, may correlate with the speaker's status in the community. In many Amazonian communities, and also among the Huallaga Quechua, the visual evidential is used sparingly—only if a person has really seen what they are talking about, or if they have sufficient authority to show that they can see what others cannot. Someone who is neither a respectable authority nor a shaman, and thus has no obvious reason to over-use a visual evidential, may be in trouble: they could be accused of being unreliable, or crazy, and suffer social exclusion (see Weber 1986: 142, and a summary in Aikhenvald 2018a). Similar principles apply to the Tariana of north-west Amazonia (see §6.7 of Chapter 6 and references there).

B. **Social constraints (taboo and avoidance).** We have just seen that the principles of indirect communication through a third party in a number of West African societies, including the Wolof, correlate with social constraints. In languages of the Vaupés region of north-west Amazonia, a shaman will be expected to use a visual evidential to describe their supernatural experience. But when talking about shamanic actions and visions, common people will use the non-visual evidential. If they do not do so, they will be in breach of expectations and social constraints (Aikhenvald 2004; Stenzel and Gomez-Imbert 2018, and §§6.4–5 of Chapter 6).

C. **Principles of interaction, and attitudes to information and its sources.** In Japanese, it is considered presumptuous and therefore pragmatically inappropriate to speak about the feelings, emotions, or intentions of someone else (even a close family member) without clear indication that one does not have direct access to the information. Evidentials indicating that one is relying on appearance, report, or hearsay are indispensable, unless one is taking the omniscient stance of a narrator (see also §6.2 of Chapter 6).

We saw, under A, how the presence of logophoric marking reflects attitudes to the ways in which information is transmitted. In many languages with grammatical evidentiality, a visual evidential has overtones of certainty, and an inferred, a nonvisual, or a reported evidential may be used to cast doubt on what is being discussed (see Aikhenvald 2004: 154–85). The conceptualization of knowledge and truth in Maaka, a Chadic language, is reflected in the use of an elaborate system of non-propositional evidentials (Storch and Coly 2014; Lüpke and Storch 2013: 245–53). The correct use of evidentials is the token of a good speaker, and a reliable person, among the Mamaindê of central Brazil (Eberhard 2009: 468, 2018). Along similar lines, the accurate use of information source markers is 'a prerequisite to a claim to human status' for the Jaqi of Bolivia (Hardman 1986: 131; see also McLendon 2003: 113, on Eastern Pomo, and Nuckolls 2018, on Pastaza Quichua) (see also §5.7 of Chapter 6). Being precise in one's information source tends to be a cross-linguistic corollary of obligatory evidential systems, especially large ones, taking us to D.

D. Beliefs, religion, spirits, and dreams. The requirement to be precise among the Tariana and their neighbours in the Vaupés region appears to be related to a common belief that there is an explicit cause for every mishap (see §§5.7–8 of Chapter 6; Aikhenvald 2015a: 298–302, 2018a: 27–30, and also Barnes 1984). Such causes often involve sorcery—real, or suspected. If speakers are remiss in using the correct marker of information source, they run the risk of being deemed sorcerers, or just unreliable and 'useless' people.

Conventionalized choices of evidentials may reflect the status of the speaker: we mentioned, in B, that in many languages of the Vaupés, shamanic actions will be described using non-visual evidential (as a speaker of Tariana explained, they are done with the shaman's 'mind' which cannot be seen). The Tariana will also use the non-visual evidential when talking about attacks of evil spirits who are 'not seen'. Speakers of Trio and Wayana, Carib languages of Suriname, French Guyana, and the adjacent regions of Brazil, talk about shamanic attacks using the non-witnessed evidential: these are said to bring about an altered state of consciousness in the victim. The shamans themselves talk about their experiences using a witnessed evidential—for them, their revelations represent an 'alternative reality' (Carlin 2018). A speaker of Dyirbal would use a non-visual marker when talking about spirits (Dixon 2014b).

In their traditional life, speakers of Kagwahiv (a Tupí-Guaraní language, from the Upper Madeira River basin) used to rely on dreams to forecast the presence of game, plan the day's hunt, and foresee illness and death. Every sentence in recounting a dream contains a marker of nonfirsthand information. Kracke (2009: 73) explains: 'the knowledge in a dream is received as a communication from beyond. Hence it cannot be coded as personal experience'. In a number of languages dreams are indeed treated as 'unconsciously acquired experience', and then told using a reported evidential (similar examples are in Pan 2018 on Formosan languages Kanakanavu, Saaroa, and Tsou; Daguman 2018 on Kankanaey, a Philippine language, and Brosig and Skribnik 2018 on Kalmyk, a Mongolic language).

Experience acquired in a dream may be marked differently depending on who the 'dreamer' is. In Shipibo-Konibo, dreams experienced by ordinary humans are not part of reality—and so they are recounted using the reported evidential =*ronki*. However, if a shaman has a dream or a vision induced by the hallucinogenic *ayahuasca*, he will retell this experience using the direct evidential (Valenzuela 2003). Similarly, shamanic dreams in Tariana, Tucano, and a few other languages from the Vaupés are cast in the visual evidential: the shamans are said to have the power of 'seeing' what has happened or will occur, through their dreams. Common people recount their dreams using the non-visual evidential (see §5.4 of Chapter 6, and Stenzel and Gomez-Imbert 2018: 382–3, Aikhenvald 2004: 346–7).

E. Means of subsistence and physical environment. There do not appear to be any demonstrable correlations between means of subsistence, or physical environment, and the marking of information source or the transmission of information. The presence of evidentiality may correlate with the form of language transmission—whether oral, or written. It appears to be the case that large evidential systems tend to occur in languages with a predominantly oral tradition (see also Daguman 2018: 291). And when writing is introduced, an evidential system may adapt to this new form of transmitting knowledge. This takes us to F.

F. Role in language awareness, language engineering, and sensitivity to societal changes. Speakers of languages with evidentiality tend to be highly aware of how evidentials are to be employed, offering explanations for their use, and their lexical reinforcement should any doubt arise as to the information source (numerous examples are in Aikhenvald 2004: 335–43). Speakers of languages with evidentials—from Amazonia to the Balkans—are aware of their absence in major languages, English, Spanish, and Portuguese, and are known to complain about their lack. One hears, from the Indians of the Vaupés, that 'white people are liars—they never tell you how they know things'. And evidentials tend to spread from one language to the next in a contact situation. Expressing one's information source, and being precise about it, becomes a speech habit, and a necessity. Evidentials have been developed in local varieties of South American Spanish and Portuguese under the influence of indigenous languages, including Quechua and Aymara (see Aikhenvald 2018b: 165–8, and references there). Along similar lines, the development of a speech report marker in Ghanaian English could be attributed to the influence of Ga and Akan (Ameka 2004: 22).

Evidentials appear to be particularly sensitive to change, as new means of knowing things come about (see also Aikhenvald 2014: 34–6, and §§5.6–7 of Chapter 6). New practices—reading, radio, telephone, television, and internet—help us understand just how pliable the systems are. A Shipibo-Konibo speaker will now use reported =*ronki* to talk about what they read in a book. And a speaker of Tariana or Tucano will use an assumed evidential, typically used for information acquired by interpretation, reasoning, and common sense. This evidential is also used to refer to something one has read or knows based on a written source (integrating writing as a new practice for the Tariana speakers into the system of marking information source). If a

Shipibo-Konibo watches something on television, this implies 'experiencing the event oneself, since one actually "sees" what is happening'—and so they would use the direct evidential =*ra*. The Tariana and the Tucano speakers would use a visual evidential. But if a Shipibo-Konibo hears something on the radio, or hears a TV report without seeing the picture, they will use the reported =*ronki*. A Tariana or a Tucano would use a non-visual evidential.

A speaker of Hinuq, a Nakh-Daghestanian language, or of Tatar, from the Turkic family, would retell something they have seen on TV or heard on the radio using the non-witnessed evidential form, as they were not there to see the event themselves (Forker 2014; Greed 2014). The introduction of writing into the Bosavi (or Kaluli) language tradition, from Papua New Guinea, has resulted in the creation of a new evidential referring to something known from this source and not known before (Schieffelin 2008; Wood 2018: 247).

We have no information concerning evidentials and language engineering. However, an evidential can become obsolete if the styles which require it fall into oblivion. In the languages of the Philippines, Daguman (2018: 691) notes, 'the formulaic and other discourse functions of the reportative in traditional oral storytelling is disappearing as fast as the verbal arts are falling out of use'; the reported evidential is hardly used in written collections of traditional stories. But it is still much alive in literary pieces of other genres—the presence of an evidential there 'contributes to making the written material sound natural rather than staid'. This takes us to §3.5.

3.5 Special speech styles

Special speech styles and their properties show strong evidence of integration with societal features, relations within a community, social categorization, interaction, and beliefs (specially focussed on in Chapters 2–5 of this volume).

A. Relations within a community, social hierarchies, and kinship categorization. The honorific style in Japanese and the choice of speech levels in Korean are motivated by the relations within the society, albeit in different ways. The special style of honorific language is a salient feature of Japanese, centring around relations within the society, social hierarchies and the in-group versus out-group differentiation—this is the topic of Chapter 2. The basis of the usage of honorific forms in Korean is much more strongly oriented to hierarchy, with particular attention to difference in age (§§4–5 of

Chapter 2 addresses the historical roots and the organization of honorifics in Japanese, and makes a comparison with Korean language and society). The appropriate usage of honorific versus humilific forms in Dzongkha, one of the major languages of Bhutan, is the backbone of *driglam namzhag*, 'the means of harmonious behaviour'—addressed in Chapter 3. The Brokpa, a minority in Bhutan, have a strong tradition of deference towards elders and those higher than the speaker on the societal hierarchy. This is reflected in the honorific system: see §5 of Chapter 4, on honorific forms of nouns and verbs in Brokpa and their origins. The choice of honorific and humiliative speech registers in Pohnpean and in Javanese reflects the established social hierarchies (Blust 2009: 118–25; Keating 1997, 1998). Noble-like speech and griot-like speech in Wolof have numerous special features, among them choice of noun class marker, use of deictics, and constituent order (Irvine 1990: 143; Ameka 2004: 18). The honorific language among the Anywa, a Nilotic-speaking group of Sudan and Ethiopia, is used by the king and those who speak to him (Storch 2013b: 99; further examples in Storch 2011: 23–8).

It is important to note that, in languages with highly developed and widely used honorific systems, these forms are often employed to assert speaker attitudes and identities that are by no means in keeping with the expression of deference or the reinforcement of established social relations. A sudden switch to honorific forms in casual interaction can signal emotional distance or anger. The elaborate show of respect for one's interlocutor and humility about oneself is frequently turned on its head as a strategy for asserting one's own superiority and social power. These strategic uses do not, however, interfere with the fundamental role that honorific styles play in establishing and reflecting social hierarchies and other types of relations within the community.

B. Social constraints (taboo and avoidance). In many Australian languages (and in Kalapalo and Kamaiurá from southern Amazonia) an avoidance style is used in the presence of certain kin relatives. Avoidance register between a man and a potential mother-in-law, or between a woman and a potential son-in-law, in a number of Australian and Amazonian languages involves distancing: not touching each other, not talking to each other directly, and not looking at each other. Above all, a special speech style is to be used in the presence of, or within earshot of, an avoidance relative. Among the Kalapalo, a Carib-speaking group in Xingu (Brazil), in-laws cannot be addressed directly, and their names cannot be uttered; circumlocutions have to be employed (Basso 2007).

The 'mother-in-law' Jalnguy style in Dyirbal had to be used instead of the everyday style (called Guwal) in the presence of an in-law relative with whom

Table 1 An example of one-to-many lexical correspondences in Guwal and Jalnguy

Guwal	Jalnguy
yuri 'eastern grey kangaroo (*Macropus giganteus*)'	
barrgan 'agile wallaby (*Macropus agilis*)'	*jaɲanbarra*
jabali 'whiptail kangaroo (*Macropus parryi*)'	
mabi 'tree-climbing kangaroo (*Dendrolagus lumholtzi*)'	

contact had to be minimized. While speaking Guwal, one needs to be as specific as possible. In contrast, Jalnguy is purposely vague, and deals in generic terms only: hence a one-to-many correspondence of numerous lexical terms between Jalnguy and Guwal (Dixon 2010a: 293, 2012: 448). An example is in Table 1: four terms for each species of kangaroo and wallaby in Guwal correspond to just one in Jalnguy.

The Jalnguy speech style in Dyirbal had the same phonetics and phonology as the everyday languages, and the differences in grammar were minimal. Every lexeme—including common nouns, adjectives, verbs, adverbals, and time words—was different between the two styles (see Chapter 5). Similar avoidance styles have been documented for other Australian languages (a comprehensive account is in Dixon 2015: 85–138), but each of them are much more limited in their expanse and application. In contrast to Dyirbal, Dzongkha and Brokpa (Chapters 3 and 4) distinguish special style forms just for verbs and for nouns, but not for other word classes.

Social constraints are at play in numerous honorific and respect languages across the African continent (see examples in Storch 2013b: 100–1, 2011: 31–4, 2017). The in-law avoidance system (known as *hlonipha*) has been described for numerous indigenous groups in Southern Africa, Ethiopia, and Tanzania (see, for instance, Mitchell 2015, 2018). A similar respect practice, called *wakaari,* was in use among the Iraqw (§5.2 of Chapter 10). The practice appears to be falling out of use, and only a few terms are still known to the speakers.

Distance between 'forbidden' relatives can be reflected in the choice of grammatical form. In talking about a forbidden relative, the Kamaiurá, a Tupí-Guaraní-speaking group from Xingu, use plural rather than singular (Seki 2000: 327, 395).

C. Principles of interaction, and attitudes to information and its sources. A special speech style is used between initiated men across Australia, and among the Tenda of south-east Senegal. This is directly related to D and E.

D. Beliefs, religion, spirits, and dreams. In East African societies, a distinct vocabulary is typically used in the presence of spirits (Storch 2011 offers numerous examples; also see Needham 1973: 307, and Keating 2002: 209–10 on the inversion of meanings, actions, and values in the spirit world, in the languages of the Pacific). Among the Tariana of north-west Amazonia, women were not permitted to witness the Yurupary ritual or to see the magic flutes associated with it. Consequently, no terms associated with the ritual could be used in the presence of women, and alternative forms were deployed.

The Murui (Witoto) people of Colombia consider the jungle at night a dangerous place inhabited by malevolent spirits and shamans who can appear in the form of a jaguar or of a snake. When the Murui have to go hunting at night, they have to disguise their voices so that evil spirits won't know that there are humans around. The 'jungle talk' is characterized by high pitch (double the fundamental frequency of normal interaction, and frequent use of interjections, imitating a non-human voice), so as to deceive a spirit (Wojtylak 2019 and §3.4 of Chapter 7). Many Australian groups used to have special speech styles used only between initiated men and taught to youths at initiation; some still do (Dixon 2002: 91–2 offers a summary).

E. Means of subsistence and physical environment. Means of subsistence and physical environment correlate with special speech styles through the intermediary of peoples' beliefs. The Kewa from the highlands of Papua New Guinea employ a special vocabulary when gathering pandanus nuts. The Murui, a Witotoan-speaking group from Colombia, have a special speech style used while hunting big animals, and interpreting dreams (Wojtylak 2015, and §3.4 of Chapter 7). Avoidance speech styles used while hunting or preparing food in the jungle have been documented for Semelai and other Aslian languages of Malaysia, and Austronesian languages of Borneo and Sumatra (Kruspe 2004: 7–10).

F. Role in language awareness, language engineering, and sensitivity to societal changes. Speakers are typically aware of the existence and rules of use of special speech styles, and are often prepared to explain these to researchers. Societal changes over the course of the past thousand years have seen the development of the system of honorifics in Japanese, originally rooted in the social hierarchy surrounding the imperial court, develop to its present use in privileging social group and interlocutor relations (detailed analysis is in §5 of Chapter 2: see also §5.2 of Chapter 4 on the development of honorifics in Brokpa).

Special speech styles can be subject to language engineering (see Storch 2017, for a general perspective and examples). An unusual initiation language, the Damin style of Lardil, was said to be invented by a legendary ancestor. It shares a number of properties with invented languages, or 'language games', which are known to be the result of language engineering or manipulation (see Hale and Nash 1997; Dixon 2002: 92). Linked to this are special 'in-group languages'. Mous (1994, 2003) describes how the Mbugu, in Tanzania, wished to set themselves apart from neighbours who speak similar Bantu languages, and developed a language with Bantu grammar but a basically Cushitic vocabulary. A 'German youth language' within the tourism spots in Mallorca is a means of constructing membership of a liminal community in a colonial environment (§3 of Chapter 11). Youth languages and other special purpose languages are a further case in point (see Kießling and Mous 2004, Storch 2013b: 104ff, and 2017, and papers in Nassenstein and Hollington 2015).

A special register may be consciously developed as a reaction to the influx of aggressive colonizers, as a means of keeping one's own identity and one's own language intact and unintelligible to the outsiders. Around 1912, the inhabitants of the Kingdom of Bamun (located in the present-day Cameroon) were under pressure from the German-speaking members of the Basle mission. To protect his own power and to manage the experience of the colonial encounter, Sultan Noya of Bamun invented a secret language and a secret writing system (Storch 2013b: 89). The Chamacoco—under pressure from the dominant Spanish-speaking society—have developed a secret register characterized by general avoidance, or phonological manipulation, of Spanish loan words so as to make their language unintelligible to outsiders (§9 of Chapter 8).

The fate of special speech styles is often affected by the attrition of relevant practices. Such 'stylistic shrinkage' (term from Campbell and Muntzel 1989: 195) goes together with cultural obsolescence. The knowledge of a ritual 'pandanus' language used by a number of peoples of the Southern Highlands province of Papua New Guinea during the harvest of pandanus nuts has decreased during the past thirty to forty years, as Franklin and Stefaniw (1992) report for Kewa and Imbongu. The stylistic reduction in Manambu has resulted in gradual obsolescence of funerary songs with their special lexicon (Aikhenvald 2014). The in-law avoidance register among the Iraqw is on its way out (see §5 of Chapter 10). The Dyirbal avoidance style Jalnguy ceased to be actively used by around 1930s. At the time when R. M. W. Dixon conducted his fieldwork on the language, older people (born about 1900) still had a good knowledge of it (see §1 of Chapter 5). As the relevant practices of in-law avoidance disintegrated, so did the special register. Along similar lines, the secret language of Bamun (Storch 2013b: 89–90) became obsolete, as the

German influence in the area faded away and the economies of power underwent further transformations.

Special styles and genres of verbal art and corresponding rituals interrelate with societal parameters in further, intricate ways. In the German tradition, the time of 'Twelvetide'—the *Rauhnächte* (literally, rough nights) between Christmas and New Year—is associated with strange apparitions, ghosts, and dreary and scary tales of horrors and trauma. The in-between status of the days 'lost' between two feasts, or milestones, is reflected in the stories one hears. German songs heard on the beaches of Mallorca, about love and belonging, reflect the local social and cultural practices and the specially created German identity in the region. Waiting and observing the contexts of language use reveals the attractions and the seductive character of names—the names of sweets and biscuits among them—which reflect almost unlimited linguistic creativity within the evolving social environment (§§2–4 of Chapter 11).

The principles of metaphorical 'cohesiveness' in the structure of Iraqw traditional songs reflect the communal nature of the society (§2 of Chapter 10), as does cursing and lifting a curse. This resonates with the centrality of 'togetherness' which permeates the grammar and the lexicon of Iraqw (§3 of Chapter 10).

Patterns of cursing and swearing may reflect attitudes to kin, and kinship categories (see, for instance, Mitchell 2020). As an instance of a 'horrible play', swearing and cursing highlight the foundations and the stereotypes of the society it ostensibly aims at undermining (Storch 2020). 'Mock' use of elements of foreign languages reflects attitudes to their speakers and the relationships within a society. Mock Chinese is used in Kinshasa Lingala to show a deprecatory attitude to the increasing presence of Chinese migrants in the region (Nassenstein 2020). Inserting Baniwa-like forms in Tariana conveys the impression of someone slightly funny and inferior (Aikhenvald 2002: 206–7). Mock Spanish in the United States highlights the unequal relationships within the society, so much so that the overtones of Spanish insertions in American English could be considered exponents of 'white racism' (Hill 2008: 128–9, 146–7). Societal stereotypes and relationships between different groups can be observed based on the ways in which languages are manipulated.

3.6 An interim summary

The integration between linguistic and societal parameters established so far is summarized in Table 2.

Table 2 The integration between language and society: An initial summary

SOCIETAL PARAMETERS	LANGUAGE PARAMETERS				
	1. Reference classification: §3.1	2. Types of possession: §3.2	3. Directing, addressing: §3.3	4. Information source: §3.4	5. Speech styles: §3.5
A. Relations within a community, social hierarchies, and kinship categorization	√	√	√	√	√
B. Social constraints (taboo, avoidance)	√	√	√	√	√
C. Principles of interaction, and attitudes to information and its sources	few	none	√	√	√
D. Beliefs, religion, spirits, and dreams	√	√	√	√	√
E. Means of subsistence, physical environment	√	√	√	none	few
F. Role in language awareness, language engineering, and sensitivity to societal changes	√	√	√	√	√

The ticks in this table show the society/language associations which we have inferred from the literature (and our first-hand knowledge) across the world. For each specific society/language parameter only some of the ticks in a given row or a given column will apply.

Most of the correlations have a straightforward explanation. The main function of reference classification devices is to categorize the objects of the real world as viewed by the speakers; hence the correlations with the structure of the society, beliefs, means of subsistence, and physical environment. Possession, and directing and addressing are directly related to the ways objects and people are treated and handled and to their relationships within societies. Marking information source is directly related to access to knowledge, and thus social hierarchies, constraints, and beliefs. Speech styles and genres reflect relations within a community and social constraints. They are particularly susceptible to changes as the society undergoes transformation, or as traditional practices and relations fade into oblivion.

We now turn to further linguistic features which could be indicative of the integration with the societies of speakers.

4 Further indicators of integration between language and society

A number of further linguistic features appear to show integration with societal traits.

THE INTERNAL COMPOSITION OF WORD CLASSES may reflect societal practices and values—covering parameters A (Relations within a community), B (Social constraints), and D (Beliefs). Many languages from South America and from the Papuan region have a small adjective class which consistently lacks colour terms. (Naturally, colour terms are assigned to other word classes.) In contrast, small adjective classes in African languages consistently include colour terms. It does appear that colour denominations have particular saliency for many African languages and the societies where they are spoken. A small adjective class is in the process of evolving in Krahn/Wobe, from the Kru family (Liberia), consisting just of three colour terms (Dixon 2010b: 74–6; Bing 1991). This is congruent with the cultural importance of colour in many East African societies (see, for instance, Turton 1980 and Payne 2006).

In traditional Manambu society, clan allegiance and name ownership used to be pivotal. The knowledge of names, totemic terms, and terms of address associated with each subclan were critical in contesting land ownership, and finding a marriageable partner. Addressing your interlocutor correctly, using the address term belonging to their mother and father, was—and still is—a key to successful communication. Address terms provide protection from evil and are thus connected to beliefs and religion. Terms of address form a special subclass of nouns, with restricted nominal properties (they cannot be pluralized, or occur with modifiers or in possessive constructions: Aikhenvald 2008: 75–7). The special relationship between the father and the first legitimate child among the Ayoreo is mirrored by the teknonymic suffix in address terms and the new name bestowed upon the father after the birth of that child (§5 of Chapter 8, this volume).

FUNCTIONAL MARKEDNESS can be partly determined by societal practices, and thus reflect parameters A (Relations within a community) and B (Social constraints). There is a fundamental distinction between two kinds of markedness in a language—formal and functional. A formally unmarked term will be the only one in its system to have zero realization (or a zero variant). In contrast, functional markedness relates to how the forms are used (not what they look like). The marked term(s) may be used in a restricted and specifiable situation, with the unmarked term used in all other circumstances. The functionally unmarked term, or category, will appear in neutralized contexts, or if one does not wish to be specific, or refers to someone or something in general.

In many familiar Indo-European languages, the masculine gender form is—or was—functionally unmarked, used to refer to people in general, a group of mixed sexes, or those whose sex is unknown as a default choice. This usage is currently perceived as sexist and is widely considered inappropriate (see discussion at F under §3.1). In Manambu, however, it is feminine gender that is both formally and functionally the unmarked choice, especially when talking about children, animals, and inanimates. But culturally important objects associated with male cults such as male houses are always referred to with masculine gender. The choice of default gender depends on the meaning of the noun, and its role in the rituals. Functional markedness shows a correlation with societal practices.

The structures and types of PERSONAL PRONOUNS and other person-reference forms tend to reflect social hierarchies and also kinship relations (our parameters A and B). In many languages of East and Southeast Asia, person-reference forms 'seem to be specifically adapted to allow people to express...messages to do with differences in social standing, respect, deference, and the like' (Goddard 2005: 19). There are often special forms whose choice depends on the identities of speaker and of addressee, and their relationships to each other. This occurs particularly in the dominant national languages, in which social hierarchy tends to be far more significant than in the languages of more egalitarian minority communities. For instance, the term *àattàmaa* in Thai is used for self-reference by a Buddhist monk when speaking to a non-intimate layman or a lower-ranking monk. The term *fàa-bàat* is used by a commoner for interlocutor reference when speaking to lower-ranking royalty (see Iwasaki and Ingkaphirom 2005). An array of pragmatic alternatives for referring to first, second, and third person effectively creates open-class systems for person reference (see Enfield 2015: 133–47, 2017: 612–14) (the ways in which pronominal systems may reflect societal structures and changes within them are discussed by Burridge and Brewer 2021 and Burke and Burridge 2021 for Australasia, and also mentioned in Chapters 2–4 of this volume, in the discussion of Japanese, Dzongkha, and Brokpa).

In a number of Australian languages, pronominal forms vary, depending on whether people belong to the same moiety or to different moieties, and to the same or to different generation levels. The Arabana of South Australia used to be divided into two moieties. Back in the old days, marrying someone from the same moiety was 'like marrying your own sister' (Hercus 1994: 12). (This restriction got relaxed somewhat as the population declined, and the traditional conventions fell into disuse.) Personal pronouns reflect these relationships. For instance, the first-person dual pronoun *alantha* 'we two' will be used if you and I belong to the same moiety. If we belong to different moieties, the form is *alakiya*. Distinct pronouns for members of the 'same moiety' and 'different moiety' also used to be a feature of Diyari (see Dixon 2002: 283–4, and references there).

The impersonal pronominal *ta*, in its meaning of 'collective subject', is just one strategy for reflecting the centrality of 'togetherness' in the culture and daily life of the Iraqw of Tanzania. This societal value is further reinforced by numerous lexical items and in the expression of possession (§4 of Chapter 10).

Small egalitarian societies typically do not encompass the notion of competition, and will often have no lexical words for 'compete' or 'win', lacking a dedicated COMPARATIVE CONSTRUCTION in their grammar (reflected parameters A and B, as mentioned in §2, and also §7 of Chapter 8).

SERIAL VERB CONSTRUCTIONS—defined as monopredicative sequences of verbs without any markers of subordination or coordination between them—are a powerful means of representing events. The ways verbs combine together tells us something about the speakers, and their ways of life. What constitutes a plausible event is often culture-specific, reflecting traditional practices, rituals, and the environment—covering sets of parameters in E and also D. A traditional Lao musical instrument *lanaat*[4] is typically played in a sitting position; serial verb constructions with verbs 'stand' or 'lie' describing this activity were not judged acceptable (see Enfield 2004b: 241–54 on this, and other examples). Listening to a sermon, *fang2-théét4,* also involves sitting. Non-sitting postures (lying down or standing up) would imply that the subject will not be properly performing the ritual. Culturally logical solutions will be the less marked options. When confronted with atypical postures, speakers overtly mention their marked character, providing an additional explanation for an atypical posture, so as to 'activate non-default cultural representation' (Enfield 2004b: 254; further discussion and summary are in Aikhenvald 2018d: 178–84; see also Jarkey 2015: 117–18, 181–2).

The size and composition of the class of NUMBER WORDS depends on the presence of a counting routine in a language. Small systems of number words are a feature of Amazonian and Australian languages with little if any counting as a social practice (see Aikhenvald 2012: 350–60; Dixon 2012: 71–5). This is in contrast to those peoples for whom counting is a salient practice—including Indo-European, Semitic, and many Papuan languages. Exact quantities of goods, contributions to exchange and to mortuary payments, and of enemies' heads one has taken, are the basis of interaction within the community. The systems of number words in many of these languages are rather elaborate. Specific rituals and arrangements may be among cultural factors contributing to the emergence of a counting system (see, for instance, Evans 2009 on the origins of an unusual six-based counting system in Southern New Guinea languages). Societies with a developed trade network require a counting system, whereas small self-contained communities often had no habit of counting and lacked number words. This is an example of a societal parameter of a different nature reflected in grammar. The conceptualization of time among the Iraqw points towards the focus on the sequence of events rather than their absolute 'timing' (§6 of Chapter 10). What kind of social feature this may correlate with is worth pursuing.[9]

---

[9] It is undoubtedly the case that some putative correlations are weaker and easier to falsify than others. Many Amazonian languages, and just a handful of languages outside Amazonia, have a special 'frustrative' marker. Its meaning was aptly captured by Sparing-Chávez (2003) as 'I want to, but I can't', for Amawaka, a Panoan language from Peru (Overall 2017 contains a detailed study of frustratives in Amazonian languages). The presence of the frustrative in the grammar of Amawaka may well be motivated by the attitudes of speakers. As Sparing-Chávez (2003: 12) put it, 'The Amahuaca people are shame oriented and it seems to me that the frustrative helps them to save face by covering up their own shortcomings. They blame others, natural forces, or circumstances. It also helps them to express

In each of these instances, a feature of the society helps explain a feature of the language which could be considered unusual if seen in a cross-linguistic perspective. Physical features of the environment can also be directly reflected in language: we address these in Appendix 1.

Further relevant linguistic issues may include:

- *In some societies direct questioning is unwelcome.* Needed information is obtained indirectly, by offering relevant information about oneself, which naturally invites a response.
- *Patterns of grammaticalization may be linked to practices and beliefs?* For speakers of Pennsylvania German, an individual is not supposed to make definite statements about the future, in agreement with a cultural value central to their belief system—'subordination of individual will to the will of God' (Burridge 2006: 184). The tentative expressions of future using *figger* 'figure', *plaenne* 'plan' and *zehle* 'count' based on English calques are 'made to measure for a group of speakers reluctant to talk about the future'. As a consequence, they can now be considered a means of obligatory expression of future, as a grammatical category.

Phonology has not been mentioned thus far, since it is hard to make any generalizations concerning how it may fit in with the parameters discussed. However, it is important to see if phonological traits can correlate with any societal features. For instance, phonological features (including unusual sounds and pitch levels) may play a role in special-purpose languages, including youth languages and special registers used in hunting (see the discussion in Storch 2011, Lüpke and Storch 2013, Wojtylak 2019, and Irvine 1990: 139, §3.4 of Chapter 7, §3 of Chapter 11). This remains a topic for further study.

5 Integration of language and society: What can we conclude?

A grammar of every language will relate to meanings and choices which reflect societal practices. This resonates with Enfield's statement that 'our

disagreement or carefully accuse someone without having face-to-face confrontation'. However, quite a few Amazonian groups whose language does have a frustrative are not particularly shame-oriented and not averse to face-to-face confrontations. Conversely, not all the groups that are averse to face-to-face confrontations have a frustrative. The correlation between having a frustrative in the grammar and people's attitude remains conjectural.

language faculty must have evolved synergistically with our general cognitive capacities for (and the demands of) complex and interactive social organisation' (2000: 149). Or, as Heine (1997:14) put it, 'the way people in Siberia or the Kalahari desert experience the world around them can immediately be held responsible for the way they shape their grammars'.

Each language will show some degree of integration with the features of the society of its speakers. It is our aim to try and understand how this integration works, what linguistic categories it affects and why.

We have identified five groups of meanings expressed in grammar which are likely to reflect five groups of societal factors (see Table 2, and §3). Each of the five groups of linguistic features tend to play a role in language awareness and language engineering, and show sensitivity to societal changes. They tend to succumb to obsolescence when a relevant cultural practice is no longer in place. Those parts of grammar which show strong integration with societal requirements and conventions are susceptible to diffusion from one language to the next when their speakers come in contact with each other (in agreement with predictions in Aikhenvald 2006: 27–8). Genders and classifiers (as reference classification devices), taboo and avoidance principles, and evidentiality are among highly diffusible categories which also show strong correlations with societal factors.

Will this work the other way around? Can a specific societal feature be expected to have a correlate in language? We suspect that the answer will tend to be 'yes'. For instance, a language spoken by a highly stratified society will have to have lexical and perhaps also grammatical means of reflecting the divisions. But what part of grammar will be co-opted to reflect this very much depends on the language, its history, and the resources at hand.

As Maarten Mous explains (§7 of Chapter 10),

'The expected diversity in social and natural contexts and behaviour will lead to the emergence of different structures in different languages. It is likely that societal structure has an influence on linguistic structure over time. Due to the necessity of time for conventions to develop, influence from society on language is not likely to be instantaneous. Moreover, such influence is ideally studied within an historical approach, which also entails that we are not looking for predictive statements but rather possible correlations of phenomena.'

The idea of integration between language and society can be developed further. As Du Bois (1985: 363) phrased it, 'grammars code best what speakers do most'. Would it also be the case that speakers do most what grammars code best? Are linguistic features which show demonstrable correlations with societal practices the ones most frequently used in natural discourse?

And do some languages have more features indicative of their integration with society than others? If so, does this degree of integration correlate with the size of the linguistic community, their networks of interaction, degree of geographic isolation, and the history of their speakers? How can the degree of interaction be affected by externally-motivated and internally-motivated change? Which factors facilitate the integration, and which impede it?

Insights into these questions will bring us a step closer to understanding 'why' each language is the way it is—the aim of this volume.

6 About this volume

We aim at cross-linguistically-based insights into how social environment, beliefs, constraints, and hierarchies are mirrored in the grammatical systems of languages. Our focus is on a range of linguistic features—some frequent, some less so—which can be demonstrably correlated with the conventions and the structure of the society where the language is spoken, and its social, and sometimes physical, environment.

The volume contains in-depth discussion of a number of languages, each considered within its areal and genetic context, from Asia to South America, Indigenous Australia, East Africa, and New Guinea. Each chapter highlights sets of integration points between language and society which appear to be particularly salient from the perspective of the researcher, and of native speakers alike.

Honorific expressions are a salient, though non-universal, linguistic feature which most typically reflects the ways in which language use is integrated within the social and cultural environment and within linguistic history. In Chapter 2, 'The grammatical expression of social relations in Japanese', Nerida Jarkey offers comprehensive analysis of the integration of honorific forms in Japanese with a range of non-linguistic parameters within the society, centring around the relations within the community, social hierarchies, and their dynamics in history (in comparison with a superficially similar system in Korean). Honorifics are the backbone of communication in Bhutanese society, where honorific usage reinforces the existing social hierarchies and directly reflects the principles of interaction, social relationships, and social constraints. In Chapter 3, 'Honorification in Dzongkha', Stephen Watters provides a detailed study of special honorific and 'humilific' forms of nouns and verbs in Dzongkha, a majority language of Bhutan, focusing on their role in interaction, and the ways in which speakers manipulate these forms for various pragmatic purposes. Honorifics are also salient in Brokpa, a minority language in Bhutan, and are one of the topics which illustrate integration points between the Brokpa language and the society it is spoken in. In Chapter 4, 'Identifying who is who in Brokpa', Pema Wangdi discusses the ways in which honorific and humiliative forms reflect social hierarchies and relationships in Brokpa society as part of social deixis. Topographic deixis—height and directionality—within the language mirrors the physical environment people live in. Comparative and superlative constructions reflect the nature of competition, another salient feature of the Brokpa cultural landscape.

Kinship-based avoidance speech style used to be a salient feature of Dyirbal. In contrast to honorific systems described in Chapters 2–4, every lexeme (not just nouns and verbs) used to have an equivalent in both the day-to-day style Guwal and the avoidance style Jalnguy. In Chapter 5, 'The semantics of the Dyirbal avoidance style: Adjectives', R. M. W. Dixon focuses on the systematic correlations between adjectives in the two styles. The correlations provide a unique insight into the semantic structure of the language. Jalnguy forms for adjectives are fewer than those for verbs and nouns, and their meanings disclose culturally revealing value judgements and cognitive underpinning rooted in the traditional society.

We then turn to the ways in which grammar reflects societal features in a selection of languages from South America. In Chapter 6, 'The ways of speaking and the means of knowing: The Tariana of north-west Amazonia', Alexandra Y. Aikhenvald addresses four groups of categories in Tariana with parallels from other, unrelated, languages spoken in the Vaupés River Basin linguistic area. Classifiers, as a major means of reference classification, reflect physical environment and subsistence. Referring to a particularly important woman as if she were a man—that is, changing genders—reflects traditional social relations. And evidentials—obligatory grammatical markers of information source—reflect the cultural requirement to be precise, as well as kinship categorization, beliefs, and language awareness. The integration between grammar and societal features in a neighbouring group is the topic of Chapter 7, 'Links between language and society among the Murui of north-west Amazonia', by Katarzyna I. Wojtylak. Classifiers reflect means of subsistence, environment, and also beliefs, while spatial adverbs mirror environmental features. The principle of collective ownership is reflected in the way possession of important items used to be marked. As the Murui get more and more exposure to the mainstream market economy, more and more objects can now be possessed by individuals: the erstwhile correlation between attitudes to possession and the ways it is marked is undergoing change and impending obsolescence. Special avoidance registers, one used while hunting and another one while travelling at night, have their roots in taboos and belief systems.

Ayoreo and Chamacoco, two Zamucoan languages from the Chaco region of South America (spanning Bolivia and Paraguay) offer a particularly fertile field for the analysis of integration, and interaction, of language in society. In Chapter 8, 'How grammar and culture interact in Zamucoan', Luca Ciucci offers an analysis of a number of grammatical features indicative of characteristics of the indigenous societies and the changes they have undergone over the years. The features include grammatical gender of non-human referents in Ayoreo and the treatment of human and non-human referents in Chamacoco; the importance of the relationship between the father and the first legitimate child as reflected in the grammatical marking on a personal name; the expression of possession; comparative constructions; and the presence of a secret register among the Chamacoco whose aim is to keep the language unintelligible to Spanish-speaking outsiders and thus secret. The loss of most traditional origin myths may have determined differential treatment of human and non-human referents in Chamacoco.

The expression of possession is a well-attested integration point between language and society. Chapter 9, 'The integration of languages and society: A view from multilingual Southern New Guinea' by Dineke Schokkin, focuses on the place of the poorly known Pahoturi family in Southern New Guinea and the expression of possession in Idi, one of the languages of the family. Idi distinguishes close and distant possession. The use of possessive markers can reflect the speaker's relationships with the possessed item, and the history of their relationship—especially salient for important attributes such as 'language' itself, the speakers' emblem within the multilingual landscape of the region.

The multiplicity of interactions between grammatical features of a language, and the characteristics of the society in which it is spoken among the Iraqw of Tanzania, are the topic of Chapter 10, by Maarten Mous. The community nature of genres of verbal art and ritual among the Iraqw and the centrality of 'togetherness' finds its correlations in a number of lexical and grammatical features, among them a collective subject marker. The conceptualization of time and its varied expression correlates with speakers' attitudes and the ways of presenting events. The importance of kinship in the social structure is mirrored by the existence of an in-law avoidance register.

Chapter 11, 'Waiting: On language and hospitality', by Anne Storch, takes a different perspective. Its focus is on the creativity of language and its complexity, in its various guises and varied environments, especially those considered liminal, transitional, and marginal—including the ambiguous time between Christmas and New Year with strange apparitions and twisted meanings of words and names. The tourist settings of the island of Mallorca offer a set of new contexts of language play and development of new identities (both foreign and local), all finding their expression through language forms—love songs and poetry of other genres among them. The 'in-between' times spent waiting offer a further playground for linguistic creativity, and interplay between spoken language, its visual representation, and the construction of place and relevant objects, all within multilingual and multicultural environments across Europe and North Africa. The integration between language and society expands into new genres and new domains—by linking together narratives and experiences within environments never approached before.

Language does not exist outside the speakers' community. As Anne Storch (§4 of Chapter 11) observes, language 'is meaningful and significant with respect to the society in which it is used, to an extent that its structure may reflect its speakers' social organization and cultural practices'. The journey towards exploring the symbiotic relationship between language and the many aspects of the social world of its speakers is the key aim of this volume, in an attempt to contribute to the crucial question: why are languages the way they are?

Appendix. Language and its geographical environment

Grammar reflects the features of geographical terrain and physical environment in a few specific ways. Nominal demonstratives, locational markers, and directional affixes on verbs may encode topographic dimensions—that is, 'uphill', 'downhill', and 'same level as the speaker'. We find these in quite a few languages spoken in hilly environments—examples come from Northeast Caucasian languages, including Archi, Akhvakh, Tindi, and Chamalal, many Tibeto-Burman, Australian, Austroasiatic languages, and languages of Papua New Guinea and the Pacific (see, for instance, Palmer 2002, Burenhult 2008, a summary in Aikhenvald 2015b: 31–3). Brokpa, a Bodish (Tibeto-Burman) language, is spoken in a mountainous terrain. Topographic distinctions are encoded in the adverbial demonstratives—whether the location is upward or downward, or higher or lower than the speaker. This is shown in §4 of

Chapter 4 (and summarized in Table 4), of this volume. The river is central for navigation and livelihood of the Murui and their neighbours in north-west Amazonia. The riverine orientation is encoded in the closed class of spatial adverbs in Murui of north-west Amazonia (§3.3 of Chapter 7, this volume).

Languages vary in how many distinctions they make. In Nungon, a Finisterre-Huon language spoken in Morobe province of Papua New Guinea, both the near distance demonstrative -*o* 'this' and the far-distance demonstrative -*u* combine with three sets of elevational markers (Sarvasy 2017: 361):

(1) Proximal series   om-o   og-o   *Nungon*
                        downhill-PROXIMAL level-PROXIMAL
                        'this downhill'   'this same level'
                        on-o
                        uphill-PROXIMAL
                        'this uphill'

     Distal series   om-u   og-u   on-u
                        downhill-FAR   level-FAR   uphill-FAR
                        'that downhill'   'that same level' 'that uphill'

Nungon is spoken in a hilly area, and it is appropriate for the speakers to specify both the distance of an object and its relative height with respect to their own location.

Dyirbal is spoken in a mountainous rainforest area with heavy rainfall and many rivers. Locational suffixes in Dyirbal reflect the location of a referent of a noun with respect to the river (upriver or downriver) and also the mountains (uphill and downhill). Central and southern dialects have twelve terms, shown in Table 3 (Dixon 2010a: 16).

The grammar thus enables a speaker to supply information concerning whether something they are talking about is up or down hill or river, and how far up or down. Note that -*u* indicates a long way, -*a* a medium distance, and (just for the hill suffixes) -*i* a short distance.

The Sepik river is the main source of livelihood, and point of reference, for the Manambu people. Hills of various dimensions pepper their habitat. No wonder demonstratives and directional suffixes on verbs in the language reflect riverine and hilly orientation. Unlike Dyirbal, one set of forms is used for 'uphill' and for 'upriver' and another one for 'downhill' and 'downriver' (see Aikhenvald 2015b: 18–21, for complicated correlations between direction and distance in Manambu demonstratives). Munya and Yonghe Qiang, from the

Table 3 Locational suffixes in Dyirbal

-bayji	short distance downhill	-dayi	short distance uphill
-bayja	medium distance downhill	-daya	medium distance uphill
-bayju	long distance downhill	-dayu	long distance uphill
-balba	medium distance downriver	-dawa	medium distance upriver
-balbu	long distance downriver	-dawu	long distance upriver
-guya across the river			
-bawal long way in any direction			

Qiangic subgroup of Tibeto-Burman family, are spoken in river valleys. Both languages have directional prefixes on verbs which indicate directions upstream and downstream from the speaker (Bai 2020; Sims and Genetti 2017: 121–2).

Galo, of the Tani subgroup of Tibeto-Burman, is spoken in the hilly regions of Arunachal Pradesh, in north-east India. Its demonstratives distinguish directions uphill and downhill, and also the distance (close or far from the speaker). Closely related Apatani is strikingly different: the demonstratives distinguish distance, but not the up-down direction. The environment offers a likely explanation. Apatani, unlike its other relatives within the subgroup, is spoken almost exclusively within a *plateau* area, with neither mountains nor rivers as sufficiently salient features of the terrain (Post 2011: 138, 151). Mising, another language from the same subgroup, employs the topographic directional terms, but again with different meanings: the direction 'uphill' in closely related languages was reinterpreted as 'upriver', and 'downhill' as 'downriver'. The explanation lies in the nature of the terrain: the overwhelmingly dominant environmental feature of the area where Mising is spoken is the Brahmaputra river, and there are virtually no hills of any noticeable size (Post 2011: 150; see also Post 2020 on the reconstruction of topographic deixis for Trans-Himalayan languages and their original environment).

Topographic deixis appears to be a shared feature of most Tani languages, but its realizations vary, depending on the environment—hilly, flat, or riverine. Along similar lines, Yalaku, a Ndu language closely related to Manambu, is spoken away from the river in a hilly area. Its demonstratives and verbs occur with suffixes indicating directions uphill and downhill—but not upriver and downriver, since the river is irrelevant to people's lifestyle.

While a topographic distinction in a language may be explained through a correlation with environment, a feature of the environment will never be enough to predict with any certainty what a language will have.

In many languages, demonstratives and directionals appear to be shaped by the salient landmarks in the geographic environment. But not always so. Iatmul is closely related to Manambu, and is spoken along the Sepik river in a hilly country. Yet, there are no topographic distinctions in the demonstratives nor in verbs. This could be an indication that the speakers moved into the region fairly recently, and haven't had the time to develop the uphill/downhill distinctions.

Correlations between the geographical terrain and grammatical systems of demonstratives or directionals appear to be a prerogative of relatively small communities, whose members all live in a similar landscape. A larger group spread over a wide territory, will be less likely to have an obligatory grammatical system relating to a specific type of terrain. Iatmul is spoken by ten times as many people as Manambu, across a much wider area. This could also be a reason for the absence of topographic distinctions in its demonstratives.

Correlations between other features of physical environment and linguistic categories are more difficult to capture. Denny (1979: 108, 112–15) attempted to link the existence of deictic classifiers in Eskimo and Toba which are fused with the distinction 'in view/not in view' by the fact that they 'hunt in open treeless environment'. On the other hand, quite a few languages with visibility distinctions in demonstratives are spoken in other kinds of environments— Dyirbal in dense rainforest, Palikur in moderately forested area, and Lilloeet in a largely open country. The question of whether the visibility distinctions in grammar correlate with any geographical feature remains open.

References

Adams, Karen L. 1989. *Systems of numeral classification in the Mon-Khmer, Nicobarese and Aslian subfamilies of Austroasiatic*. Canberra: Pacific Linguistics.

Adams, Karen L. 1992. 'A comparison of the numeral classification of humans in Mon-Khmer'. *Mon-Khmer Studies* 21: 107–29.

Agha, Asif. 2007. *Language and social relations*. Cambridge: Cambridge University Press.

Aikhenvald, Alexandra Y. 2000. *Classifiers. A typology of noun categorization devices*. Oxford: Oxford University Press.

Aikhenvald, Alexandra Y. 2002. *Language contact in Amazonia*. Oxford: Oxford University Press.

Aikhenvald, Alexandra Y. 2004. *Evidentiality*. Oxford: Oxford University Press.

Aikhenvald, Alexandra Y. 2006. 'Grammars in contact: A cross-linguistic perspective', in Alexandra Y. Aikhenvald and R. M. W. Dixon (eds), *Grammars in contact: A cross-linguistic typology*. Oxford: Oxford University Press, 1–66.

Aikhenvald, Alexandra Y. 2008. *The Manambu language, from East Sepik, Papua New Guinea*. Oxford: Oxford University Press.

Aikhenvald, Alexandra Y. 2010. *Imperatives and commands*. Oxford: Oxford University Press.

Aikhenvald, Alexandra Y. 2012. *The languages of the Amazon*. Oxford: Oxford University Press.

Aikhenvald, Alexandra Y. 2013. 'Possession and ownership in cross-linguistic perspective', in Alexandra Y. Aikhenvald and R. M. W. Dixon (eds), *Possession and ownership: A cross-linguistic typology*. Oxford: Oxford University Press, 1–64.

Aikhenvald, Alexandra Y. 2014. 'Double talk: Parallel structures in Manambu songs'. *Language and Linguistics in Melanesia* 32.2: 86–109.

Aikhenvald, Alexandra Y. 2015a. *The art of grammar: A practical guide*. Oxford: Oxford University Press.

Aikhenvald, Alexandra Y. 2015b. 'Distance, direction, and relevance: How to choose and to use a demonstrative in Manambu'. *Anthropological Linguistics* 57: 1–45.

Aikhenvald, Alexandra Y. 2016. *How gender shapes the world*. Oxford: Oxford University Press.

Aikhenvald, Alexandra Y. 2017. 'A typology of noun categorization devices', in Alexandra Y. Aikhenvald and R. M. W. Dixon (eds), *The Cambridge handbook of linguistic typology*. Cambridge: Cambridge University Press, 361–404.

Aikhenvald, Alexandra Y. 2018a. 'Evidentiality: the framework', in Alexandra Y. Aikhenvald (ed.), *The Oxford Handbook of evidentiality*. Oxford: Oxford University Press, 1–46.

Aikhenvald, Alexandra Y. 2018b. 'Evidentiality and language contact', in Alexandra Y. Aikhenvald (ed.), *The Oxford handbook of evidentiality*. Oxford: Oxford University Press, 148–72.

Aikhenvald, Alexandra Y. 2018c. 'Comparison, contrast and similarity in Yalaku'. *Linguistic Discovery* 16.1: 1–13.

Aikhenvald, Alexandra Y. 2018d. *Serial verbs*. Oxford: Oxford University Press.

Aikhenvald, Alexandra Y. 2021. 'One of a kind: On the utility of specific classifiers'. *Cognitive Semantics* 7: 232–57.

Aitchison, Jean. 1999. 'Review of Anna Wierzbicka. *Understanding cultures through their key words: English, Russian, Polish, German and Japanese*. Oxford: Oxford University Press'. *International Journal of Lexicography* 12: 87–9.

Ameka, Felix K. 2004. 'Grammar and cultural practices: The grammaticalization of triadic communication in West African languages'. *Journal of West African Languages* XXX.2: 5–28.

Ameka, Felix K. 2013. 'Possessive constructions in Likpe (Sɛkpɛlé)', in Alexandra Y. Aikhenvald and R. M. W. Dixon (eds), *Possession and ownership: A cross-linguistic typology*. Oxford: Oxford University Press, 224–42.

Ameka, Felix K. 2017. 'Logophoricity', in Alexandra Y. Aikhenvald and R. M. W. Dixon (eds), *The Cambridge handbook of linguistic typology*. Cambridge: Cambridge University Press, 513–37.

Anderson, L-G. and T. Janson. 1997. *Languages in Botswana. Language ecology in Southern Africa*. Botswana: Longman.

Asher, R. E. 1985. *Tamil*. London: Croom Helm.

Azeb Amha. 2001. *The Maale language*. Leiden: CNWS.

Azeb Amha. 2013. 'Directives to humans and to domestic animals – the imperative and some interjections in Zargulla', in Marie-Claude Simeone-Senelle and Martine Vanhove (eds), *Proceedings of the 5th International Conference on Cushitic and Omotic languages, Paris, 16–18 April 2008*. Cologne: Köppe, 211–29.

Bai, Junwei. 2020. 'A grammar of Munya'. PhD thesis, James Cook University.

Barnes, Janet. 1984. 'Evidentials in the Tuyuca verb'. *International Journal of American Linguistics* 50: 255–71.

Basso, Ellen. 2007. 'The Kalapalo affinal civility register'. *Journal of Linguistic Anthropology* 17: 161–83.

Bauman, Richard and Charles Briggs. 1990. 'Poetics and performance as critical perspectives on language and social life'. *Annual Review of Anthropology* 19: 59–88.

Bickel, Balthasar. 1999. 'Cultural formalism and spatial language in Belhare', in Balthasar Bickel and Martin Gaenszle (eds), *Himalayan space: Cultural horizons and practices*. Zürich: Museum of Ethnography, 75–104.

Bickel, Balthasar. 2000. 'Grammar and social practice. On the role of "culture" in linguistic relativity', in Susanne Niemeier and René Dirven (eds), *Evidence for linguistic relativity*. Amsterdam: John Benjamins, 162–91.

Bickel, Balthasar. 2001. 'Deictic transposition and referential practice in Belhare'. *Journal of Linguistic Anthropology* 10: 224–47.

Bing, Janet M. 1991. 'Color terms and lexical classes in Krahn/Wobé'. *Studies in African Linguistics* 22: 277–96.

Bisang, Walter. 2017. 'Classification between grammar and culture. A cross-linguistic perspective', in Tanja Pommerening and Walter Bisang (eds), *Classification from antiquity to modern times*. Berlin: De Gruyter, 199–230.

Blust, Robert. 2009. *The Austronesian languages.* Canberra: Pacific Linguistics.

Boas, Franz. 1938. 'Language', in Franz Boas (ed.), *General anthropology.* Boston, New York: D. C. Heath and Company, 124–45.

Boas, Franz. 1942. 'Language and culture', *Studies in the history of culture: The disciplines of the humanities.* Menasha: The George Banta Publishing Co, 178–84.

Boas, Franz and Ella Deloria. 1941. *Dakota grammar.* Washington: US Govt. Print. Office.

Boroditsky, L. 2003. 'Linguistic relativity', in L. Nadel (ed.), *Encyclopedia of cognitive science.* Hoboken, NJ: Wiley, 917–22.

Bradley, David. 2001. 'Counting the family: Family group classifiers in Yi (Tibeto-Burman) languages.' *Anthropological Linguistics* 43: 1–17.

Braun, Friederike. 1988. *Terms of address. Problems of patterns and usage in various languages and cultures.* Berlin: Mouton de Gruyter.

Breedveld, Anneke. 1995. *Form and meaning in Fulfulde.* Leiden: CNWS.

Brosig, Benjamin and Elena Skribnik. 2018. 'Evidentiality in Mongolic', in Alexandra Y. Aikhenvald (ed.), *The Oxford handbook of evidentiality.* Oxford: Oxford University Press, 554–79.

Brosnahan, P. 1961. *The sounds of language.* Cambridge: W. Heffer and Sons Ltd.

Brown, Roger. 1976. 'Reference: In memorial tribute to Eric Lenneberg'. *Cognition* 4: 125–53.

Brownie, John and Marjo Brownie. 2007. *Mussau grammar essentials.* Ukarumpa: SIL - PNG Academic Publications.

Bulygina, T. V. and A. D. Shmelev. 1997. *Linguistic conceptualization of the world (on the basis of Russian grammar).* (Jazykovaja konceptualizacija mira (na materiale russkoj grammatiki)). Moscow: Jazyki russkoj kuljtury.

Burenhult, Niclas. 2008. 'Spatial coordinate systems in demonstrative meaning'. *Linguistic Typology* 12: 99–142.

Burke, Isabelle and Kate Burridge. 2021. 'Privileging informality—cultural influences on the structural patterning of Australian English', Pam Peters and Kate Burridge (eds), *Exploring the ecology of World Englishes in the 21st Century: Language, society, culture.* Edinburgh: Edinburgh University Press, 324–44.

Burridge, Kate. 2006. 'Language contact and convergence in Pennsylvanian German', in Alexandra Y. Aikhenvald and R. M. W. Dixon (eds), *Grammars in contact: A cross-linguistic typology.* Oxford: Oxford University Press, 179–200.

Burridge, Kate and Caroline Brewer. 2021. 'Where grammar meets culture: Pronominal systems in Australasia and the South Pacific revisited', Pam Peters and Kate Burridge (eds), *Exploring the ecology of World Englishes in the 21st Century: Language, society, culture.* Edinburgh: Edinburgh University Press, 260–79.

Campbell, Lyle and Martha Muntzel. 1989. 'The structural consequences of language death', in Nancy Dorian (ed.), *Investigating obsolescence. Studies in language contraction and death.* Cambridge: Cambridge University Press, 181–96.

Carlin, Eithne B. 2004. *A grammar of Trio, a Cariban language of Suriname.* Frankfurt am Main: Peter Lang.

Carlin, Eithne B. 2018. 'Evidentiality and the Cariban languages', in Alexandra Y. Aikhenvald (ed.), *The Oxford Handbook of evidentiality.* Oxford: Oxford University Press, 315–32.

Carroll, John B. 1963. 'Linguistic relativity, contrastive linguistics, and language learning'. *International Review of Applied Linguistics in Language Teaching* 1: 1–20.

Cheshire, J. 2008. 'Still a gender-biased language? Updates on gender inequalities and the English language'. *English Today* 93: 7–10.

Ciucci, Luca. 2019. 'A culture of secrecy: The hidden narratives of the Ayoreo'. *International Journal of Language and Culture* 6: 175–94.

Ciucci, Luca and Pier Marco Bertinetto. 2019. 'Possessive classifiers in Zamucoan', in Alexandra Y. Aikhenvald and Elena Mihas (eds), *Genders and classifiers: A cross-linguistic typology.* Oxford: Oxford University Press, 144–75.

Clyne, Michael, H-L. Kretzenbacher, C. Norrby, and D. Schüpbach. 2006. 'Perceptions of variation and change in German and Swedish address'. *Journal of Sociolinguistics* 10: 287–319.

Coates, Jennifer. 2003. 'Address', in William J. Frawley (ed.), *International encyclopedia of linguistics,* 2nd edition. Oxford: Oxford University Press, 33–4.

Cowell, Andrew. 2007. 'Arapaho imperatives: Indirectness, politeness and communal "face" '. *Journal of Linguistic Anthropology* 17: 44–60.

Craig, Colette G. 1986. 'Jacaltec noun classifiers: A study in language and culture', in Colette G. Craig (ed.), *Noun classes and categorization: Proceedings of a symposium on categorization and noun classification, Eugene, Oregon, October 1983.* Amsterdam: John Benjamins, 263–94.

Daguman, Josephine. 2018. 'The reportative in the languages of the Philippines', in Alexandra Y. Aikhenvald (ed.), *The Oxford Handbook of evidentiality.* Oxford: Oxford University Press, 674–92.

Dench, Alan. 2013. 'Possession in Martuthunira', in Alexandra Y. Aikhenvald and R. M. W. Dixon (eds), *Possession and ownership: A cross-linguistic typology.* Oxford: Oxford University Press, 126–48.

Denny, J. P. 1979. 'The 'extendedness' variable in classifier semantics: Universal semantic features and cultural variation', in Mathiot, M. (ed.), *Ethnology: Boas, Sapir and Whorf revisit(ed.)* The Hague: Mouton, 97–119.

Deutscher, Guy. 2010. *Through the language glass: Why the world looks different in other languages.* New York: Metropolitan books.

Dixon, R. M. W. 1994. *Ergativity*. Cambridge: Cambridge University Press.

Dixon, R. M. W. 2002. *Australian languages: Their nature and development*. Cambridge: Cambridge University Press.

Dixon, R. M. W. 2008. 'Comparative constructions: A cross-linguistic typology.' *Studies in Language* 32: 787–817.

Dixon, R. M. W. 2010a. *Basic Linguistic Theory*. Volume I. *Methodology*. Oxford: Oxford University Press.

Dixon, R. M. W. 2010b. *Basic Linguistic Theory*. Volume II. *Grammatical topics*. Oxford: Oxford University Press.

Dixon, R. M. W. 2012. *Basic linguistic theory*. Volume III. *Further grammatical topics*. Oxford: Oxford University Press.

Dixon, R. M. W. 2014a. 'The basics of a language', in N. J. Enfield, Paul Kockelman, and Jack Sidnell (eds), *The Cambridge handbook of linguistic anthropology*. Cambridge: Cambridge University Press, 29–47.

Dixon, R. M. W. 2014b. 'The non-visible marker in Dyirbal', in Alexandra Y. Aikhenvald and R. M. W. Dixon (eds), *The grammar of knowledge*. Oxford: Oxford University Press, 171–89.

Dixon, R. M. W. 2015. *Edible gender, mother-in-law style & other grammatical wonders. Studies in Dyirbal, Yidiñ, & Warrgamay*. Oxford: Oxford University Press.

Dixon, R. M. W. 2016. *Are some languages better than others?* Oxford: Oxford University Press.

Dixon, R. M. W. 2017. 'What Dyirbal uses instead of commands', in Alexandra Y. Aikhenvald and R. M. W. Dixon (eds), *Commands: A cross-linguistic typology*. Oxford: Oxford University Press, 127–45.

Du Bois, J. 1985. 'Competing motivations', in John Haiman (ed.), *Iconicity in syntax*. Amsterdam: John Benjamins, 343–66.

Eberhard, David M. 2009. 'Mamaindê Grammar: A Northern Nambikwara language and its cultural context'. PhD dissertation, Vrije Universiteit Amsterdam.

Eberhard, David M. 2018. 'Evidentiality in Nambikwara languages', in Alexandra Y. Aikhenvald (ed.), *The Oxford handbook of evidentiality*. Oxford: Oxford University Press, 333–56.

Enfield, N. J. 2000. 'On linguocentrism', in Susanne Niemeier and René Dirven (eds), *Evidence for linguistic relativity*. Amsterdam: John Benjamins, 126–57.

Enfield, N. J. 2004a. 'Ethnosyntax: Introduction', in N. J. Enfield (ed.), *Ethnosyntax: Explorations in grammar and culture*. Oxford: Oxford University Press, 3–30.

Enfield, N. J. 2004b. 'Cultural logic and syntactic productivity: Associated posture constructions in Lao', in N. J. Enfield (ed.), *Ethnosyntax. Explorations in grammar and culture*. Oxford: Oxford University Press, 231–58.

Enfield, N. J. 2014. *Natural causes of language. Frames, biases, and cultural transmission*. Language Sciences Press.

Enfield, N. J. 2015. *The Utility of meaning. What words mean and why.* Oxford: Oxford University Press.

Enfield, N. J. 2017. 'Language in the Mainland Southeast Asia area', in Alexandra Y. Aikhenvald and R. M. W. Dixon (eds), *The Cambridge handbook of linguistic typology.* Cambridge: Cambridge University Press, 601–23.

Evans, Nicholas. 2009. 'Two p(l)us one makes thirteen: Senary numerals in the Morehead-Maro region'. *Linguistic Typology* 13: 321–35.

Evans-Pritchard, E. E. 1940. *The Nuer. A description of the modes of livelihood and political institutions of a Nilotic people.* New York and Oxford: Oxford University Press.

Forker, Diana. 2014. 'The grammar of knowledge in Hinuq', in Alexandra Y. Aikhenvald and R. M. W. Dixon (eds), *The grammar of knowledge.* Oxford: Oxford University Press, 52–68.

Franklin, K. J. and R. Stefaniw. 1992. 'The 'pandanus languages' of the Southern Highlands Province, Papua New Guinea—a further report', in Tom E. Dutton (ed.), *Culture change, language change. Case studies from Melanesia.* Canberra: Pacific Linguistics, 1–6.

Geraghty, Paul. 2000. 'Possession in the Fijian languages'. *Sprachtypologie und Universalienforschung* 53 3/4: 243–50.

Goddard, Cliff. 1983. 'A semantically-oriented grammar of the Yankunytjatjara dialect of the Western Desert language'. PhD thesis, Australian National University.

Goddard, Cliff. 2005. *The languages of East and Southeast Asia. An introduction.* Oxford: Oxford University Press.

Greed, Teija. 2014. 'The grammar of knowledge in Tatar', in Alexandra Y. Aikhenvald and R. M. W. Dixon (eds), *The grammar of knowledge.* Oxford: Oxford University Press, 69–88.

Gruzdeva, Ekaterina. 2004. 'Classifiers in Nivkh', in Alexandra Y. Aikhenvald (ed.), *Nominal classification*, Special issue of *Sprachtypologie und Universalienforschung* 57, 2/3: 300–29.

Gumperz, John J. and Stephen C. Levinson 1996. (eds). *Explorations in linguistic relativity.* Cambridge: Cambridge University Press.

Haiman, John. 1983. 'Iconic and Economic Motivation'. *Language* 59: 781–819.

Hale, Ken and David Nash. 1997. 'Lardil and Damin phonotactics', in Darrell Tryon and Michael Walsh (eds), *Boundary rider. Essays in honour of Geoffrey O'Grady.* Canberra: Pacific Linguistics, 247–59.

Hardman, M. J. 1986. 'Data-source marking in the Jaqi languages', in Wallace L. Chafe and Johanna Nichols (eds), *Evidentiality: The linguistic coding of epistemology.* Norwood: Ablex Publishing, 113–36.

Heine, Bernd. 1997. *Cognitive foundations of grammar.* Oxford: Oxford University Press.

Hercus, Louise. 1994. *A grammar of the Arabana-Wangkanguru language, Lake Eyre basin, South Australia.* Canberra: Pacific Linguistics.

Hill, Jane H. 2008. *The everyday language of white racism.* Oxford: Wiley-Blackwell.

Irvine, Judith T. 1978. 'Wolof noun classification: The social setting of divergent change'. *Language in Society* 7: 37–64.

Irvine, Judith T. 1990. 'Registering affect: Heteroglossia in the linguistic expression of emotion', in Catherine A. Lutz and Lila Abu-Lughod (eds), *Language and the politics of emotion.* Cambridge: Cambridge University Press and Paris: Éditions de la maison des science de l'homme, 126–61.

Irvine, Judith T. 1998. 'Ideologies of honorific language', in Kathryn A. Woolard and Paul V. Kroskrity (eds) *Language ideologies. Practice and theory.* Oxford: Oxford University Press, 51–67.

Iwasaki, Shoichi and Preeya Ingkaphirom. 2005. *A reference grammar of Thai.* Cambridge: Cambridge University Press.

Jarkey, Nerida. 2015. *Serial verbs in White Hmong.* Leiden: Brill.

Jarkey, Nerida. 2017. 'Imperatives and commands in Japanese', in Alexandra Y. Aikhenvald and R. M. W. Dixon (eds), *Commands: A cross-linguistic typology.* Oxford: Oxford University Press, 169–88.

Juntanamalaga, P. 1988. 'Social issues in Thai classifier usage'. *Language Sciences* 10: 313–30.

Keating, Elizabeth. 1997. 'Honorific possession: Power and language in Pohnpei, Micronesia'. *Language in Society* 26: 247–68.

Keating, Elizabeth. 1998. *Power sharing: Language, rank, gender and social space in Pohnpei, Micronesia.* New York: Oxford University Press.

Keating, Elizabeth. 2002. 'Space and its role in social stratification in Pohnpei, Micronesia', in Giovanni Bernardo (ed.), *Representing space in Oceania: Culture in language and mind.* Canberra: Pacific Linguistics, 201–13.

Kießling, Roland & Maarten Mous. 2004. 'Urban youth languages in Africa'. *Anthropological Linguistics* 46, 3: 303–41.

Kracke, Waud H. 2009. 'Dream as deceit, dream as truth: The grammar of telling dreams.' *Anthropological Linguistics* 51: 61–77.

Kruspe, Nicole. 2004. *A grammar of Semelai.* Cambridge: Cambridge University Press.

Lakoff, Robin Tolmach. 1973. 'Language and woman's place'. *Language in Society* 2: 45–80.

Lakoff, Robin Tolmach. 1975. *Language and woman's place.* New York: Harper and Row.

Langacker, R. W. 1977. *Studies in Uto-Aztecan grammar*, vol.1 *An Overview of Uto-Aztecan grammar*. Dallas: Summer Institute of Linguistics and the University of Texas at Arlington.

Lee, Yunseok. 2014. *Classifiers in Korean*. Munich: Lincom Europa.

Lu, Tian-Qiao. 2012. *Classifiers in Kam-Tai languages. A cognitive and cultural perspective*. Boca Raton: Universal Publishers.

Lucy, John A. 1992a. *Grammatical categories and cognition. A study of the linguistic relativity hypothesis*. Cambridge: Cambridge University Press.

Lucy, John A. 1992b. *Language diversity and thought. A reformulation of the linguistic relativity hypothesis*. Cambridge: Cambridge University Press.

Lucy, John A. 1996. 'The scope of linguistic relativity: An analysis and review of empirical research', in John J. Gumperz and Stephen C. Levinson (eds), *Rethinking linguistic relativity*. Cambridge: Cambridge University Press, 37–69.

Lüpke, Friederike and Anne Storch (eds). 2013. *Repertoires and choices in African languages*. Berlin: De Gruyter.

Maiden, Martin and Cecilia Robustelli. 2007. *A reference grammar of Modern Italian*, second edition. New York: MacGraw Hill.

Marnita, R. 1996. *Classifiers in Minangkabau*. MA thesis, Australian National University.

Mathiot, M. (ed.). 1979. *Ethnology: Boas, Sapir and Whorf revisited*. The Hague: Mouton.

McLendon, S. 2003. 'Evidentials in Eastern Pomo with a comparative survey of the category in other Pomoan languages', in Alexandra Y. Aikhenvald and R. M. W. Dixon (eds), *Studies in evidentiality*. Amsterdam: John Benjamins, 101–30.

Messineo, Cristina. 2011. 'Aproximación tipológica a las lenguas indígenas del Gran Chaco. Rasgos compartidos entre toba (familia guaycurú) y maká (familia mataco-mataguayo)'. *Indiana* 28. 183–226.

Michael, Lev. 2013. 'Possession in Nanti', in Alexandra Y. Aikhenvald and R. M. W. Dixon (eds), *Possession and ownership: A cross-linguistic typology*. Oxford: Oxford University Press, 149–66.

Mihas, Elena. 2017. 'Imperatives in Ashaninka Satipo (Kampa Arawak) of Peru', in Alexandra Y. Aikhenvald and R. M. W. Dixon (eds), *Commands: A cross-linguistic typology*. Oxford: Oxford University Press, 83–105.

Mitchell, Alice. 2015. 'Words that smell like father-in-law: A linguistic description of the Datooga avoidance register'. *Anthropological Linguistics* 57: 195–217.

Mitchell, Alice. 2018. 'Allusive references and other-oriented stance in an affinal avoidance register'. *Journal of Linguistic Anthropology* 28: 4–21.

Mitchell, Alice. 2020. '"Oh, bald father!": Kinship and swearing among Datooga of Tanzania', in Nico Nassenstein and Anne Storch (eds), *Swearing and cursing– Contexts and practices in a critical linguistic perspective*. Berlin: De Gruyter Mouton, 79–102.

Mous, Maarten. 1994. 'Ma'a or Mbugu', in P. Bakker and M. Mous (eds), *Mixed languages: 15 case studies in language intertwining*. Amsterdam: IFOTT, 175–200.

Mous, Maarten. 2003. *The making of a mixed language: The case of Ma'a/Mbugu* Amsterdam: John Benjamins.

Müller, André and Rachel Weymuth. 2017. 'How society shapes language: Personal pronouns in the Greater Burma Zone'. *Asiatische Studien-Études Asiatiques* 71: 209–32.

Nassentein, Nico. 2020. 'Mock Chinese in Kinshasa: On Lingala speakers' offensive language use and verbal hostility', in Nico Nassenstein and Anne Storch (eds), *Swearing and cursing – Contexts and practices in a critical linguistic perspective*. Berlin: De Gruyter Mouton, 185–208.

Nassenstein, Nico and Andrea Hollington (eds). 2015. *Youth language practices in Africa and beyond*. Berlin: De Gruyter Mouton.

Needham, Rodney (ed.). 1973. *Right and left: Essays on dual symbolic classification*. Chicago: University of Chicago Press.

Nuckolls, Janis B. 2018. 'The interactional and cultural pragmatics of evidentiality in Pastaza Quichua', in Alexandra Y. Aikhenvald (ed.), *The Oxford handbook of evidentiality*. Oxford: Oxford University Press, 202–21.

Overall, Simon E. 2017. 'A typology of frustrative marking in Amazonian languages', in Alexandra Y. Aikhenvald and R. M. W. Dixon (eds), *The Cambridge handbook of linguistic typology*. Cambridge: Cambridge University Press, 477–512.

Palmer, Bill. 2002. 'Absolute spatial reference and the grammaticalisation of perceptually salient phenomena', in Giovanni Bennardo (ed.), *Representing space in Oceania. Culture in language and mind*. Canberra: Pacific Linguistics, 107–57.

Pan, Chia-jung. 2018. 'Evidentiality in Formosan languages', in Alexandra Y. Aikhenvald (ed.) *The Oxford handbook of evidentiality*. Oxford: Oxford University Press, 657–73.

Pauwels, Anne. 1998. *Women changing language*. London: Longman.

Payne, Doris L. 2006. 'Color terms', in Keith Brown (ed.), *Encyclopedia of language and linguistics*, second edition. Oxford: Elsevier, 605–10.

Post, Mark W. 2011. 'Topographical deixis and the Tani languages of North East India', in Gwendolyn Hyslop, Stephen Morey, and Mark W. Post (eds), *North East Indian Linguistics*. New Delhi, India: Cambridge University Press, 137–54.

Post, Mark W. 2020. 'The distribution, reconstruction and varied fates of topographical deixis in Trans-Himalayan (Sino-Tibetan). Implications for the reconstruction of an early Trans-Himalayan environment'. *Diachronica* 37: 146–87.

Rind-Pawlowski, Monika. 2019. 'Possession in Khinalug', in Lars Johanson, Lidia Federica Mazzitelli, and Irina Nevskaya (eds), *Possession in languages of Europe and North and Central Asia*. Amsterdam: John Benjamins, 239–66.

Rivière, Peter. 1969. *Marriage among the Trio. A principle of social organization.* Oxford: Clarendon Press.

Rosaldo, Michelle. 1973. 'I have nothing to hide: The language of Ilongot Oratory'. *Language in Society* 2: 193–222.

Rosaldo, Michelle. 1982. 'The things we do with words: Ilongot speech acts and speech act theory in philosophy'. *Language in Society* 11: 203–37.

Salzmann, Zdenek. 2004. *Language, culture and society.* 3rd edition. Boulder, Colorado: Westview Press.

Sapir, E. 1921. *Language.* New York: Harcourt, Brace, and World.

Sarvasy, Hannah. 2017. *A grammar of Nungon, a Papuan language of Northeast New Guinea.* Leiden: Brill.

Schieffelin, Bambi B. 2008. 'Speaking only your own mind: Reflections on talk, gossip and intentionality in Bosavi (PNG)'. *Anthropological Quarterly* 81: 431–41.

Schmidt, A. 1985. *Young People's Dyirbal. An example of language death from Australia.* Cambridge: Cambridge University Press.

Schokkin, Dineke. 2014. 'A grammar of Paluai, the language of Baluan Island, Papua New Guinea'. PhD thesis, James Cook University.

Schokkin, Dineke and Ton Otto. 2017. 'Relatives and relations in Paluai'. *Oceanic Linguistics* 56: 228–46.

Seiler, H. 1977. *Cahuilla grammar.* California: Malki Museum Press.

Seki, L. 2000. *Gramática da língua Kamaiurá.* Campinas: Editora da Unicamp.

Sims, Nathaniel and Carol Genetti. 2017. 'The grammatical encoding of space in Yonghe Qiang'. *Himalayan Linguistics* 16: 99–140.

Slobin, Dan I. 1996. 'From "thought and language" to "thinking for speaking"', in John J. Gumperz and Stephen C. Levinson (eds), *Rethinking linguistic relativity.* Cambridge: Cambridge University Press, 70–96.

Sohn, Ho-Min. 1994. *Korean.* London and New York: Routledge.

Sparing-Chávez, M. 2003. 'I want to but I can't: The frustrative in Amahuaca.' *Summer Institute of Linguistics Electronic Working Papers* SILEWP 2003-002, 13 pp.

Stenzel, Kristine and Elsa Gomez-Imbert. 2018. 'Evidentiality in Tukanoan languages', in Alexandra Y. Aikhenvald (ed.), *The Oxford handbook of evidentiality.* Oxford: Oxford University Press, 357–87.

Storch, Anne. 2011. *Secret manipulations*. New York: Oxford University Press.

Storch, Anne. 2013a. 'Possession in Hone', in Alexandra Y. Aikhenvald and R. M. W. Dixon (eds), *Possession and ownership: A cross-linguistic typology*. Oxford: Oxford University Press, 208–23.

Storch, Anne. 2013b. 'Doing things with words', pp. 77–122 of Lüpke and Storch (eds), 2013.

Storch, Anne. 2014. *A grammar of Luwo. An anthropological approa*ch. Amsterdam: John Benjamins.

Storch, Anne. 2017. 'Typology of secret languages and linguistic taboos', in Alexandra Y. Aikhenvald and R. M. W. Dixon (eds), *The Cambridge handbook of linguistic typology*. Cambridge: Cambridge University Press, 287–321.

Storch, Anne. 2020. 'Aesthetics of the obscure: Swearing as horrible play', in Nico Nassenstein and Anne Storch (eds), *Swearing and cursing – Contexts and practices in a critical linguistic perspective*. Berlin: De Gruyter Mouton, 103–20.

Storch, Anne and Jules Jacques Coly. 2014. 'The grammar of knowledge in Maaka (Western Chadic, Nigeria)', in Alexandra Y. Aikhenvald and R. M. W. Dixon (eds), *The grammar of knowledge*. Oxford: Oxford University Press, 190–208.

Sun, Jackson T.-S. 2018. 'Evidentials and person', in Alexandra Y. Aikhenvald (ed.), *The Oxford handbook of evidentiality*. Oxford: Oxford University Press, 47–64.

Trechter, Sara. 1995. 'The pragmatic functions of gender deixis in Lakhota'. PhD dissertation, University of Kansas.

Trudgill, Peter. 2004. 'Linguistic and social typology: The Austronesian migrations and phoneme inventories'. *Linguistic Typology* 8: 305–20.

Trudgill, Peter. 2009. 'Sociolinguistic typology and complexification', in Geoffrey Sampson et al. (eds), *Language complexity as an evolving variable*. Oxford: Oxford University Press, 99–109.

Trudgill, Peter. 2011. *Sociolinguistic typology: Social determinants of linguistic complexity*. Oxford: Oxford University Press.

Turton, David. 1980. 'There's no such beast: Cattle and colour naming among the Mursi'. *Man*, New Series 15.2: 320–38.

Ullrich, Jan. 2008. *New Lakota dictionary*. Bloomington: Lakota Language Consortium.

Valenzuela, Pilar. 2003. 'Evidentiality in Shipibo-Konibo, with a comparative overview of the category in Panoan', in Alexandra Y. Aikhenvald and R. M. W. Dixon (eds), *Studies in evidentiality*. Amsterdam: John Benjamins, 33–62.

Weber, David J. 1986. 'Information perspective, profile, and patterns in Quechua', in Wallace L. Chafe and Johanna Nichols (eds), *Evidentiality: The linguistic coding of epistemology*. Norwood: Ablex Publishing, 137–55.

Wierzbicka, Anna. 1997. *Understanding cultures through their key words: English, Russian, Polish, German, and Japanese*. Oxford: Oxford University Press.

Wojtylak, Katarzyna Isabela. 2015. 'Fruits for animals: Hunting avoidance speech style in Murui (Witoto, Northwest Amazonia)'. *Proceedings of the forty-first annual meeting of the Berkeley Linguistics Society. General Session. Special Session. Fieldwork methodology*, edited by Anna E. Jurgensen, Hannah Sande, Spencer Lamoureux, Kenny Baclawski, and Alison Zerbe: 545–61.

Wojtylak, Katarzyna Isabela. 2019. 'A secret "jungle-at-night" register of the Murui people from Northwest Amazonia'. in Alexandra Y. Aikhenvald and Anne Storch (eds), *The Mouth*. Special issue *Taboo in language and discourse*. 4: 77–90.

Wood, Michael. 2018. 'Stereotypes and evidentiality', in Alexandra Y. Aikhenvald (ed.), *The Oxford handbook of evidentiality*. Oxford: Oxford University Press, 243–57.

2

The grammatical expression
of social relations in Japanese

Nerida Jarkey

1 Introduction

This chapter discusses the topic of the integration of language and society through an in-depth analysis of an individual, non-universal linguistic
feature—the special speech style of honorific language in Japanese. The analysis
points to the integration of this linguistic feature with a range of non-
linguistic parameters in Japanese society, centred around relations within the
community, as well as social hierarchies and organization (see Chapter 1). The
ways in which this linguistic feature has changed along with changes in
Japanese society over the course of a millennium are considered, revealing
evidence of mutual influence over time. Reference is also briefly made to
another linguistic feature in Japanese—the donatory verb system—that works
together with the honorific system, supported by and in support of one of the
most significant non-linguistic parameters discussed, that of ingroup affiliation
in Japanese society.

Honorifics have been characterized as 'social indexicals'—indexing
speakers' social identity and relationship with others (Agha 2006: 310)—and
as expressing 'social deixis' (Traugott and Dasher 2002: 226–78). However,
the question of what kinds of social identity, relationships, and deictic perspectives honorifics index in contemporary Japanese is by no means a
straightforward one. In particular, it is crucial to distinguish between cultural ideologies regarding what is indexed by these forms and their real-world
use in interaction (Duranti 1992; Keating 1998: 37–67; Agha 2006: 307–8).
As Keating (1998: 39) notes,

> With social relationships explicitly marked in language, it is possible to
> have two data sets: (1) speakers' beliefs about how the system is organized

Nerida Jarkey, *The grammatical expression of social relations in Japanese*. In: *The Integration of Language and Society: A Cross-Linguistic Typology*. Edited by: Alexandra Y. Aikhenvald, R. M. W. Dixon, and Nerida Jarkey, Oxford University Press.
© Nerida Jarkey 2021. DOI: 10.1093/oso/9780192845924.003.0002

and used, and (2) information about how speakers actually deploy these mechanisms, and negotiate social relations.

In the case of Japanese, the terminology surrounding the honorific language system expresses the strong cultural ideology that this system functions to acknowledge an established social hierarchy and allows speakers to behave appropriately within it. This does, indeed, seem to have been the purpose for which honorifics initially arose in Japanese, as in many other languages in which they occur. Furthermore, there is no doubt that they still serve this purpose in some cases.

The ongoing ideological focus on the link between honorifics and hierarchy is evident in many of the expressions employed in contexts in which honorifics are used in contemporary Japanese society (such as in the workplace). Such expressions as *meue/meshita* 'superior/inferior' (lit: 'above the eyes/below the eyes') and *jooge kankei* 'hierarchical relationships' (lit: 'above-below relationships') all clearly refer to metaphorically 'vertical' social relations (Matsumoto 1988: 413). Furthermore, the terms used for the various types of predicate honorifics themselves also reflect the social attitudes that one is expected to express towards one's social 'superiors' within such a hierarchy: *teineigo* 'polite language', *sonkeigo* 'respectful language', *kenjoogo* 'humble language', *teichoogo* 'courteous language'.

When it comes to the issue raised by Keating (quoted above) of 'how speakers actually deploy these mechanisms, and negotiate social relations', much attention has been paid in the literature to the ways in which speakers of Japanese use honorifics in everyday situations to pursue their own interactional agendas and to create and modify their own personal and institutional identities (e.g. Barke 2010; Cook 2013; Okamoto 1999, to name but a few). Scholars have found that Japanese honorifics, like those in many other languages with honorific systems, sometimes function in interaction to enact a wide range of social behaviours: to assert power or manipulate an interlocutor, to assume an institutional role, to share truisms, and even to convey anger, rejection, and sarcasm. However, this chapter focuses not on honorific use in moment-by-moment interaction, but rather on the ways in which honorifics are consistently used by speakers throughout the speech community, but which, even so, do not always conform to speakers' stereotypical perceptions concerning their function.

The speech style of honorific language in Japanese initially developed in the context of a strict, 'vertical' social hierarchy surrounding the imperial court. However, this chapter proposes that political and societal changes in pre- and early-modern Japan, and subsequent developments during the country's rapid modernization, were associated with the growing importance of ingroup/outgroup social relationships as well as with a dramatic increase in interaction with non-intimates in the public sphere. These changes in Japanese society were accompanied by changes in the Japanese language, including an increasing attention to both ingroup/outgroup distinctions and to 'horizontal' social relations in the use of the Japanese honorific system. Processes of grammaticalization, involving the development of some types of referent honorifics (subjective) into addressee honorifics (intersubjective), have accompanied these changes (Traugott and Dasher 2002: 226–78). The system has broadened its functions significantly, from simply acknowledging social hierarchy to indexing social and psychological 'distance', with a strong focus on deference to the addressee.

Following this introduction, the chapter goes on to give a short description of the typological features of Standard Japanese in §2, followed by an examination of the four types of honorifics in this language and the 'stereotypical indexical force' (Agha 2006: 308) of each type in §3. In §4, the Japanese notions of *uchi* 'ingroup' and *soto* 'outgroup' are introduced, and their importance in the use of both the honorific and donatory verb systems are shown. Section 5 gives an overview of some key changes in Japanese society over time, since around the turn of the first millennium to the modern period, that are proposed here to be associated with changes in the functions of honorifics in Japan.

2 The Japanese language

As the standard language of the nation, Japanese is spoken in at least some domains by most of the 126 million inhabitants of Japan. The long and mountainous Japanese island chain is home not only to Standard Japanese, but also to numerous regional dialects and to the Ryukyuan languages in the far south. All of these are classified as Japonic, but the wider genetic relationships of the family are still a matter of debate.

Japanese is a synthetic, agglutinating language with a basic constituent order of SV, AOV. Core arguments have nominative-accusative alignment. A particularly common sentence type involves the topic-comment structure: CS=TOP CC COP. Post-positional particles are used to mark not only topics but also core and peripheral arguments, resulting in a relatively free constituent order, as long as the verb is final. Omission of subjects and objects that can be contextually retrieved is the norm, and there is a strong preference not to refer overtly to speech participants in most cases.

The language has three major word classes: nouns (an open class with non-inflecting, free stems), verbs, and adjectives (both closed classes with inflecting, bound stems). Open-class sub-types of nouns are verbal nouns and adjectival nouns. The former describe actions and events and form predicates with the light verb *su-ru* 'to do'; the latter, though functioning like adjectives, are formally similar to nouns, and require copula support when used both attributively and predicatively. Minor word classes include modal auxiliaries, auxiliary verbs, adverbs, conjunctions, interjections, numerals, numeral classifiers, measures, and quantifiers.

Verbs are the only word class that can take honorific suffixes, indexing both referent and addressee honorific meanings. The addressee honorific form of the copula is used with predicative adjectives, as with nouns and adjectival nouns.

3 Types of predicate honorifics in Japanese

The categories of honorific language described in this section are restricted to those expressed via the predicate, with a focus on verbs. While honorific forms expressed via nominal arguments are also important, the system in Japanese is fundamentally centred around the predicate and is most fully elaborated on verbal predicates.

Predicate honorifics in Standard Japanese can be divided into four types, illustrated in examples (1)–(4). Examples are given of suppletive honorific lexemes as well as productive grammatical forms in the categories in which both of these occur. The examples given here are not authentic, but rather illustrate the 'stereotypical indexical force' (Agha 2006: 308) of the forms for each type.

3.1 Polite language (Addressee honorifics)

The first and by far the most commonly used type of predicate honorific in contemporary Japanese is *teineigo* 'polite language'. This form is completely independent of the nature of the referents in the proposition; its stereotypical function is to index the deference of the speaker directly (and only) to the addressee and it is thus classified as an addressee (rather than a referent) honorific. In the examples in (1), the honorific component is in bold.

(1)   *Teineigo* 'Polite language' (Addressee honorifics)

    a. Onishi   sensei=wa   ik-i-**mashi**-ta
        O.   teacher =TOP   go-INFIN-AHON-PAST
        Professor Onishi went.

    b. Onishi   sensei=wa   Nihon-jin   **des**-u
        O.   teacher =TOP   Japanese-person   COP:AHON-NPAST
        Professor Onishi is Japanese.

    c. Sora=ga   hare-**mashi**-ta
        sky=NOM   clear-AHON-PAST
        The sky cleared.

    d. Kyoo=wa   getsuyoobi   **des**-u
        today=TOP   Monday   COP:AHON-NPAST
        Today is Monday.

In example (1a), even though the subject referent (marked here as the topic), Professor Onishi, is given the honorific title *sensei* 'teacher', there is no respect shown to her in the predicate stem *ik-u* 'to go'.[1] The only expression of deference in the predicate is to the addressee, through the addressee honorific suffix *-mas-u*. This suffix is a highly productive addressee honorific form, able to occur on all verbs in the language. In (1b), the addressee honorific form of the copula, *des-u* (reduced from the addressee honorific form of the formal copula *de ar-i-mas-u*), again shows deference only to the addressee, not to Professor Onishi. In examples (1c) and (1d) there is no human referent, the suffix *-mas-u* and copula *des-u* again expressing deference only to the addressee.

3.2 Respect language (Subject honorifics)

The second type of predicate honorifics, *sonkeigo* 'respect language', often called 'subject honorifics' in English-language analyses, is a referent honorific that stereotypically indexes the speaker's deference to the subject referent, as in the sentences in (2). In all examples the target of respect is underlined and the honorific component(s) of the predicate are in bold.

---

[1] Explanation is in order as to why the subject of these subject honorific predicates is marked with the topic particle =*wa* rather than the nominative particle =*ga* in the examples given. By far the most common target of the deference indexed by a subject honorific is a definite, human subject, and the topicalization of such a subject is particularly common in Japanese. Whether topicalization occurs or not, of course, ultimately relates to discourse factors.

(2) *Sonkeigo* 'Respect language' (Subject honorifics)

    a. <u>Onishi sensei</u>=wa   **irasshat**-ta

        O.   teacher =TOP   come/go/be:RESP-PAST

        <u>Professor Onishi</u> **came/went/was** [here/there].

    b. <u>Onishi sensei</u>=wa   tegami=o   **o**-kak-i-**ni.nat**-ta

        O.   teacher=TOP letter=ACC HON-write-INFIN-RESP-PAST

        <u>Professor Onishi</u> **wrote** a letter.

    c. <u>Onishi sensei</u>=wa   tegami=o   kak-**are**-ta

        O.   teacher =TOP letter=ACC write-RESP-PAST

        <u>Professor Onishi</u> **wrote** a letter.

Example (2a) illustrates a suppletive subject honorific verb *irasshar-u*, which exhibits loss of distinction between more than one non-honorific equivalent, in this case between three distinct non-honorific verbs meaning 'to come', 'to go', and 'to be'. This relates to a tendency in honorific registers in many languages to speak somewhat more vaguely than in everyday speech. Other suppletive subject honorific verbs, not all of which exhibit loss of distinction, include *nasar-u* 'to do', *meshiagar-u* 'to eat, drink', *osshar-u* 'to say', *kudasar-u* 'to give'.

While the first example, (2a), illustrates a suppletive form, examples (2b and c) show two, alternative productive strategies for creating a subject honorific verb form. In (2b), a circumfix, *o-…-ni.nar-u* is attached to the infinitive stem of the verb. The prefix *o-* is a general honorific prefix and the suffix *-ni.nar-u* is grammaticalized from the lexical verb *nar-u* meaning 'to become'.[2] In (2c), the suffix, *-(r)are-ru*, which is also used to mark passive and potential meanings, is attached to the verb root. These two productive strategies both function to lower the degree of agency, and thus responsibility, attributed to the subject (Ikegami 1991: 314; Yamamoto 2006: 24–9, 103), and thus to depersonalize the action attributed to it (Traugott and Dasher 2002: 244).

3.3 Humble language type I (Object honorifics)

The third type of predicate honorifics in Japanese is *kenjoogo I* 'humble language type I', commonly called 'object honorifics' in English. Like subject

---

[2] Verbal nouns of Sino-Japanese origin appear in combination with the light verb *su-ru* 'to do' when used as predicates, e.g. *shinpai su-ru* (concern do-NPST) 'to be concerned'. The *sonkeigo* 'respect' form for these verbs employs the Sino-Japanese form of the honorific prefix, *go-*, instead of the native *o-* and the suppletive *sonkeigo* 'respect' form of the light verb *su-ru* 'do', which is *nasar-u*, e.g. *go-shinpai nasar-u* (HON-concern do:RESP-NPST).

honorifics, these are also a type of referent honorific. Verbs of this type all express some kind of interaction between the subject referent and a non-subject referent (generally a direct or indirect object), as shown in the examples in (3). The form stereotypically indexes the speaker's humility concerning the action of the subject referent (italicized below) in relation to the non-subject referent who is the target of respect (underlined).

(3) *Kenjoogo I* 'Humble language type I' (Object honorifics)
    a. <u>Onishi sensei</u>=ni   tegami=o   **itadai**-ta
        O.   teacher = DAT letter=ACC receive:HUMI-PAST
        [*I*] **received** a letter from <u>Professor Onishi</u>.

    b. <u>Onishi sensei</u>=ni   oreijoo=o
        O.   teacher = DAT letter.of.thanks=ACC
        o-okur-i-**shi**-ta
        HON-send-INFIN-HUMI-PAST
        [*I*] **sent** a letter of thanks to <u>Professor Onishi</u>.

    c. *Imooto*=wa   <u>Onishi sensei</u>=o
        younger.sister=TOP O.   teacher = ACC
        o-mach-i-**shi**-ta
        HON-wait.for-INFIN-HUMI-PAST
        [*My*] *younger sister* **waited for** <u>Professor Onishi</u>.

As in the case of subject honorific forms, both suppletive (3a) and productive (3b and c) object honorific forms occur. Other examples of suppletive forms include *mooshiage-ru* 'to speak to', *sashiage-ru* 'to give to', *zonjiage-ru* 'to think about, know', and *ukaga-u* 'to inquire, implore, visit', the latter two exhibiting loss of distinction.[3] The productive strategy again utilizes a circumfix, with the same, initial honorific prefix *o-* that occurs in the productive subject honorific forms (§3.2), and the suffix *-su-ru*, grammaticalized from the lexical verb meaning 'to do'. Thus, while the subject honorific suffixes (*-ni.nar-u* and *-(r)are-ru*) work to lower the sense of agency attributed to the respected subject, this object honorific suffix serves to retain the sense of agency/responsibility of the humbled subject.

As seen in examples (3a and b), the default subject referent of an object honorific verb is the speaker. However, example (3c) shows that a referent

---

[3] Notice the compounding involved in some of the object honorifics—*mooshiage-ru* 'to tell', *sashiage-ru* 'to give to', *zonjiage-ru* 'to think about, know'—in which the second element, *age-ru* 'to give, to raise up', introduces the sense of deferential interaction with the non-subject referent that is characteristic of this honorific type.

other than the speaker can occur as subject, provided it is someone who can be considered the speaker's 'ingroup' member—here the speaker's younger sister (see §4 regarding the notion of 'ingroup').

3.4 Humble language type II (Courteous honorifics)

Kenjoogo II 'humble language type II' is the fourth and final type of predicate honorific in Japanese. This type is also called *teichoogo* 'courteous language' and has been referred to simply (though somewhat confusingly) as 'humble forms' in some literature in English (for example in the much-quoted work of Ide 1982).[4] Like the third type—object honorifics—courteous honorifics stereotypically index the humility of the subject referent. However, they differ from object honorifics in that, while they express the action of the subject in a humble way, they do not express interaction with a respected party and thus have no referential target of deference. Both honorific components— the courteous honorific verb and the addressee honorific suffix -*mas-u*—are highlighted in bold in the examples in (4), and the humbled referent is italicized.

(4) *Kenjoogo II* 'Humble language type II' (Courteous honorifics)
   a. **Mair-i-mashi**-ta
       come/go:HUMII-INFIN-AHON-PAST
       [*I*] **came/went**.

   b. Kyoodai=de   manan-de
       Kyoto.University=LOC   learn-GERUND
       or-i-mas-u
       be:HUMII-INFIN-AHON-NPAST
       [*I*] **am** studying at Kyoto University.

   c. *Imooto*=wa   Hanako=to
       younger.sister=TOP   H.=COMP
       moosh-i-mas-u
       be.called:HUMII-INFIN-AHON-NPAST
       [*My*] *younger sister* **is called** Hanako.

---

[4] This is confusing because the word *kenjoogo* itself means 'humble language / humble forms', so the English term 'humble forms' sounds like a cover term for both *kenjoogo* I (object honorifics) and *kenjoogo* II (courteous honorifics). The term 'courteous honorifics' has been chosen instead for use in this chapter.

There is no productive grammatical strategy for creating courteous honorifics; all are suppletive lexical items like those in (4a–c). Some involve loss of
distinction, as in (4a and c) (the verb *moos-u* in (4c) meaning 'to say' in other
contexts). Additional examples include *itas-u* 'to do' and *zonjir-u* 'to think,
know'. As in the case of object honorifics, the default subject referent is the
speaker (4a and b) but an ingroup referent can also readily occur (4c).

As there is no referential target of deference in the case of courteous
honorifics, the humility conveyed can only be understood as expressing deference, in an indirect way, towards the addressee. For this reason, this type of
honorific has properties akin to both referent and addressee honorifics.
It is a referent honorific, like subject and object honorifics (§3.2 and §3.3) in
that the social deixis applies to a referent (the subject), stereotypically indexed
as the humbled party. However, it is like an addressee honorific (§3.1) in
that it also functions (albeit indirectly) to express deference towards the
addressee.

Notice in all the examples given, that this form is accompanied by the
addressee honorific suffix *-mas-u*. While subject and object honorifics can
occur without an addressee honorific suffix, as shown in the examples in (2)
and (3), this would be simply incongruous with this courteous type of honorific
predicate in contemporary Japanese. This is precisely because the form clearly
functions to show courtesy to the addressee.

In formal contexts such as public announcements, verbs of this type have
come to be used with a non-human subject, as shown in (4d).

(4)   d.   Densha=ga   **mair-i-mashi**-ta
           train=NOM   come/go:HUMII-INFIN-AHON-PAST
           The train (has) **come/gone.**

With no human referent that can be interpreted as the humbled participant in
the event, the only possible interpretation here is that the speaker's humility is
expressed to the addressee in a slightly less indirect way, rather than via the
humbling of a human subject referent.

Even when a non-human subject appears, such as *densha* 'train' in (4d),
this type still differs in two ways from an addressee honorific suffix like *-mas-u*
(§3.1). First, as noted, the suffix *-mas-u* indexes the speaker's stance of deference towards the addressee directly, while the verb *mair-u* does so (more or
less) indirectly, through the speaker's expression of humility. Second, even
though the humility expressed by the predicate *mair-u* cannot here be taken
as relevant to the subject but only to the speaker, the propositional meaning

of the predicate 'go/come' still applies, of course, to the subject (the train). The suffix -*mas-u*, on the other hand, has no propositional meaning at all; its meaning relates only to the interactional relationship between the speaker and the addressee.

What we see in examples of this type is an important step in the process of grammaticalization involved in the development of productive addressee honorific forms, as well as in the transition from subjective to intersubjective social deictic meaning (Traugott and Dasher 2002: 226–78). These processes have been an integral part of the development of honorifics in Japanese; they are described more fully in §5, which also examines the socio-historical background associated with this and other changes. Before exploring this issue further, we will first look into the fundamental importance of ingroup/ outgroup relations in the use of honorifics in Japanese today.

4 Speaker's ingroup as centre of interactional/social deixis: Ingroup vs outgroup

In Japanese society, one's *uchi* 'ingroup' are those with whom one identifies most closely within a particular context. The ingroup *par excellence* is the family, generally conceived in contemporary Japan as the nuclear family but historically as the extended family. Other typical ingroups are often viewed as extensions of the family, such as the company for which one works and the nation of Japan.

An ingroup often only comes into focus as such when the context evokes a salient *soto* 'outgroup'. Thus, a member of a sporting team will identify more clearly with the whole team as ingroup when competing with another team than when participating in a practice session. The notion of the ingroup of 'our school' is more likely to be activated when comparisons are made with another school than when internal comparisons are made. In the latter context, the ingroup of the class or the year-group is more likely to be activated.

Ingroup affiliation is relevant to a range of linguistic systems in Japanese, including the use of kin terms (different terms for one's own kin than for another's) and of donatory verbs. The examples in (5) show that there are two donatory verbs in Japanese which are both translated as 'give' in English, but which differ depending on the relationship of the speaker to the recipient. The raised hash in these examples symbolizes pragmatic infelicity (rather than ungrammaticality).

(5) a. Tanaka   san=ni   hon=o   age-ta / #kure-ta
         T.   TITLE=DAT   book=ACC   give-PAST
         [I] gave Mr Tanaka a book.

     b. Yamada   san=wa   Tanaka   san=ni   hon=o
         Yamada   TITLE=TOP   Tanaka   TITLE=DAT   book=ACC
         age-ta / #kure-ta
         give-PAST
         Ms Yamada gave Mr Tanaka a book.

     c. Yamada   san=wa   hon=o   kure-ta / #age-ta
         Yamada   TITLE=TOP   book=ACC   give-PAST
         Intended meaning: Ms Yamada gave [me] a book.

     d. Yamada   san=wa   imooto=ni   hon=o
         Yamada   TITLE=TOP   younger.sister=DAT   book-ACC
         kure-ta / #age-ta
         give-PAST
         Ms Yamada gave my little sister a book.

While the unmarked donatory verb, *age-ru* 'give', is used when an outgroup member is recipient (5a and b), a special centripetal donatory verb, *kure-ru* 'give (to me)', is used when the self and ingroup members are recipient (5c and d).

We have already seen the relevance of the notion of ingroup in some examples of honorific predicates above. Two of the four types of honorifics introduced in §3 stereotypically index the humility of the subject referent: object honorifics (§3.3) and courteous honorifics (§3.4). In both these types we observed that the default subject referent is the speaker, but that an ingroup member, such as the speaker's younger sister, is also appropriate as a subject referent. Thus, it is not the speaker alone, but the speaker and their ingroup members, that function as the deictic centre for honorific use.

Just as important as the nature of the referents that *can* occur with each type of honorific is the nature of the referents that can *not* occur. The examples in (6) show that the interactional/social deictic meaning of each honorific type is compatible with a different set of referent types when it comes to ingroup/outgroup status (at least when they appear, as they do in these examples, without any clear context that might be incompatible with their stereotypical indexical force). As above, all the honorific components of each predicate are in bold, targets of respect are underlined, and targets of humility are italicized. Because the addressee honorific *-mas-u* form must be used whenever courteous honorifics appear (see §3.4), this form is given in all the examples in (6), for consistency.

(6) a. <u>Onishi sensei</u>=wa   Amerika=ni   #**mair**-i-**mashi**-ta/
         O.   teacher=TOP   America=DAT   go:HUMII-INFIN-AHON-PAST
         ik-i-**mashi**-ta/   irassha-i-**mashi**-ta
         go-INFIN-AHON-PAST   go:RESP-INFIN-AHON-PAST
         <u>Professor Onishi</u> **went** to America.

     b. *Imooto*=wa   Amerika=ni   **mair**-i-**mashi**-ta/
         younger.sister=TOP   America=DAT   go:HUMII-INFIN-AHON-PAST
         ik-i-**mashi**-ta/   #**irassha**-i-**mashi**-ta
         go-INFIN-AHON-PAST   go:RESP-INFIN-AHON-PAST
         My little sister **went** to America.

     c. Amerika-ni-**mair**-i-**mashi**-ta   /
         America=DAT go:HUMII-INFIN-AHON-PAST
         ik-i-**mashi**-ta /   #**irassha**-i-**mashi**-ta
         go-INFIN-AHON-PAST   go:RESP-INFIN-AHON-PAST
         Intended meaning: [*I*] **went** to America.

The subject referents in (6a and b) clearly differ in terms of their ingroup/
outgroup status. In (6a), *Onishi sensei* 'Professor Onishi', is signalled as an
outgroup referent by the use of a deferential title after the name. *Imooto*
'younger sister' in (6b), on the other hand, is a close family member and so
invariably regarded as ingroup when speaking to anyone outside the family.
The subject referent in (6c) is assumed by default to be the speaker in the
absence of any context that suggests otherwise (such as an incompatible
honorific predicate).

The courteous honorific verb *mair-u* 'to go:HUMII', which stereotypically
indexes the humility of the subject, is pragmatically infelicitous with an outgroup subject, (6a), but appropriate with an ingroup subject, (6b), just as
when the speaker is subject, (6c). It is most likely to be used when the
addressee is outgroup, particularly in a formal context. The non-honorific
verb *ik-u* 'to go' is appropriate in all examples, (6a–c), regardless of whether
the subject is ingroup, outgroup, or speaker, providing neither the nature of
the addressee nor the formality of the interaction calls for a more deferential form. Finally, the respectful subject honorific verb *irasshar-u* 'to go:RESP'
is acceptable with a subject referent who is outgroup to the speaker, (6a),
and is most likely to be used if that referent is an ingroup member to the
addressee, or in a formal context. This honorific type would not be used, of
course, with reference to an ingroup member of the speaker, (6b), or with
self-reference, (6c).

The examples in (7) show that the notions of ingroup and outgroup in Japanese are by no means fixed, but can vary according to the interlocutor (modified from Ide (1982: 374)).

(7)   a.   To a colleague in the same company:
           <u>Nakayama shachoo</u>=wa   Amerika=ni
           Nakayama company.head=TOP   America=DAT
           irassha-i-**mashi**-ta
           go:RESP-INFIN-AHON-PAST
           <u>Company President Nakayama</u> **went** to America.

      b.   To a client of the company:
           Nakayama=wa   Amerika=ni   **mair**-i-**mashi**-ta
           Nakayama=TOP   America=DAT   go:HUMII-INFIN-AHON-PAST
           Nakayama **went** to America.

When talking to a colleague in the same company about the company president, the speaker and addressee regard each other as ingroup members, and their boss as outgroup. The speaker thus uses a deferential title when referring to the boss, and a subject honorific form to show appropriate respect, as in (7a). When speaking to a different interlocutor—a client from outside the company—the speaker reorients to the boss as an ingroup member, not only dropping the deferential title but also using a courteous honorific, which functions to humble the actions of the boss as subject, shown in (7b).

These examples highlight the importance of the relationships between the participants in the speech event and those in the 'real-world' event (the referents) in determining the appropriate type(s) of honorific to use. Perhaps even more significantly, they also highlight the importance of ingroup affiliation relative to other factors that influence the choice of honorific forms. Example (7b) shows that the 'vertical' status of the boss compared to the speaker is of no consequence in comparison to the ingroup/outgroup relations involved. Factors related to the differences in age, social status, and power between a referent and the speaker can all play a part in whether honorifics are used or not, as do contextual factors such as the formality of the setting, the topic, the medium of interaction, and so on (Ide 1982: 366–77). While these factors apply to the use/non-use of honorifics by interlocutors, when it comes to the *type* of referent honorific used for a particular referent (one that functions to show respect or humility regarding that referent), ingroup/outgroup status is the single most significant variable. The only case in which respectful referent honorifics are invariably used is when reference is made to the Japanese imperial family. This practice is referred to as *zettai keigo* 'absolute honorifics', and applies in all circumstances, regardless of whom one is speaking to.

The importance of ingroup/outgroup relations in the choice of honorifics is one of the ways in which the Japanese honorific system differs significantly from the Korean one (Brown 2008: 380–3; Park 1990: 123–4). Group affiliation is not important in honorific usage in Korean; compared to a Japanese speaker, a Korean speaker pays little attention to the ingroup/outgroup relationships between participants in the speech event and referential targets of deference.

The main criterion for honorific usage in Korean is difference in age. In the case of referent honorifics, differences in age between the speaker and the targeted referent and between referents are both relevant.[5] Other factors relating to hierarchy, such as social status and power are also taken into account. It is thus important not to neglect to show respect for one's parents and grandparents as referents, even when one's addressee is someone outside the family. Likewise, one is expected to use respectful honorifics when speaking about one's boss, even when speaking to someone who belongs to another company. By showing appropriate respect in this way, one humbles oneself in relation to one's referent, and so demonstrates good demeanour (in the sense of Goffman 1956). The appropriate form is decided on the basis of the 'vertical' relationship between the speaker and the referent (or the relative relationship of two referents). The relationship of the speaker to the addressee (superior/inferior, ingroup/outgroup) is not relevant to the choice of referent honorifics, only to that of addressee honorifics in Korean.

The difference between Japanese and Korean in this respect is clearly attributable to the relative importance of different social factors: ingroup/outgroup relations in Japan vs hierarchical relations in Korea. As Park (1990: 124) observes, however, the reasons for this difference are far less apparent:

> Due probably to their long Confucian tradition of valuing collectivism or interrelatedness (a pattern of interpersonal dependency) among people (Smith 1983 and Wetzel 1984), groupness (*uchi* and *soto*) is strongly reflected in Japanese. There is an intriguing difference: although Confucianism has

---

[5] When it comes to the use of addressee honorifics in Korean, differences in age between the addressee and the targeted referent must also be taken into account with regard to the relative level of honorifics used, to ensure that the addressee's age status is acknowledged if higher than that of the referent.

long flourished and become very much a part of the daily lives of people both in Japan and Korea, yet the emphasis on group solidarity is far less in Korea than in Japanese honorific usage.

The historical and social factors associated with this 'intriguing difference' involving the prominence of group affiliation in Japanese society are the topic of the next section.

5 A brief history of some social factors associated with changes in the functions of honorifics in Japan

Honorifics in Japan, as in a number of other societies with highly developed honorific systems, developed in the context of an elaborate social hierarchy surrounding the imperial court. The use of this system was already well established by the Heian period (794–1185), a period of some (though limited) degree of centralization around the then-newly established capital of Kyoto. At that time, the use of honorific language was probably confined primarily to members of the imperial court and the aristocratic families, along with the retainers and servants who interacted with them.

The honorific forms used in the Heian period functioned to show appropriate deference in an 'upwards' direction, with those of lower rank humbling the self (as a referent) and others of similar or lower status (Morris 1971: 283, fn. 74) and showing respect concerning a higher status party, in accordance with the importance placed on acknowledgement of each person's precise rank within a complex hierarchical system (Morris 1971: 383–6). Murasaki Shikibu, the author of the Heian classic novel *The Tale of Genji* (c. 1008), conveys this as received wisdom in the voice of one of her characters, a young nobleman (Suematsu 1973: 40):

> Public business can only be tranquilly conducted when the superior receives the assistance of subordinates, and when the subordinate yields a becoming respect and loyalty to his superior, and affairs are thus conducted in a spirit of mutual conciliation.

Another major Heian writer, Sei Shōnagon, well known for the witty and cutting observations scattered throughout her *Pillow Book* [c. 1002], included the following in her list of 'Hateful things' (Morris 1971: 47):

It is particularly unpleasant to hear some foolish man or woman omit the proper marks of respect when addressing a person of quality.[6]

As Sei Shōnagon goes on to reveal, the use of honorific forms simply in an attempt to express good demeanour, while it may occasionally be heard at that time, was considered laughable in the strictly hierarchical courtly circles in which she interacted (Morris 1971: 47–8):

No less odious, however, are those masters who, in addressing their servants, use phrases such as 'When you were good enough to do such-and-such' or 'As you so kindly remarked'. No doubt there are some masters who, in describing their own actions to a servant, say, 'presumed to do so-and-so'!

Sometimes a person who is utterly devoid of charm will try to create a good impression by using very elegant language; yet he only succeeds in being ridiculous. No doubt he believes this refined language to be just what the occasion demands, but, when it goes so far that everyone bursts out laughing, surely something must be wrong.

Here the words that Sei Shōnagon attributes to such 'odious' masters— omowas-u 'to (be good enough to) do' and notama-u 'to (kindly) remark'— inappropriately signal the master's respect for the actions of the servant. The verb habe-ru 'to serve' (translated here as 'to presume to do'), on the other hand, signals (again inappropriately) the humility of the master concerning his own actions in interacting with his servant. The accepted use of habe-ru was to refer to one's own or another's actions only in relation to a social superior (Morris 1971: fn. 74, 283). Notice that what was considered correct use at this

---

[6] According to Traugott and Dasher (2002: 240), Tsujimura (1971: 15) claims that, in the subsequent line, Sei Shōnagon indicated that 'she disliked it when servants used [respectful] forms in reference to their masters when speaking to outsiders; she thought that [humble] forms should be used instead'. Traugott and Dasher (240) suggest that this is an 'early indication of in-group/out-group sensitivity'. The original text (Section 262) is actually rather vague at this point, simply saying 『わが使ふ者などの、「何とおはする」「のたまふ」など言ふ、いとにくし。』'(When) one's servants and such say things like 'come:RESP', 'say:RESP', it is truly hateful'. Modern Japanese translations take this to mean that the servants concerned are using these respectful forms about their own husbands (rather than their masters), leaving open the interpretation that Sei Shonagon's complaint was about servants inappropriately raising the status of such lowly people as their husbands above that of a much higher status interlocutor (the one they served, such as herself). Traugott and Dasher do go on to note that the norm throughout the Heian period (Late Old Japanese / Early Middle Japanese), was that respectful forms were used to refer to subject referents of high position, regardless of the ingroup/outgroup status of those referents in relation to the speaker or addressee. Likewise, they found the norm for the use of humbling forms was for subject referents of lower position than the non-subject referent, again with the ingroup/outgroup relationship to the speech-act participants not being a factor.

time (Late Old Japanese/Early Middle Japanese) was not determined by the ingroup/outgroup relations that are so important in contemporary Japanese (see §4). Sei Shōnagon's complaints indicate that correct usage was dependent on whether or not one succeeded in acknowledging the proper social hierarchy amongst referents, regardless of one's relationship with any of those referents.

There is evidence that ingroup/outgroup relations became somewhat more relevant to the use of honorific language over the course of the Kamakura (1185–1333) and Muromachi (1336–1573) periods (the period of Late Middle Japanese), during which time the power of the military clans and samurai class grew and an early form of the Japanese feudal system was initially established. Referring to the language of the late sixteenth century, the Portuguese Jesuit missionary and scholar, João Rodrigues, in his *Arte da Lingoa de Iapam* [Art of the Japanese language], observed that the Japanese tended not to use honorifics when talking about an ingroup member when the addressee was an outsider (Takiura 2001: 27–8, cited in Koyama 2004: 419). This suggests that a significant step had already taken place by this time in the relevance of ingroup/outgroup distinctions in the use of honorifics and in attention to the face of the addressee. However, the simple avoidance of honorific reference to an ingroup member is still a far cry from what we see today: the deliberate use of humble reference to the actions of an ingroup superior as a strategy for showing deference to one's addressee (see §4, example (7)).

Far too many intertwined factors are at play to identify precisely the historical and societal factors that have brought about the special significance of ingroup/outgroup relations in contemporary Japanese society, leading to their dominance over hierarchical relations in the use of honorifics today, along with the more widely recognized change from a focus on deference to the referent to that on deference to the addressee. However, it is worthwhile identifying some dynamics that are likely to have contributed to the current situation.

For this we need to turn to Tokugawa period (1603–1868), in many senses the mint from which modern Japan emerged. While precedents can be found in earlier times, this long period of peace encouraged the development of some methods of social control conducive to a peculiar, and perhaps extraordinary, strengthening of the us/them representation.[7] One key contributing factor was the then firmly established feudal political structure—the

---

[7] My sincere thanks to Olivier Ansart for his most generous support in my understanding of these issues in Japanese political and social history.

division of the country, under the often nominal authority of the shogun (overlord or hereditary military dictator), into de facto independent countries—the fiefs of the *daimyoo* 'feudal lords' (often themselves containing semi-autonomous sub-fiefs)—and largely autonomous villages in which the majority of the population lived. While this feudal political structure encouraged a strong sense of collective identity at all these different levels (fief, sub-fief, and village), this trend was compounded in the social structure by the prevalence of status groups—hierarchically arranged groups in which people were born and would die. Starting with the samurai, themselves divided into dozens of mutually impermeable, micro-status groups, these groups included professional groups, mendicants, pariahs, doctors, and so on.

Whether in the political units of the feudal structure, or in the social units of the status hierarchy, the principle was that, as long as the service due to the higher level was rendered (military service for the feudal lords; taxes for most of the other groups), each political or social group was left to its own devices. All group members were keenly aware that they had to live together as a united and harmonious group, to self-manage their affairs or their quarrels smoothly, for any disorder, any serious infightings, would be punished, regardless of the rights or wrongs of the parties involved.

The units to which most of the population were assigned, the peasant villages, provided a clear illustration of this deliberate policy. Villages were, in most cases, inhabited by only peasants; members of the military elite status groups—the *bushi* (warriors who served a particular lord)—had to leave the villages where they owned lands and people, to live close to their lords in the local town. The villages had just one function to perform so that they could be left in peace, free to manage their affairs: the payment of tribute taxes (Ooms 1996). Each village was itself divided (according to organizational principles previously established in the military) into smaller units that came to be called *gonin gumi* 'a group of five [households]'—though the number of families in one group could actually vary considerably—and placed under a principle of collective responsibility (Lu 2015: 208–10, 214; Ooms 1996: 80).[8] If any household could not pay their share of the village tax, other households in the group, with the support of other groups if needed, must make up the shortfall. If the amount offered by the whole village fell short, there was no interest in which group of five or which household was responsible; instead,

---

[8] The *gonin-gumi* 'group of five (households)' system in feudal Japan had *some* similarities to the 'frankpledge' system in medieval England (Schofield 1996: 408–10) and to the *băojiă* system in Ming Dynasty China and beyond (Brook 2005: 36–8).

the entire village was held to account. Thus, pressure came from those within one's own group, before it could come from above.

The same systematic encouragement of collective responsibility and peer pressure could also be seen in civil matters, such as sales and purchases of land, marriages and divorces (see Fuess 2004: 29, 38–9); none of those things could happen without the agreement of other members of the group. And when crimes were committed by one member, the others would be punished as well. If a disagreement could not be solved by the group and an appeal was made to the higher level, all parties would be punished (see, for example, Ooms 1996: 263). Similar practices were deliberately introduced in the burgeoning towns—in suburbs, in professional guilds, etc.

This method of social organization involving shared responsibility within a group, along with a strong sense of group belonging, so successful in the Tokugawa period, was reproduced in the subsequent Meiji period (1868–1912) in a range of institutions, continuing in the military and introduced into the education system as well as public and private companies. It remains embedded in Japanese socialization and institutional life today. From the very first days of elementary school, for example, the teacher divides the class into *han* 'groups, squads', each composed of four to eight children. Each *han* collaborates on educational, as well as social and physical activities. *Han* groups are also assigned classroom duties, such as serving the lunch or cleaning the floor. Most schools do not employ cleaners or janitors, and teacher intervention is kept to an absolute minimum, so these duties are serious responsibilities. Both approbation and blame go to the group as a whole. This results in shared pride in group accomplishments as well as considerable peer pressure to do one's best, to ensure that one's own *han* is not shamed in comparison with others (Benjamin 1997: 53–86; Lewis 1995: 74–100). These patterns of highly collaborative behaviour within one's own group along with a sense of separation from members of other groups, learnt through this process of socialization from a young age, are precisely those expected in adulthood, particularly in the context of employment (Benjamin 1997: 64–6).

To further understand the relationship between changes in Japanese society and changes in honorific language—the greater attention both to recognizing ingroup/outgroup distinctions and to showing deference to the addressee—we need to return to our historical overview. As the relative peace of the Tokugawa period continued, many of the elite samurai class became unemployed, although their high social status was maintained. The growing merchant class, on the other hand, was gaining in economic power even though its members had extremely low social status. Not surprisingly, merchants began emulating samurai habits and language styles, with a view to increasing their social capital. Even then, it was still very unlikely that honorific language was used to any significant extent by the vast majority of the population (around eighty per cent in the peasant class (Saito 2009: 169)) in spite of the continuation of the highly stratified nature of the society.

It was at the time of the remarkably rapid modernization and centralization of the Meiji Period (1868–1912) that the use of honorific language started to become significantly more widespread in Japanese society. Language standardization was a major aim of the Meiji government, and of the subsequent Taisho (1912–26) and early Showa (1926–1930s) governments, along with a broad range of other ideologically driven goals related to modernization, growth of capitalism, nationalization, universal education, and strong, central control. Members of the erstwhile samurai class, along with many from former aristocratic and land-owning families, had by this time become prominent in elite, government circles, so that their social status was again accompanied by real power. The motivation to emulate linguistic habits associated with these upper classes, already evident in the merchant class of the Tokugawa period, became stronger still.

At a time of insecurity due to rapid societal change it is not uncommon to turn to symbols of an imagined past with a view to re-establishing a sense of continuity into the present. Koyama (2004) observes that, from around 1890 (late Meiji) and especially from 1920 onwards (late Taisho/early Showa), honorifics began to be thought of as a 'linguistic emblem of the Japanese national character' (416). As is often the case, it was women, in particular, who were charged with the responsibility of maintaining this conservative connection with the past. The increasing separation of gender roles—with men assigned to work outside the home and women to all matters inside the home—meant that women were expected to develop a new role and identity as *sengyoo shufu* 'professional housewives', and to conform to the ideology of *ryoosai kenboo* 'good wife, wise mother'. Apart from Western (particularly German) women, the only models available of women who had previously been devoted to domestication were the wives of prominent aristocrats and former samurai. Women's magazines vigorously promoted these models and, in this way, contributed to educating women in the speech styles characteristic of the upper classes, especially honorific language (Ishii and Jarkey 2002; Jarkey 2015).

Koyama (2004: 416–17) explains that, even while this conservative ideology and concomitant linguistic practices were growing, a range of other changes in the use of honorifics were also taking place, all of which can be attributed to modern rather than conservative ideologies, including egalitarianism and agentive individualism (in which personal identities and relationships are seen as constructed rather than pre-supposed). Four key, interwoven changes that Koyama describes are:

- the rise of addressee honorifics in relation to referent honorifics, with speakers showing deference to the addressee (both indirectly as a referent and directly as addressee) but not to referents who were not participants in the speech event (see also Inoue 1999). I would add here that another condition under which a referent could receive deference, of course, was when that referent was an ingroup member of the addressee.
- the increase in symmetric uses rather than asymmetric ones between speech participants.
- the move to symmetric *non-use* of honorifics in the private sphere amongst kin, leading to the strong association of the honorific style with the public sphere.
- greater focus on the second-order indexicality of honorifics, as an aesthetic sign of good demeanour: good upbringing, refinement, education, and so on.

Koyama (2004: 418–19) also points to a rise in commercial contexts in the use of the honorific forms of donatory verbs (see §4), forms that simultaneously serve to indicate both deference and group identity. This leads to clear associations between complex honorific use and cities (rather than rural areas) and 'overlaps with second-order indexical entailments' of the standard variety (rather than with dialects). Koyama characterizes this as a 'quasi-diglossic situation', in which self-monitored language—the standard variety along with honorific usage—is valorized as appropriate for public performance, while non-standard varieties and non-honorific usage are relegated to the private domain. As noted by Wetzel (2004: 52), in a society undergoing modernization, the greatly increased interaction between people who are complete strangers or mere acquaintances is one of the key reasons for the need for a 'public', standard language. It is also a key reason for an honorific system that pays greater attention to maintaining polite distance with non-intimates and somewhat less to acknowledging and reinforcing established hierarchical relations.

The explicit education in 'correct' honorific usage has become a key aspect in the right of passage into Japanese adulthood, particularly into the working world of commerce and business (Wetzel 2004: 89–116) and in other forms of public language use. In this context, great attention has been paid (for example in the Japanese media) to changes in honorific usage, such as the one mentioned briefly in §3.4, by which courteous forms have come to be used with non-human subjects. Example (4d) is repeated here:

(4) d. Densha=ga   **mair-i-mashi**-ta
         train=NOM   come/go:HUMII-INFIN-AHON-PAST
         The train (has) **come/gone**.

In fact, this change is part of a process that has been in progress since the Heian period, by which non-honorific words give rise, through metaphorical transfer, to referent honorifics (indexing the subjective attitude of the speaker to a referent), which, in turn, become the source of addressee honorifics (indexing intersubjective meaning, independent from propositional content) (Traugott and Dasher 2002: 231; Tsujimura 1968, 1971). The productive addressee honorific suffix -*mas-u* of contemporary Japanese itself originated in an object referent honorific verb *mairas-u* 'to give' (Shirane 2005: 520), via an intermediate stage of use as a courteous honorific (Traugott and Dasher 2002: 258–72).

We can observe this change in progress in contemporary Japanese, as certain courteous honorifics take on a growing role in expressing deference to the interlocutor. This currently occurs most commonly in formal contexts, such as in public announcements and speeches, and parliamentary debates. Speakers enacting these genres are strongly motivated to express good demeanour and seize upon the opportunity to leverage the second-order indexical meaning of honorifics. Forms that are associated with the humility of the speaker are commandeered to serve in displaying additional deference to the addressee, over and above the well-worn, everyday use of the -*mas-u* addressee honorific.

Prime candidates for this change in usage are suppletive honorific forms that can also be used as auxiliary verbs, such as the courteous honorific verbs *mair-u* 'to come/go:HUMII' and *or-u* 'to be:HUMII'. In the examples in (8) we see three instances of this phenomenon, demonstrating what may well be the penultimate stage in the full grammaticalization of these forms as addressee honorifics. All honorific forms are highlighted in bold.

(8) a. In a weather report (Traugott and Dasher 2002: 240):
Saikin   zuibun   atataka-ku nat-te
recently rather   warm-ADV become-GERUND
mair-i-masi-ta.
come:HUMII-INFIN-AHON-PAST
Recently, [it/the weather] **has become** rather warm.

     b. Prime Minister Noda Yoshihiko, addressing opposition MP
Yamamoto Yuji; House of Representatives Budget Committee
Meeting, 12 November 2012:
… o-hanashi=o   s-**are-**te
HON-speech=ACC   do-RESP-GERUND

or-i-**mas-**u
be:HUMII-INFIN-AHON-NPAST
[you] **are saying**….

     c. The Emperor Naruhito in a press conference just prior to his
ascension to the throne (23 February 2019):
…<u>ryooheika</u>=ga   **nasat-**te   **or-are-**ru
Their.Majesties=NOM do:RESP-GERUND be:HUMII-RESP-NPAST
yoo.ni…
in.the.manner
[(I) humbly intend to fulfill my duty]…just as <u>Their Majesties</u> [the
retiring Emperor and Empress] **have been doing**…

Example (8a) is interesting to compare with (4d), in which the lexical verb
mair-u 'to go/come:HUMII' is predicated of the subject *densha* 'train'. As noted,
while the humility indexed by *mair-u* is not relevant to the subject in (4d), but
only to the speaker, the propositional meaning 'to go/come' still applies to that
subject (the train). In (8a) the auxiliary use of *mair-u* represents a step further
from pure propositional meaning in that it metaphorically represents the change
in the weather as 'coming' towards the time of the speech event. The humble
meaning of *mair-u* simultaneously functions here to reinforce the deference
shown to the addressee through the fully grammaticalized suffix *-mas-u*.

A doubtless more innovative phenomenon is illustrated in (8b), in which
the auxiliary use of the courteous honorific *or-u* 'to be' is combined with a
main verb in a respectful subject honorific form, *s-are-ru* 'to do-RESP' (see
§3.2). This combination succeeds in indexing deference to the addressee in
three ways: first, directly, through the respectful subject honorific (as the
addressee *is* the subject referent—the one who 'is saying'); second, indirectly

through the use of the courteous honorific; and finally, directly with the addressee honorific -*mas-u* suffix.

In (8c) we see an extension of this combination of respectful forms with courteous auxiliaries. Here the courteous auxiliary *or-u* is not only combined with a respectful subject honorific main verb, *nasar-u* 'to do:RESP', but itself undergoes productive subject honorification with the respectful suffix -*(r)are-ru*. The new Emperor thus reinforces his display of respect to his parents, the subject referents 'Their Majesties', while in no way neglecting to express his own humility, and his indirect deference to his addressees. This example is, furthermore, a rare instance illustrating the use of *zettai keigo* 'absolute honorifics' in reference to the imperial family. The expression of respect to the institution of the throne is of even greater importance than the expression of ingroup humility concerning his family members. Even though the new Emperor shows no hesitation in articulating his personal humility and deference to his subjects, as a display of his good demeanour, he does not neglect to show proper respect to the throne, embodied in the form of his parents, the retiring Emperor and Empress.

Changes like these to Japanese honorific usage, which are severely censured when they initially emerge, eventually become fully accepted as 'correct' usage themselves. To my knowledge the new Emperor's elaborate combination of honorific types at the time of his ascension to the throne went entirely unremarked. When I discussed the combination of forms he used with native-speaker linguists, the most notable response I received was that this must be correct usage now, as the Emperor uses it. While this particular combination is still restricted to use in a very limited range of genres today, I have no doubt that it will emerge as a productive addressee honorific form in the not-too-distant future.

6 Conclusion

Honorifics are a non-universal linguistic feature and, as such, one that may well exhibit correlations with specific, non-linguistic societal traits (Chapter 1). This chapter has shown evidence of a strong integration point between the Japanese language and society, related to the functions of the Japanese honorific system. Moreover, the analysis has demonstrated that changes in Japanese society since the Heian period can be seen to be associated with significant changes in the functions of the honorific system.

The system began as a way of indexing respect for social superiors and humility on the part of inferiors; it allowed interactants to acknowledge allotted social positions within a complex, hierarchical social system—the

Japanese imperial court. This focus on the role of honorifics in reinforcing metaphorically vertical social relations has been maintained in the language ideologies of contemporary Japan.

In fact, over the course of more than a thousand years, the Japanese honorific system has developed into one that has far broader functions, most of which relate in some way to indexing social 'distance'. While expressing vertical social distance remains one important function of honorific use in Japan today, the expression of closeness to ingroup, and distance from outgroup, has become even more important. Distance is also expressed in metaphorically horizontal relations between speaker and addressee, with honorifics now being commonly used in symmetrical ways in the public sphere. Associated with this change there has been a clear process of grammaticalization, still in progress today. Through this process, lexical honorifics that express the speakers' subjective judgement concerning their relationship to referents develop over time into grammatical honorifics that express intersubjective meanings, unrelated to the propositional content, but relevant only to the relationship between speaker and addressee.

Acknowledgements

This chapter was developed from a paper presented at the Workshop on The Integration of Language and Society held at the Language and Culture Research Centre at James Cook University, 21–23 August 2019. My thanks to all participants at the Workshop, and especially to Alexandra Aikhenvald and R. M. W. Dixon, as well as Kasia Wotjtylak, Pema Wangdi, and Stephen Watters. The ideas presented here on the social factors associated with the importance of the ingroup/outgroup system in modern and contemporary Japan were greatly inspired by conversations with Olivier Ansart. Sincere gratitude for additional and very helpful input also goes to Hyunsu Kim, Hiroko Kobayashi, Kimiyo Matsui, Harumi Minagawa, Duk-Soo Park, and Yoko Yonezawa.

References

Agha, Asif. 2006. *Language and social relations*. Cambridge: Cambridge University Press.

Barke, Andrew. 2010. 'Manipulating honorifics in the construction of social identities in Japanese television drama', *Journal of Sociolinguistics*, 14(4): 456–76.

Benjamin, Gail. 1997. *Japanese lessons: A year in a Japanese school through the eyes of an American anthropologist and her children*. New York: New York University Press.

Brook, Timothy. 2005. *The Chinese state in Ming society*. London: Routledge Curzon.

Brown, Lucien. 2008. 'Contrasts between Korean and Japanese honorifics', *Rivista degli studi orientali* 1(4): 369–85.

Cook, Haruko M. 2013. 'A scientist or salesman? Identity construction through referent honorifics on a Japanese shopping channel program', *Multilingua* 32(2): 177–202.

Duranti, Alessandro. 1992. 'Language in context and language as context: The Samoan respect vocabulary', in Alessandro Duranti and Charles Goodwin (eds), *Rethinking context: Language as an interactive phenomenon*. Cambridge: Cambridge University Press, 77–99.

Fuess, Harald. 2004. *Divorce in Japan: Family, gender, and the state, 1600–2000*. Stanford: Stanford University Press.

Goffman, Erving. 1956. 'The nature of deference and demeanor', *American Anthropologist* 58: 473–502.

Ide, Sachiko. 1982. 'Japanese sociolinguistics: Politeness and women's language', *Lingua* 57(2): 357–85.

Ikegami, Yoshihiko. 1991. ' "DO-language" and "BECOME-language": Two contrasting types of linguistic representation', in Yoshihiko Ikegami (ed.), *The empire of signs: Semiotic essays on Japanese culture*. Amsterdam: John Benjamins, 285–326.

Inoue, Fumio. 1999. *Keigo wa kowaku-nai: Saishin yōrei to kiso-chishiki* [Honorifics are not scary: Recent examples of use and basic information]. Tokyo: Kodansha.

Ishii, Kazumi and Nerida Jarkey. 2002. 'The housewife is born: The establishment of the notion and identity of the *shufu* in modern Japan', *Japanese Studies* 22(1): 35–47.

Jarkey, Nerida. 2015. 'The Housewife's Companion: Identity construction in a Japanese women's magazine', in Dwi Noverini Djenar, Ahmar Mahboob, and Ken Cruickshank (eds), *Language and identity across modes of communication*. Berlin: De Gruyter Mouton, 179–202.

Keating, Elizabeth L. 1998. *Power sharing: Language, rank, gender, and social space in Pohnpei, Micronesia*. New York: Oxford University Press.

Koyama, Wataru. 2004. 'The linguistic ideologies of modern Japanese honorifics and the historic reality of modernity', *Language & Communication* 24(4): 413–35.

Lewis, Catherine C. 1995. *Educating hearts and minds: Reflections on Japanese preschool and elementary education*. Cambridge: Cambridge University Press.

Lu, David J. 2015. *Japan. Vol. 1, The dawn of history to the late Tokugawa period: A documentary history*. London: Routledge.

Matsumoto, Yoshiko. 1988. 'Reexamination of the universality of face: Politeness phenomena in Japanese'. *Journal of Pragmatics* 12(4): 403–26.

Morris, Ivan. 1971. Translator and editor of *The pillow book of Sei Shōnagon*. Kingsport, Tennessee: Penguin Classics.

Okamoto, Shigeko. 1999. 'Situated politeness: Manipulating honorific and non-honorific expressions in Japanese conversations'. *Pragmatics* 9(1): 51–74.

Ooms, Herman. 1996. *Tokugawa village practice: Class, status, power, law*. Berkeley: University of California Press.

Park, Mae-Ran. 1990. 'Conflict avoidance in social interaction: A sociolinguistic comparison of the Korean and Japanese honorific systems', in Hajime Hoji and Patricia M. Clancy (eds), *Japanese/Korean Linguistics*. Stanford: Center for the Study of Language and Information, 111–27.

Saito, Osamu. 2009. 'Land, labour and market forces in Tokugawa Japan', *Continuity and Change* 24(1): 169–96.

Schofield, Phillipp R. 1996. 'The late Medieval view of the frankpledge and tithing system: An Essex case study', in Zvu Razi and Richard M. Smith (eds), *Medieval society and the manor court*. Oxford: Clarendon Press, 408–49.

Shirane, Haruo. 2005. *Classical Japanese: A grammar*. New York: Columbia University Press.

Smith, Robert J. 1983. *Japanese society: Tradition, self, and the social order*. Cambridge: Cambridge University Press.

Suematsu, Kenchō. 1973. Translator of *Genji monogatari* [The tale of Genji]. Boston: Tuttle.

Takiura, Masato. 2001. ' "Keii" no hokorobi: Keigo-ron to poraitonesu to "keii hyoogen" ' [The unravelling of 'respect': Honorific theories, politeness, and 'respectful expressions']. *Gengo* 30(12): 26–33.

Traugott, Elizabeth Closs and Richard B. Dasher. 2002. *Regularity in Semantic Change*. Cambridge: Cambridge University Press.

Tsujimura, Toshiki. 1968. *Keigo no shi-teki kenkyuu* [Historical studies of Japanese honorifics]. Tokyo: Kyōbunsha.

Tsujimura, Toshiki. 1971. Editor of *Keigo-Shi* [The History of Japanese Honorifics]. Kōza Kokugoshi, 5 [Monograph Series on the History of the Japanese Language 5]. Tokyo: Taishūkan Shoten.

Wetzel, Patricia J. 1984. '*Uti* and *soto* [in-group and out-group]: Social deixis in Japanese'. PhD dissertation, Ithaca: Cornell University.

Wetzel, Patricia J. 2004. *Keigo in Modern Japan: Polite language from Meiji to the present*. Honolulu: University of Hawaii Press.

Yamamoto, Mutsumi. 2006. *Agency and impersonality: Their linguistic and cultural manifestations*. Amsterdam: John Benjamins.

3

Honorification in Dzongkha

Stephen Watters

1 Introduction

Language and society are integrated and mutually supportive of one another in more than non-trivial ways. The two are not only reflective of one another, but mutually reinforce one another. The linguistic parameter of honorification in Dzongkha, the national language of Bhutan, exemplifies this integration, and will be the focus of this chapter. Honorification, as it will be used here, involves the marking of social status, respect, or deference between interlocutors in conversation (Agha 1994: 277), as well as toward the referents of clausal arguments (Shibatani 2001). Honorific language is a vital cultural tool in expressing politeness and etiquette in Bhutanese society.

The relationship between language and society with regard to honorification is overt in Bhutanese society. Much of honorific usage in formal settings reinforces notions of social hierarchies through politeness behaviour toward those of relatively higher social standing. However, the chapter will show that politeness is also a feature of conversation among social equals, particularly in the use of honorifics to mitigate the perception that the speaker is imposing on the interlocutor. It will also be shown that the honorification of nouns draws on the Tibetic system which has been shown by DeLancey (1998) to have a classificatory function based on cultural and social values.

After an introduction to Dzongkha in §2, §3 introduces the practice of Bhutanese etiquette, known in Dzongkha as *driglam namzhag*.[1] An understanding of *driglam namzhag* serves as a backdrop to the value placed on honorific language. Honorific words and constructions are the topic of §4. §4.1 describes how honorific nouns are a reflection of human interaction with the referent; their derivation through compounding demonstrate that honorific roots have a classificatory function. §4.2 shows that while the basic honorific

---

[1] Dzongkha is represented with the Roman Dzongkha orthography, developed with the help of van Driem for the Dzongkha Development Commission. See van Driem (1991).

Stephen Watters, *Honorification in Dzongkha*. In: *The Integration of Language and Society: A Cross-Linguistic Typology.* Edited by: Alexandra Y. Aikhenvald, R. M. W. Dixon, and Nerida Jarkey, Oxford University Press. © Stephen Watters 2021. DOI: 10.1093/oso/9780192845924.003.0003

vocabulary overlaps with that of Lhasa Tibetan, new honorific vocabulary has developed in Dzongkha. It shows that honorific nouns are a semi-open class, adding to the referents that occur in an honorific form. §4.3 illustrates that Dzongkha has honorific and humilific verbs, the latter forms of which are a special subclass of verbs that give focus to the relative social gap between clausal referents. Finally, §5 discusses honorific language usage in two conversations where the interlocutors are social equals: one conversation is drawn from the movie *chö da jikten* 'The Divine and the Mundane'; the other conversation is extracted from an unscripted and natural conversation over a game of Carrom (a cue-based tabletop game popular throughout South Asia).

Data for honorific vocabulary comes from dictionaries produced by the Dzongkha Development Commission, as well as their honorific glossary. Sentence examples come from natural language texts, whether written or spoken, drawing heavily from examples in Watters (2018). Most spoken examples come from conversation which is interactional rather than monologic.

2 Genetic affiliation and typological profile of Dzongkha

Dzongkha is spoken as a mother-tongue in eight of the twenty districts of Bhutan (van Driem and Tshering 1998: 3); these eight districts cover the main river valleys of western Bhutan. Dzongkha is one among many Central Bodish languages spoken in the central and eastern Himalayas and the erstwhile nation of Tibet (Bradley 1997: 4; Tournadre 2013). It shares with many Central Bodish languages an affinity with the literary language of Tibet from which a great deal of its honorific vocabulary comes. The literary language developed primarily as a religious language containing translated Buddhist texts as well as natively developed treatises. The literary form continues to serve as a symbol of pan Tibetan-Buddhist identity, although modern literary languages with an admixture of literary forms and spoken language have emerged in many Central Bodish languages. Dzongkha is no exception to this, drawing significantly on its Buddhist literary heritage as evinced in the development of modern Dzongkha. The varieties of the language that have more of the literary forms than the local language are commonly known throughout the Tibetan-Buddhist world as 'Chöke' (or as variously pronounced). Honorific language is frequent in Chöke, and is known as *zhesa*.

The traditional inhabitants of western Bhutan are known as *Ngalong*. They are no longer the only speakers of Dzongkha, however, as the language is used as a lingua franca throughout the country where it is also privileged as a national language. Many L2 speakers of Dzongkha are strong advocates of its use as a national language (van Driem and Tshering 1998: 3).

Van Driem and Tshering (1998: 2) report 160,000 native speakers of Dzongkha in Bhutan. Eberhard et al. (2019) report that the overall population of Dzongkha speakers is 237,080, which includes small communities in the neighbouring countries of India and Nepal.

2.1 Typological summary

Dzongkha has two limited noun classification systems. One marks gender on a small subset of human nouns, and the other categorizes a semi-open set of words for purposes of honorifics. It is these words that are one of the foci of this chapter.

Verbs reflect three basic event schemas that profile agents, themes, and locations, and can be further differentiated on the basis of whether theme or location receives prominence. There are four values of transitivity: zero-valent verbs (weather verbs), intransitive, transitive, and ditransitive. Light verb constructions and complex verbs, composed of a noun verb juxtaposition, make up a significant portion of the verbal lexicon. One of the honorific constructions of the language entails the replacement of the common noun with an honorific noun in a complex verb.

Other word classes are: adjective, adverb, relator noun, pronoun, demonstrative, ideophone, adposition, interrogative, numeral, auxiliary, conjunction, and interjection. Dzongkha has an abundance of copular and existential verbs that, in addition to clausal function, also encode egophoric and evidential distinctions. These verbs may also combine with one another, extending the evidential distinctions to such categories as inference, assumption, and prediction. The copulas and existentials function periphrastically in the tense aspect system where they also serve to make distinctions in egophoricity and evidentiality. Tense and aspect are coded by a complex system of suffixes, auxiliaries, and post-verbal enclitics each of which distinguish egophoric and evidential values in addition to temporal contrasts.

Basic phrasal constituent order in Dzongkha is AOV/SV, although constituent order is not fixed, and clausal arguments need not be expressed.

3 *Driglam namzhag* 'The means of harmonious behaviour'

As Bhutan emerges from the mystique of an isolated Buddhist kingdom, one of the principle issues the nation faces is the way in which modern development can be harmonized with traditional culture (Aris 1998: 11–25;

Ura 1998). An important element of this harmonization is the practice of Bhutanese etiquette, known in Dzongkha as *driglam namzhag* 'the means of harmonious behaviour'. The manual on *driglam namzhag*, a publication of the Special Commission for Cultural Affairs, in its own words is 'a code of conduct on how to speak, eat, drink, behave, walk, sit, etc . . .' (Special Commission for Cultural Affairs 1999: 150). The English introduction explains how this relates to modernization:

> "Driglam Namzhag" is, indeed, a means to maintain, in all their purity, the bonds between the governers and the governed, between superiors and subordinates, between teachers and students, between parents and children, between friends, and between husbands and wives. It enhances development activities because of the shared interests and the common path or value system of society and of the nation. It is aimed at preserving what is good in our own way of thinking, derived from the Buddhist philosophy that is inherent in Bhutanese culture. The Royal Government of Bhutan has put a great deal of effort into policy, believing that it can preserve our distinct cultural identity as a sovereign nation through the process of modernisation (xxxix).

The efforts of the Dzongkha Development Commission (DDC) reflect the development of Dzongkha both as a process of language engineering to accommodate new vocabulary, and as a process of maintenance and revitalization of the 'pure' ways of speaking. Their efforts include manuals on correct usage of the language such as the *drukgi yigkur namzhag* 'Bhutanese letter writing'. The glossary on Dzongkha Honorifics, on which some of this chapter is based, gives a fairly comprehensive listing of common words and their honorific counterparts, although it gives no information about their usage (DDC 2011).

Honorific vocabulary and grammatical constructions are an important part of public life in Bhutan as a linguistic expression of *driglam namzhag*. Honorifics are abundant in media, public speeches, and writing. Children are taught to use them in their Dzongkha education classes. Members of society who have professional lives that bring them into the domains of public life control the honorific lexicon and grammar well; it is a necessity, even a requirement. Bhutanese who do not participate in public life, particularly as civil servants, are less adept at using honorific vocabulary and constructions. Nevertheless, honorifics are used among these members of society, even if less frequently.

A brief excursus into language usage demonstrates that honorific language plays an important role in reifying a notion of what constitutes harmony, and a belief that this harmony is uniquely preserved in Bhutan through the language and culture. Honorific language is valued as one of the means of maintaining Bhutanese etiquette. However, honorific vocabulary is largely absent in spontaneous natural conversation. While the honorific system, no doubt, promotes social distance and ranking in more formal settings, in the context of social equals, it can be used to mitigate the perception that the speaker is imposing on the interlocutor (see §5).

4 Honorific words and constructions

The focus of this section is on referent honorifics in contrast to addressee or bystander honorifics. Referent honorifics are those that mark clausal nominal referents with honorification (Comrie 1976; Shibatani 2001). Dzongkha does not have any honorific forms that are used only in the presence of a particular bystander. It does have a post clausal particle, *lâ*, that gives honorification to the addressee, as will show up in a few examples of language usage below.

Dzongkha has a well-developed system of honorific nouns comprised of a semi-open class of over five hundred lexical items. The honorific verbal system is significantly smaller than this with a closed class of around twenty monomorphemic forms, several of which can be used in serial verb constructions to augment common verbs with honorification. Moreover, honorific noun incorporation can also augment many complex verbs, adding to the number of verbs that can take an honorific meaning. The honorific noun vocabulary exhibits a two-way contrast between common and honorific nouns, as will be shown in §4.1. While many of these honorific nouns are borrowed from Lhasa Tibetan, others are newly developed in Dzongkha (§4.2). Verbs index the honorification of clausal referents; one set gives honorification to the A or S argument, and will be referred to as honorific (see §4.3); the other set marks relative status between clausal arguments, profiling the lower status of the referent of the A or S argument in relation to the referent of the non-A/S argument, and will be referred to as humilific (see §4.4).

4.1 Honorific nouns

The honorific nouns of Dzongkha are comprised of a class of words with well over five hundred items. The honorific system closely approximates the system documented by DeLancey (1998) for Lhasa Tibetan. In addition to shared honorific roots, the Dzongkha system has in common with Lhasa Tibetan a semantic categorization similar to a classifier system. What is distinct about the Tibetic system in comparison to other classifier systems is that it classifies nouns on the basis of how humans interact with these referents, i.e. a categorization that is social and cultural, rather than perceptual (DeLancey 1998: 109). As such, honorific nouns are only those nouns which involve the human world, and more specifically the world of those who hold places of social honour. Since gender marking on nouns in Dzongkha is primarily for human nouns (and their social or work roles), it is not surprising that the honorific system also pays attention to humans, the objects closely associated with them, and what they do. The function of categorizing humans and the world with which they immediately interact drives the system.

One characteristic feature of the Tibetic system (at least for Lhasa Tibetan and Dzongkha) is that, generally speaking, honorific nouns do not carry a broader semantic meaning than their common counterparts. (This is different than honorific verbs some of which carry a range of event meanings, e.g. *jön* 'come, go HON' or *zî* 'see, look HON'.) In fact, in some cases, compounding with an honorific root results in a more specific term than the common term from which it is derived, e.g. *söchu* 'drinking water HON' from *chu* '(any) water' where *sö* is an honorific root for food or eating. The honorific root *chap* is the more generic term for 'water' and may substitute for *chu*; when compounded, once again, a more specific term is derived, e.g. *chapchu* 'chang (homemade beer) HON'. It is partly the absence of a hyponymous relationship in honorific nouns that gives the honorific system a classificatory nature.

Honorific nouns are formed through compounding with at least one root from a small closed class of honorific roots. The small set of honorific roots is very similar, if not identical, with the set of honorific roots in Lhasa Tibetan. The common nouns with which they may combine, however, can be different, and the structural ways in which they may combine are significantly more complex than that documented in DeLancey (1998) for Lhasa Tibetan (see Watters 2018: 157–9). (Honorific vocabulary particular to Dzongkha will be illustrated in §4.2.) Honorific nouns come from three sources: body parts, daily items, and a few honorific verbs. Only the former two are discussed in this section; they are given in Table 1. Daily items have to do with such things as food, meat, water, fire, dinner, and horse.

The honorific monosyllabic roots for body parts and daily items form the basis of compounding and classificatory derivations for honorific words. Many honorific roots only substitute for the common roots which have the

Table 1 Monosyllabic honorific words that form the basis of the classificatory system

Body parts			Food/household/daily items		
Common	Honorific	Gloss	Common	Honorific	Gloss
zu	*ku*	body	*to*	*sö*	food
kangm	*zh'ap*	foot	*sha*	*trum*	meat
lap	*chak*	hand	*chu*	*chap*	water
ökô	*gul*	neck			
sem	*thuk*	mind, spirit	*g'i*	*shen*	knife
gutô	*'û*	head	*me*	*shuk*	fire
mîtô	*cen*	eye			
'namco	*nyen*	ear	*ta*	*chip*	horse
nhapa	*shang*	nose			
kha	*zh'ĕ*	mouth	*ngak*	*kâ*	speech
ce	*jak*	tongue			
so	*tshem*	tooth			
rüto	*dung*	bone			
ro	*pur*	corpse			

Table 2 General substitution of the honorific root *ku*

Common → *ku*	Common root meaning	Common honorific suppletion	Compound gloss
zû →	body	*zûtop* → *kutop*	stamina
lü →	body	*lütshê* → *kutshê*	stature
ke →	waist	*kerâ* → *kurâ*	belt
ngo →	face	*ngopar* → *kupar*	portrait
sha →	flesh	*shadok* → *kudok*	complexion
cha →	pair	*charo* → *kuro*	friend
mi →	person	*mitshe* → *kutshe*	life
rang →	oneself	*rangcang* → *kucang*	solitary, aloof
yön →	knowledge	*yönten* → *kuyön*	knowledge
go →	portion	*gokê* → *kukê*	allotment

equivalent sense, e.g. *tshem* 'tooth HON' substitutes only for a few compounds with *so* 'tooth'. A handful of honorific roots, however, may substitute for a larger range of common roots, increasing the semantic range of nouns that encode honorification. As illustrated in Table 2, *ku* may replace not only the two common synonyms for 'body', but also the remainder of the items in Table 2. The words at the bottom of Table 2 have meanings that are not semantically related, directly at least, to the physical human body. Knowledge, for example, which may just as well have been categorized as related to the mind, takes *ku* to derive an honorific.

The fact that *ku* replaces many common nouns is taken as indicating that *ku* semantically categorizes a fairly broad range of nouns, and not that *ku* itself has a broad meaning. That is, for the pragmatic purposes of honorification, the *ku* derived nouns are those that are classified as being related to notions of the human body rather than specific parts of the body. As far as honorification is concerned, *ku* classifies the broadest range of referents.

Other monosyllabic honorific roots compound with common roots in more transparent ways than *ku*; they replace a more semantically uniform set of words, usually relating the referent to a specific body part. Examples are given in Tables 3 to 6. The choice of honorific root depends largely on human interaction with that referent. Some referents are categorized on the basis of what part of the body interacts with it. Others are categorized on the basis of what one does with that referent, especially things that humans eat or drink.

Referents that take *'u* 'head HON' as an honorific classifier, shown in Table 3, include such nouns as 'hat' and 'pillow', and physical sensation in the head (dizziness), as well as more abstract things which are construed metaphorically as involving the head. The common equivalents of 'dizziness', 'leader', and 'trick' are comprised of a compound with the common root *gu/go* 'head'; the honorific form replaces the common form for 'head', e.g. *'ukhor* ← *gukhor* 'dizziness'. Other honorific forms entail the addition of the honorific root for head, e.g. *'uhang* ← *hang* 'pillow'.

Table 3 Referents that take *'u* 'head HON' as an honorific classifier

Common	Honorific	Gloss	Common	Honorific	Gloss
hang	*'uhang*	pillow	*sham*	*'usham*	hat
gukhor	*'ukhor*	dizziness	*gothri*	*'uthri*	leader
gukor	*'ukor*	trick	*'na*	*'unâ*	promise
		construed linguistically as turning the head			

Referents that take *'chak* 'hand HON' as an honorific classifier (Table 4) include parts of the hand such as 'finger', clothing worn on the hand such as 'glove', as well as a host of things which are handled with the hand: 'money', 'hand purse', 'bow', 'arrow', 'gun', 'rosary', 'pen', and 'book'. Note that there are many other things which might be handled by the hand, but these are specifically things that persons of social status might touch and interact with.

Table 4 Referents that take *chak* 'hand HON' as an honorific classifier

Common	Honorific	Gloss	Common	Honorific	Gloss
zumo	*châzup*	finger	*shup*	*châshup*	gloves
ngü	*chângü*	money	*d'ă*	*châdâ*	gun/arrow
zh'u	*châzhu*	bow	*pchem*	*châthreng*	rosary
peca	*chakpe*	scroll, book	*nyugu*	*chaknyuk*	pen

Referents that take *zh'ap* 'foot HON' as an honorific classifier (Table 5) include parts of the foot, clothing worn on the foot, as well as 'servant'.

Table 5 Referents that take *zh'ap* 'foot HON' as an honorific classifier

Common	Honorific	Gloss	Common	Honorific	Gloss
zumo	*zh'apzup*	toe	*pümo*	*zh'apü*	knee
omso	*zh'apso*	socks	*bj'aro*	*zh'apchi*	servant, slave

Nouns that take *sö* 'food HON' as an honorific classifier (Table 6) refer primarily to items that can be ingested: various foods, as well as 'medicine' and 'poison'. The referents 'kitchen' and 'firewood' are also categorized in this manner.

Table 6 Nouns that take *sö* 'food HON' as an honorific classifier

Common	Honorific	Gloss	Common	Honorific	Gloss
j'a	*söja*	tea	*chu*	*söchu*	drinking water
pche	*söpche*	white flour	*mâ*	*sömâ*	butter
d'u	*södu*	poison	*men*	*sömen*	medicine
thaptshang	*söthap*	kitchen	*shing*	*söshing*	firewood
tshok	*sötshok*	dinner, supper	*lhâma*	*sölhak*	leftovers

Referents categorized with *chip* 'horse HON' (Table 7) refer specifically to the equestrian world, but have also been extended to both traditional and modern forms of transportation: 'yaks and horses', and 'cars'.

Table 7 Referents that take *chip* 'horse HON' as an honorific classifier

Common	Honorific	Gloss	Common	Honorific	Gloss
ga	*chipga*	saddle	*tara*	*chipra*	horse stable
yak d'a ta	*chipa*	yaks and horses animals that get ridden	*numkhor*	*chipkhor*	car

In summary, there is a small set of common monomorphemic roots for body parts and household items that have equivalent honorific words. This small set of honorific words forms the basis of honorification of nouns, deriving honorific words in a compounding relationship from a much larger set of common words. The honorific noun compounds have specific referents; the honorific noun is not in a hyponymous relationship with its equivalent common noun.

The honorific monomorphemic forms function like classifiers categorizing nouns on the basis of how humans interact with them. One component of the system is based on what body part interacts with the referent, i.e. 'hand' interacts with 'pen'. It is a system that refers specifically to things that people of social status might use, and not, for example, to the digging utensil a labourer uses. Another component is based on the human utility of the referent, i.e. food items or transportation. As such, the categorization of honorific nouns in the Dzongkha system is cultural and social rather than based on perceptions of animacy, shape, consistency, or other schemas typical of classifier systems.

4.2 New honorific nouns

As noted earlier, much of the honorific vocabulary is identical to what is found in Lhasa Tibetan, as well as geographical speech varieties of other Central Bodish languages. Some Dzongkha forms are distinct from Lhasa Tibetan, however, illustrating that this part of the lexicon is a result of more than borrowing of Tibetan lexical items. Rather, it is the Tibetic system of classifying common items according to cultural and social values that is present, and to some extent productive, in Dzongkha.

New nouns may be added to the honorific class using the cultural and social classificatory system. Equestrian activities, for example, were an important part of the life of nobles in traditional society, and continue to be important in many parts of the Tibetic world. In Dzongkha, the honorific equestrian root <chibs> has taken on an extended use not found in standard Tibetan, deriving the honorific word for 'car', e.g. <chibs.'khor> *chipkhor* 'car HON' (lit. ride (a horse) HON + wheel) from <snum.'khor> *'numkhor* 'car' (lit. oil + wheel), where <chibs.rta> *chipta* is the honorific for horse. The referent 'cow' may also take an honorific form that is not present in standard Tibetan, e.g. <gsol.bam> *söbam* 'cow HON' from *ba* 'cow'. An honorific form for 'cow', no doubt, reflects the social relevance of cattle in traditional Bhutanese society. Note that 'cow HON' accords honorification to the owner of the cow, and not the cow itself.

Table 8 Extant variation in honorific words derived from *châk* 'hand HON'

	Gloss	Dzongkha	Tibetan	# of Tibetan dictionaries
châklen	'practice HON'	√	√	5
châkkhaw	'walking stick HON'	√	√	3
châkdâ	'arrow HON'	√	√	3
châkyik	'letter HON'	√	√	1
châksho	'dice HON'	√	√	1
châkyok	'butler to royalty HON'	√	-	-
châkrin	'price HON'	√	-	-
châkgen	'responsibility HON'	√	-	-
châkthiu	'seal HON'	√	-	-

Additional examples are given with *châk* 'hand HON' in Table 8. The forms found in Dzongkha vary in the extent to which they are also found in Tibetan dictionaries. Thus, some honorific Dzongkha words are found in a variety of dictionaries, such as the *Bögya Tshikdzö Chenmo* (the Great Tibetan Dictionary), as well as a compilation of Tibetan dictionaries as accessed online through *The Tibetan and Himalayan Library* (THL 2020). The top five words in Table 8 are found in at least one Tibetan dictionary. The bottom four words are not found in any of the dictionaries accessed through the THL website or in Goldstein's *Tibetan-English Dictionary of Modern Tibetan* (1984). The fact that every form is not present in every Tibetan dictionary is illustrative of the fact that, while the honorific classificatory system is common between Central Bodish speech varieties, the specific referents of what is classified as honorific may vary from region to region, and dictionary to dictionary. The extent to which new vocabulary and usage has developed around *driglam namzhag* is a potentially fruitful avenue of further research.

4.3 Honorific verbs and constructions

Like nouns, there is a small closed set of monomorphemic honorific roots that form the basis of the honorific system in verbs. The set of forms I am aware of are given in Table 9; there may be a few others, but the class size will not change significantly. The transitive set gives honorification to the A argument of a clause, and the intransitive set, the S argument. Unlike honorific nouns, a number of honorific verbs are in hyponymous relationship with common verbs. The common forms *ong* 'come' and *jo* 'go', for example, may both be replaced by the intransitive HON form *jön*. The control and

Table 9 Honorific monomorphemic verbs

Common	Honorific	Gloss
	Transitive	
tang, bjin	*nang*	'send, give (verbalizer)'
cap, be	*ze*	'do' (verbalizer)
ta, thong	*zî*	'look, see'
nyen, g'o	*sen*	'listen, hear'
long, lhong	*zheng*	'rise, raise'
bak, khî	*'nam*	'carry, lead'
'lap, shê	*sung*	'speak, talk, say'
len	*zhê*	'take'
se	*trong*	'kill'
nyo	*'lu*	'buy'
zhön	*chip*	'ride'
	Intransitive	
jo, ong, lhö	*jön*	'go, come, arrive'
dö	*zhû*	'sit'
ke	*thrung*	'be born, give birth'[2]
j'ong, shi	*shâk*	'die'
nyê	*zim*	'sleep'
'ngu	*shum*	'cry'
jê	*'nyê (thuk 'nyê)*	'forget'
na	*'nyung*	'be sick'
jang	*(ku) sil*	'be cold'

non-control verbs *ta* 'look' and *thong* 'see', respectively, are replaced by the single form *zî* 'look, see HON'. However, approximately half of honorific monomorphemic verbs replace only one common verb.

The honorific register of the clause is often coded in both the lexical choice of the referent noun and clausal verb. The clause in (1) is a canonical and elicited example of the use of honorifics wherein the clausal arguments, both core and oblique, accord with the referent honorification of the intransitive predicate. Note, also that the clause is followed by the optional post-clausal particle *lâ*, which is the one addressee-focused construction of the language. Only the words with grammatical function are not encoded with HON forms in example (1).

(1)   na   zimcung   na   bjön-m
      2:sg:HON   house:HON   POSTP:IN   go.come: HON-IMPERV
      îmme   lâ
      AUX:EXO   AHON
      You:HON are going:HON to (your) house:HON, laa:ahon.
      E00-1

---

[2] The common and honorific verbs *ke* and *thrung* are ambitransitive, taking both transitive and intransitive senses without valence increasing or decreasing constructions.

Not all clausal constituents need to index the honorification of the referent, particularly with transitive clauses. The HON verb, *nang* 'give', encodes the honorification of the A argument in example (2); the O argument, *nêp tshu* 'patients', is common. Note the use of the full name of the A argument, who is the fourth king of the country, and ruling king at the time of the article (March, 1994). The clause in (2) is the last clause of a multi-clausal sentence, the previous clauses of which make use of the Dzongkha equivalent of the title 'their majesties' for the king and his wives. Honorific titles are an important feature of honorific language, but are beyond the scope of this chapter.

(2)   [jig.mi.do.ji.wang.chuk]a   gêyong tsocen   menkhang
      Jigme Dorji Wangchuk   national chief   hospital
      nang yö-mi   [nêp=tshu=gi]o   dön=lê
      POSTP:IN EXIST:EGO-REL   the.sick=PL=GEN   purpose=ABL
      tshewang=ci   yang   'nang-yi
      life.blessing=INDEF also   give:HON-PAST:EGO
      [Jigme Dorji Wangchuk]a gave:hon life blessings for the [patients]o in
      the chief national hospital.
      Kuensel, March 1994

In addition to monomorphemic root verbs, Dzongkha has a medium-sized class of complex verbs that are composed of a noun-verb sequence. The noun is analysed as an incorporated object. Representative examples are given in Table 10. Such verbs are honorific by virtue of the incorporated noun, rather than the lexical verb. That is, the honorific verb for 'thirst' is composed of *zhel* 'mouth HON' + *kom*, where *zhel* is an honorific noun replacement of the common noun *kha* 'mouth'; the verb *kom* remains the same in both the common and honorific form. The set of verbs that are composed of the incorporated object *sem* 'mind' take honorification by replacing *thuk* 'mind HON' for *sem*; there are several dozen of these verbs. Some honorific forms, such as *thuk nyê/gê* 'be happy', replace both the noun and the verb with

Table 10 Representative examples of honorific complex verbs

Common	Honorific	Literal	Gloss
kha kom	*zhel kom*	mouth + thirst	'thirst'
sem gö	*thuk gö*	mind + regret	'regret'
kâm câng	*zhǎp câng*	foot + stretch	'sprawl'
kha cham	*zhĕ cham*	mouth + get long	'be in accord'
sem gâ	*thuk nyê / gê*	mind + be happy	'be happy'

honorific equivalents. Most complex incorporated-noun-verb structures are intransitive.

Common monomorphemic intransitive verbs do not have the grammatical means of honorification through the incorporated noun. Monomorphemic intransitive verbs derive an honorific meaning with the incorporation of *ku*. As demonstrated above (§4.1), *ku* is the broadest of honorific classifiers, replacing common forms whose meanings entail broad notions of the body. Intransitive common verbs can be made honorific by incorporating *ku* as an additional argument in the verb phrase, *ku* being co-referential with the clausal S argument.

(3)   a. alo   tsangchu   nang   thim-so-nu
         child   river   in   drown-INCH-PAST:EXO
         The child drowned in the river.

      b. 'lam   tsangchu   nang   ku   thim-so-nu
         Lama   river   in   body:HON   drown-INCH-PAST:EXO
         The lama drowned:hon in the river.
         E00-1

In (3a), the S argument, the common noun *alo* 'child', concords in register with the common verb *thim* 'drown'; noun incorporation is absent. In (3b), an additional noun argument *ku* precedes the verb; it is coreferential with the S argument *'lam* 'lama'. The overall semantics of the common verb does not change with the incorporation of *ku*, but only adds reference to the drowning of an honorific referent.

The incorporation of *ku* into an intransitive verb phrase is reminiscent of classificatory noun incorporation, a phenomenon first recognized by Mithun (1984), and also explored in Aikhenvald (2003: 150). In this morphosyntactic process, '[a] relatively general N stem is incorporated to narrow the scope of the V…but the compound stem can be accompanied by a more specific external NP which identifies the argument implied by the IN [incorporated noun]….Since only general N's are incorporated for this purpose, a classificatory system often results' (Mithun 1984: 863). Here in Dzongkha, the incorporated *ku* form takes a classificatory function, categorizing the S argument referent as honorific.

(4)   zh'ap   gîta   shor
      foot:HON   slip   befall
      to slip:hon

Other honorific nouns may also function in the honorification construction, as in (4). Here, the honorific root for foot, *zhʼap*, is incorporated into the complex verb *gîta shor* 'slip'. The difference between the verbs given in Table 10 and *ku thim* in (3b) or *zhʼap gîta shor* in (4) is that the former are lexicalized forms, and the latter are a grammatical construction.

Another means of making a common verb honorific entails serial verb constructions (SVCs) with a small set of honorific verbs. The honorific *jön* 'come, go' may be juxtaposed to common verbs of motion such as *lok* 'return', e.g. *lok jön* 'return HON'. Transitive verbs that do not have an equivalent honorific form may juxtapose the roots *nang* (HON of *tang* 'send') or *ze* (HON of *cap* 'hit, do' or *be* 'do') to the head of predicate.

(5) [cap   ze-mi]   ga   yang   mî
     save   do:HON-REL   who   also   neg:exist:ego
     There is no one [who (will) save:hon (me)].
     E00-1

In (5), the honorific verb *ze* augments the common verb *cap* with an HON value, referencing the internal A argument of the relative clause, marked in [ ]. The *cap ze* juxtaposition exhibits some of the features of an SVC such as monoclausality, single eventhood, and the sharing of arguments. However, the primary semantic function is honorification, rather than deictic, aspectual, or other commonly described semantic functions of SVCs.

(6) zhung   thrê   de   dumdra=ci   mâ   phap
     government   tax   DEM   a.bit=INDEF   down   bring.down
     'nang   go-p   dû   zề   îmme
     give:HON   need-NOMZ   EXIST:EXO   QUOT   COP:EXO
     It seems (the government) needs to lower:hon government tax a bit.
     Kuensel, Feb 1994

Similarly in (6), the verb *phap* has no monomorphemic replacement honorific form, but takes honorification with the juxtaposition of the honorific verb *'nang* 'give'. The clausal constituent that receives honorification is the unexpressed referent 'the government'. In both (5) and (6), the semantic content of the honorific verb is bleached, although there are clear distinctions between what common verbs combine with *ze* or *'nang*. Their primary function is to augment the common verb with honorification of the subject referent.

Thus, like honorific nouns, there is a small closed set of honorific verbs that is used to expand the honorific repertoire, and index the honorification of clausal referents. There are a number of strategies that have been described here, although the description is not exhaustive. Replacement is one means of indexing honorification, either with an honorific verb root for a common verb root, or with an honorific noun root for a common noun root in a complex (noun-verb) verb. The incorporation of an honorific noun, primarily *ku*, into the intransitive verb phrase is another strategy. Finally, a common verb may take a serial verb construction with an honorific verb the semantics of which are largely bleached. The use of one strategy over another is posited to largely be a function of lexical characteristics of the predicate head.

4.4 Humilific verbs

In addition to honorific verbs, Dzongkha has a small, five member set of humilific verbs, as given in Table 11. Humilific verbs are those that index the honorification of two referents in relation to one another; one referent is thought of as higher in relation to the other (Keating 1998: 68–9; Hugoniot 2003). In Dzongkha, it is always the referent of S/A that is portrayed as lower than the referent of the non-S/A argument; the humilific verb frequently entails the deferential presentation of the speaker as referent of S or A. The referent of the non-S/A argument is usually human, but may be a sacred object such as an 'altar'. Humilific verbs have common and honorific equivalents, e.g. the humilific form *zh'u* 'speak HUM' has both *sung* 'speak HON' as an honorific and *'lap* 'speak' as a common equivalent.

The humilific verb *zh'u* is the most frequently attested humilific verb, often functioning to mark a deferential stance between the speaker and addressee.

Table 11 Humilific verbs

Common	Honorific	Humilific	Gloss
'lap	*sung*	*zh'u*	'say, talk, speak'
bjin, trö	*'nang*	*phü*	'give, offer'
len	*zhê*	*z'è*	'take, receive'
pchê	*jêkha nang*	*jê*	'meet'
jô	*jön*	*câr*	'go, come, visit'

(7) [na=gi   sung-do   zumbe=ra]ₐ
     2:sg:HON   speak:HON-PROG:EGO   like=EMPH
     dawgem=gi   kejur   be-ni=gi   internship   re
     dawgem=ERG   translation   do-INFIN=GEN   internship   just
     thop-pacin   gokab   bom=ci   îmme
     obtain-COND   opportunity   big=INDEF   COP:EXO
     [z'ê   zh'u-ni   ing]b
     QUOT   say:HUM-FUT   AUX:EGO
     [Like you:HON said:HON]a, 'It would be a great opportunity if Dawgem
     could have just an internship in translation,' [(I) say:HUM (to you)]b.
     L16-1

There are two parameters of honorification in operation in the clause in
(7). The first parameter, in the clause marked as a, profiles the elevated social
status of addressee, who is the referent of the A argument of the first clause of
the sentence. The referent takes the 2nd person pronoun *na* HON'; the clausal
predicate *sung* 'speak HON' also indexes the honorification of the argument.
The second parameter, in the clause marked as b, profiles the relative social gap
between the speaker and the addressee. Note that the speaker is the unexpressed referent of the A argument of clause b. The construction in clause b
is quotative, but functions to portray the deferential attitude of the speaker
toward the 2nd person referent/addressee. It mitigates any face threat the
speaker's implied request imposes on the addressee.

(8) nga=gi   charô   be-ni   be-w   ing
     1:sg=ERG   friend   do-FUT   do-IMPERV   AUX:EGO
     z'ê   debe   zh'u-yi
     QUOT   like.that   say:HUM-PAST:EGO
     'I am here to be his friend,' I told:HUM like that (to the official).
     C16-1

The sentence in (8) also consists of a direct quote clause in the first line
followed by the quotative *z'ê* and inflected main clause humilific speech verb
zh'u as the matrix verb (in the second line). The main clause encodes the first
clause as a quote, indexing the deferential manner of the speaker in relation to
the unexpressed non-S/A referent of the clause (to the official). The speaker in
this example is telling a story about being in an administrative office seeking
permission to travel with a friend; the speaker is the A argument. The one
who is being addressed in the story is an official who has the power to give or

refuse permission. The official is the non-S/A argument, whose relatively higher status is in focus.

The humilific verb may also encode the relative status of two honorific clausal referents, as in example (9).

(9) jagâr=gi   'makde   33-p=i   kӧchap   gopӧn
     India=GEN   military.unit   33-NOMZ=GEN   director   leader
     gunglӧn   em   âr   sharma   chok
     general   M   R   Sharma   great:HON
     druk=gi   'makde=i   gӧm   be
     Bhutan=GEN   military=GEN   guest   ADV
     gêkhap   nang   nyim   6=gi   ring=lu
     country   POSTP:IN   day   6=GEN   length=DAT
     [zîkor   nang-pâr   jӧn   yӧ-p
     visit:HON   give:HON-PURP   come.go:HON   AUX:EXIST:EGO-IMPERV
     zhin-du]a   [thimphu=lu   'mi.'wang.zh'ap   sâ
     after-DAT:LITERARY   Thimphu=DAT   majestic.king   place
     câr-yi]b
     go.to:HUM
     The Major General of the Indian military unit 33, the honorable HON M
     R Sharma, as a guest of the Bhutanese military, [having toured:HON the
     Bhutanese kingdom for six days]a, [visited:HUM his majesty in Thimphu.]b
     Kuensel, July 1995

In context, the Indian army general is accorded honorification in titles in a series of appositional noun phrases, as in the first two lines of (9). Later in the sentence, in clause a, honorification of the S argument is indexed with the honorific complex verb *zîkor nang* 'tour' and the honorific verb *jӧn* 'come, go HON'. The final clause of the sentence, clause b, however, reports of the general's visit to his majesty the king wherein the event is expressed with the humilific *câr* 'go.to hum'. Although the general is accorded honorification elsewhere in the sentence, the humilific encodes the relatively higher status of his majesty the king in relation to the general. Note that *câr* is an intransitive verb and is showing deference to the referent of the oblique phrase, *'mi.'wang.zh'ap sa* 'the place of his majesty the king'.

Thus, the humilific verbs express a relative status between clausal referents, specifically the relatively lower status of the referent of the S/A argument in relation to the referent of the non-S/A argument. The relative status may be expressed even if the referent of relatively lower status also receives honorification elsewhere in the sentence. When the S/A argument references the speaker, as in (8), the humilific verb expresses deference to the referent of the non-S/A argument, and in frequent usage, deference to the referent who is the addressee, as in (7).

5 Honorific ideology versus usage

Thus far, the chapter has described the structural elements of honorific vocabulary in Dzongkha, noting in particular the way body part roots function in the nominal system. Nouns take honorification by way of replacement or compounding with an honorific body part root associated with interacting with the referent. Verbs take honorification by means of replacement, serial verb constructions with honorific verbs, or through the incorporation of honorific nouns. In this section, the chapter turns to a brief description of honorifics in language usage.

Examples that typify politeness and social hierarchy have been given in the section on honorific and humilific verbs. In example (2), repeated here for convenience as (10), the king is given honorification in the verb ʼnang ʻgive HON'.

(10) jig.mi.do.ji.wang.chuk   gêyong   tsocen   menkhang
      Jigme Dorji Wangchuk   national   chief   hospital
      nang   yö-mi   nêp=tshu=gi   dön=lê
      POSTP:IN   EXIST:EGO-REL   the.sick=PL=GEN   purpose=ABL
      tshewang=ci   yang   ʼnang-yi
      life.blessing=INDEF   also   give:HON-PAST:EGO
      Jigme Dorji Wangchuk gave:hon life blessings for the patients in the
      chief national hospital.
      Kuensel, March 1994

The verb along with his titles in previous clauses of the sentence reflects his elevated social position as king. Example (9) with the humilific verb zhʼu ʻsay HUM' also elevates his position above another person of social honour. Honorific language usage in public domains, such as Dzongkha medium newspapers, tends toward the coding of social distance and hierarchy, reifying the importance of driglam namzhag in national life and the value of maintaining the appropriate ʻbonds' between members of society.

The two sequences in (11) and (12), however, illustrate a different environment for the use of honorifics. Although they still function to encode politeness, they are used between social equals. One sequence is taken from the movie *chö da jikte* 'The Divine and the Mundane'. The sequence entails interaction between three monks as they wait for the results of their annual exam and they consider their future plans. The other sequence is extracted from a conversation involving four men who are engaged in a game of Carrom. Both social contexts are informal, and the interlocutors are social equals. The difference is that the movie sequence is carefully scripted, and in part, produced to preserve and support national identity through the Dzongkha language medium. The Carrom sequence is unscripted, spontaneous, and natural.

(11) a. de   dang   g'aci   ze-pi=gi   charzhi
          DEM   and   what   do:HON-NOMZ=GEN   plan
          yö   ga   lâ?
          EXIST:EGO   INTER   AHON
          So, what do (you) plan to do:hon? (S1)

      b. ma   shê   d'a
          NEG   know   now
          I'm not sure. (S2)

      c. dangja   khenpo=lu   châk zh'u-wa   song-yi
          last. time abbot=DAT   serve:HUM-PURP   go:SUPL-PAST:EGO
          The other time I went to serve:hum the abbot. (S2)

      d. khenpo=gi   te   tsham=ci   zhê-wacin
          abbot=ERG   PART   retreat=INDEF   take:HON-COND
          drâk   zê   sung-de
          good   QUOT   say:HON-PROG:EXO
          The abbot says:hon, 'It's good if (you) go:hon on a retreat.' (S2)

      e. ngöndü=ci   tang   ong   dre   zê   no
          initiation=INDEF   send   AUX:PRED   EPSTM   QUOT   think
          dö   be
          sit   ADV
          I was thinking that I'd probably get initiated. (S2)

      f. S3 worries about passing his exam in a sequence of 7 clauses

      g. thâ   khö   khö   ong   lâ
          edge   finish   finish   STAT:EXO   AHON
          You'll graduate. (S2)

h. thuksam   zhê   mi   go   ba   te
    thought:HON   take:HON   NEG   need   NOMZ   PART
    You don't need to worry:HON. (S2)
    'The Divine and the Mundane'

In the sequence in (11), the three monk friends use honorifics with one another. S1 uses the honorific verb *ze* 'do HON' in (11a) to ask his friends what they will do after their exam results are posted. The verb indexes the honorification of S1's interlocutors. S2 uses the humilific verb *châk zh'u* 'serve HUM' in (11c) to index his visit to the abbot, showing a deference for his teacher. This is followed by S2's report of what the abbot said in (11d), marking the direct quote with the honorific verb *sung* 'say HON'. Finally, S2 comforts S3 in (11h), telling him to not worry about whether he has passed his exams or not; S2 uses nominal and verbal honorifics in the complex noun-verb sequence.

What is of interest here in the sequence in (11) is that the script for the monk characters has them using honorifics with one another in an informal setting. That is, the use of honorifics in this script does not portray a hierarchical distinction between them. The monks are equal with one another, but nevertheless ascribe honorification to one another. It is not clear whether use of honorifics is a monastic rule or not, but in personal interactions with monks in the monastery, I have not observed their use among peers. More true to personal observation is the expression of honorifics and humilifics in relation to persons of higher social and or religious ranking, as in (11c) and (11d). The movie script exhibits a language ideology reifying the use of honorifics in domains of national and cultural significance. Their use here is less about differences in social standing, as the exhibition of *driglam namzhag*. The monks serve as linguistic examples of speech etiquette and 'harmony between fellow beings'.

In contrast to the monks are the four men who play a game of Carrom. Their game is interspersed with friendly banter, and posturing about who is better than the other player, although one player is clearly better than the rest. The interlocutors give one another commands, instructions, prohibitives, and make fun of one another. There is no politeness, at least as it would be defined by propriety. But for a few honorific commands, honorific language usage is absent. The sequence in (12) contains one of the few clauses where an honorific verb is used.

(12)   a. d'aben   jangkha   cap-Ø   'mare
          so.then   count   do-IMP   warning
          So then, take a count. (S1)

       b. handrid   ma   lang   ga?
          hundred   NEG:PAST   enough   INTER:POLAR
          Has one hundred not been reached? (S1)

       c. atsi   zhu-me
          little.bit sit:HON-IMP:REQUEST
          Just wait:hon a bit (while I count). (S2)
          C16-12

Here, S1 has won a game of Carrom by being the first to acquire one-hundred points. First, S1 tells his interlocutors in (12a) to count his score, using the common verb *cap* 'do' in an imperative construction, followed by the post verbal warning particle *'mare*. Second, S1 asks in (12b) with negative polarity whether or not one-hundred points are acquired. The grammatical mood of the clause is interrogative, but the question is rhetorical. S1 intends to convey the obvious that one-hundred points have been reached. But, S2 contests S1's claim in (12c), and tells S1 to wait while he counts the points. Here, the honorific verb *zhu* 'sit HON' is used even though the imperative construction takes the familiar request marker *-me*.

The use of an honorific verb in (12c) illustrates a linguistic means of politeness by mitigating a potential 'face threatening act' (FTA). FTAs are verbal interactions such as ordering, advising, criticizing, promising that have the potential of affecting the face of the conversational interlocutor (Brown and Levinson 1987: 68–9; Song 2017: 67–8). Here S2 contests S1's claim to have won the game, but knows that his efforts are potentially confronting, not only with his interlocutor in this sequence (S1), but also with the other players of the game who have observed S1 win. The potential social risk of S2's order to wait is mitigated with the use of honorific verb.

The majority of honorific vocabulary in language usage in situations of familiarity is found in imperative constructions like the construction in (12c), suggesting that honorific usage in this interactional environment is suited to the speaker's perception of what Brown and Levinson (1987: 76) call 'imposition of the task'. While speaker's perception of social power and distance are a central part of Brown and Levinson's theory of politeness, these appear to be largely irrelevant in interaction among social peers in Dzongkha. What seems to be at play is the 'seriousness' of the request, i.e. the extent to which the speaker perceives his/her command to impose on the interlocutor.

Although Dzongkha honorific vocabulary is used extensively in formal settings to reify distinctions in social hierarchy, the two conversational sequences given here illustrate usage in informal situations among interlocutors without social distance. In the movie script, honorific usage is reciprocal, and not one way. The monks serve as linguistic examples of the harmonious behavior of *driglam namzhag*; usage is ideologically driven. In the game of Carrom, the use of an honorific among peers is unscripted, and shows how honorifics are used to mitigate a potential FTA, and as such that they are linguistic means of expressing politeness.

6 Conclusion

This chapter demonstrates that the linguistic parameter of honorifics is a point of integration between Bhutanese society and Dzongkha. At one level, the integration is overt, especially as demonstrated by governmental policy to preserve and maintain *driglam namzhag*; honorifics are an overt linguistic expression of the value placed on this etiquette. They index the social hierarchy of clausal referents, and encode speaker politeness toward them. However, there is much that remains unstudied about how *driglam namzhag* manifests itself in language usage, both in the interactions of civil servants in the administrative offices of the government, and among common interlocutors in local village settings. In the interaction among social equals studied here in natural conversation, the use of honorifics exhibits features of politeness, but with a focus on mitigating the speaker's perception of imposing on the interlocutor, rather than maintaining social distance or hierarchy.

The chapter also shows that honorific nouns have a classificatory function that is based on body part or human utility, illustrating that the classificatory system in this language is cultural and social. The class of honorific nouns is semi-open with new forms that may be added to reflect the referents of modern Bhutanese society. In addition, honorific and humilific classes of verb differentiate between two aspects of honorification. Honorific verbs focus on the elevated status of the referent. Humilific verbs are inherently relative, profiling the comparative social gap between clausal referents.

References

Agha, Asif. 1994. 'Honorification', *Annual Review of Anthropology* 23: 277–302.

Aikhenvald, Alexandra Y. 2003. *Classifiers: A typology of noun categorization devices*. Oxford: Oxford University Press.

Aris, Michael. 1998. *The raven crown: The origins of Buddhist monarchy in Bhutan*. Chicago: Serindia Publications, Inc.

Bradley, David. 1997. 'Tibeto-Burman languages and classification', in David Bradley (ed.), *Tibeto-Burman languages of the Himalayas*, [Papers in Southeast Asian linguistics No. 14, Pacific Linguistics Series A-86]. Canberra: Australian National University, 1–71.

Brown, Penelope and Stephen Levinson. 1987. *Politeness: Some universals in language usage*. Cambridge: Cambridge University Press.

Comrie, Bernard. 1976. 'Linguistic politeness axes: speaker-addressee, speaker-referent, speaker-bystander', *Pragmatics Microfiche* 1.7:A3.

DeLancey, Scott. 1998. 'Semantic Categorization in Tibetan Honorific Nouns', *Anthropological Linguistics* 40(1): 109–23.

Dzongkha Development Commission. 2011. *phal.skad zhe.sa'i rnam.gzhag skar. ma'i 'od.zer; Dzongkha Honorifics*. Thimphu, Bhutan: DDC.

Eberhard, David M., Gary F. Simons, and Charles D. Fennig (eds). 2019. *Ethnologue: Languages of the world. Twenty-second edition*. Dallas, Texas: SIL International. <http://www.ethnologue.com>

Goldstein, Melvyn C. 1984. *English-Tibetan dictionary of Modern Tibetan*. Dharamsala, India: Library of Tibetan Works and Archives.

Hugoniot, Kenneth. 2003. *At the crossroads of pragmatics, syntax and semantics: The Tibetan humiliative honorific verb zhu*. MA thesis, University of California, Santa Barbara.

Keating, Elizabeth. 1998. *Power Sharing: Language, rank, gender and social space in Pohnpei, Micronesia*. Oxford: Oxford University Press.

Mithun, Marrianne. 1984. 'The evolution of noun incorporation', *Language* 60(4): 847–94.

Shibatani, Masayoshi. 2001. 'Honorifics', in R. Mesthrie and R. E. Asher (eds), *Concise encyclopedia of sociolinguistics*. Oxford: Elsevier Science & Technology 552–558.

Song, Sooho. 2017. 'The Brown and Levinson theory revisited: A statistical analysis', *Language Sciences* 62: 66–75.

Special Commission for Cultural Affairs. 1999. *sgrig.lam rnam.gzhag lag.len 'thab. thangs; Driglam Namzhag (Bhutanese Etiquette): A Manual*. Thimphu, Bhutan: National Library of Bhutan.

The Tibetan and Himalayan Library. 2020. 'The Tibetan and Himalayan Library'. <http://dictionary.thlib.org/search_definitions (02/2020)>

Tournadre, Nicolas. 2013. 'The Tibetic languages and their classification', in Thomas Owen-Smith and Nathan Hill (eds), *Trans-Himalayan linguistics. historical and descriptive linguistics of the Himalayan area*. Berlin, Boston: De Gruyter Mouton, 105–30.

Ura, Karma. 1998. 'Development and decentralisation in medieval and modern Bhutan', in Michael Aris and Michael Hutt (eds), *Bhutan: Aspects of culture and development*, Kiscadale Research Series Edition. 5: 24–49. Stirlingshire, Scotland: Kiscadale Ltd.

van Driem, George. 1991. *Guide to official Dzongkha Romanization*. Gaylegphug, Bhutan: Sherab Lham Press.

van Driem, George and Karma Tshering. 1998. *A grammar of Dzongkha*. Leiden: Research School CNWS, School of Asian, African, and Amerindian Studies.

Watters, Stephen. 2018. *A grammar of Dzongkha (dzo): Phonology, words, and simple clauses*. PhD dissertation, Rice University.

4

Identifying who is who in Brokpa

Pema Wangdi

1 Introduction

Brokpa is a Bodish (Tibetic) language belonging to the Tibeto-Burman language family, also known as Trans-Himalayan (van Driem 1994, 1998; Eberhard, Simons, and Fennig 2019; Shafer 1955, 1966; Tournadre 2014). Brokpa is spoken by approximately 3,500 people in the highlands of Merak and Sakteng in Eastern Bhutan. Dondrup (1993) reports about 1,855 more Brokpa speakers living in small parts of Arunachal Pradesh in Northeast India.

Brokpa is a close linguistic relative of Dzongkha, the national language of Bhutan. Brokpa is spoken in direct contact with Tshangla belonging to the Bodic Division within the Tibeto-Burman family (Shafer 1955, 1966; Benedict 1972; van Driem 1998, 2011; Andvik 2010). Brokpa is also spoken in direct contact with Dakpa, an East Bodish language (Shafer 1955; van Driem 1994; Hyslop 2013), in Bhutan as well as in Northeast India.

Animal husbandry and subsistence farming form the main means of livelihood for the Brokpa people. The Brokpa people predominantly practise transhumance, moving with their livestock from one grazing land to another in a seasonal cycle. They take their livestock to highlands in spring and summer and to lowlands in autumn and winter. The Brokpa people follow Buddhism.

Brokpa is a traditional small-scale society. There are no stratified social classes and no local chiefs. There are community councils known as Gewog Tshogde in the main villages. The members of the Gewog Tshogde (Community Council) are all elected by the people for a fixed term of five years. Every decision is taken democratically. The heads and the staff of District and Subdistrict offices are bureaucrats with specific executive and judicial functions.

Pema Wangdi, *Identifying who is who in Brokpa*. In: *The Integration of Language and Society: A Cross-Linguistic Typology.*
Edited by: Alexandra Y. Aikhenvald, R. M. W. Dixon, and Nerida Jarkey, Oxford University Press. © Pema Wangdi 2021.
DOI: 10.1093/oso/9780192845924.003.0004

This chapter[1] deals with the ways in which the Brokpa language and the society are closely related and mutually reinforcing in relation to three Parameters (A , B, and E) outlined in Chapter 1 of this book:

Parameter A — Relations within a community, social hierarchies, and kinship categorization;
Parameter B — Social constraints (taboo and avoidance);
Parameter E — Means of subsistence and physical environment.

Linguistic categories examined, as points of integration with these non-linguistic parameters, include: a comparative construction which correlates with relations within the community and social categorization (Parameter A); the honorific forms and social deixis (Parameters A and B); and topographic deixis (Parameter E).

Section 2 provides a brief overview of the key linguistic features of Brokpa. Section 3 examines the comparative construction as indicative of attitudes and societal practices of the past and the present. Section 4 investigates demonstratives indicating height and distance (deictic reference). Section 5 describes social deixis by focusing on honorific speech. Section 6 offers brief conclusions.

2 Key linguistic features

Brokpa is an agglutinating language with some fusion. Brokpa has three open lexical classes of nouns, verbs, and adjectives, and a semi-open class of adverbs. Closed classes include personal pronouns, demonstratives, interrogatives, relators (relator nouns), time words, number words, quantifiers, connectives, and interjections. Grammatical categories typically associated with nouns are case, possession, number, definiteness, natural gender, and augmentative and diminutive marking. Grammatical categories typically associated with verbs include aspect, modality, mood, evidentiality, and egophoricity.

Some grammatical categories occurring with nouns occur with verbs in different functions and with different meanings. For example, some case

---

[1] Linguistic data for this chapter come from a textual corpus of about four hours of recordings of different genres with corroborative grammatical and lexical elicitation. The information on the non-linguistic parameters are based on immersion fieldwork and participant observation. They are also based on the personal observation and knowledge acquired as a citizen of Bhutan and as a native and near-native speaker of Tshangla and Dzongkha, which are spoken in the same sociocultural and topographical environments.

markers may occur with verbs and mark different types of dependent clauses. All verbs and a smallish group of adjectives can be negated with a bound morpheme. Negation of an adjective has scope over a word whereas negation of a verb has scope over an entire clause or a sentence. Many of the grammatical categories occurring with nouns can appear with adjectives modifying the head in an NP, with agreement determined by the head noun. Both nouns and adjectives can function as a copula complement argument within a copula construction, but pre-modifiers such as *násmeti* 'very' and *deɕmeti* 'extremely' apply only to adjectives and not to nouns. There are a number of word-class-changing derivational suffixes, specific to each open class.

New words can be derived through the morphological processes of compounding, reduplication, change of tone, internal change, and affixation. Transitivity value of a predicate can be understood from the presence or absence of ergative marking on the NP argument in the subject slot. In addition to dedicated markers, certain grammatical information such as transitivity and imperative mood can be marked by tone, voicing, and aspiration. Grammatical relations are shown by a system of case marking.

There are certain areas of the lexicon in Brokpa which particularly reflect the sociocultural values and lifestyles of its speakers. For example, Brokpa has a wealth of lexical items related to livestock, indicative of their transhumant lifestyle. There is also a rich set of vocabulary items related to polygamy, directly indicating that Brokpa embraces this practice. However, the lexicon is outside the scope of this chapter and we will limit ourselves to examining the connection between some grammatical systems and societal practices.

3 Comparison and recreational activities

As noted in Chapter 1 and in Dixon (2008), small egalitarian societies tend to have little in the way of comparative constructions, perhaps because notions such as competition and hierarchy are not important in these societies. Brokpa is a small egalitarian society, so we may not expect notions such as competition and hierarchy to be important, and yet the language does have a comparative construction. We can associate a comparative construction in Brokpa with two relevant societal factors: (a) the traditionally competitive recreational activities; and (b) the comparison of people through social deixis (§5). Both (a) and (b) suggest that a comparative construction is not a recent grammatical phenomenon in Brokpa nor is it a result of borrowing or influence from other languages. This is also not the case with the concepts of winning and losing, as they are clearly expressed in Brokpa.

Horse racing known as *tabraŋ~tabaŋ* (also *tagyuk*) has been popular among the Brokpa people for hundreds of years. Typically, men would take part in horse racing at a place called Jomo Tathaksa when they go on the Jomokora pilgrimage with family members, relatives, and friends. Jomokora is a pilgrimage trip to Jomo Phodrang, a sacred mountain crag believed to be the dwelling place of the protecting deity Ama Jomo. Ama Jomo was an ancestral Brokpa lady who guided the Brokpa ancestors when they first came to the present settlement areas more than 600 years ago. Ama Jomo is now worshipped as the local deity and every Brokpa man and woman goes to the mountain crag of Jomo Phodrang at least once a year, or whenever they can, to receive blessings from her.

It is believed that when Ama Jomo and her entourage arrived at Jomo Tathaksa, her warriors took part in a horse race to keep her entertained. After that, it was continued as a tradition.

Brokpa has a unique genre of oral literature known as *kʰapɕo* 'singing dialogue', similar to 'ballads'. It is quite common for young men and women to have a *kʰapɕo* competition, as a form of entertainment, in the evening during the Jomokora pilgrimage, as well as during other social events. Brokpa people love singing and dancing. Any family or community celebration is not complete without men and women bursting into song and dance. Men and women sing and take turns in dancing and, more often than not, this leads to a joyful competition.

The Brokpa people also have great fondness for other competitive sports such as *betʰa* 'wrestling'. Wrestling is generally held as a form of entertainment but it is also a way of demonstrating prowess among men. Occasionally, during big national celebrations, organized wrestling competitions are held; and Brokpa men are famed for being hardcore wrestlers. Some have emerged victorious in such big wrestling matches in the past.

Archery is a favourite pastime among Brokpa men. Every Brokpa village has one or more archery grounds and men indulge in this popular national sport whenever they can. They also organize archery competitions against neighbouring villages. There are other sports played in groups such as *kʰur* 'darts' and *degor* 'circular stone', which are also popular among young men.

In all such societal practices, including games and sports, one person or one team tries to be better than another. Spectators need to talk about who is faster/fastest, stronger/strongest, better/best and this results in making direct comparisons between two or more participants. Comparison of participants in sporting events is extended to other phenomena. Not only are there several words with the meanings of 'competition', 'win', 'lose', 'draw', etc., in the vocabulary, in addition to these, Brokpa also has grammatical means of coding comparison.

Dixon (2008, 2012: 343) provides three basic elements in a prototypical comparative scheme: the two participants being compared and the property in terms of which they are compared. The participants are, first, the one which is compared (Comparee) and, second, what the Comparee is being compared against (Standard); the property is the Parameter of comparison; a prototypical comparative scheme may also involve an Index of comparison (more, less, etc.). The Parameter in a mono-clausal comparative construction may be a copula complement, the head of an intransitive predicate, or a verb within a serial verb construction (Dixon 2008).

In Brokpa, the Parameter of comparison is realized as an adjective which takes a morphological marking of index of comparison. There are two contrasting suffixes, comparative and superlative. The adjective in a comparative construction, typically making up the whole of a copula complement argument, is marked by the suffix -ɕo. The adjective in a superlative construction is shown by suffix -da (and its allomorphs, -ta and -tʰa). In other words, comparative and superlative in Brokpa are distinguished by morphological marking of Index on adjectives. The suffix –kyaŋ 'too/also' is also used as a superlative strategy.

Table 1 provides examples of adjectives and their comparative and superlative forms.

Note that adjectival roots undergo phonological processes before the suffixation of comparative and superlative markers. For example, the final syllable from the adjectival root is omitted, as in tompo → tom-, or a diphthong is made a monopthong, as in kʰeu → kʰe-. In some cases, the coda consonant from the root is replaced by another consonant, as in ɽamo → ɽap- (Wangdi forthcoming).

Table 1 Brokpa adjectives and their comparative and superlative forms

Bare form	Meaning	Comparative	Superlative
ɽamo	'thin'	ɽap-ɕo	ɽap-ta, ɽap-kyaŋ
tompo	'short'	tom-ɕo	tom-da, tom-kyaŋ
kʰeu	'cheap'	kʰe-ɕo	kʰe-da, kʰe-kyaŋ
dʒokpʰo	'quick'	dʒok-ɕo	dʒok-tʰa, dʒok-kyaŋ
guibu	'slow'	gui-ɕo	gui-da, gui-kyaŋ
sarbo	'new'	sar-ɕo	sar-da, sar-kyaŋ

Examples (1a) and (1b) show suffix -ɕo marking a comparative construction contrasting two participants:

(1) a. zo=læ   yáʔ   ɖak-**ɕo**   yin
        Zo=ABL   yak   good-COMPAR   COP.EGO
        Yak is better than Zo. (a cross-bred bull)

     b. Tashi=læ   Lham   ɕe: tɕʰe-**ɕo**
        Tashi=ABL   Lham   energy   big-COMPAR
        Lham is stronger than Tashi.

In (1a), the adjective ɖak-ɕo 'better', with the Index suffix, makes up the whole copula complement argument and is involved in the comparison of two participants, zo (Standard) and yá: (Comparee). The ablative enclitic =læ (Mark) marks the Standard of comparison.

Examples (2a) and (2b) show suffix –ta and -da marking the superlative construction in which the best among many or a unique participant or an item out of a set is identified:

(2) a. gonor   gaŋyu   naŋ=næ   yáʔ   ɖak-**ta**
        farm.cattle   all   inside=ABL   yak   good-SUPER
        Of all the farm cattle, yak is the best.

     b. Merak   naŋ=næ   ɕe: tɕʰe-**da**
        Merak   inside=ABL   energy   big-SUPER
        Lham   yin
        Lham   COP.EGO
        Lham is the strongest (one) from Merak.

Lham from the village of Merak came first in the wrestling category of the Strong Men Competition held at the national level in Bhutan. He also won titles at the local and regional levels. So the speaker takes it for granted that Lham is the strongest man in Merak and uses the superlative form, as in (2b). It is also a known fact that Lham is a strong man who can throw down a yak on the ground just by holding the horns with his hands. So the speaker uses the egophoric copula yin which denotes a personal knowledge (or a privileged access to knowledge).

Examples (3a) and (3b) show suffix -kyaŋ used as a marker of superlative strategy:

(3) a. muz   ʔani   ʔadʑaŋ   yak-**kyaŋ**   yona
        non-self   aunt   uncle   good-SUPER   COP.FACTUAL
        They, aunty and uncle, are excellent/super good (people).

b. golam   yin-ne=ye   sarbu-sar-**kyaŋ**=raŋ
   clothes   COP.EGO-COND=EMPH   new~new-SUPER=EMPH
   gon=næ   ɖo-go-pʰi-na
   wear=ABL.SEQ   go-MOD:OBLIGATION-NOMZ-FACTUAL
   Even the clothes, you must wear the newest one.

The adjective with the suffix -*kyaŋ* typically modifies the head noun within an NP and shows that the referent of the head noun is of the most excellent type or quality, the same function achieved by the suffix -*da*. The existence of traditional competitive practices correlates with the presence of well-defined comparative and superlative constructions.

4 Physical environment and deictic reference

Brokpa is spoken in a mountainous terrain. There are special monomorphemic lexical words like *gyen* to refer to 'slope up' and *tʰur* to 'slope down' which do not involve compounding with words meaning 'up' or 'down'. The villages are scattered and are separated by high mountains, dense forests, and fast-flowing rivers. Brokpa has several words encoding relative height, stance, and direction in its demonstrative system. Some demonstratives include information regarding whether a referent is on the same level as the speaker or whether it is higher or lower than the speaker, which is typical of small communities living in mountainous terrain (Dixon 2016). These demonstrative words directly correlate with social deixis (§5).

Some body-part terms are used with the locative/allative marker to refer to the upper or lower part of something, especially rivers and mountains. For example, *go=la* 'head=LOC' can be used to mean the upper reaches of a valley, river, mountain, valley, etc., and *dʑuk=la* 'tail =LOC' can be used to refer to the lower reaches. In the same manner, the nouns *to:* 'upper part', *bar* 'middle part' and *mǽ* 'lower part' of something can occur with the locative/allative enclitic =*la* and refer to the upper part, middle part, or lower part of a mountain, river, village, and so on.

Two types of demonstratives are of relevance here, the nominal demonstratives and the local adverbial demonstratives (Dixon 2003, 2010: 224). Nominal demonstratives make a two-way spatial contrast, 'near speaker' and 'away from speaker'. There are two sets of nominal demonstratives, one set commencing with a voiced apico-alveolar stop /d/ and another with a glottal stop /ʔ/. The first set are named 'archaic nominal demonstratives' and the second 'innovative nominal demonstratives' for an easy distinction.

Table 2 provides the two sets of nominal demonstratives.

The nominal demonstrative forms *di* and *de* are common to many Bodish languages including Dzongkha (van Driem and Tshering 2019; Watters 2018), Classical Tibetan (Beyer 1992; DeLancey 2003a), and Lhasa Tibetan (DeLancey 2003b); this is the reason why they are described as 'archaic nominal demonstratives' in Brokpa. The functions of nominal demonstratives are also fulfilled by the innovative demonstratives *ʔoti* and *ʔupʰi*, sometimes reduced to *ʔot* (further reduced to *ʔo*) and *ʔu*. The archaic set of nominal demonstratives *di* 'proximal' and *de* 'distal' do sporadically retain their deictic functions, but are neutralized into a single form *di* which takes on the role of a definite article. However, the forms *di* and *de* can be used for deriving other demonstratives, as we will see later in this section.

A nominal demonstrative in Brokpa can occur in an NP with a noun or a pronoun, and can make up an NP on its own. The syntactic functions of nominal demonstratives will not be explored here. Of relevance are those adverbial demonstratives that code height and stance in addition to the spatial pointing references. Following Post (2011, 2019), and Aikhenvald (2015: 188), the demonstratives which include information about height and stance determined topographically, among other criteria, will be referred to as markers of 'topographic deixis'.

First, we briefly look at the local adverbial demonstratives that do not code height. Table 3 gives a list of local adverbial demonstratives that make a two-way spatial contrast.

Table 2 Nominal demonstratives in Brokpa

	ARCHAIC	INNOVATIVE	MEANING
PROXIMAL	*di*	*ʔoti ~ woti*	this
DISTAL	*de*	*ʔupʰi*	that

Table 3 Local adverbial demonstratives in Brokpa

FORM	ETYMOLOGY	FEATURE	MEANING
ʔol(a), ʔotil(a)	this + loc	PROXIMAL	'here'
dil(a)	this + loc	PROXIMAL	'here'
ʔon		PROXIMAL	'here'
dotil		PROXIMAL	'here'
ʔupʰil(a)	that ı loc	DISTAL	'there'
ʔun(la)	that + loc	DISTAL	'there'

Table 4 The expression of topographic deixis in Brokpa

FORM	ETYMOLOGY	FEATURE	MEANING
yal, ya:te	up + loc/all	UPWARD	'up there/upwards'
mal, ma:te	down +loc/all	DOWNWARD	'down there/ downwards'
ʔoyil(a)	this + up + loc	UPWARD + DISTAL	'up there'
ʔumil(a)	that + down + loc	DOWNWARD + DISTAL	'down there'
pʰal(a)	that.side + loc/all	SAME LEVEL + DISTAL	'over there/thither'
tsʰul(a)	this.side + loc/all	SAME LEVEL + PROXIMAL	'over here/hither'
ditɕʰok(la)	this + direction + loc/all	SAME LEVEL + PROXIMAL	'here/this side'
pʰetɕʰok(la)	that + direction + loc/all	SAME LEVEL + DISTAL	'there/that side'
gyente	up.slope + all	UPHILL	'uphill'
tʰurte	down.slope + all	DOWNHILL	'downhill'

All the local adverbial demonstratives, provided in Table 3, can form an NP on their own. They can have spatial pointing reference and include stance in relation to the speaker, proximal or distal, but do not have height reference such as upward or downward or higher or lower than the speaker. The nominal demonstrative and the local adverbial demonstrative which do not mark topographic deixis are introduced because the two-way spatial contrasts achieved by them have parallels with comparative constructions in which two participants are compared (§3) and with social deixis based on bipartite social categorizations (§5).

Table 4 provides a list of markers of topographic deixis in Brokpa. Similar to the regular local adverbial demonstratives in Table 3, the forms sensitive to topographic deixis are derived from the nominal demonstratives and directional adverbs by means of the locative/allative case marker =*la*[2]. Some are formed by means of the allative =*te*. With *ditɕʰok* 'this side' and *pʰetɕʰok* 'that side', the entire locative/allative marker including the initial consonant is optional. The allative =*te* also forms a prosodic unit with the root.

All the demonstratives in Table 4 encode relative height, stance, and direction in addition to spatial reference and can be analysed as exponents of topographic deixis (Aikhenvald 2015: 188; Post 2019). Consider:

(4) a. nor=di   den   nám   soː   **yal**
         cattle=DEF   DEM:ABL   season   spring   **up.there**

---

[2] The locative/allative case enclitic =*la* has coalesced with the root and the final vowel /a/ is optional leading to syllable reduction.

la=la   za-zin
mountain=LOC   climb-DUR
Then while taking the cattle up there to the mountain…

b. den   gun   **maːte**   ton   **maːte**
PART   winter   **downward**   autumn   **downward**
loʔ=næ   te
return=ABL.SEQ PART
So then in winter and autumn, we return downwards…

In these two examples, (4a) and (4b), the speaker is talking about the trans-humant lifestyle. He uses the demonstrative *yal* to refer to the practice of taking the cattle up in the spring season and *maːte* to refer to bringing them back down in autumn and winter. In both the expressions, *yal* and *maːte* have a deictic function and combine reference to height and to distance.

The demonstratives *ditɕʰok* 'this side' and *pʰetɕʰok* 'that side' have deictic functions as examples (5a) and (5b) illustrate:

(5) a. den   **ditɕʰok**   kʰim=la   dok=næ
DEM:ABL   this.side   house=LOC   reach=ABL.SEQ
Then, after arriving at the house this side …

b. Yeshi Khandom Numa=gi   **pʰetɕʰok**=di=la
Yeshi Khandom Numa=GEN   that.side=DEF=LOC
bæyuː   yoː
hidden.village   COP:EXIST.EGO
There is Hidden Village on the other side of Yeshi Khandoma Numa.

Both *ditɕʰok* and *pʰetɕʰok* encode the same height level. They can refer to this side or that side of something at the same level as a point of reference such as a river in between. These two terms can also function as markers of social deixis, and can be used with a deictic effect for distinguishing people (for instance, they are employed in categorizing kinship relations, referring to consanguineal relations as 'people this side' and to affinal relations as 'people that side').

5 Social deixis and the honorific system

As mentioned in §3, Brokpa is a small egalitarian society. At the same time, there is a strong culture of showing deference towards elders and seniors. As a result, several bipartite and tripartite systems of social categorizations have been developed. Examples of terms reflecting a bipartite categorization include *tɕʰe-tɕʰuŋ* or *bom-tɕʰuŋ* 'big-small', *tʰo-mǽn* 'high-low', and *ɖak-ʐæn* 'stronger-weaker'. We also find examples of tripartite categorization (where three distinctions are made). Examples of tripartite categorizations include *tɕʰe-ɖiŋ-tɕʰuŋ-sum* 'the three—big, medium, and small', *tʰo-mǽn-bar-sum* 'the three—high, low, and middle', *teŋ-ɦok-bar-sum* 'the three—upper, lower, and middle'.

Terms associated with such categorizations are used as markers of social deixis. They are used as referential terms and, in certain contexts (such as addressing an audience), they can be used as forms of address. Most of these terms can also be used, with deictic effect, to refer to the height or size of a natural phenomenon such as mountains, rocks, and trees.

The bipartite and tripartite categorizations are for the purpose of according deference to people who are 'elders' not only in terms of age, but also in terms of responsibility, experience, knowledge, contribution, and suchlike. The terms used in this chapter such as 'social status', 'higher status', 'lower status', 'big', 'small', 'superior', and 'inferior' include these parameters in the context of Brokpa and Bhutanese society and not in the sense of a rigid social class system. The honorific forms have additional functions of expressing politeness or 'social niceties' (Dixon 2010: 201–3).

For some speakers, the bipartite and tripartite terms sound too hierarchical and appear to reflect stratified social classes. On the face of it, these concepts sound ordered and hierarchical. However, at a deeper level, they reflect a culture of according deference towards others, particularly elders. This reflects a way of thinking in which people who are elders in terms of the parameters mentioned above are duly recognized and formally acknowledged.

The first person, the speaker, is always included in the 'small' or the 'low' category in both bipartite and tripartite categorizations. Placing oneself in the bottom-most category stems from a culture of self-effacing or self-deprecating known as *kʰeŋpa tɕuŋwa* literally 'casting away of pride' in Classical Tibetan. This self-deprecating culture is associated with a politeness register referred to as humilifics, as in Mabzhi Amdo Tibetan (Samdrup and Suzuki 2019). Brokpa too has a culture of showing humility by belittling oneself. Among others, humility is shown by using lexical items—usually adjectives— such as *preŋbu, dʰukpu, kyambu* (all meaning 'poor'), *kukpa* 'dumb', and *ʐænba* 'feeble/ weaker'.

The speaker and the people from the 'small' category are supposed to use the honorific forms (§5.1) while interacting with people from the 'middle' and the 'big' categories; and those in the 'middle' category are supposed to do the same with those from the 'big' category'. However, this is not a hard-and-fast rule and the conventions for personal interaction are extremely complex. For example, social status can be absolute for some while relative for others. A person may be in the 'big' category in one context and in the 'middle' or even 'small' category in another.

Note that the honorific system is the same across all the Bodish languages of Bhutan and beyond, in which the language of liturgy is Classical Tibetan also known as Chöke (literally 'Dharma Language'). Classical Tibetan originally written in d^ha-$ɲiŋ$ 'old orthography' and now in d^ha-sar 'new orthography' was once used as a medium of instruction in Bhutan. Classical Tibetan continues to be the medium of monastic education in the Brokpa-speaking community and other language communities in the Himalayas. Looking at the shared honorific forms in the spoken languages, the honorific forms clearly spread through Classical Tibetan.

There may be subtle variations in the honorific forms depending on the phonology of the main languages. However, the forms and functions of the honorific nouns and verbs and their derivational processes are essentially the same across all these languages despite differences in the main lexicon, construction patterns, and grammatical elements.

Some publications[3] dealing with social deixis including honorifics in Bodish languages are DeLancey (1998), Denwood (1999: 215–17), van Driem and Tshering (2019: 399–404), Watters (2018), and Agha (1993). Nepali, an Indo-Aryan language, which is not genetically related to Brokpa but spoken in some parts of Bhutan, also has morphological means for expressing deference (van Driem 2019).

5.1 Morphophonology of honorific forms

The phonology and phonotactics of the honorific nouns and honorific verbs do not differ from those of the ordinary nouns and verbs. Typically, mono-morphemic honorific nouns and verbs in Brokpa are monosyllabic, to the exclusion of affixes, clitics, and other derivational processes. New honorific nouns and verbs are derived from a given set of monomorphemic honorific

---

[3] General discussions on 'honorifics' include Comrie (1976), Brown and Levinson (1987: 276–80), Levinson (1983: 89–94), Frawley (1992: 117–21), Agha (1994, 1998), and McCready (2019). Some discussions related to honorifics and politeness in Japanese include Matsumoto (1988, 1989), Dunn (1998, 1999), and Jarkey (2015, 2017).

nouns and verbs by means of compounding and affixation. There are no monomorphemic honorific adjectives from which other honorific adjectives can be derived. What may appear like a derived honorific adjective, such as *ku-tɕʰem* 'HON-big', is actually an honorific noun. Similarly, there are no honorific forms for the members of other word classes.

5.1.1 Honorific nouns

Generally, nouns from the semantic types of HUMANS (and their PARTS), ARTEFACTS, and concrete objects and abstract phenomena which are related to humans have honorific forms. There are more monosyllabic monomorphemic honorific nouns than disyllabic ones in Brokpa. Table 5 gives some monomorphemic and monosyllabic honorific nouns from these semantic domains.

Note that the honorific noun *suŋ* 'speech/talk:HON' can also be used as an honorific verb root *suŋ*, 'tell: HON', an instance of double duty or zero derivation.

There are also a few monomorphemic honorific nouns which are disyllabic, e.g. *tɕʰöme* (cf. *karme*) 'butter lamp', *námza* (cf. *golam*) 'cloth'. No monomorphemic trisyllabic honorific nouns have been attested in Brokpa; and there are more monosyllabic monomorphemic honorific nouns than disyllabic ones. As mentioned in §5.3, a largish set of honorific nouns can be derived from the honorific noun roots *ku* 'body: HON', *suŋ* 'speech: HON', and *tʰuk* 'mind: HON'.

Table 6 gives examples of honorific nouns derived on the basis of the monomorphemic honorific root *ku*.

The meaning of every derived honorific compound in Table 6 is the same as that of the ordinary form which is the second component of the compound. There are exceptional cases in which the second component of the compound is not the ordinary form. Furthermore, in some cases, the second component is another suppletive form. I will discuss these later in this section.

Table 5 Monosyllabic monomorphemic honorific nouns in Brokpa

Honorific noun	Ordinary form	Meaning
ku	*luspa*	'body'
tɕʰak	*lakpa*	'hand'
ʑæl	*kʰa*	'mouth'
ɕaŋ	*ná*	'nose'
yap	*ʔapa*	'father'
ʑap	*kaŋba*	'leg'
ʔu	*go*	'head'
suŋ	*ló*	'speech'
tʰuk	*sem/samba*	'mind'

Table 6 Honorific nouns derived on the basis of honorific root *ku* in Brokpa

Derived	Ordinary form	Meaning
Honorific noun		
ku-wóŋ	woŋ	'power'
ku-par	par	'photo'
ku-tsʰe	tsʰe	'life'
ku-tsʰou	tsʰou	'nephew'
ku-tɕʰem	mi bombo	'VIP'
ku-pʰuŋ/ku-duŋ/ku-pur	pʰuŋba/roː	'dead body'
ku-pʰo	suipʰa	'stomach'
ku-tɕʰak	lakpa	'hand'

Table 7 Honorific nouns derived on the basis of honorific root *suŋ-* in Brokpa

Dervived	Ordinary form	Meaning
Honorific noun		
suŋ-pʰrin	pʰrin	'message'
suŋ-læn	læn	'answer/response'
suŋ-tɕʰoː	tɕʰoga	'liturgy/recitation'
suŋ-ɖö	tun-ɖö	'discussion'
suŋ-ɕæ	ɕæba	'description'
suŋ-kæ	kæ	'voice'
suŋ-gyun	kʰa-gyun	'verbal tradition'

The first component *ku* is a light CV syllable. When it enters into compounding, there is no phonetic lengthening, as in isolation, and it functions like a grammaticalized prefix. Table 7 provides examples of honorific nouns derived on the basis of the honorific root *suŋ*.

Table 8 provides examples of honorific nouns derived on the basis of the monosyllabic honorific root *tʰuk*[4].

The form *tɕʰak*, which is the honorific form of *lakpa* 'hand', is also a robust honorific root which can derive a largish set of honorific nouns. Table 9 gives examples of honorific noun stems derived by means of compounding with *tɕʰak*[5].

---

[4] The dorso-velar /k/ is phonetically realized as glottal stop [ʔ] word-finally and it is severely weakened in some compounds while completely lost in others leading to phonological compensatory lengthening, e.g *tʰuk-dʑe* ['tʰuː.dʑe].

[5] An additional phonological process taking place in a derived honorific compound is consonant epenthesis. The final /k/ from the honorific root is omitted and, instead of the anticipated compensatory lengthening, the apico-alveolar /n/ is inserted as part of the phonological adaptation. e.g. *tɕʰan-dʱa* 'HON-arrow'.

Table 8 Honorific nouns derived on the basis of honorific root *tʰuk* in Brokpa

Derived Honorific noun	Ordinary form	Meaning
tʰuk-sam	*samba*	'thought'
tʰuk-món	*mónlam*	'aspiration'
tʰuk-tæ	*lótæ*	'trust'
tʰuk-gen	*genkʰa*	'responsibility'
tʰuk-gyö	*gyöpa*	'regret'
tʰuk-dok	*dokpa*	'doubt'
tʰuk-dʰö	*dʰöba*	'desire'
tʰuk-gyæ	*ŋagyæ*	'pride'
tʰuk-dʐe	*ɲiŋdʐe*	'compassion'
tʰuk-don	*sam-don*	'expectation'

Table 9 Honorific nouns derived on the basis of form *tɕʰak* in Brokpa

Derived Honorific noun	Ordinary form	Meaning
tɕʰak-ɖi	*ɖi*	'knife'
tɕʰak-tʰam	*tʰiu*	'seal'
tɕʰak-gʰam	*gʰam*	'wooden box'
tɕʰak-ɖil	*ɖilbu*	'bell'
tɕʰak-dʰup	*dʰugu*	'bracelet'
tɕʰa-n-dʰa:	*dʰa:*	'arrow'
tɕʰak-pe	*petɕʰa*	'book/scripture'
tɕʰak-pʰreŋ	*pʰreŋa*	'rosary beads'

All common monomorphemic honorific noun roots listed in Table 5 and others can form honorific compounds in the same way, although the degrees of productivity vary. The patterns of compounding and phonological processes before compounding are the same as those in Table 7.

Based on the examples given in Tables 6, 7, 8, and 9, we can conclude that the monomorphemic honorific roots, typically occurring as the first element of the derived honorific compound noun, share some similarities with class nouns or noun classifiers (Aikhenvald 2000: 87, 2017: 81–97). DeLancey (1998) describes such phenomena in Tibetan as class nouns.

Brokpa provides clear evidence that the honorific noun derivation process is also a noun categorization device. Most concrete objects and abstract

Table 10 Honorific nouns derived from honorific verb roots in Brokpa

Derived Honorific noun	Ordinary form	Meaning	Honorific Verb root	Ordinary Verb root	Meaning
ʐuk-ʈʰi	kaŋtʰi	'chair'	ʐuk	dʰo	'to sit'
ʐuk-tan	tan	'mattress'			
dzön-lam	lam	'path'	dzön	ɖo	'to go/walk'
dzön-tɕʰaŋ	tɕʰaŋ	'farewell drink'			
zim-kʰaŋ	ɲa:-kʰaŋ	'bedroom'	zim	ɲa:	'to sleep'
zim-ʈʰi	ɲa:-ʈʰi	'bed'			
ɲé-tsʰor	ga-tsʰor	'gratitude'	ɲé:	ga:	'be happy'
ʐeŋ-dʐa	loŋ-dʐa	'bed tea'	ʐeŋ	laŋ	'to wake up'

phenomena that are related to the body take the honorific form *ku* 'body:HON', and most abstract nouns related to speech combine with the honorific root *suŋ* 'speech-HON'. Most mental states, including emotions, feelings, and intellectual processes combine with *tʰuk*, the honorific form of 'mind'.

In the same manner, most concrete nouns including artefacts associated with 'hand' take the honorific form *tɕʰak* 'hand: HON' as the first component of the honorific compound. Note that *tɕʰak* in *ku-tɕʰak* 'HON -prostration' is an ordinary term meaning 'prostration' and is a homonym of the honorific term for 'hand'. This principle applies to all other body parts, which generally have a monomorphemic honorific form; as well as to other monomorphemic honorific roots which participate in the honorific noun derivation process.

The honorific verb roots also take part in the derivation of honorific nouns. An honorific verb can enter into compounding with an ordinary noun and derive honorific noun stems. Table 10 provides examples of honorific noun stems derived from honorific verb roots via compounding.

In this type of honorific compound noun, the honorific verb root appears as the first component and the ordinary noun root as the second component of the compound. The base is the nominal component because its meaning is the referential meaning of the compound. The verbal component adds 'honorificity' to the compound.

Honorific nouns can also be derived by means of lexical nominalization. Nominalizers are realized as suffixes forming one grammatical word with the host and the derivation process involved will be affixation. The categories of nominalization involved in honorific noun formation are agentive nominalization as in (6a), locative/place nominalization as in (6b), and, as shown in (6c), manner nominalization (Comrie and Thompson 1985, 2007; Aikhenvald 2007):

(6) a. ɕak-**kan**
        die: HON-NOMZ:AG
        the late/one who died

     b. t̪ʰuŋ-**sa**
        be.born-NOMZ:LOC
        birthplace/village

     c. suŋ-**tʰaŋ**
        speak: HON - NOMZ:MANNER
        style of speaking

We can now make some generalizations about the morphology of honorific nouns. Honorific nouns involve only two derivational process—compounding and affixation. There is no reduplication, inherent or total. All honorific compound nouns fall into the category of endocentric compounds (Aikhenvald 2007, 2015: 123). An honorific compound noun denotes the same item referred to by the second component, which is an ordinary noun. The first component of the compound, which is a monomorphemic honorific noun or verb root, adds an honorific sense to the compound.

There are three compounding patterns in the formation of Brokpa honorific nouns:

In Pattern A, the honorific root is added to an ordinary form as is, e.g. *suŋ-læn* 'HON -answer' in which the ordinary form *læn* does not undergo any phonological process before compounding.

In Pattern B, the ordinary component of the compound is already a compound noun; and the first component of the ordinary compound is replaced by the honorific root in the derived honorific compound stem, e.g. *suŋ-ɖö* (cf. *tun-ɖö* 'discussion').

In Pattern C, the final syllable from the ordinary component which is disyllabic is omitted before compounding with the honorific root, e.g. *suŋ-tɕʰoː* (cf. *tɕʰoga* 'liturgy/recitation'), *suŋ-ɕæ* (cf. *ɕæba* 'description') wherein the second/final syllable -*ga* and -*ba* are dropped.

The Brokpa honorific noun compounding patterns are similar to some patterns of honorific noun formation in Tibetan (Brokpa Pattern A to Tibetan Pattern I, B to IV, and C to III (DeLancey 1998)), but one Tibetan pattern (Compounding Pattern III of Tibetan), in which honorificity is built on the second component of the compound noun, is not found in Brokpa. However, in Brokpa, an honorific form may enter into compounding with another honorific root such as *ku-tɕʰak* 'hand', wherein the root *tɕʰak* is already the honorific form of *lakpa* 'hand'. In this type of compound, both the components are honorific. Following the general pattern, we can assume that honorificity is indicated by the first component or both, but not exclusively by the second component.

An honorific root may also enter into compounding with an ordinary root which is not an expected root but is synonymous with or semantically related to the expected ordinary root. For example, in *ku-tɕʰem* 'VIP', the expected ordinary form would be *bom* from *bombo* 'big', but *tɕʰem* from *tɕʰenmo* which is a synonym of *bombo*, appears in the honorific compound. Structurally, it is like Pattern C.

The honorific nouns derived from honorific verb roots, provided in Table 10, follow these same compounding patterns (A–C). All the derived honorific nouns are disyllabic.

There are some additional phonological processes involved. The first syllable from the ordinary component may be omitted and there may be changes in the vowel quality. For example, in *ku-pʰo* 'HON-stomach' in which the first syllable *sui-* from the ordinary form *suipʰa* is omitted and the final vowel /a/ changes to /o/. In other instances, the second syllable of the ordinary form is omitted, but the final consonant from the first syllable is also omitted and there is a change in vowel quality. For example, in *ku-rü*, the honorific form of *ruspa* 'bone', the final syllable *pa* is omitted; and the coda consonant /s/ from the resulting syllable *rus* is also dropped leading to change in vowel quality from /u/ to /ü/.

The honorific nouns, both monomorphemic and derived, have the same inflectional possibilities as the ordinary nouns including case, gender, number, and markers of other grammatical systems which may be realized as affixes or clitics. The honorific nouns, as well as honorific verbs, bear the same suprasegmental features as ordinary nouns and verbs including tone and stress.

5.1.2 Honorific verbs

There is a closed set of monosyllabic monomorphemic honorific verbs. No disyllabic honorific verb roots that are monomorphemic are found in Brokpa. Table 11 provides some common monomorphemic honorific verb roots, which are all monosyllabic.

Honorific verb stems are derived from the monomorphemic honorific verb roots and noun roots via compounding. The honorific verb stems basically follow the same compounding patterns as the honorific nouns.[6] We have seen that all resulting honorific noun compound stems contain the maximum of two syllables and two morphemes. If a monosyllabic honorific root forms a compound with a disyllabic ordinary (or non-honorific) root and the expected

---

[6] The phonological processes that occur in some honorific noun formation, such as deletion or changes in vowel qualities, are not found in honorific verb formation.

Table 11 Monomorphemic honorific verb roots in Brokpa

Honorific verb	Ordinary form	Meaning
náŋ	*dʑin*	'to give'
suŋ	*láp*	'to tell'
ʐu	*láp*	'to tell'
sen	*ɲæn*	'to listen'
zim	*ɲa:*	'to sleep'
ʐeŋ	*loŋ*	'to wake up'
ɖe:	*ge:*	'to age'
dʑon	*ɖo*	'to go'
ʐuk	*dʰo:*	'to sit'

number of syllables of the resulting form is three, a syllable from the ordinary compound is reduced and the resulting form is always disyllabic. In contrast, a derived honorific verb stem can be disyllabic, trisyllabic, or more. There can also be more than two morphemes in an honorific verb compound.

An honorific verb stem can be derived through 'lexical compounding' (Aikhenvald 2007; Mithun 1984) by incorporating an honorific noun into an honorific verb stem. The honorific compound verb stem can be endocentric as in (7a); or it can be an exocentric compound as in (7b) with the meaning of the derived honorific compound verb different from either of its components (Aikhenvald 2007, 2015: 123):

(7)   a.   tʰuk-ɲé:
           mind: HON-be.happy:HON
           to be pleased

      b.   tɕʰa-ʐu
           hand:HON-receive:HON
           to serve

Further relatively uncommon honorific verb stems can be formed by compounding an honorific noun and an ordinary verb root. This clearly suggests that honorificity is indicated by the first component of the compound. An honorific compound verb of this type can be endocentric as in (8a) or, although semantically predictable, it can be exocentric as in (8b). In this kind of compound, the first component is an honorific noun and the second is an ordinary (non-honorific) verb:

(8)   a.   **goŋma**-tʰel
           thought: HON-scorn
           to get angry

   b. **tʰuk-pʰam**
      mind: HON-defeat
      to be disappointed

(9) a. **ʐæl-keŋ**
      face/mouth: HON-be.embarrassed
      to be embarrassed

   b. **tʰuk-den**
      mind: HON-be.true
      to be true

In (9a), the honorific noun root *ʐæl* is incorporated into the ordinary verb *keŋ*, as is *tʰuk* into *den* in (9b). In both, the meaning of the derived complex honorific verb remains the same as the meaning of the ordinary verb. The incorporated honorific noun root adds honorificity in both cases.

An honorific verb stem can be formed by adding a derived honorific compound noun to an honorific verb root. This type of honorific compound verb stem will have three roots and two of the three roots may be lexicalized. The first component of the compound can be an honorific noun, the second an ordinary noun, and the third an honorific verb, as in (10a) and (10b). The entire resulting compound functions as a single honorific verb:

(10) a. tʰuk-món-náŋ
       mind: HON-aspiration-do:HON
       to bless

     b. ku-ʈʰü-náŋ
       body:HON-wash-do:HON
       to bathe
       Lit. 'to body-wash'

The honorific verb *náŋ*[7] 'give/do' is the most productive root. It can combine with most verb roots or verb stems and form honorific predicates. The honorific verb root *náŋ* can combine with an ordinary verb root, e.g. *kʰur-náŋ* 'carry-do:HON = carry'; or with an honorific verb root, e.g. *zik-náŋ* 'watch: HON-do: HON = watch'. A verb stem may also have an honorific verb root before compounding with *náŋ*, e.g. *tʰuk-kʰur-náŋ* 'mind:HON-carry-do:HON =

---

   [7] The form *náŋ* is the honorific form of verb *dzin* 'give' as well as the honorific form of verb *gya* 'do'. It is glossed 'do' throughout for consistency.

shoulder responsibility'. If a verb root that forms a compound with *náŋ* is already an honorific root or if a verb stem already has an honorific root, *náŋ* serves to further reinforce the honorific meaning.

The honorific verb root *náŋ* can also occupy a predicate slot on its own, as in (11):

(11)   ʔama dʑomo   mo=raŋ=ge=raŋ
       Ama.Jomo   3:SG:FEM=REFL=ERG=EMPH
       kaktɕʰa-**náŋ**-ŋai
       restriction-do:HON- PERV
       Ama Jomo herself stopped.

The honorific verb *náŋ* can occur in different types of predicate. It combines with an intransitive verb as in *yar-náŋ* 'run-do:HON = run'; with a transitive verb as in *ʈʰiː-náŋ* 'guide-do:HON = guide'; or with an extended transitive (ditransitive) verb as in *ton-náŋ* 'show-do:HON = show'.

There are more monomorphemic honorific nouns than monomorphemic honorific verbs. New honorific verbs are derived only through compounding. This is in contrast to the formation of honorific nouns, which involves both compounding and affixation. Most predicates can be made honorific by adding one or more monomorphemic honorific verb roots, particularly *náŋ* 'do:HON'. The honorific verb roots and stems take the markers of all the grammatical systems associated with ordinary verbs.

5.2 The use and the function of honorifics

The analysis of honorifics can be undertaken in terms of three main axes: (a) speaker-referent; (b) speaker-addressee; and (c) speaker-bystander (Comrie 1976; Brown and Levinson 1987; Levinson 1983; Frawley 1992). Levinson (1983: 90) and Brown and Levinson (1987: 181) add a fourth axis: (d) speaker-setting. Type (a) is referred to as 'referent honorifics', (b) as 'addressee honorifics', (c) as 'bystander honorifics', and (d) as 'setting honorifics' (situation honorifics). Addressee honorifics and referent honorifics are also referred to as 'utterance honorifics' and 'argument honorifics' respectively (McCready 2019).

In a referent honorific expression, respect is conveyed to the addressee by referring to the target of the respect; in an addressee honorific, respect is conveyed without necessarily referring to any referential target; in a bystander

Table 12 A three-way contrast in the verbs of GIVING and SPEAKING in Brokpa

	Downward	Upward	Horizontal
GIVE	*náŋ*	*pʰuː*	*dʑin*
SPEAK	*suŋ*	*ʐu*	*láp*

honorific, the intended target of respect is the participants in audience role or the non-participating hearers; and setting honorifics are triggered by the setting or the circumstances in which a conversation is occurring. Typical examples of setting honorifics include formality levels of Japanese or the diglossic variants of Tamil (Levinson 1983: 93).

Honorifics in Brokpa convey deference, humility, and politeness. They also convey formality and social distance. All types of honorifics are encoded in Brokpa through one, or more, of these three techniques: (i) variant honorific forms (lexical); (ii) compounding or affixation (morphological); and (iii) the polite particle *lá* (syntactic). The first two (lexical and morphological) encode referent honorifics. The third technique, the use of particle *lá*, encodes addressee honorifics and setting honorifics. We will first illustrate referent honorifics by using the verbs of SPEAKING and GIVING. Then we will briefly illustrate addressee honorifics and setting honorifics.

Verbs of SPEAKING and GIVING make a three-way contrast involving two honorific forms and one ordinary form. Theoretically, one honorific form is to describe the speaking/giving from a higher to a lower (downward), another from a lower to a higher level (upward), and the ordinary form to be used with the equals (horizontal). Table 12 shows verbs of SPEAKING and GIVING making these three distinctions.

The use of an honorific verb has a semantic basis. There are three semantic roles with regard to these two verbs. For the verb 'give', the three semantic roles are Donor, Gift, Recipient; and for the verb 'speak', the semantic roles are Speaker, Addressee, and Message/Medium (Dixon 2010: 127). A particular verb form will be used depending on the referent of each semantic role, in terms of the bipartite and tripartite social deixis, and its syntactic functions. Consider:

(12) a. [Dasho=ge] DONOR:A   diriŋ   [ŋa=la]RECIPIENT:E
          Dasho=ERG   today   1:SG=DAT
          [gokap]GIFT:O   **náŋ-ŋai**
          opportunity   give:HON-PERV
          Today, Dasho[8] gave me (an) opportunity.

---

[8] Dasho here is used as a term of address for someone important.

b. [pʰadʑu=la]RECIPIENT:E   [ɲénsem=tɕik]GIFT:O   pʰa=te
   astrologer=DAT   report=INDEF   that.side=ALL
   pʰuː=næ
   give:HON=ABL.SEQ
   After giving a report to the
   astrologer...

c. [söri=di]GIFT:O   gaŋyu   [lumbe=i   mi=bak=la]RECIPIENT:E
   tip=DEF   all   village=GEN   person=PL=DAT
   dʑin=næ
   give=ABL.SEQ
   By giving all the tips to the people of the village...

The Donor role is in A function, the Gift is assigned to O function, and the Recipient is in E function marked by the dative =*la* in all the three examples of (12). Note that A is not overtly stated in (12b) and (12c). In (12a), the downward honorific verb *náŋ* is used because the Donor is perceived to belong to 'big/high' category in the eyes of the Recipient who is the speaker. In the same manner, the upward honorific form *pʰuː* is used in (12b) because *pʰadʑu* 'astrologer', fulfilling the Recipient role, is an important person in the village who is always accorded deference by the people. In (12a), the speaker is the Recipient and the verb *náŋ* shows respect to the Donor as well as humility of the Recipient.

If the Gift in (12a) were to someone other than the speaker, the choice of the honorific verb would depend on the relative status of the Donor and the Recipient, according to the speaker's perception. If the Donor is perceived to be of higher status than the Recipient, then the same downward honorific verb *náŋ* will be used. If the Recipient is perceived to be higher than the Donor, then the upward honorific verb *pʰuː* will be used. If the Donor and the Recipient are somewhat equal, the speaker will still use one of the two honorific forms and not the 'horizontal' form to show humility with regard to himself. The choice between the 'downward' form and the upward form may be determined by whether or not one of the two referents (Donor, Recipient) is with the speaker at the time of speaking.

Similarly, in (12b), the verb *pʰuː* shows both the humility of the Donor and respect to the Recipient. If the Donor in A function were people with whom the speaker identifies (e.g. the people in the speaker's village), the speaker will still use the upward honorific form *pʰuː*. If the Donor is someone other than the speaker or those with whom the speaker identifies, the choice of the honorific form will again depend on the relative status of the Donor and the Recipient. If the Donor has higher status than *pʰadʑu* 'the astrologist', as does the chief lama of the village, the speaker will shift to the 'downward' honorific form *náŋ*.

In (12c), the speaker is talking about the local wedding practices. The Gift in O function must preferably be in an honorific form when the predicate is realized by an honorific verb. The parents of the groom, the underlying Donor in A function in (12c), leaves tips for the friends and neighbours of the bride when they go to fetch her. Since both the Donor and the Recipient are village folks, viewed at equal level in terms of social deixis, the horizontal (ordinary) form *dʑin* is used. When the predicate is realized by an ordinary verb, the Gift in O function must preferably be an ordinary noun.

The same principle holds for the transitive verb of speaking. The Speaker is in A, the Addressee in E, and the Message/Medium in O function. If the referent of the Speaker role in A function is supposedly from the big/high category, then the honorific form *suŋ* is felicitous. If the referent of the Addressee role in E function is perceived to be from that same big/high category, the honorific form *ʑu* is felicitous. If the referent of either of these two semantic roles is perceived to be from the middle/equal/small category, then the ordinary form *láp* is more felicitous. The Message/Medium must preferably be in an honorific form when one of the honorific verbs is used.

Only the verbs of GIVING and SPEAKING make three-way contrasts. Other monomorphemic verb roots and derived verb stems make two-way contrasts—ordinary versus honorific. We can also find intransitive predicates realized by monomorphemic honorific verb roots or derived honorific verb stems. Consider:

(13) a. láma **ɕum-pʰi**
          lama cry:HON-PERV
          The Lama cried.

      b. mákpon=bak=daŋ tɕʰatsaŋ
          general=PL=CONJ complete
          söwa-ɲúŋ=næ
          food:HON-be.hungry:HON=ABL.SEQ
          The generals and all felt hungry.

In (13a), the predicate slot is filled by an intransitive monomorphemic honorific verb *ɕum*; and in (13b), a derived verb stem or a complex predicate, in which the incorporated honorific noun *söwa* does not have argument status, fills the predicate slot. As with the referent of transitive subject A of an honorific transitive predicate, the referent of an intransitive subject s must be from the 'big/high' category.

Examples (12a) and (12b) are instances of both referent honorifics and bystander honorifics. The Donor in A function in (12a) and the Recipient in E function in (12b) which are the targets of honour can be speech act participants as well as bystanders. Examples (13a) and (13b) are bystander honorifics. The referents of the s arguments in (13) and (13b), the targets of honour, are not the speech act participants. The referent of these s arguments can be non-participant hearers or they can be absent from the conversational moment.

Brokpa has a polite particle *lá* shared with all the Bhutanese languages. Its function is similar to the polite particle *khá* or *khráp* in Thai (McCready 2019: 43; Levinson 1983: 91) except that there is no natural gender distinction of the speaker in Brokpa. In Thai, the closed syllable *khráp* can only be used by male speakers and the open syllable *khrá* only by female speakers.

The polite particle *lá* in Brokpa occurs in vocative expressions after a personal name, e.g. *Tashi lá* 'Tashi POLITE', after a term of address as in *Dasho lá* 'Dasho POLITE', and after a kinship term *ʔapa lá* 'father POLITE'. The particle *lá* also occurs with a predicate, *ta-gu lá* 'see-IMPERV POLITE'. When *lá* occurs with an NP, its scope is only over a word or a phrase, but when it occurs with a predicate its scope extends over an entire clause. When it has scope over an entire clause, the polite particle *lá* functions as a marker of an addressee honorific in Brokpa:

(14) a. pʰa=yi=la=ya   toptɕa=ʑik   yoŋ-gu
          there=GEN=LOC=EMPH   food=INDEF   be.there-FUT.IMPERV
          lá
          POLITE
          There will be a meal there also.

      b. ʔotɕins   lap-ki   lá
          like.this say-PRES.IMPERV   POLITE
          It is said like this.

In both (14a) and (14b) neither the speaker nor the addressee is a referent and the particle *lá* can also be used in these kinds of sentences. This is distinct from, though often compatible with, the referent honorifics.

Brokpa does not have a distinct marker of setting honorifics such as a marker of formality level. However, in a situation where formality needs to be maintained, one uses honorific verbs and honorific nouns wherever possible complemented by the particle *lá*, as in (15). There can also be a change in prosody such as a flat intonation at the end of the clause:

(15) ʔo-ḍou   **suŋ-náŋ**-na   námpardakpa
      DEM-same   tell:HON-give: HON-COND   perfect
      yoŋ-ro=se   ẓu-yo   lá
      be.there-IMPERV=QUOT   say: HON-EGO   POLITE
      I would like to say that, 'If you say like this, it will be perfect'.

Essentially, in (15), the speaker is trying to achieve a maximum level of formality using whatever honorific resources the language has.

It is important to bear in mind that if the s/A argument is a respectable person who is doing something with the referent of the honorific noun in an instrumental function, the predicate should be cast as honorific:

(16) ɲǽn-sen-kʰan=bak=kʰe   **tʰuk=ke**
      ear:HON-listen: HON-NOMZ:AG=PL=ERG   mind:HON=INST
      zöba-ẓe-náŋ
      patience-take:HON-do:HON
      Those who listen, please be patient
      Lit. Those who listen, please feel patience with the mind.

In (16), the referent of the A argument who does the listening is the audience, which is the target of honour. The honorific noun *tʰuk* 'mind' in instrumental function triggers the predicate *zöba-ẓe-náŋ* to be in the honorific. If any of the two honorific verb roots in the predicate is replaced with an ordinary verb root, as in **zöba-za-náŋ* or **zöba-ẓe-dʑin*, it will sound incongruous and can even be considered ungrammatical.

A couple of caveats must be noted concerning the use of honorific language. Employing honorific forms with someone who is very close, such as close relatives or close friends, might be viewed as a distancing strategy. One is generally expected to use ordinary forms among family members. While it is not uncommon to find the use of honorific forms with one's parents or elder family members, particularly if the parent is a religious practitioner such as a lama, using honorific language among family members and close relatives may sound ludicrous to others.

As mentioned at the beginning of this section, it is not uncommon for people from the 'big/high' category to use honorific forms with those from the 'medium/small' category. However, care must be taken lest this be perceived as an expression of disdain or mockery, akin to similar effects produced by gender reversals in some languages (Aikhenvald 2019). It also runs the risk of creating an unfriendly environment for conversation. In any case, the use of honorific forms in an infelicitous situation, whether among close friends and relatives or from high to low, will sound oddly formal and become a social distancing strategy.

5.3 Origin and development of honorifics

The honorific system is a deep-rooted feature of Brokpa and other Bodish languages. Its origin and development can be associated with Buddhist values. Akin to social categorizations in the spoken languages, Buddhism has a distinguished tradition of enumerating various, but related, phenomena in terms of numbers. The number word and the enumerated concepts together function as a lexical unit. Common examples include *gewa tɕu* <dge ba bcu> 'Ten Virtues', *mi-gewa-tɕu* <mi dge ba bcu> 'Ten Non-virtues', *ʈaɕi-ta:-gyæ* <bkra shis rtags brgya> 'Eight Auspicious Symbols', *rintɕʰen-ná-dün* <rin chen sna bdun> 'Seven Precious Possessions'. There are hundreds of such expressions which consist of enumerated concepts. Some common ones have become part of the vocabulary of spoken languages, including Brokpa.

Perhaps the most important of such enumerated sequences is *kön-tɕʰo:-su:m* <dkon mchog gsum> 'Three Precious Jewels'. The Three Precious Jewels are the Buddha Jewel, the Dharma Jewel, and the Sangha Jewel. The Buddha Jewel refers to Buddha, the Dharma Jewel to the Buddhist teachings including all the Buddhist scriptures, and the Sangha Jewel refers to the monastic community.

In the Brokpa tradition, as is the case with other Bodish language communities, the monastic community includes all of the *láma* 'lama', *geɕe* 'learned teacher', *geloŋ* 'monk', *ʔanim* 'nun', *gomtɕʰen* 'noncelibate monk', and *dʑambeyáŋ/pʰadzu* 'astrologer'. All the three Jewels are precious to every person and people pray to them and seek refuge with them all the time.

A further concept enumerated in terms of three, related to the Three Precious Jewels, is *dordʑe sum* <rdo rje gsum> 'Three Indestructible Realities' which refers to the 'body', 'speech', and 'mind' of a buddha. The ordinary term for body, speech, and mind in most Bodish languages including Brokpa are *lü* 'body' (with synonyms such as *luspu*), *ŋaʔ* 'speech' (with synonyms such as *ló* and *poŋpoŋ*), and *yi:* 'mind' (with synonyms such as *sem*). The term *dordʑe sum* is related to the Three Precious Jewels in general—'body' relates to Sangha Jewel, 'speech' to Dharma Jewel, and 'mind' to Buddha Jewel.

Given the infelicitous effects of employing the ordinary terms to refer to the body, speech, and mind of a buddha or any of the Three Precious Jewels, it is only natural for speakers to come up with variant forms. So there is a variant form for each of the Three Indestructible Realities—*ku* for 'body', *suŋ* for 'speech', and *tʰuk* for 'mind'. These three words became the honorific forms of the ordinary terms *lǚ*, *ŋaʔ*, and *yi:* respectively.

The development of honorific forms extends to anything related to the Three Jewels, over and above body, speech, and mind. Honorific forms have developed not just for the words describing these concrete objects, but also for words describing actions and states associated with the Three Jewels.

For example, Avalokiteshvara, originally one of the closest disciples of Buddha and now worshipped as the Deity of Compassion, is called Chenrezig ['tɕɛːn.rɛː.ziː] literally meaning 'Watching with the Eyes'. He is given the epithet *tɕʰak-toŋ-tɕæn-toŋ* <phyag stong spyan stong> 'Thousand Hands and Thousand Eyes'. The reason for him having a thousand eyes is that he watches over all the people with compassionate concern. Apart from the number word *toŋ* 'thousand', only the honorific forms—*tɕæn* <spyan> 'eye', *tɕʰak* <phyag> 'hand', and *zik* <gzigs> 'to watch'—are used in his name and epithet, instead of the ordinary forms *mík* 'eye', *lakpa* 'hand', and *ta* 'see/watch'.

There are a host of monomorphemic nouns and verbs all associated with the Three Jewels, body parts as well as artefacts, and also actions and states associated with the body parts and artefacts of the Three Jewels. Other honorific nouns and honorific verbs are derived from the given set of monomorphemic honorific nouns and verbs by means of compounding and affixation (such as nominalization). As illustrated in §5.1.1, a largish set of honorific nouns can be derived from *ku* 'body:HON', *suŋ* 'speech:HON', and *tʰuk* 'mind:HON'. The honorific forms, although originating in these spiritual contexts, have become part of the everyday language style in Brokpa and other Bodish languages.

5.4 Forms of address

Brokpa does not have special honorific pronouns. This is a little surprising since it has honorific forms for most nouns and verbs, either monomorphemic or derived. The form *kʰoŋ* 'he/she/it' which is the third person honorific pronoun in Classical Tibetan is the ordinary third person plural pronoun

in both Brokpa and Dzongkha. Classical Tibetan also has 2nd person honorific pronoun <khyed> distinguished with a vowel from its ordinary 2nd person pronoun <khyod>; but they are neutralized in the ordinary 2nd person
pronoun $k^hyö$ in Brokpa and Dzongkha. Dzongkha has innovated a polite or
honorific second person *nâ* (van Driem and Tshering 2019: 100; Watters
2018: 190), but there is no such innovation in Brokpa. In addition to its pronouns with regular three persons, Brokpa makes use of *raŋ* 'self' and *muzu*
'other' as independent personal pronouns with a wide range of functions.

However, Brokpa makes use of other terms of address or honorific titles[9] as
a strategy for avoiding the use of pronouns to refer to respected persons. The
forms of address (honorific titles) are distinct from linguistic honorifics, but
they are related because the target of an honorific title is usually the target of
respect in honorific speech. All the forms of address or the honorific titles in
Brokpa are used as a forms of address in the 2nd person and as terms of reference in the 3rd person. McCready (2019: 79–103) describes honorific titles
such as Japanese *sensei* 'teacher' or Thai *mɔ̌ɔ* 'doctor' as 'role honorifics'.

There are three common honorific titles which are used for the king—
miwaŋ, *ŋádaʔ*, and *zap* (all similar to 'Majesty'). The term *zap* is used in isolation, more as a referential term than a term of address. The other two, *miwaŋ*
and *ŋádaʔ*, can be used in isolation or they can be juxtaposed and compounded with *rinpotɕʰe* literally 'precious' and derive a single term of address
miwang ŋadaʔ rinpotɕʰe which is exclusively used for addressing the king. The
term *gyætsun* is used only for addressing the queen. The honorific title *miwaŋ*
can be used for addressing the queen and the members of the king's family.

The prime minister and the ministers would be addressed as *midze*
'Excellency' (literally 'Human Lord').[10] There is a special group of individuals
who have received a special award from the king, a red scarf and a symbolic
sword, in recognition of their outstanding contributions in different fields.
These people are addressed as *ɖakɕo* <drag shos> which is, interestingly, an
adjectival root *ɖak* with comparative index marker *-ɕo* (involving omission of
the final syllable *-po* from the adjective *ɖakpo* 'better' applied before the morphological process of suffixation). Note that these are not honorific adjectives
but honorific titles or honorific terms of address, which is a subclass of noun.

Members of parliament are addressed with a term coined recently which is
bit of a mouthful, *tɕʰötötɕangi tʰümi* literally 'Praise-worthy Member'. People

---

[9] Most terms of address and honorific titles are shared with other Tibeto-Burman languages
spoken in Bhutan.
[10] The term for 'minister' is *lónpo* and not *midze*.

respectfully address members of parliament, other senior civil servants, senior corporate employees, and in fact anyone perceived as respectable with the title *ɖakɕo*. A term *tɕʰog* literally 'supreme' may be added to the name of anyone occupying a 'big/high' slot preceded by a relevant term of address.

There are also several terms of address used among the people. Some common ones are *lópon* (lit. 'teacher'), akin to the Japanese *sensei* or the Thai *aacaan*, both meaning 'teacher', (McCready 2019: 4), *ʔau* (lit. 'elder brother'), *ʔap(a)* (lit. 'father'), *ʔam(a)* (lit. 'mother'), *ʔaɕi* (lit. 'elder sister'). English terms including *sar* 'sir', *medam* 'madam', *ʔaŋkal* 'uncle', *ʔanʈi* 'aunty' are popularly used. Another address term *sayab* [sɐˈjəp] originally from Arabic *sahib* 'companion', borrowed via Hindi in which it is used as an honorific title, was once popularly used in Brokpa possibly due to proximity to the Indian state of Arunachal Pradesh. Now it is less popular and has been replaced by the English loan *sar* 'sir'.

6 Conclusion

The Brokpa language and society are intricately related and mutually reinforcing. The language which is a result of a distillation of the thought processes of its speakers from generation to generation shapes the society as a whole.

The culture of deference, politeness, and self-effacement, all of which have their roots in the Brokpa belief system, is reflected in the social deixis and honorific systems. Some aspects of social deixis have striking parallels with the topographic deixis. The comparative construction, reflecting the sociocultural practices of the past and the present, is yet another means of categorizing people possibly for the same purpose—that of showing deference to the deserving ones.

There are two-way and three-way contrasts in all the three grammatical systems we have seen—the comparative construction, topographic deixis including demonstratives, and social deixis.

A mono-clausal comparative construction in which the Parameter of comparison is modified by the index marker *-ɕo*, compares two participants. This is the prototypical comparative scheme (Dixon 2008) of Brokpa which fits into its system of making bipartite categorization. A comparative construction involving the superlative form of an adjective *-da* relates to the system of making tripartite categorization. When the Parameter is modified by the index marker *-da*, the participants or entities are compared in terms of three degrees of gradable properties—the unmarked form, the comparative form, and the superlative form.

In the same manner, nominal demonstratives and some local adverbial demonstratives make a two-way contrast, proximal and distal, which again conforms with the bipartite classification system. Topographic deixis, part of the local adverbial demonstratives, involve three height levels—higher, lower, or same level as the speaker. The speech act participants, in particular, and the people in the world in general, are categorized into twos (bipartite) and threes (tripartite). The bipartite categorization—big versus small or high versus low—is a broad and simple way of categorization for the purpose of employing the honorific forms and the tripartite classification—'big, middling, small' or 'high, medium, low'—is a subtler or a finer system of categorization.

These three grammatical systems, among others, are reflective of one common social value—that of identifying who is who and according due deference using honorific forms and constructions.

Acknowledgements

I would like to thank Alexandra Y. Aikhenvald, R. M. W. Dixon, and Nerida Jarkey for reading the draft of this chapter and for providing helpful comments.

References

Agha, Asif. 1993. 'Grammatical and indexical convention in honorific discourse'. *Journal of Linguistic Anthropology* 3(2): 131–63.

Agha, Asif. 1994. 'Honorification'. *Annual Review of Anthropology* 23: 277–302.

Agha, Asif. 1998. 'Stereotypes and registers of honorific language'. *Language in Society* 27: 151–93.

Aikhenvald, Alexandra Y. 2000. *Classifiers: A typology of noun categorization devices.* Oxford: Oxford University Press.

Aikhenvald, Alexandra Y. 2007. 'Typological distinctions in word-formation', in Timothy Shopen (ed.) *Language typology and syntactic description* III. Cambridge: Cambridge University Press, 1–65.

Aikhenvald, Alexandra Y. 2015. *The art of grammar: A practical guide.* Oxford: Oxford University Press.

Aikhenvald, Alexandra Y. 2017. 'A typology of noun categorization devices', in Alexandra Y. Aikhenvald and R. M. W. Dixon, (eds), *The Cambridge handbook of linguistic typology.* Cambridge: Cambridge University Press, 361–404.

Aikhenvald, Alexandra Y. 2019. 'Endearment, respect, and disdain through linguistic gender'. *ReVEL, edição especial* 17, n. 16, 2019. <www.revel.inf.br>

Andvik, Erik. 2010. *A grammar of Tshangla*. Leiden/Boston: Brill.

Benedict, Paul K. 1972. *Sino-Tibetan: A conspectus*. Cambridge: Cambridge University Press.

Beyer, Stephan V. 1992. *The Classical Tibetan language*. New York: State University of New York.

Brown, Penelope and Stephen C. 1987. *Politeness: Some universals in language*. Cambridge: Cambridge University Press.

Comrie, Bernard. 1976. 'Linguistic politeness axes: Speaker-addressee, speaker-referent, speaker-bystander'. *Pragmatics Microfiche* 1, No. 7: A3–B1.

Comrie, Bernard and Sandra A. Thompson. 1985. 'Lexical nominalization', in Timothy Shopen (ed.), *Language typology and syntactic description*, III. Cambridge: Cambridge University Press, 349–98.

Comrie, Bernard and Sandra A. Thompson. 2007. 'Lexical nominalization', in Timothy Shopen (ed.), *Language typology and syntactic description*, III:. Cambridge: Cambridge University Press, 334–81.

DeLancey, Scott. 1998. 'Semantic categorization in Tibetan honorific nouns'. *Anthropological Linguistics* 40: 109–23.

DeLancey, Scott. 2003a. 'Classical Tibetan', in Graham Thurgood and Randy J. Lapolla (eds), *The Sino-Tibetan languages*. London: Routledge, 255–69.

DeLancey, Scott. 2003b. 'Lhasa Tibetan', in Graham Thurgood and Randy J. Lapolla (eds), *The Sino-Tibetan languages*. London: Routledge, 270–88.

Denwood, Phillip. 1999. *Tibetan*. Amsterdam: John Benjamins.

Dixon, R. M. W. 2003. 'Demonstratives: A cross-linguistic typology'. *Studies in Language* 27 (1): 61–112.

Dixon, R. M. W. 2008. 'Comparative constructions: A cross-linguistic typology'. *Studies in Language* 32: 787–817.

Dixon, R. M. W. 2010. *Basic linguistic theory, vol. 2. Grammatical topics*. Oxford: Oxford University Press.

Dixon, R. M. W. 2012. *Basic linguistic theory, vol. 3. Further grammatical topics*. Oxford: Oxford University Press.

Dixon, R. M. W. 2016. *Are some languages better than others?* Oxford: Oxford University Press.

Dondrup, Rinchen. 1993. *Brokeh language guide*. Itanagar: The Director of Research, Arunachal Pradesh.

Dunn, Cynthia Dickel. 1998. 'Ideology and practice in Japanese honorific use', in M.C. Chalasani, J. A. Grocer, and P. C. Haney (eds), *SALSA V: Proceedings of the Fifth Annual Symposium About Language and Society–Austin (Texas*

Linguistic Forum 39), 50–9. Austin TX: Linguistic Department, University of Texas at Austin.

Dunn, Cynthia Dickel. 1999. 'Coming of age in Japan: Language ideology and the acquisition of formal speech registers', in Jef Verschueren (ed.) *Language and ideology: selected papers from the 5th international pragmatics conference,* I. Antwerp: International Pragmatics Association, 89–97.

Eberhard, David M., Gary F. Simons, and Charles D. Fennig (eds). 2019. *Ethnologue: Languages of the world. Twenty-second edition.* Dallas, Texas: International. <http://www.ethnologue.com>

Frawley, William. 1992. *Linguistics semantics.* London: Routledge.

Hyslop, Gwendolyn. 2013. 'A preliminary reconstruction of East Bodish'. *Trans-Himalayan linguistics: Historical and descriptive linguistics of the Himalayan area,* 155–80.

Jarkey, N. 2015. 'The housewife's companion: Identity construction in a Japanese women's magazine', in Dwi Noverini Djenar, Ahmar Mahboob, and Ken Cruickshank (eds), *Language and identity across modes of communication.* Berlin: Mouton de Gruyter, 179–201.

Jarkey, N. 2017. 'Imperatives and commands in Japanese', in Alexandra Y. Aikhenvald and R. M. W. Dixon (eds), *Commands: A cross-linguistic typology.* Oxford: Oxford University Press, 169–88.

Levinson, Stephen C. 1983. *Pragmatics.* Cambridge: Cambridge University Press.

Matsumoto, Yoshiko. 1988. 'Reexamination of the universality of face: Politeness phenomena in Japanese'. *Journal of Pragmatics* 12: 403–26.

Matsumoto, Yoshiko. 1989. 'Politeness and conversational universals–observations from Japanese'. *Multilingua* 8-2/3: 207–21.

McCready, Elin. 2019. *The semantics and pragmatics of honorification: Register and social meaning.* Oxford Scholarship Online: Oxford University Press. DOI: 10.1093/oso/9780198821366.001.0001.

Mithun, Marianne. 1984. 'The evolution of noun incorporation'. *Language* 60: 847–94.

Post, Mark W. 2011. 'Topographical deixis and the Tani languages of North-East India', in Gwendolyn Hyslop, Stephen Morey, and Mark W. Post (eds), *North East Indian linguistics,* 3: 137–54. New Delhi: Cambridge University Press India.

Post, Mark W. 2019. 'Topographical deixis in Trans-Himalayan (Sino-Tibetan) languages'. *Transactions of the Philological Society* 117: 1–22. DOI: 10.1111/1467-968X.12155.

Samdrup, Tshering and Hiroyuki Suzuki. 2019. 'Humilifics in Mabzhi pastoralist speech of Amdo Tibetan'. *Linguistics of the Tibeto-Burman Area* 42:2: 222–59.

Shafer, Robert. 1955. *Classification of the Sino-Tibetan languages.* WORD, 11:1: 94–111. DOI: 10.1080/00437956.1955.11659552.

Shafer, Robert. 1966. *Introduction to Sino-Tibetan (Part 1)*. Wiesbaden: Otto Harrassowitz.

Tournadre, N. 2014. 'The Tibetic languages and their classification'. *Trans-Himalayan linguistics: Historical and descriptive linguistics of the Himalayan area*, 105–29.

van Driem, George. 1994. 'Language policy in Bhutan', in Michael Aris and Michael Hutt (eds), *Bhutan: Aspects of culture and development*. Gartmore: Kiscadale Publications, 87–105.

van Driem, George. 1998. *Dzongkha*. Leiden: Research CNWS, School of Asian, African, and Amerindian Studies.

van Driem, George. 2011. 'Tibeto-Burman subgroups and historical grammar'. *Himalayan Linguistics* 10 (1): 31–9. (Special Issue in Memory of Michael Noonan and David Watters).

van Driem, George. 2019. 'The dynamics of Nepali pronominal distinctions in familiar, casual and formal relationships', in Paul Bouissac (ed.), *The social dynamics of pronominal systems: A comparative approach*. Amsterdam: John Benjamins, 151–203.

van Driem, George and Karma Tshering. 2019. *The grammar of Dzongkha: Revised and expanded, with a guide to Roman Dzongkha and to phonological Dzongkha*. (4th edition) Santa Barbara: Himalayan Linguistics, University of California.

Wangdi, Pema. Forthcoming. *A grammar of Brokpa*. PhD thesis, James Cook University.

Watters, Stephen A. 2018. *A grammar of Dzongkha: phonology, words, and simple clauses*. PhD dissertation, Rice University.

5

The semantics of the Dyirbal
avoidance style

Adjectives

R. M. W. Dixon

1 Introduction

Dyirbal was spoken in north-east Queensland, within a territory which extended from just north of the present town of Cardwell to just north of Innisfail along the coast, and inland as far as Ravenshoe, Herberton, and Mount Garmet. The country was mostly luxurious rain forest, partly sclerophyll woodland.

There were ten dialects (perhaps more). Between 1963 and 2002 I was able to gather extensive materials on three dialects, and good materials on three more. Only limited data is available for the remainder.

Direct contact had to be avoided between certain types of relatives—real and classificatory mother-in-law, son-in-law, father-in-law, and daughter-in-law. Two people in such a relation should not sit close; they must not look at each other, nor speak directly with each other. When talking to anyone in the presence of an avoidance relative, a special speech type had to be employed, called—in all dialects—*Jalnguy* /ˈjalŋuy/ (Ja). My main Jirrbal teacher, Chloe Grant, referred in English to Jalnguy as 'Mother-in-law language', and that is a useful colloquial label, except that it is not a separate language but rather a speech style or register.

In all other circumstances the everyday speech style (Ev) was employed; this is called *Guwal* in southern and *Ngirrma* or *NgiRma* in northern dialects.

The Jalnguy speech style ceased to be actively spoken around 1930. However, a number of older people (born about 1900 or earlier) still had good knowledge of it, which they were eager to share with me. I recorded one monologue and three dialogues in Jalnguy, and obtained the Ja equivalents of more than two thousand lexemes for three dialects; in north to south order:

R. M. W. Dixon, *The semantics of the Dyirbal avoidance style: Adjectives*. In: *The Integration of Language and Society: A Cross-Linguistic Typology*. Edited by: Alexandra Y. Aikhenvald, R. M. W. Dixon, and Nerida Jarkey, Oxford University Press.
© R. M. W. Dixon 2021. DOI: 10.1093/oso/9780192845924.003.0005

Ngajan (N), spoken around the Russell River, Mamu (M), around the South Johnstone River, and Jirrbal (J), around the Tully River.

The relationship of Ja to Ev styles is:

(a) For each dialect, Ev and Ja show **the same phonology and phonetics**.
(b) With a tiny handful of exceptions (see Appendix), **the grammar is identical** across styles. That is, every suffix and every grammatical word (pronouns, demonstratives, particles) exhibits no variation.
(c) **Every lexeme**—that is, every common noun, adjective, verb, adverbal, and time word—**is different** between styles, except for the four grandparent/grandchild terms and *jañja/yañja* 'now'. (Note that proper names, of people and of places, are the same in Ev and in Ja.)

Many Australian languages have an avoidance vocabulary but it normally consists of, at the most, a few score lexemes. These are substituted for the corresponding everyday word in normal discourse. (See Dixon 1980: 58–65, 479–80; 2002: 92–4; 2019: 63–4, 177–9, and further references therein.) Dyirbal (and its northerly neighbour Yidiñ) are the only languages known in which the Ev and Ja speech styles are quite separate; one may not employ an Ev word when speaking Ja, nor the reverse.

However, it is not the case that Ja has as many lexical forms as Ev. In fact it has far less, perhaps only a quarter as many. What happens is that typically a single word in Ja corresponds to a group of words in Ev. For instance, the Ev style for the M dialect has a distinct name for every species of honey-producing bee, including *gandirri* 'small yellow native bee', *wagurru* 'red native bee', and *mayi* 'introduced English bee'. But Ja has a single term, *mugilmbarram*, corresponding to all these Ev nouns.

The basic principle is as follows. In everyday discourse one should be as specific as possible, vagueness being regarded as a mental deficiency. In contrast, communication employing the avoidance style is at a more abstract level. This harmonizes with the social context in which Ja is used; it is appropriate to speak just in general terms within a kinship-avoidance situation.

Some important items do have their own Ja name. For instance, the black walnut tree (*Endiandra palmerstonii*)—which produces a fruit that is part of the staple diet—is *guway* in Ev and *gadaginay* in Ja, a one-to-one plant correspondence. However, in most instances there is a many-to-one Ev-to-Ja correspondence. For instance, Ja noun *guruŋun* is applied to six varieties of oak tree, each of which has its own name in Ev (and there is no generic term in Ev).

Many-to-one correspondences pervade the whole lexicon. In Ev there are a dozen verbs describing types of seeing, including *buran* 'see, look at', *waban* 'look up at', *gindan* 'look at after dark with the aid of a light', and *rugan* 'watch'. Corresponding to all of these, Ja uses a single generic term, *ñuriman* 'see'.

It is, of course, possible to be more exact in Ja if this should be necessary. An adjective or a relative clause could be added to a Ja lexeme to indicate, for instance, what species of oak tree is at issue, or which variety of the general act of seeing is involved.

The beauty of the Dyirbal system is that the underlying semantic system of the language is mapped onto lexemes at two different levels of generality. Examination of Ev-Ja correspondences reveals the taxonomic principles through which speakers of Dyirbal categorize the world around them and the ways in which they semantically organize—and perceive—states and activities.

Although many-to-one correspondences are foundational, there are a number of other ways of linking Ev and Ja lexemes. The techniques employed vary between the word classes and their subclasses. In section §4 there are brief discussions of how verbs and nouns are dealt with. Then the main focus of the chapter, in §5, is on how Ja reveals the underlying semantic organization of the adjective class.

Fieldwork on Ja was a rewarding experience. Speakers insisted that no Ev word should ever be included when speaking in Ja. They searched their memory for an appropriate Ja correspondent for each Ev lexeme. It became an intellectual challenge which they were eager to undertake and thoroughly enjoyed. Some times they could not provide a single-word Ja correspondent for some Ev word and then offered a circumlocution (using just Ja lexemes). For example, when we came to consider the Ev adjective *ŋuyiñ* 'gazing at, staring at', this was rendered by the Ja sentence: *ŋayguna ñurima-n baŋgul, diŋal gilgarri-mban*, which means 'He is looking at me, his eyes are jumping out at me'.

2 Background data on Jalnguy

The following abbreviations are used:

N   everyday style in Ngajan dialect (called NgiRma)
M   everyday style in Mamu dialect (called Ngirrma)
J   everyday style in Jirrbal dialect (called Guwal)

Nja avoidance style in Ngajan dialect (called Jalnguy)

Mja avoidance style in Mamu dialect (called Jalnguy)

Jja avoidance style in Jirrbal dialect (called Jalnguy)

I carried out a lexical comparison, across the Ev and Ja styles, for those items in N, M, and J for which monomorphemic Ja correspondents had been given:

THE SAME EV LEXEME

N

208/278 = 75%	M
128/197 = 65%	183/222 = 82%	J

THE SAME JA LEXEME

Nja

192/278 = 69%	Mja
75/197 = 38%	109/222 = 49%	Jja

It can be seen that M is closer to J than to N in terms of Ev lexemes; this would be expected since J and M are contiguous, whereas a further dialect, Waribarra (for which no Ja information is available) intervenes between M and N. What is of particular interest is that, when Ja lexemes are examined, Mja is much more similar to Nja than it is to Jja.

It is likely (see Dixon 1972: 351) that the Dyirbal language was originally spoken by a single tribe in the southern part of its present territory. Speakers of Dyirbal then expanded north, the original tribe split into a number of separate tribes, and the modern dialects gradually evolved. It seems probable that the Ja vocabulary grew to its present size quite recently—after the dialects split—and has done so in different ways in different dialects. The figures above suggest that the M and N dialects developed their Ja partly as a joint venture, whereas the J dialect has pursued a more separate course.

The Yidiñ language was spoken directly to the north of Dyirbal. When I began work, Yidiñ was further along the path towards oblivion than was Dyirbal. However, two old speakers did remember a certain amount of their avoidance style (also called Jalnguy); details are in Dixon (1977: 501–7, 1991). Similarly to speakers of Dyirbal, they maintained that no Ev lexeme could be used when speaking Ja.

I carried out a lexical comparison between the two languages for those items for which Ev and monomorphemic Ja forms were known, parallel to the count quoted above between dialects of Dyirbal. The number of lexemes which are identical or nearly identical between corresponding styles of the two languages are:

	Ev	Ja
Yidiñ and the adjacent N dialect of Dyirbal	38/163 = 23%	60/163 = 37%
Yidiñ and all dialects of Dyirbal	42/163 = 26%	66/163 = 40%

We can see that Yidiñ and Dyirbal are more similar in Ja than in Ev lexemes. In light of the intra-Dyirbal figures it was suggested that the northern dialects of Dyirbal—M and N—developed their Ja partly as a joint venture, whereas the J dialect pursued a more separate course. The figures just given indicate that, as Ja vocabularies grew, there was a good deal of borrowing between Yidiñ and neighbouring dialects of Dyirbal.

An investigation into the forms of Ja lexemes reveals a number of sources. Quite often, a Ja term in one dialect is identical to an Ev lexeme in a different dialect of Dyirbal, or in Yidiñ or another neighbouring language. Sometimes a Ja term in Dyirbal is identical with a Ja term in Yidiñ. And there are quite a few instances of a Ja term having apparently been formed by phonological deformation of the corresponding Ev lexeme in the same dialect; for instance, verb 'return' is *banagañu* in Ev and *walagañu* in Ja, adjective 'hungry' is *ŋamir* in Ev and *gabir* in Ja. (Details are in Dixon 1990, 2015: 112–38.)

3 Phonological and grammatical information

3.1 Phonology

All but two dialects of Dyirbal have sixteen phonemes. The three vowels are front high *i*, back high *u*, and low *a*. The thirteen consonants comprise:

- Four stop/nasal pairs—bilabial *b*, *m*; apico-alveolar *d*, *n*; lamino-palatal *j*, *ñ*; and dorso-velar *g*, *ŋ*.
- Two semi-vowels—lamino-palatal *y* and velar/labial *w*.
- An apico-alveolar lateral *l*.
- Two rhotics—apico-alveolar trill *rr* and apico-postalveolar continuant *r*.

This inventory is maintained in all dialects except for the most northerly two. Ngajan has undergone compensatory changes whereby a series of long vowels was introduced (*ii, uu,* and *aa*) and the contrast between the two rhotic phonemes was neutralized. The single rhotic in N is written as *R*. These changes are illustrated in the name of the rufous fantail bird (*Rhipidura rufifrons*). It *is burujiŋgal* in M and J, but *buuRjiŋgaa* in N. (Waribarra, the dialect between N and M, has also evolved long vowels, but maintains two rhotic phonemes.)

3.2 Grammar

There are four open classes of lexemes which divide into two pairs:

- Verbals, made up of:
  — Verbs.
  — Adverbals. These are adverb-like words which generally accompany a verb and modify it—for example 'do properly', 'start to do', 'do too soon'.
- Nominals, made up of:
  — Nouns.
  — Adjectives.

Each verbal is strictly transitive or strictly intransitive (with only a handful of exceptions). They divide into two conjugations, which correlate with—but do not coincide with—transitivity classes. Verbs and adverbals show the same derivational and inflectional morphology. A verb phrase may include several verbals so long as they have the same transitivity value and final inflection.

Nouns and adjectives have identical derivational and inflectional morphology. They may co-occur in a noun phrase and then share the same case inflection. A major criterion for deciding whether a certain nominal should be categorized as a noun or as an adjective, involves gender.

Each noun belongs to one of four genders, shown by a marker used with the noun:

GENDER	MARKER	BASIC CONCEPTS
I	*bayi*	male humans; non-human animates
II	*balan*	female humans; fire; drinkable liquids; fighting
III	*balam*	edible plant food including honey
IV	*bala*	everything else, including body parts, stone, earth, language, noises, and flesh food (meat and fish); and bees

There are, in addition, a number of semantic principles involved in assigning genders: association through legend, belief, or physical similarity, or highlighting an important property (such as being edible or being harmful). Full details are in Dixon (2015: 31–43).

Fruit and vegetable foods—in gender III, marked by *balam*—are produced by plants, which are gender IV, *bala*. Honey, *balam guru*, is produced by bees, and—because of this congruence—all bees are *bala* (they are the only animates which are not *bayi* or *balan*). In §1, *mugilmbarram* was mentioned as the Ja correspondent for several species of bee, each of which has a distinct name in Ev. The same Ja noun, *mugilmbarram* is also used for honey. However, gender marking clearly distinguishes between product and producers:

Ja	Ev
balam mugilmbarram 'honey'	*balam* guru 'honey'
	⌈ *bala gandirri* 'small yellow native bee'
bala mugilmbarram 'all bees'	├ *bala wagurru* 'red native bee'
	⌊ *bala mayi* 'introduced English bee', and more

Generally each noun belongs to a single gender. An adjective can potentially modify a noun of any gender. An adjective generally occurs with a noun, but the noun may be anaphorically omitted so that the adjective is the only lexeme in the NP; it then takes a marker determined by the gender of the understood (but unstated) head noun.

Thus, in most cases gender provides a criterion for deciding whether a given nominal is to be regarded as noun or as adjective—a noun occurs with only one of the gender markers, an adjective with any of them. However, the criterion is not quite watertight. There are a few nouns which may be used with either of two gender markers, e.g. *bayi jaja* 'male child', *balan jaja* 'female child'; and *bala muja* 'the timber from a bush guava tree (*Eupomatia laurina*), *balam muja* 'the fruit from this tree'. From the other end, there are a few adjectives which may only be used of a human, with I or II gender marker; for example, *jilbay* 'experienced/expert at a task'.

Any nominal may be made into an intransitive verb by adding suffix *-bin* 'become', or into a transitive verb by adding suffix *-m(b)an* 'make'. These two derivational processes are used a great deal with adjectives, and only rather sparingly with nouns. Some adjectives occur more often as a derived intransitive verb (with *-bin*), than as a plain adjective; e.g. *burrun* 'busy'.

There is also a small lexical class of Time Words, whose Ja correspondents are outlined in Dixon (2015: 103), and grammatical systems involving words—pronouns, interrogatives, demonstratives, and particles (such as 'not', 'don't', 'maybe', and 'might well have happened').

4 How Jalnguy deals with verbs and nouns

As a background to the detailed discussion of how Ja treats adjectives, we briefly mention the techniques Ja employs with verbs and with various types of nouns.

4.1 Verbs

I asked for the Ja correspondent of each of several hundred Ev verbs. (Every verb was of course placed in a sentence, rather than being quoted as an isolated element.) Typically, one Ja verb was given as the correspondent for each of a group of Ev verbs, with similar meanings.

Here is a selection of Ev verbs for which *ñuriman* was given as Ja correspondent (there were half-a-dozen more):

Ev verb		Ja correspondent
buran	see, look at, notice, read	ñuriman
waban	look up at	ñuriman
barrmin	look back at	ñuriman
gindan	look at after dark with the aid of a light	ñuriman
rugan	watch someone who is going	ñuriman
jaymban	find	ñuriman

I then asked things the other way round: 'What would be the Ev correspondent of the Ja verb *ñuriman*?' The answer was '*buran*'. 'What about *waban*?' I then asked. 'Oh yes, that's *ñuriman* too.'

I pursued the matter further: '*Buran* and *waban* are different words in Ev; how could this be brought out in Ja?' My teacher thought for a moment and then explained: '*Buran* would be plain *ñuriman*, but for *waban* you could say *yalu-ŋulañ-gala-mban ñuriman*'. The first word starts with *yalu-* 'to a place here', following by *-ŋulañ-*, which is a special Ja element inserted into such a locational marker, then *-gala* 'up', and finally the transitive verbalizer *-mban*; the word means 'do to up here'.

Similar results were obtained for every other pair. *Buran* was *ŋuriman*, with no further specification, but for the other Ev verbs an appropriate addition was provided to *ñuriman*:

Ev verb	Ja correspondent
buran	ñuriman
waban	yalu-ŋulañ-gala-mban ñuriman 'look up here at'
barrmin	yalu-ŋulañ-ŋarru-mban ñuriman 'look back here at'
gindan	ŋarrgana-gu ñuriman 'look at with a light'
rugan	ñuriman bawal-bi-ŋu 'look at (someone) who is going'
jaymban	ñuriman mulwa-li 'see (something) in order to pick it up'

It is useful to describe *buran* as a 'nuclear' item. It is the general Ev verb for 'seeing' with the other Ev verbs being more specific articulations of it. The Ja style simply has the nuclear verb, with further specification being added to it as needed.

The same results were obtained for every semantic set. There is a many-to-one Ev-Ja correspondence, but one of the Ev verbs is the nuclear item, with a general meaning which corresponds to that of the unique Ja verb.

This provides merely a glimpse of one of the techniques which Ja used for dealing with verbs. Fuller accounts are in Dixon (1971, 1973, 1982: 63–139, 2015: 104–10).

4.2 Fauna and flora

The organization of a language reflects the nature of the society in which it is used. I gathered names in Ev for about 560 individual plants found in the rainforest environment. Almost 200 of these have parts which may be eaten, and it is this which motivates a special gender, III 'edible plant food', with marker *balam*.

Areas of specialization in Ja vocabulary also reflect what is of cultural importance. There are probably a higher number of one-to-one Ev-to-Ja correspondences for flora than for any other lexical domain. About twenty plants producing staple foods each has a unique Ja correspondent; they include:

Ev name		Ja correspondent
balam bara	yellow walnut, *Beilschmiedia bancroftii*	balam gaŋgi
balam daguli	watergum, *Syzygiun gustavoides*	balam giŋama
balam jugur	wild yam, *Dioscorea transversa*	balam wandu

Otherwise, there are many-to-one correspondences. As mentioned above, six varieties of oak trees, each with its own name in Ev, are grouped together as *bala gurruŋun* in Ja. All are in the family *Protaceae*, and are appreciated for their hard timber. Six species of lawyer vine (in the family *Calamus*) are grouped together in Ja as *balam ŋunjanum*. One name in Ja, *balam gumulam*, covers no fewer than thirty plants which have fruit that can be just picked and eaten when ripe (in contrast to staple foods which require lengthy preparation by soaking, scraping, roasting etc.); each has its own name in Ev.

We saw that—for every set of verbs in Ev sharing a single correspondent in Ja—there is one 'nuclear' Ev verb, with the non-nuclear verbs being definable in terms of it. Nothing of this kind applies for nouns. The six species of oak tree, six varieties of lawyer vine, thirty-plus plants with fruit that does not require special preparation, are all on a par. There is not one member of the set which has prime importance.

An artefact may typically be made from a certain plant, which is accorded the same name in Ja as the artefact. Or a plant may have the shape of a body part and be thus named, or be the favourite food of some creature, and be named the same in Ja. For example:

Ev NAME		Ja CORRESPONDENT
bayi maŋañ	boomerang (typically made from brown walnut)	bayi muyuu
bala ŋañjaRa	brown walnut, *Endiandra tooram*	bala muyuu
bayi yulman	woomera (typically made from cherry penda)	bayi jumala
balam wanjan	cherry penda, *Syzygium kuranda*	balam jumala
bala maŋa	ear	bala walin
balam gundumu	wild banana, *Musa banksii*	balam walin
bayi mabi	tree-climbing kangaroo, *Dendrolagus lumholtzi*	bayi jaŋanbaRa
bala mabilmabil	delarbrea, *Delarbrea michieana*	bala jaŋanbaRa

I was told that the wild banana looks like an ear, and that the small berries on the delarbrea tree are a favourite food for the tree kangaroo. Note that, in each instance, gender serves to distinguish the Ja labels.

One tree is named in Ja by an adjective which describes the taste of its fruit. Ja adjective *ŋumuy* corresponds to two Ev adjectives: *jamar* 'bitter tasting' and *muymur* 'sour (and salty) tasting'; see examples (29) and (30) in section 5.5. The large Davidson plum tree, *Davidsonia pruriens*, is *balam wuray* in Ev, and simply *balam ŋumuy* in Ja; the adjective is here being used as a noun to characterize the astringent taste of the fruit.

There is rather less specification in Ja for fauna than for flora. Basically, the many-to-one Ev-to-Ja principle applies. In Ja, *bayi yuŋga* corresponds to six names in Ev for types of wallaby and kangaroo, *bayi jibuñ* is used for eleven kinds of possums, *bayi guwaga* for more than twenty species of frogs (and for tadpoles), *bayi mayaja* for seven varieties of edible grubs, and *bayi balbiji* for five sorts of eels. Just as for flora there is no 'nuclear' Ja term within a many-to-one correspondence set. Each possum, each frog, and so on, is accorded equal status.

It is interesting to enquire why there are more one-to-one Ev-to-Ja correspondences for flora than for fauna. This is because each of the staple foods has a distinctive character—in terms of how it grows, methods for harvesting, and the processes which need to be applied to render it edible. In contrast, every one of the eleven species of possum, for example, is hunted in more-or-less the same way, and cooked in identical fashion.

There are (or were) occasional one-to-one correspondences for fauna. The echidna, an egg-laying mammal on land, is unique; it is called *balan gumbi-yan* in Ev and *balan ginga* in Ja. When the European invaders brought with them pigs, these were assigned the name *balan bigibigi*. Their short sharp bristles were regarded as similar to the spines on an echidna and in Ja they were also included under *balan ginga*. In similar fashion, the Ja term for 'dingo, dog' was extended to cover another introduced animal, the horse.

Some fauna were assigned descriptive labels in Ja, typically involving a verb plus agentive nominalizer *-muŋa*. The kookaburra (which wakes a bushman by its laugh-like cry at the brink of dawn) is *bayi guŋgaga* in Ev and *bayi yirrguñji-muŋa* 'they who laugh' in Ja. Several types of hawks and all species of wasps and ticks are subsumed under *bayi ñanbal-muŋa* 'they who pierce' in Ja, while the mosquito, march flies, several types of biting ant, and the centipede are all *bayi guyjul-muŋa* 'they who bite'.

Other descriptive labels in Ja are based on a noun plus suffix *-barra* 'associated with'. *Bala jinbay* is Ja for 'ground' and *balan jinbay-barra* is used for several types of bird which lay their eggs on or near the ground, while *bayi jinbay-barra* is the Ja term for several kinds of crickets, which do the same.

There are many ways in which the language reflects fables and beliefs. For instance the sun is held to be a legendary woman and the moon her husband; on this basis they are assigned to genders II and I respectively, like humans. Birds are believed to incorporate the spirits of dead human females; the Ja term *balan muyguyŋgun* corresponds to Ev *balan guyŋgan* 'spirit of a dead woman' and also to Ev *balan dundu* 'bird'. Willy wagtail birds gyrate in a manner reminiscent of how initiated men dance on a corroboree ground, which for J is *balan buya* in Ev and *balan burula* in Ja. The three willy wagtails, each with its own name in Ev, are grouped together in Ja as *balan burula-barra* 'associated with the corroboree ground'.

4.3 Other nouns

Terms for the major body parts are central elements in the lexicon of every language, with metaphorical extensions to parts of plants, artefacts, and the environment. For example, *bala guwu* 'nose' in Ev is also used for things of similar shape: the nipple on a breast, the beak of a bird, the point of a spear, the prow of a canoe, the operative end of a firestick, and the peak of a mountain. The Ja correspondent is *bala ŋarrŋgalan*, which also covers the bridge of the nose, *bala yadin* in Ev.

The Ev noun *bala jina* has a fair range of meaning: foot of a person and of some animals (bandicoot, crocodile, turkey), also foot mark and animal track. The Ja term is *bala winarra*; besides *bala jina* this was given as Ja for five further Ev nouns:

- *bala ŋuru* 'heel, heel mark'
- *bala gadam* 'sole of foot'
- *bala murun* 'paw of dog; foot of goat, horse, cattle, pig'
- *bala magal* 'back paw of wallaby and kangaroo'
- *bala bunjurru* 'boot, shoe'

One Ja term corresponds to separate Ev names for head hair, beard, moustache, body hair, and pubic hair. Distinct names in Ev for the tail of a mammal, the tail of a snake, the tail of a fish or eel, and the tail of a crocodile share the Ja correspondent *bala jibibu*, which is also used for penis, *bala wundu* in Ev. In Ja, *bala ŋuju* links three Ev terms: *bala ñurruy* 'snot, nasal mucus (and bad cold)', *bala ñumba* 'spittle', and *bala galgi* 'phlegm'. There are many similar examples.

Spears of different shapes and sizes each has its own role: a split-point spear for pinioning eels, one with a multi-point head for fish, a spear with echidna-quill spikes fastened with wax around the top, one with a backwards hook attached which makes it hard to extract. Each has its own name in Ev and Ev also includes a generic term *balan baŋgay* '(any) spear'. As would be expected, Ja just has a single term, *balan waybay*, corresponding to *balan baŋgay*.

Balan yibay was given as Ja for the general Ev noun *balan buni* 'fire' and also for the more specialized one *balan yiŋgiñ* 'flying spark'. When I asked how to distinguish these in Ja, *balan buni* was just *balan yibay*, with the Ja for *balan yiŋgiñ* being expanded (by adding a relative clause) to be *balan yibay gilgarrin-ja-ŋu* 'fire which jumps a lot'. *Balan jujamu* is the Ja for Ev noun *balan bana* 'water' and also corresponding to Ev designations for 'lagoon', 'swamp', and 'dew'. *Bala bayŋgin*, Ev for 'sweat' is rendered by *bala jujamu* in Ja, as is *bala gayŋgir* 'tears' in Ev.

Some phenomena receive the same Ja designation by virtue of their looks. For example, *balan garrmban* is Ja for 'steam' which is *balan jawuy* in Ev (gender marker *balan* since it is associated with water). And *bala garrmban* is Ja for Ev *bala garran* 'smoke' (with the 'residue' gender marker *bala*).

Ev loan words *balam jubayga* 'tobacco' and *balam jiga* 'cigarette' are *balam garrmban* in Ja, by virtue of the smoke they produce. Note here *balam*, for gender III, showing that smoking tobacco is classed together with eating.

Some Ev nouns are simply accorded descriptive labels in Ja. For *bala buŋurray* 'snore' in Ev I was given the Ja sentence *bayi nayŋul-ŋa-ñú yulmba-ŋu* 'having lain down, he throws it out'. Others get only an adjective—Ev noun *bala burumba* 'stump of a tree' was named in Ja just by the adjective *ñingal* 'short'.

The intention in §4 has been simply to outline some of the techniques used to deal with verbs and nouns in Ja. Examples were given across dialects, since only the general principles involved were in focus. This has been a lead-up to §5, which provides a detailed study how Ja analyses adjectives, taking full cognizance of differences between N, M, and J (those dialects for which there is information on the Ja style).

We can recall, from §3.1, that *R* in N corresponds to *rr* and *r* in M and J, and that N often has a long vowel where M and J have a vowel plus *l*, *r*, or *y*.

5 The semantics of adjectives in Jalnguy

Examination of the Ja correspondences given for adjectives from Ev shows that the Ja lexicon is less rich and less well-developed when dealing with adjectives than with verbs and nouns.

There are, of course, Ja correspondents for Ev adjectives expressing the most common qualities, found across languages world-wide. There are a number of many-to-one Ev-to-Ja correspondences, which can be semantically revealing. Speakers provided sentential definitions for some adjectives (in terms of verbs), often quite ingenious.

But for many Ev adjectives referring to rather recondite qualities, my consultants could offer no appropriate Ja term. What they did instead was provide an evaluative judgement, most often *maŋgay* 'not good', sometimes *ŋundarriñ* 'good' (or occasionally a dimensional description, 'big' or 'little'). The principle of not using any Ev words in Ja discourse was thus maintained by commenting on the worth of a quality, rather than specifying what the quality is.

5.1 Dialect similarities and differences

For some of the most central adjectival concepts, the same Ev and Ja terms are found across all three of the dialects N, M, and J. For instance:

(1)   N, M, J   *buga* 'rotten, gone bad (fruit or meat), dead (and
                            putrefying) body'
      Nja, Mja, Jja   *gundum*

M and J have an Ev adjective *guyi* 'dead (lacking life)' and this was also accorded Ja correspondent *gundum* (*guyi* does not occur in N). And an adjective with more specialized meaning was included under *gundum* in Ja:

(1a) M *ralŋga*; J *dalŋa* 'dried used of a tree which is dead but still standing'
      Mja, Jja *gundum* (plus *dalmbirr* 'tree')

In the next example all three dialects have the same Ev adjective but there is one Ja term in Nja and Jja (the most northerly and southerly of the three dialects) and another in Mja (which comes between them):

(2)   N, M J *dinu* 'cold'
      Nja, Jja *gungi*; Mja *ŋilu*

There is in M and J another adjective *gurrul* 'really cold (used of a person, as they may double up their body to try to keep warm)'; this is also *ŋilu* in Mja and *gungi* in Jja.

Since nouns and adjectives share the same morphology, it is a straightforward matter for a word to do 'double duty' as a member of both word classes. This is encountered only occasionally in Ev. One example parallels *fat* in English; in the Ev style for all three dialects we have adjective *jami* 'fat' and noun *bala jami* 'fat'. Such double duty is more frequent in Ja. For example the adjectives 'cold' are also used for the noun 'wintertime, cold weather, frost':

(2)   a.   N *bala yiwaa*; M, J *bala birrgil* 'winter, cold weather, frost'
Nja, Jja *bala gungi*; Mja *bala ŋilu*

In M, 'widow' is *balan bilmbu* and 'widower' is *bayi bilmbu*. These are rendered by *balan ŋilu* and *bayi ŋilu* in Mja; with no spouse to keep them warm a person is likely to be cold. Also in M, the Ev term for 'nautilus shell (a mollusc with edible flesh inside)' is *balan gubaguba*; it is *balan ŋilu* in Mja since the shell is so cold to the touch. The Ja adjective extends its meaning in another direction for N, corresponding to Ev noun *bala wuŋgu* 'shade', Nja has *bala gungi*.

An unusual feature of Dyirbal is that there are in Ev nineteen specialized adjectives for 'big' with respect to different kinds of fauna. For example, *gunuji*, in all three dialects, is 'big used of eels', while *maŋara* in M and J, *maŋaRa* in N is 'big used of wallabies and kangaroos'. There is also a general term 'big', with different dialectal forms in Ev but the same form in Ja:

(3)   N *baŋan*; M, J *bulgan* 'big, large (also elder sibling), lots of'
Nja *gagiR*; Mja, Jja *gagir*

GagiR/gagir is, as would be expected, the Ja correspondent for the nineteen specialized adjectives 'big'. It was also given as Ja for 'deep (water)', which in is Ev *ŋagu* for N and M, *ŋurin* for J.

Some adjectival concepts show different forms across dialects both in Ev and in Ja. For example 'no good' (Dyirbal speakers hardly ever use the adjective *bad* in their English, preferring *no good*):

(4)   N *juŋgin*; M *walgay*; J *wuygi* 'no good (also used for old person, ill person, bad omen)'
Nja *yaRbuR*; Mja, Jja *maŋgay*

Maŋgay is the most pervasive word in Ja, being given as the Ja correspondent for many adjectives with specialized meanings (and *yaRbuR* is not far behind it). This will be exemplified throughout the remainder of the chapter.

5.2 Semantic sets

The majority of the many-to one Ev-to-Ja correspondences for verbs and for nouns apply across all three dialects. Often the same Ja form is used. For example, verb *jaymban* 'give' is the Nja, Mja, and Jja correspondent for half-a-dozen Ev verbs which describe ways of transferring ownership—'send', 'give through an opening', 'provide food for relatives', 'share out', etc., as well as the nuclear verb with a general meaning, *wugan* 'give'. And *bala mugilmbar-ram* in Mja, *bala mugiimbaRam* in Nja, are used for all species of bees, and also for honey (then with gender marker *balam*).

Sometimes the actual form in Ja varies between dialects but the many-to-one grouping is maintained. Whereas Mja and Jja have *ñuriman* for 'see, look at', Nja uses *wuugan*; but it covers the same set of Ev verbs as does *ñuriman*. For 'edible grubs', Nja and Mja have *bayi mayaja* and Jja *bayi jamuy*; both cover the same set of grub types, each with its own name in Ev.

The contrast of many-to-one Ev-to-Ja correspondences between word classes is striking. Whereas those for verbs and nouns are largely similar across all three dialects, those for adjectives are in many cases dialect-specific.

The semantic associations shown by many-to-one correspondences for adjectives can be illustrated through a handful of examples.

(5) Nja *bigaa* given for   N   *giRgil* 'broken, split or torn (into two or more pieces)'

                                       N   *gajala* 'cracked (stone, glass, egg, ground, wood); feelings hurt (of a person)'

                                       N   *gumban* 'sliced (e.g. lawyer vine sliced fine for weaving a dilly-bag)'

This is straightforward. The Nja adjective *bigaa* describes the unity of some thing (or equanimity of a person) being disturbed, corresponding to Ev adjectives dealing with three different kinds of disturbance.

Example (6) is concerned with cause and effect. When heat is applied to something it dries it; heat leads to evaporation for a body of water, so that what was deep becomes shallow. Jja adjective *ñigala* links Ev adjectives describing these individual qualities:

(6) Jja *ñigala* given for   J   *biŋgir* 'hot (sun, water, steam, charcoal, food, etc.)'

                                       J   *ŋarrala* 'dry (ground, swamp, river, clothes)'

J   *gadala* 'dry (rain has finished), dried up
     (of a creek)'

J   *jala* 'shallow (water)'

In (7), Mja adjective *wurrgal* connotes something happening in a manner which is less than acceptable or at a speed which is less than typical:

(7)   Mja *wurrgal* given for   M   *wunma* 'moving slowly'

                                    M   *wunay* 'slow at doing something (climbing, cutting, talking, etc.)'

                                    M   *jalmbuy* 'unable to do something as it should be done (because of tiredness or incapacity)'

                                    M   *malu* 'dragging behind, going slower and slower (from laziness or pretended tiredness)'

In example (8a) a mental attitude is seen as similar to a physical state—a person's wish for social interaction (and for talking) has evaporated:

(8) a. Nja *dulun* given for   N   *bumba* 'dry (e.g. a campsite which has been dried by the sun, a reservoir gone dry, dry throat when thirsty)'

                                 N   *jamaa* 'sulking, not talking to people after being offended'

      The Mja correspondent for *bumba* has a different range of meanings:

    b. Mja *nalŋga* given for   M   *bumba* 'dry (e.g. a campsite which has been dried by the sun, a reservoir gone dry, dry throat when thirsty)'

                                 M   *yagar* 'lightweight; mental state when worrying about what has happened to a relative'

The association here is basically physical; when something wet becomes dry it weighs less. It is the Ev adjective *yagar* which extends from the physical to the mental. This Mja term is also used for a noun. The Ev loanword *balam burin* 'bread' was given as *balam nalŋga* in Mja since it is a dry foodstuff. (See also example (38).)

It will be seen that the range of Ev correspondents for an adjective in Ja demonstrates the nature of adjectival concepts in Dyirbal. One of the most fascinating examples is that in example (9) for *jagarri*:

(9)   Mja *jagarri* given for   M   *jami* 'fat' (adjective); *bala jami* 'fat' (noun)'

                                       M   *bala galan* 'the fat inside a cassowary' (noun)

                                       M   *dulburr* '(person) of short and fat build'

                                       M   *bambun* 'in good health (used especially of someone regaining good health after illness)' [see also (36)]

                                       M   *jugal* 'straight (e.g. a road or a stick)'

                                       M   *nungu* 'intact, with no holes (can be a blanket or a road or a bridge)'

                                       M   *jalgirr* 'tough, can't be broken (e.g. timber)'

                                       M   *darrŋgara* 'clean (of water)'

                                       M   *duru* 'feeling happy, pleased, satisfied, glad'

                                       M   *gulngan* 'well-behaved: respectful, kind-hearted, grateful'

See also example (18).

The essential meaning of Mja adjective *jagarri* appears to be 'satisfactory'. Meat or eels with lots of fat are a much-valued food. It is considered good for a person to be healthily fat. Ideally, a stick or a road should be straight, an artefact or material lacking imperfections, and water free from contamination. It is appropriate to apply it to a person when they are contented in themselves, and behave in a socially acceptable way towards others. (Note that there are quite different Ev and Ja adjectives for 'good'.)

(Nja does have adjective *jagaRi* which was given as the Ja equivalent of just two Ev adjectives, *jami* 'fat' and *yangaRa* 'straight'.)

J and M share the Ev adjective *burrmu* 'forgetful, failing to understand' but with different Ev correspondents:

(10)   Jja *gurrŋu* given for   J   *burrmu* 'forgetful, failing to understand'

                                       J   *ñurrŋu* 'preoccupied, too busy to notice'

(11)   Mja *dilbin* given for   M   *burrmu* 'forgetful, failing to understand'

                                       M   *baba* 'deaf, losing memory, losing wits'

                                       M   *munamuna* '(angry and) determined to do something'

It appears that *gurrŋu* in Jja relates to a lack of awareness, whereas Mja *dilbin* describes a state of mind—being blind to everything outside an obsession (for *munamuna*) or not being able to focus the mind (for *burrmu* and *baba*).

5.3 Definitions

Sometimes, a consultant could not offer a single-word Ja correspondent for a given Ev word. There may not have been one or, if there was, they could not recall it to mind. In such cases they might offer what could be called a 'definition' within Ja (using a Ja verb and Ja nouns). A few examples will illustrate the variety of ways in which this was done.

(12)   J   *yabarr* 'spreading arms and legs wide, while standing or walking (typically children)'

     Jja   *jabarra-jabarra*ₛ *diinda-rri-ñu* (REDUP-leg stand-INTR-PRES) 'legs are standing'

In (12), the Jja gives a partial characterization of the Ev adjective, whereas in (13) the Mja provides a clear paraphrase.

(13)   M   *binjil* 'being in love with; desiring sexually'

     Ma   *wajarr*ₛ *ñawarray-marri-ñu bagun* (heart/feelings come.out-INTR-PRES HER.DAT) '(his) feelings come out for her'

In the next two examples there is an illustration of part of the scope of the Ev adjective. The Mja in (14) describes one of the ways of being elusive. In (15) the Jja mentions one aspect of the skill described by Ev *jumburu*; a good hunter has to be able to locate the prey (as stated in the Jja) and also to kill it (which is implied).

(14)   M   *ñuriñ* 'elusive (can get out of the way of a thrown spear, can disappear so that no one knows where they have gone)'

     Mja   *bawal-bawal.ni-n, gulu ñuurima-n* (REDUP-go-PRES, NOT see-PRES) '(someone) goes, and can't be seen'

(15) J   *jumburu* 'skilled/lucky in hunting'
      Jja   *bayi-mban*_S *ñurima-rri-muŋa* (HE-EMPH see-INTR-AGENT) 'he's
             the one who always sees'

Ev adjective *garrbi* has a very specific meaning. Someone who locates
a 'sugar-bag' (as it was called) would mark the tree to show it was theirs,
planning later to return to and garner. In (16), the Mja clearly describes this.

(16) M   *garrbi* 'earmarked: used of a sugar-bag (beehive) that has been
             located by some person, and earmarked by that person to
             return to and harvest later (once it has been earmarked, no one
             else should touch it)'
      Mja   *ganba-gabun-ŋunu ŋaja*_S *mugilmbarrram-gu bawalbi-ñ*
             (yesterday-ANOTHER-FROM I honey-DAT go-FUT) 'I'll go
             back for the honey from a few days ago'

The Mja for (17) is fully informative. (It is instructive to compare this
with the Nja given for 'pregnant', which was the succinct *duwuR-ba*, literally
'stomach-WITH')

(17) M   *muygam* 'pregnant'
      Mja   *duwurr*_S *gagir-bi-n ñalmaru-ba; wajay ñalmaru-gu julbamba-rri-gu*
             (stomach big-BECOME-PRES child-WITH; in.a.few.days
             child-DAT put.down-INTR-PURP) '(her) stomach has become
             big with child; in a few days she'll give birth to a child (lit. put
             down a child)'

Sometimes the same definition was given for two dialects. 'He always
gives' in Ja clearly renders Ev adjective 'generous'. Note that in M the Mja
adjective 'satisfactory'—illustrated in example (9)—is added, as a comment on
the worth of this quality.

(18) M, J   *wugija* 'generous (always shares everything)'
      Mja   *bayi*_S *jaymal-muŋa* (HE give-AGENT); *jagarri* (satisfactory);
             'he always gives; satisfactory'
      Jja   *bayi*_S *jaymal-muŋa* (HE give-AGENT) 'he always gives'

As shown in (18), Mja and Jja share the verb *jayman* 'give'. The definitions quoted in (19) for 'thirsty' in Nja and Mja are identical. However, this is not immediately apparent because of the different forms of lexemes in the two Ja styles. Noun 'water' is *nuba* in Nja but *jujamu* in Mja (it is *bana* in Ev for both dialects); and verb 'drink' is *wuɲaɲu* in Nja but *miljaɲu* in Mja (again the Ev verb in the same in all dialects, *guɲjan*).

(19) N   *ŋayiRañ* 'thirsty'
      M   *ŋayirañ* 'thirsty'
      Nja   *ŋaja$_s$ nuba-gu wuɲa-naa-gu* (I water-DAT drink-ANTIPASS-
            PURP) 'I want to drink water'
      Mja   *jujamu-gu ŋaja$_s$ milja-nay-gu* (water-DAT I drink-ANTIPASS-
            PURP) 'I want to drink water'

(The fact that pronoun *ŋaja* 'I' comes first in the Nja sentence and second in the Mja one is of no significance. The order of words is remarkably free across Dyirbal.)

The Ev adjective *marma*, in (20), has a range of meanings. Mja describes one aspect of this (he won't share) and Jja another facet (he consumes too much himself).

(20) M, J   *marma* 'mean, selfish, wants to keep everything for himself;
             overindulges'
      Mja   *bayi$_s$ gulu jayma-rri-ñu* (HE NOT give-INTR-PRES) 'he never
             gives (anything)'
      Jja   *bayi$_s$ ŋandi-yirri-ñu yulmi-na-ñu* (HE do.too.much-INTR-PRES
             eat-ANTIPASS-PRES) 'he eats too much'

For some Ev adjectives, a one-word Ja correspondent was given in one or two dialects but a definition in another. This can be illustrated for 'heavy' and 'full'. The Mja definition given for 'heavy' in (21) states a consequence of something being heavy, while the Jja definition for 'full' in (22) describes an example of being full.

(21) N   *biRjan* 'heavy'
      M, J   *ñañjal* 'heavy'
      Nja   *dimbuu*
      Mja   *yandamba-n julwa-n* (try.do.but.can't-PRES lift.up-PRES) 'trying
             to lift it up but can't'
      Jja   *ñanjarray*

(22)   N   *jaagadaa* 'full (bag, box, mouth, but not stomach)'
       M, J   *gurrburu* 'full (bag, box, mouth, but not stomach)'
       Nja   *guduRuy*
       Mja   *gudurruy*
       Jja   *balam-dayi jawa-ŋga jajirra-ga* (EDIBLE-UP mouth-LOC
              bag-LOC) 'the food is in the bag right up to its mouth'

5.4 'No, nothing'

Monosyllabic response words *ŋa* 'yes' and *ŋu* 'alright' are the same across all dialects and in both Ev and Ja styles. However 'no' is more complex:

(23)   N, M, J   *yimba* 'no, nothing'
       Nja, Mja   *gamañjal*; Jja *jilbu*

Besides providing a negative response, 'no', the Ev word *yimba* can mean 'nothing' and then functions a little like a nominal. It can take emphatic suffix *-jilu/-ju* or contrastive/emphatic *-ban* (or both). And in J it can accept just one of the nominal case inflections, locative *-ŋga*. *Yimba-ŋga* indicates '(there is) nothing there'. Both *jilbu* and *gamañjal* play a role in Ja correspondents for adjectives.

Dyirbal has no verb 'know'. A speaker must be specific, stating what it is they know and how they know it. However, there are two adjectives 'don't know' and each was given *jilbu* as Jja correspondent:

(23)   Jja *jilbu*   given for   J *ŋañum* 'don't know', in answer to a question such
                                 as 'What's the name of that person/place?' or
                                 'How far away is that place?' or 'How do you
                                 make a boomerang?'
                                 J *juru* 'don't know', in answer to a question such as
                                 'Where is a certain person or place?, 'Was the
                                 creator being a man?'

There is a contrasting pair of Ev adjectives *ŋalma* 'belonging to oneself' and *yurrga* 'belonging to someone else'. The Jja correspondent for *yurrga* was given as *jilbu bala baŋul* (no THING HIS) 'no, it's his (sc. not mine)'.

Gamañjal also featured in a number of Ja correspondents for Ev adjectives:

(24)   N, M   *muña* 'finished, all gone (e.g. all the food is eaten, all the
                        people are dead)'
         Nja, Mja   *gamañjal*

(25)   M   *warru* 'empty (dilly-bag or water-bag); having holes in it
                        (vessel or blanket)'
         Mja   *gamañjal*

(26)   M, J   *gumun* 'blocked, shut (e.g. a road is blocked, a door is shut,
                        standing dumbfounded (mouth shut), being unable
                        to urinate)'
         Mja   *gamañjal-bin* 'become nothing'
         Jja   *jawa-ŋaŋgay* (mouth-WITHOUT) 'with no opening'

The Mja in (26) adds intransitive verbalizer *-bin* 'become' to *gamañjal*.
(Note that *-bin* is not attested with *yimba* in Ev.) The Jja here is a
description.

5.5 *Maŋgay* 'no good' and other evaluatives

Adjective *maŋgay* 'no good' in Mja and Jja—see (4)—is by far the most common word occurring in the Ja correspondents given for Ev adjectives. An Ev
adjective describing something which is unwelcome may simply be given the
Ja correspondent *maŋgay*; that is, Ja comments on the worth of the quality
rather than saying what the Ev adjective actually connotes. We can give just a
selection of the instances of this:

(27)   Jja *maŋgay* given for   J *julŋgu* 'nauseous, making one want to vomit
                                      (e.g. decaying flesh)'
                                 J *diñan* 'really dirty (of a place)'
                                 J *jiŋu* 'promiscuous, randy'
                                 J *malŋgal* 'always telling lies, answering
                                      questions untruthfully, making up things'
                                 J *jingarra* 'not wanting to accompany someone'

(28)   Mja, Jja *maŋgay* given for   M, J *dangal* 'stale, gone off, mildewed'
                                      M, J *marrgi* 'very thin (from illness)'

Sometimes one dialect has a specific Ja adjective and another will resort to *maŋgay*, as in:

(29)   M, J *jamar* 'bitter tasting (like quinine or lemon)'
     Mja *maŋgay*; Jja *ŋumuy*

(30)   M, J *muymur* 'sour (and salty) tasting'
     Mja *maŋgay*; Jja *ŋumuy*

It was mentioned in section 4.2 that *balam ŋumuy* is the Jja term for Ev *balam wuray* 'Davidson plum tree, *Davidsonia pruriens*.'

A Ja noun may be modified by *maŋgay* to describe something unwelcome:

(31)   Mja *jujamu maŋgay*   given for   M *ŋuju* 'dirty (water)'
     (water no.good)
     Mja *walin maŋgay*   M *gulbay* 'won't listen, pretends to
     (ear no.good)   be deaf'
     Jja *bilumu maŋgay*   J *wangay* 'crippled in one leg'
     (hip.bone no.good)

A regular Ja correspondent was given for some Ev adjectives and then *maŋgay* was added, as an ancillary comment. For example:

(32)   J   *jaŋa* 'making fun of things, making something into a joke in play, telling an obvious untruth in a joking way'
     Jja   *giyi$_s$ wiyama-ñu jalguba-ñu* (THIS.MAN do.why-PRES talk-PRES); *maŋgay* (no.good) 'why is this man talking in this way; (it's) no good'

Sometimes *maŋgay* was given first as the Ja correspondent for an Ev adjective, this then being expanded by an illustration of the negative quality, as in:

(33)   J   *birubuga* 'extremely lazy (won't do anything for himself, expects others to do it for him)'
     Jja   *maŋgay* (no.good); *baŋgun-dayi malŋi-nay-ma-li bayi yulmban-gani-ñu* (SHE.ERG-UP bring-ANTIPASS-APPLIC-PURP HE lie.down-CONTINUALLY-PRES) '(he's) no good; he just lies down all the time (expecting) her to bring (food to him)'

YaRbuR, the Nja adjective 'no good'—see (4)—has similar properties to *maŋgay* in Mja and Jja, although it is less common. For instance, the Ev adjective *muuga* 'blind' was given in Nja as *diŋaa yaRbuR* 'eye no good'.

The Ja for 'good' is the same across the three dialects (with the automatic alternation of rhotics):

(34)   N guRiñ; M, J jigil 'good'
        Nja ŋundaRiñ; Mja, Jja ŋundarriñ

Ja adjective, *ŋundaRiñ* or *ŋundarriñ* is sometimes given as the sole Ja correspondent of some quality which is valued (although there are fewer examples of this than of *maŋgay* and *yaRbuR*). These include:

(35)   Jja *ŋundarriñ*   given for   J *balgara* 'smooth, clear, empty, unimpeded'
                                        J *dungun* 'ripe (of a fruit)'
                                        J *jaŋal* 'sweet (honey, sugar, a drink, etc.)'
                                           [See example (45)]
                                        J *yayburru* 'willing, kind, generous'
                                        J *jalmiyuru* 'especially good looking (used
                                           of person, bird, animal)'
        Nja *ŋundaRiñ*   given for   N *manbaa* 'pretty (for example, of a girl)'

This Ja adjective may also be used with body parts. The Ev adjective *yarrgan* 'with a good memory, doesn't forget things, reliable' in J was accorded the Jja correspondent *jarrgumu ŋundarriñ* 'ears good'.

It was earlier noted that whereas precise specification is valued in Ev, the Ja style operates in more general terms. This is taken to an extreme for those adjectives which are just rendered as 'no good' or 'good' in Ja. The context would be likely to make clear whether 'no good' or 'good' was describing a property of a person or thing and what sort of property it was. It was not appropriate to conduct a really detailed discussion in Ja, just a general conspectus for which the available Ja correspondents suffice.

The most general dimensional adjectives also cover a range of meanings. Ev and Ja words 'big' were given in (3). The Ja terms have their meanings extended; for example:

(36)   Nja *gagiR* 'big'   given for   N *judajala* 'of large volume (e.g. a bag or
                                    bushy hair)'
                                 N *ŋagu* 'deep (water, hole)'
                                 N *bambun* 'in good health (used especially
                                    of regaining full health after an illness)'
                                    [see also (9)]

'Little' has the same form across all dialects (but for rhotic alternation) in
Ev and in Ja:

(37)   N, M, J *midi* 'little small (and younger sibling), a little of'
       Nja *wumbaR*; Mja, Jja *wumbarr*

This Ja adjective may also be used for various Ev adjectives referring to a
limited size. For instance:

(38)   N *wubil*; M, J *yagar*   'lightweight; mental state when worrying about
                                what has happened to a relative'
       Nja *wumbaR*; Mja *nalŋga*; Jja *walŋgu*

Example (8b) showed that Mja *nalŋga* also covers Ev adjective *bumba* 'dry'. Jja
walŋgu appears to be a unique correspondent for *yagar*. But for Nja I was just
given *wumbaR* 'little, small'. A similar example is:

(39)   N, M, J *gundun* 'short'
       Nja *ñingaa*; Mja *ñingal*; Jja *wumbarr*

Nja and Mja here have a specific correspondent (Mja *ñingal* was also given for
Ev adjective *burrin* 'near, close by' and—as mentioned in §4.3—for the noun
bala burumba 'a stump'). But just the general term *wumbarr* 'little, small' was
offered for Jja.

   Both *gagirr* 'big' and *wumbarr* 'little' are employed in the following Ja definition of an Ev noun:

(40)   M   *bayi/balan mirru* 'child who never grows big'
       Mja   *bayi_s wumbarr-bi-n, gulu gagirr-bi-n* (HE small-BECOME-PRES
            NOT big-BECOME-PRES) 'he is small and doesn't get big'

Adjective *wumbarr* was given in the Mja correspondent for two Ev nouns, *giñju* 'chick' and *guri* 'pet', but with a difference:

(41)   M *bayi/balan giñju* 'chicken, pup; young member of any non-human
          variety—wallaby, possum, dog, bird, even snake'
       Mja *bayi/balan wumbarr* 'little one'

(42)   M *bayi/balan guri* 'any young animal kept as a pet (also used of stuffed
          animals as toys)'
       Mja *ŋaygu wumbarr* (MY little) 'my little one'

The addition of possessive pronoun *ŋaygu* 'my' indicates that *guri* describes a small animal which is associated with a person, as a pet. (In this environment, only juvenile creatures could be pets.)

5.6 More complex correspondences

As would be expected, not every word has the same range of meaning across all dialects. This applies for the Ev adjective *guli*. Three senses may be recognized:

(43)   *guli*   (a)   in N, M, J: 'angry, savage, wild (of a person, dog,
                                       snake, etc.)'
                (b)   in N, M: 'sweet (sugar, honey, a drink)'
                (c)   in J: 'sharp (point or blade)'

The Ja correspondent for Ev adjective *guli* was given as *ŋulma* in all three dialects. However, just saying this does not fully explain things. It is sensible to recognize three separate dictionary entries:

(44)   N, M, J *guli* 'angry, savage, wild' (of a person, dog, snake, etc.)'
       Nja, Mja, Jja *ŋulma*

(45)   N, M *guli*; J *jaŋal* 'sweet (sugar, honey, a drink)'
       Nja, Mja *ŋulma*; Jja *ŋundarriñ* ('good')

(46)   N *gaRga*; M *garrga*; J *guli* 'sharp (point or blade)'
       Nja, Mja, Jja *ŋulma*

We see that:

- In Nja and Mja, *ŋulma* is the correspondent for both (a) and (b) senses of *guli* in Ev. And also for sense (c) which is expressed by *gaRga/garrga* in Ev. That is, *ŋulma* in Nja and Mja covers all of (a), (b), and (c), for which there are two separate adjectives in Ev.
- In Jja, *ŋulma* only relates to (a) and (c), the senses that are expressed by *guli* in Ev. For sense (b) J has *jaŋal* in Ev and the consultant just offered the evaluative *ŋundarriñ* 'good' in Jja. (See example (35).)

6 Summation

It was mentioned in §1 that other Australian languages have an avoidance vocabulary involving just a limited number of lexemes, these being substituted for the corresponding everyday word in everyday discourse. This may have been the case in proto-Dyirbal, as the first step on the way to the present-day situation.

The evidence suggests that the full Ja vocabulary developed quite late, after proto-Dyirbal had split into the modern set of dialects. Today, Ev and Ja are distinct styles, with no lexical overlap. The important point—repeatedly stressed to me by speakers—is that when speaking in the presence of an avoidance relative, only Ja words could be used. It was not permissible to include any Ev lexeme (except for the four grandparent/grandchild terms and *yañja/jañja* 'now').

We have seen that different techniques were employed in creating Ja correspondents for the various open word classes, and that most attention was given to verbs and to nouns. There was a Ja verb corresponding to each 'nuclear' verb in Ev, with a non-nuclear Ev verb being 'defined' in terms of the appropriate nuclear one. For nouns, including fauna and flora, there were in many cases just many-to-one Ev-to-Ja correspondences, on a fairly obvious basis. Only the most important foodstuffs were awarded a unique Ja correspondent.

It appears the Ja vocabulary was less well-developed for adjectives than for verbs and nouns. There were Ja correspondents for the most basic adjectival concepts (which are expressed in every language). Added to these were many-to-one correspondences which reflect the cognitive bent of Dyirbal speakers. For verbs and nouns the classification shown by Ja are in most cases pretty standard: one Ja term for all possums, one for all frogs, one for all lawyer vines, and so on. In contrast, the groupings for Ev adjectives—shown by a shared Ja correspondent—are illuminating and culture-specific. For instance, the fact that, as shown in (9). Mja *jagarri* links together 'fat', 'straight', 'intact', 'happy', and 'well-behaved'.

Basic adjectives—for dimension, age, colour, value, physical properties, etc.—are a sine qua non. Beyond these, Ev has many adjectives with rather specific, culturally-sensitive meanings. We can add one more to the several quoted above.

In all dialects, Ev noun *bala yabala* is 'flat ground'. The Mja correspondent for this was given as *bala nayŋu-rri-yarra-y* (throw-INTR-START-NOMINAL-IZER) 'started to be thrown out'. Just in M and J, *yalbara* is also used as an Ev adjective:

(47)   M, J *yalbara* 'everything is alright now after a period of trouble; everything is on an even plane again ('flat again'); for example: a dispute has been resolved and there are no grudges remaining; a period of mourning has finished and life returns to its normal course; feeling better now after having been sick; "free land", meaning that anyone can go there without needing permission'

Adjectives of this type are, in essence, luxuries. They are not absolutely necessary, and their meanings can be re-phrased. Such sophistication adds elegance to conversation in Ev, but is not needed within the more guarded register of Ja.

When asked how to express Ev adjective *yalbara* in Ja, the J consultant gave just the evaluative term *ŋundarriñ* 'good'; see (35). The correspondent proffered for Mja had two parts: *jagarri* 'satisfactory' as in (9), followed by *gulu ŋulma-bi-n* (NOT angry-BECOME-PRES) 'not angry now', which describes one of the circumstances for which *yalbara* would be appropriate. (This is the sense of *ŋulma* from (44).) (Note that adjective *jagarri* is not attested for Jja.)

As mentioned before, the nature of Ja correspondences for Ev lexemes provides a unique insight into the underlying semantic structure of the Dyirbal language, and its cognitive underpinnings. This is most apparent with adjectives. The fact that Ja forms for adjectives are sparser than those for verbs and nouns gives rise to value judgements and 'definitions' (in terms of Ja verbs) which are culturally revealing.

Appendix. Grammatical differences between Everyday and Avoidance styles

All grammatical affixes and clitics are identical between styles with one exception. In Ev, a noun marker (for example *yalu* 'TO.PLACE.HERE') may be immediately followed by a locational bound form (for example, *-gala* 'UP'), giving *yalu-gala*. The same applies for Jja. However, Mja inserts *-ŋulañ-* between the two parts, giving *yalu-ŋulañ-gala* (see the example in §4.1). Interestingly, *ŋulañ-* also features in Yidiñ Ja; see Dixon 1977: 503–4.

All personal pronouns and also 'who' and 'where' are the same in Ev and Ja. However, other interrogatives differ:

- N, M, J *miña* 'what'. Nja *mindiR*; Mja Jja mindirr.
- N, M, J *miñañ* 'how many'. Jja *minay*.
- N *miñaa*; M, J *miñay* 'when'. Jja also *minay*.

There are eighteen non-inflecting particles which apply over a clause; they include *gulu* 'not' and *yanda* 'tried and failed'. All are the same in Ev and Ja except for three:

- N *waRa*; M, J *warra* 'inappropriate S or O'. Nja *waRanda*; Mja *warranda*.
- N, M, J *mugu* 'couldn't help doing it'. Nja *buba*; Mja *mumba*.
- N *ŋuRi*; M, J *ŋurri* 'do in turn'; Nja *ŋuRñji*; Mja, Jja *ŋurrñji*.

(Where information on the Ja of some dialects is not given above, it is because it is not known.)

Conventions

DIALECTS (in north to south order):
N, Ngajan; M, Mamu; J, Jirrbal
SPEECH STYLES:
Ev, everyday style (NgiRma in N, Ngirrna in M, Guwal in J)
Ja, avoidance ('mother-in-law') style; Jalnguy in all dialects
Nja, Ngajan Jalnguy; Mja, Mamu Jalnguy; Jja Jirrbal Jalnguy

References

Dixon, R. M. W. 1971. 'A method of semantic description', in Danny D. Steinberg and Leon A. Jakobvits (eds), *Semantics, an interdisciplinary reader in philosophy, linguistics and psychology*. Cambridge: Cambridge University Press, 436–71.

Dixon, R. M. W. 1972. *The Dyirbal language of North Queensland*. Cambridge: Cambridge University Press. Reissued in 2009.

Dixon, R. M. W. 1973. 'The semantics of giving', in Maurice Gross, Morris Halle, and Marcel-Paul Schützenberger (eds), *The formal analysis of natural languages*. The Hague: Mouton, 205–23.

Dixon, R. M. W. 1977. *A grammar of Yidiñ*. Cambridge: Cambridge University Press. Reissued in 2010.

Dixon, R. M. W. 1980. *The languages of Australia*. Cambridge: Cambridge University Press. Reissued in 2010.

Dixon, R. M. W. 1982. *Where have all the adjectives gone? And other essays in semantics and syntax*. Berlin: Mouton. [Includes revisions of 1971, 1973.]

Dixon, R. M. W. 1990. 'The origin of "mother-in-law vocabulary" in two Australian languages', *Anthropological Linguistics* 32: 1–58.

Dixon, R. M. W. 1991. *Words of our country: Stories, place names and vocabulary in Yidiny, the Aboriginal language of the Cairns/Yarrabah region*. St Lucia: University of Queensland Press. Reissued as an e-book in 2012.

Dixon, R. M. W. 2002. *Australian languages: Their nature and development*. Cambridge: Cambridge University Press.

Dixon, R. M. W. 2015. *Edible gender, mother-in-law style, and other grammatical wonders: Studies in Dyirbal, Yidiñ, and Warrgamay*. Oxford: Oxford University Press. [Includes revision of 1990.]

Dixon, R. M. W. 2019. *Australia's original languages: An introduction*. Sydney: Allen & Unwin.

6

The ways of speaking and the means of knowing

The Tariana of north-west Amazonia

Alexandra Y. Aikhenvald

1 Preamble

Language, the society which speaks it, and the environment where the speakers live, are closely integrated and mutually supportive. Non-universal facets of a language may correlate with specific traits of social organization, beliefs, and life-style, including physical environment and subsistence. Each of these may be codified in grammar.

Chapter 1 of this volume addressed five groups of linguistic parameters and linguistic categories which show demonstrable correlations with non-linguistic societal traits: (1) reference classification; (2) types of possession; (3) directing and addressing; (4) information source, transmission of information, and inter-action patterns; and (5) special speech styles. This list is hardly exhaustive. For instance, the ways in which an event can be structured reflects cultural practices and environmental features (see Aikhenvald 2018a, for some examples).

Integration points are defined as features demonstrably indicative of the integration between language and society. They can be realized in specific semantic distinctions made within a grammatical category. And the frequency of a construction or a grammatical form may correlate with cultural conven-tions. For instance, in Tariana and Tucano, evidentials fused with tense in both languages, and in Tucano also with person, have to occur in every sen-tence, and thus very high in frequency. A cultural requirement for precision in stating one's information source can be seen as a correlate of this grammatical feature, and its obligatory—and thus recurrent—marking: we return to this in §5. The increased frequency of a form or a pattern may be considered a con-comitant factor in the maintenance and enhancement of an integration point.

Alexandra Y. Aikhenvald, *The ways of speaking and the means of knowing: The Tariana of north-west Amazonia*. In: *The Integration of Language and Society: A Cross-Linguistic Typology*. Edited by: Alexandra Y. Aikhenvald, R. M. W. Dixon, and Nerida Jarkey, Oxford University Press. © Alexandra Y. Aikhenvald 2021. DOI: 10.1093/oso/9780192845924.003.0006

As Du Bois (1985: 363) put it, 'grammars code best what speakers do most'. What they do most relates to their ways of life, beliefs, and social structure.

My focus here is on a number of integration points in Tariana, the only Arawak language spoken in the multilingual Vaupés River Basin area. After a brief background on Tariana and its neighbours and relatives in §2, I offer a summary of what the language is like, in §3. Three grammatical devices are then looked at as integration points. Each is highly frequent in every speech genre. The first two, discussed in §4, encompass reference classification— genders and classifiers. Tariana combines a small closed system of two genders (feminine and non-feminine) with a large system of multiple classifiers. The manipulation of genders correlates with the status of men and women, or their social gender (parameter A in Chapter 1). The multiple classifier system reflects the environment and means of subsistence (parameter E in Chapter 1).

A salient feature of Tariana and the neighbouring languages from the same region is evidentiality, or grammaticalized marking of information source. The choice of evidentials reflects (a) principles of interaction and attitudes to information (parameter C), (b) beliefs, spirits, and dreams (parameter D), and (c) access to information depending on the kinship relationship between speaker and addressee and speaker's status (parameter A). Evidentials are sensitive to language awareness and societal change (parameter F). These issues are discussed in §5. The final section contains a summary.

2 The Tariana of north-west Amazonia: Their relatives and neighbours

Tariana is an endangered Arawak language from north-western Amazonia (Brazil). Once a powerful language group, it is now reduced to about seventy speakers in two villages (Santa Rosa and Periquitos).

Tariana is spoken within the Vaupés River Basin linguistic area in north-west Amazonia known for its linguistic exogamy and multilingualism. The area spans adjacent regions of Brazil and Colombia (see Aikhenvald 2002, 2015, forthcoming).

The traditional Vaupés River Basin linguistic area is characterized by language-based exogamy between speakers of Tariana and those belonging to the East Tucanoan subgroup (including Tucano, Piratapuya, Wanano, and Desano). The general principle is that one can only marry someone who belongs to a different language group. One's affiliation to a language group is inherited through one's father, and gives one the right to be called a competent speaker and an owner of the language (more in Aikhenvald 2002, 2003, 2015: 75–83; comparable patterns of multilingualism are mentioned in §3 of Chapter 9).[1] Speakers say: 'those who speak the same language as us are our brothers, and we do not marry our sisters'. People who marry someone whose father speaks the same language as themselves are referred to as being 'like dogs' (*tsinu kayu-peni* 'dog like-PL.ANIM') (or, as phrased by the late Maria da Silva Brito, 'like Americans', *Americano kayu-peni*). According to the traditional language etiquette, one speaks one's father's language to one's father and siblings, and the addressee's father's language to other people.

Languages spoken in this area within the traditional marriage network include the East Tucanoan languages Tucano, Wanano, Desano, Piratapuya, Tuyuca (and a few others), and the Arawak language Tariana. Speakers of these languages participate in the exogamous marriage network, which ensures obligatory multilingualism. Each group has their preferential marriage partners, coming from a particular group. For the Tariana of Periquitos, preferential partners are the Wanano. For the Tariana of Santa Rosa, these are the Piratapuya. The late Maria da Silva Brito was a Piratapuya, by her father's group and language. Her mother was a Tariana, and her competence in Tariana was remarkable, though she herself downplayed it, as it was not 'her' language.

Traditionally, when a woman came to live in her husband's village, she was likely to encounter relatives who spoke the same language; her children would learn her language from her and would be fluent in it (more on this in Aikhenvald 2002 and references there, and Chernela 2004). A special status of women within the Vaupés society is defined by the fact women come from a different group, and are, in a sense, outsiders: we return to this in §4.2.

The main features of the Vaupés River Basin linguistic area defined by the exogamous marriage network are summarized in Aikhenvald (2015: 82; 2019b: 97).[2] All the Vaupés people share subsistence patterns (slash-and-burn agriculture).

The classificatory kinship system is the basis for interactions and social relations between the members of the marriage network within the Vaupés River Basin area—as in many other Amazonian groups. Kinship system is of

---

[1] The Colombian part of the area was first made famous by Sorensen (1967/72). However, Tariana is not spoken in Colombia, and the situation in Brazil is markedly different.
[2] A number of languages whose speakers belong to the Makú cultural complex are marginal members of the area, as they are not involved in the marriage network, do not practice linguistic exogamy, and are considered 'inferior' (a detailed discussion is in Aikhenvald forthcoming, 2015: 73–83, and references there).

Dravidian type (based on cross-cousin marriage). All the Tariana and the Desano are blood relatives. All the East Tucanoans are their affines. One's immediate core family (parents, siblings, children, and spouse) and classificatory family at large in Tariana can be distinguished through two grammatical means.

- Using the intensifier *-pu* with the term for a core, or a close, relative.

For instance, *haniri* can refer to one's blood father, one's father's older brothers, and one's classificatory father and his brothers. To talk about one's blood father, one will say *haniri-pu* (father-INTENS) 'real father'.

- Using a nonvisual evidential to refer to internal states of oneself and a member of one's core family—see §5.2.

This appears to be a feature shared with other languages of the Vaupés.

Every speaker of Tariana is fully proficient in at least one language from the unrelated East Tucanoan family. Languages one speaks are kept strictly apart. A striking feature of the Vaupés linguistic area is a strong cultural inhibition against language mixing, viewed in terms of borrowing forms, or inserting bits of other languages (especially East Tucanoan), into one's Tariana. This inhibition operates predominantly in terms of recognizable loan forms. The long-term interaction based on institutionalized societal multilingualism between unrelated languages—East Tucanoan versus Tariana—has resulted in rampant diffusion of grammatical and semantic patterns (rather than forms) and calquing of categories. Comparison of Tariana with closely related Arawak languages of Wapuí subgroup (such as the Baniwa of Içana-Kurripako dialect continuum, Piapoco, and Guarequena) helps identify which features have diffused into Tariana from Tucanoan languages and which are inherited from the proto-language.

3 What the Tariana language is like

Tariana is agglutinating with some fusion, and highly synthetic. Similarly to other Arawak languages, the few prefixes are cross-referencing markers, the attributive prefix *ka-* and its negative counterpart, the privative *ma-*. Other categories are expressed through suffixes or enclitics. Grammatical relations are marked with prefixes (on a split-S basis, as in most Arawak languages), and with cases. A topical non-subject case (*–naku* for traditional speakers,

–nuku for innovative speakers) is used to mark objects, beneficiaries, and other non-subject constituents more topical than the subject. A focussed subject case (*–ne/–nhe* for traditional speakers, *–ne* for innovative speakers) marks the subject which is in contrastive focus. Case-marking is one of the features Tariana developed as a consequence of its contact with East Tucanoan languages.

Almost the same set of prefixes marks possessor on (a) inalienably possessed nouns and (b) A/S$_a$ on verbs, and also the subject argument on nominalizations formed on prefixed verbs. The indefinite prefix is used on nouns, but is obsolescent on verbs. Table 1 shows the set of pronominal prefixes and of personal pronouns.

Open word classes are nouns and verbs. Nouns divide into inalienably possessed nouns (body parts, most kinship terms, important possessions, e.g. *nupitana* (1sg+name) 'my name'), which take the full set of prefixes (shown in Table 1), and optionally possessed nouns which do not take prefixes. Noun categories include case (topical non-subject, focussed subject, locative and instrumental-comitative), animacy, gender (feminine vs non-feminine), number (singular, collective, non-singular; associative non-singular for kinship terms and proper names only), nominal tense (future, past, unmarked/present), diminutive, augmentative, excessive, approximative, and classifiers (bound morphemes in multiple contexts). Underived adjectives constitute a closed class of about twenty members. Manner adverbs and time words are semi-open classes; closed classes include postpositions (most of them similar to obligatorily possessed nouns), demonstratives, interrogatives, quantifiers, and number words.

Table 1 Cross-referencing prefixes and pronouns

	SINGULAR		PLURAL	
	A/Sa/R	pronouns	A/Sa/R	pronouns
1nf/general	*nu–*	*nuha*	*wa–*	*w(a)ha*
1f				*w(a)ha-ma-pe* (we-CL: FEM-pl)
2nf/general	*pi–*	*piha, phia*	*i–*	*iha*
2f				*iha-ma-pe* (you.pl-CL: FEM-pl)
3nf	*di–*	*diha, dihya*	*na–*	*n(a)ha*
3f	*du–*	*duha, duhua*		*n(a)ha-ma-pe* (they-CL: FEM-pl)
impersonal	*pa–*	*p(a)ha*	-	-
indefinite(nouns only)	*i–*	-	-	-

Verbs divide into prefixed and prefixless. Prefixed verbs can be transitive, ambitransitive ($A = S_a$ or $O = S_a$), or active intransitive (S_a). Prefixless verbs are typically stative intransitive (of S_o or S_{io} type); some are $A = S_o$ ambitransitives. Categories of verbs are: person, number, and gender of A/S_a (for prefixed 'active' verbs), tense fused with evidentiality, degree, aspect, manner of action, valency-changing derivations (causative, applicative, and passive), degree, and negation. Verb structure is quite elaborate—with over twenty suffixal and enclitic positions.

Constituent order within clauses, and word order within noun phrases containing adjectives and modifiers from closed classes, is pragmatically determined. Traditional speakers have a slight tendency towards predicate-final order. Speakers of innovative Tariana prefer verb-final order (this feature is a sign of the Tucano influence).

4 Reference classification in Tariana as an integration point

A notable feature of Tariana, shared with related Arawak languages and their unrelated Tucanoan neighbours, is the co-existence of a small system of genders and a large system of classifiers in multiple contexts (cf. Aikhenvald 2019a). In §4.1, I offer an overview of the two kinds of reference classification in the language. The ways in which their meanings are integrated within societal practices and the environment are addressed in §§4.2–3.

4.1 Gender and classifiers in Tariana: A snap-shot

Feminine and non-feminine genders are distinguished in personal prefixes and personal pronouns—see Table 1. The two genders are also distinguished in a few more, limited, contexts. Derivational gender markers occur on kinship nouns; the nominal past marker and the relative clause marker inflect for gender. Gender is inherited from Proto-Arawak.

Classifiers in multiple contexts are a feature Tariana shares with other languages of north-west Amazonia (especially Tucanoan, Witotoan, and Tariana's closest relative Baniwa of Içana/Kurripako). Tariana has a large set of over 100 established classifiers.[3]

---

[3] In addition to these classifiers, Tariana employs the 'repeater', or 'autoclassifier', technique for nouns not subsumed under established classifiers, and for any inanimate noun under special

Classifiers are used (a) with number words, (b) with demonstratives, interrogatives, and modifiers of other closed word classes, (c) with adjectives, (d) in possessive constructions, and (e) as derivational markers on nouns. Example (1) comes from pedagogical materials created by a Tariana speaker. It illustrates the classifier *-dapana* 'habitat' in functions (b), (c), (d), and (e). Classifiers are in bold.

(1) ha-**dapana**   hanu-**dapana**   wa-ya-**dapana**
      DEM.INAN-CL:HABITAT   big-CL:HABITAT   1pl-POSS-CL:HABITAT
      di-tape-**dapana**-pena-nuka
      3sgnf-medicine-CL:HABITAT-NOM.FUT-PRES.VIS
      This big house of ours is a future hospital.

Classifiers can be used with a noun root to make its general meaning more specific. The following examples show how this happens.

(2) haiku   'tree, wood in general'
      haiku-**na**   'a tree'
      tree-CL:VERT
      haiku-**pi**   'palm-tree'
      tree-CL:LONG.THIN
      haiku-**kwa**   'flat cut on a tree'
      tree-CL:FLAT.SURFACE

Classifiers derive nouns from verbs, as in (3), and nouns from other nouns, as in (4).

(3) ka-ra-ka-**whya**
      ATTRIB-fly-THEMATIC-CL:CANOE
      plane (lit. flying canoe)

(4) ka-ra-ka-**whya-puna**
      ATTRIB-fly-THEMATIC-CL:CANOE- CL:ROAD
      airstrip (lit. road for flying canoe)

discourse conditions. Ongoing grammaticalization of some repeaters into classifiers makes it difficult to determine the exact number of classifiers (see Aikhenvald 2003).

Classifiers are also word-class changing derivations (see also (3)). In (5), the classifier -*ite* 'CL:ANIMATE' derives an adjective from a noun *di-tape-dapana* 'hospital' which contains the classifier -*dapana* 'habitation'.

(5) (tsiãri)   di-tape-**dapanite**
     (man)   3sgnf-medicine-CL:HABITAT+CL:ANIMATE
     (a man) belonging to a hospital; one who lives or works at a
     hospital, a nurse

Classifiers have numerous functions, and are often used anaphorically. Several classifiers can occur together, as shown in (4), (5), as well as in (6a) and (6b).

(6) a. wa-ya-**sawa**
         1pl-POSS-CL:GROUP
         our group (referring to a clan or a language group)

     b. wa-ya-**sawa-ite**
         1pl-POSS-CL:GROUP-CL:ANIMATE
         one belonging to our language group or to our clan

Genders and classifiers are independent systems. The choice of both is semantically transparent. They differ in their locus of marking and in their semantics— see Table 2.

In terms of their semantics, classifiers categorize inanimate referents in terms of their animacy, gender, shape, function, arrangement, etc. Animate referents are categorized in terms of their animacy and gender, and also arrangement (such as 'group' in (6a,b)).

In contrast, gender assignment is based on sex, or natural gender: an animate female will be assigned to the feminine gender, and the non-feminine

Table 2 Contrasting genders and classifiers in Tariana

Property	Genders	Classifiers
A. Locus of marking	cross-referencing prefixes (Table 1) personal pronouns (Table 1) derivational suffixes on nouns nominal past forms, relative clause markers	number words, adjectives, demonstratives, possessive constructions, nouns (as derivational markers), and in plural pronouns (Table 1)
B. Semantics	feminine versus non-feminine	animacy, gender, shape, function, arrangement, specific items

gender is used for all other animates and also for inanimates. Non-feminine is the functionally unmarked choice (in contrast to a few other languages of the Arawak family, including Lokono, Palikur: Green 2019, Aikhenvald and Green 2011, and Kampa languages: Mihas 2017).

The assignment of a classifier to a referent may vary, depending on the feature one wishes to highlight. This is one of the functions of classifiers—to disambiguate a polysemous referent (see Aikhenvald 2000: 307–37). The noun *uni* can refer to water (a mass noun) and to a waterway. A waterway *uni* accompanied by the adjectiuve *hanu-* 'big' can be referred to with different classifiers depending on its shape and size—see (7) (see also Table 7 in Aikhenvald 2019a).

(7) *uni hanu-pua* (big-CL:WATERWAY)   'big river'
     uni hanipa (big+CL:LARGE.SPACE)   'big, large river, large pool
                                             of water'

     uni hanu-kha (big-CL:CURVED)   'big, curved river'
     uni hanu-wani   'big river (as a location)'
        (big-CL:ABSTRACT.PLACES)
     uni hanu-nai (big-CL:LAKE)   'big, lake-like river'
     uni hanu-dawa (big-CL:CORNER)   'big bay in a river'
     uni hanu-pina (big-CL:SWAMP)   'big, swampy river'
     uni hanu-puna (big-CL:ROAD)   'big river (road-like) for
                                             canoe to travel'

     uni hanu-kwa (big-CL:FLAT.SURFACE)   'big river (with flat surface)'
     uni hanu-peku (big-CL:THIN.STRETCH)   'big narrow stretch of a river'
     uni hanu-thiwa (big-CL:HOLLOW)   'big ravine-like waterway'

The collective marker *-peri* is applicable to mass nouns only. When used with a modifier to *uni*, it describes the properties of a particular type of water, e.g. *uni pumeni-peri* (water sweet-COLLECTIVE) 'sweet water, juice, soft drink' and *uni kada-peri* (water black-COLLECTIVE) 'black water (in a river), coffee'.

In contrast, gender assignment is usually fixed. One notable exception appears to reflect societal values and can be considered an integration point.

4.2 Manipulation of gender as an integration point

Throughout Tariana stories and lore, women appear as strange and potentially dangerous beings who tend to wreak havoc and adversely affect the natural flow of things. Manioc (the starch staple across the area) is hard to peel, thanks to a woman—the daughter-in-law of the creator of the manioc Kali— breaching his ban on eating the first manioc until the time was ripe. If a man dreams of a woman before going hunting, he will fail to kill any game. Women are often referred to as *manihta-kadite* (NEG+think/reason-NEG+CL:ANIM) 'someone who does not think' and *pa-kalite-ka mhema-kadite* (IMPERS-talk-SEQ NEG+listen/hear-NEG-CL:ANIM) 'someone who does not listen to advice'.

In contrast, the term *tsiãri* 'man' has a positive value associated with courage and resilience. This is often contrasted with *inaru* 'woman'—in a story, a turtle encourages himself to be courageous and behave like man, not like a woman (examples are in Aikhenvald 2013: 65, 2019c: 103). The functionally unmarked term for 'person' is the same as 'man'. This is comparable to the use of 'generic' man and generic 'he' in many languages of the world, and a bone of contention in the recent literature and practice: (see Aikhenvald 2016: 185–211, and a case study in Cheshire 2008; see also §3.1 of Chapter 1).

Women are prohibited, under the threat of death, from catching a glimpse of the sacred Yurupary flutes or any paraphernalia of the Yurupary rites (they are believed to have been the owners of the flutes until men had snatched them from them). The Tariana used to have a special taboo register: a set of terms, most of them associated with the Yurupary rites, which women were not supposed to see, were, traditionally, 'hidden' from women, and for which replacement forms were in use (Aikhenvald 2019b contains a full account of what is known of these forms; further examples of women treated as a 'dangerous other' are in Aikhenvald 2013). Women's physical states (being pregnant or menstruating) are often referred to as *puaya* 'adverse, strange, different from normal'.

Even nowadays, women—wives and mothers—are blamed for the decline of the Tariana language, as they are said to be at fault for not passing the children's fathers' language on to the children. When Elvia, a Tucano woman and a teacher in the Tariana school in Iauaretê, was getting married to a Tariana man, her father said to her, 'You will now kill his language, this is what women do' (Aikhenvald 2016: 180–1). In actual fact, the demise of the Tariana language was due to a combination of factors—including the policy of the Salesian missionaries of the order of Dom Bosco to put an end to the heathen multilingualism and impose Tucano (already a majority language), taking children to dormitories away from their parents. Add to this the lengthy absences of men forced into employment on rubber and other plantation by white invaders. At present, the rhetoric of accusation appears to be shifting: that children hardly know any Tariana is said to be the fault of the school system. Since most teachers are women anyway, this may well come to the same thing.

This attitude to women may have its roots in the society where the language is spoken. Among the Tariana, and throughout all traditional communities in the Vaupés, women used to come from a language group different from men. Brüzzi (1977: 371–4) goes as far as saying that women have traditionally been 'outsiders' and 'strangers' within their husbands' villages.[4] It stands to reason that women are potentially dangerous outsiders. The status of women among the Tariana and within the Vaupés linguistic area in general is unlike what Ciucci describes for the Ayoreo—another example of reference classification as an integration point between language and society (§8 of Chapter 8, this volume).

A particularly important and respected female can be 'promoted' to the status of an honorary man, by using the non-feminine singular cross-referencing prefix *di-* and the non-feminine singular pronoun *diha* 'he' (see Table 1). The gender switch, from feminine to masculine, can be considered a point of integration between language and societal attitudes in Tariana.

The woman-creator Nanayo appears in a number of stories (depicted by different speakers as either the daughter or the wife of the Trickster-Creator *Yapirikuri*). As different groups of people, including the Indians and the white people, emerge from the waters around the Ipanoré rapids, she names the people, tells them where they will live, and distributes the goods. She is referred to with the feminine pronoun *duha* 'she' and the feminine cross-referencing prefix *du-*, up until a turning a point in a story. She shows the people a coin (note the Portuguese word for 'money', *dinheiro,* accompanied by the classifier *-kwema* 'round object') and asks how much it is worth. At this point, she is referred to with the non-feminine prefix and the non-feminine pronoun—as if to highlight her importance and agency. Cross-referencing prefixes are in bold in this section.

(8) Ne-sina   **du**-sata   dhuma   *feminine marking*
     then-REM.P.ASSUM   3sgf-ask   3sgf+hear
     Then she asked,
     Hĩ   Yeposeri   dinheiro-kwema   pa:-kwema
     DEM:ANIM   Indian   money-CL:ROUND   one-CL:ROUND

---

[4] An incisive account of the status of women among the Wanano, an East Tucanoan group in the Vaupés, by Chernela (2003), is applicable across the board to all the riverine groups, including the Tariana (see also Chernela 2011; C. Hugh-Jones 1979: 49–52; Brüzzi 1977: 373).

di-sue-ta-sina   ne-nuku   *non-feminine marking*
3sgnf-stay+CAUS-CAUS-REM.P.ASSUM   then-TOP. NON.A/S
He (=she) put a coin (to) this Indian,

dinheiro   pa:-kwema
money-CL:ROUND   one-CL:ROUND
di-sue-ta-sina
3sgnf-stay+CAUS-CAUS-REM.P.ASSUM
He (=she) put the coin,

Dihya   Yeposeri-nsuku   **diha**
he/the   Indian- TOP. NON.A/S   he
di-sata-sina   dhima   **di**-keñua
3sgnf-ask-REM.P.ASSUM   3sgnf+hear   3sgnf-start
He (=she) started asking the Indian,

Hĩ   kayda-nha   kaweni,
DEM:ANIM   how.much-PRES.VIS.INTER   be.worth
di-a-sina.
3sgnf-say-REM.P.ASSUM
How much is it worth, he (=she) asked

The Indian didn't know what the coin was worth. The white man did, and this is why white people are said to be rich in money. The woman creator then goes on to distributing bows and arrows to Indians. (At that point gender marking switches back to feminine; different versions of this origin myth are discussed in Aikhenvald 2013: 70–2). The gender switch always comes at the climax of the story, when the Woman-Creator asks the crucial question. At the point when the Woman creator tells the people that they were to be the way they are now, she is also referred to with the non-feminine *di-*, as shown in (9).

(9)   diwesewya-nuku   hya-ka-mhade   i-dia-niki
       then-TOP. NON.A/S   2pl-DECL-FUT   2pl-stay-COMPL
       di-a-sina   nekana   *non-feminine marking*
       3sgnf-say-REM.P.ASSUM   3pl+chief
       'And then 'you will stay (the way you are)', said (he=she) the chief (woman Nanayo).

No gender switches were attested in the stories where Nanayo was behaving in a 'wayward' womanly way, going against orders given by the Creator.

In a story about a shaman told by the late Cândido Brito (the most knowledgeable elder), the non-feminine singular cross-referencing is employed to refer to an important female participant, the shaman's wife. The term for 'wife' bears the feminine derivational marking, and yet the agreement marker on the verb is non-feminine.

(10) kani-nha   nu-daki-ru,   *non-feminine*
      where-PRES.VIS.INTER   1sg-grandchild-FEM
      di-a-pidana   di-sa-do-peru
      3sgnf-say-REM.P.REP   3sgnf-spouse-FEM-OLD:FEM
      'Where is my granddaughter?', said (he=she) his old wife (feminine).

We can recall from §2 that, according to the Vaupés principles of language allegiance, Tariana was not Maria's language (her father was a Piratapuya). Her mother was a Tariana, and she herself knew the Tariana language very well indeed, and used to help her sons remember the traditional terms which had slipped them. She was often referred to with non-feminine prefixes, in her absence (when commenting on her proficiency in Tariana). In (11), a non-feminine prefix was used to say how happy she was about me coming back.

(11) duha   mača-peri   puwhi   **di**-wa-nipe-ne-mha
      she   good-COLL   be.glad   3sgnf-enter-NOMZ-INST-PRES.NONVIS
      alia
      EXIST
      She is very happy indeed. (lit. (She) is with good feeling of (his=hers) being glad)

In many languages of the world, linguistic gender reversal is a mark of offence, praise, endearment, affection, affinity, solidarity, or camaraderie (see detailed discussion in Aikhenvald 2016: 101–9, and references there; see also Nübling 2017, Christen 1998 on endearing overtones of gender switches in Swiss German and other German dialects). Similar to Tariana, women can be referred to with masculine rather than with feminine gender among the Jarawara, an Arawá-speaking group of southern Amazonia, 'as a mark of affinity and of respect towards them' (Dixon 2004: 287). Switching from masculine to non-masculine gender in reference to men in Machiguenga and Ashéninka Perené is a feature of joking register in contexts meant to be somewhat grotesque (Glenn Shepard, p.c. in Aikhenvald 2016: 102; Mihas 2019). In each of these cases, one might look for a societal explanation to do with the status of women. The lowly societal status of women in the Perené society may well be responsible for a somewhat offensive jocular effect of gender switch from masculine to non-masculine gender (Mihas 2019: 142–3).

To summarize: switches from feminine to non-feminine gender in Tariana are indicative of the special status of individual women to whom this can be applied. As soon as a woman is considered important or knowledgeable, she will be treated—grammatically—on a par with a man, the 'unmarked' human being. Gender switch implies adding value.

Let's now turn to the parameters within Chapter 1 (§3.1 there). Gender switch in Tariana reflects A, relations within the community. As Tariana is gradually becoming obsolescent, the gender switches are falling out of use. Speakers of Innovative Tariana do not use them and accept them as grammatical in the stories told by their elders only because of the elders' authority.

In all likelihood, the demise of gender switch in Tariana is linked with three groups of societal factors indicative of Parameter F—sensitivity to social change:

(a) a gradual but imminent disintegration of linguistic exogamy, exacerbated by the loss of indigenous languages other than Tucano;

(b) obsolescence of origin myths and traditional stories among the Tariana, exacerbated by the demise of knowledgeable elders who could authoritatively tell such stories (see also §5.6);

(c) changing roles of women within the indigenous society, their growing economic independence (thanks to the activities of the Women's Association supported by the Catholic church), and enhancement of employment opportunities, especially as teachers. Women taking men's place and acquiring a higher status in the society is no longer a rarity.

The loss of the gender switch alerts us to another issue—that of 'disintegration' of the foundations of the society which may result in the obsolescence and eventual loss of integration points (see §4 of Chapter 7 on Murui, an unrelated language spoken in the Colombian Amazonia). Similar instances of 'disintegration' have been attested in other languages affected by obsolescence (see §3.1 of Chapter 1, on the radical reduction of numeral classifier system in the obsolescent Nivkh, concomitant with the loss of traditional fishing practices).

4.3 Meanings of classifiers as an integration point

Correlating physical properties encoded in classifier systems with physical—or cultural—environment of the speakers is hardly easy. Denny (1979: 108–15) attempted to determine links between the environment and the parameter of visibility in deictic classifiers, and also between interioricity as a parameter in classifier systems and existing technologies, land ownership, and social rank. Suggestive as they may sound, such hypotheses are hard to prove. It is in the domain of highly specific classifiers—categorizing particular objects and the ways they can be perused—that we are likely to find indisputable correlations between environment, subsistence techniques, and language.

Similar to the majority of neighbouring languages with classifiers, classifiers in Tariana are assigned to a noun referent on the basis of universal properties—animacy, gender, shape, and arrangement. Forty-nine of about 100 classifiers characterize the referent in terms of its functions. The meanings of many of these reflect environmental features, means of subsistence and ways of life, and cultural preoccupations of speakers. They can be considered integration points, along the lines of §3.1 in Chapter 1.[5]

The Tariana are river-dwellers. The Tariana-speaking villages are located on the banks of the Vaupés, the major river. Canoes are a major means of transportation. The existence of a classifier for 'canoe', -*whya*, can be considered an integration point: we would not expect a society of desert dwellers to have such a classifier. The classifier is extended to cover any means of transportation, including a car, *ka-koloka-whya* (ATTRIB-roll-THEM-CL:CANOE) 'car' (a rolling canoe) and a 'plane ('a flying canoe' in (3)) (similar to Murui-Muina and other Witotoan languages spoken in the neighbouring area: see Wojtylak 2020 and Chapter 7, this volume).

Furthermore, classifiers reflect a taxonomic categorization of plants (something that could be done lexically in other languages). Classifiers distinguish a palm from a tree, as we saw in (2). Environmental features reflected in classifiers mirror numerous aspects of the waterways, relevant for a navigator. The classifiers which refer specifically to environmental properties are listed in Table 3 (see also (7)). Each of these classifiers are used in multiple contexts outlined in §4.1. Shape classifiers can also refer to features associated with a river: this is what we see in the first five lines of (7).

---

[5] See Aikhenvald (2000: 272–5), for general principles of semantic choice of classifiers; further references and examples of how classifiers reflect features of societies and the way people live are in Aikhenvald (2000: 342–6). A comprehensive list of classifiers in Tariana is in Aikhenvald (2003: 89–92, 2019b).

Table 3 Classifiers which reflect environmental features

CLASSIFIER	SEMANTICS
RIVERINE FEATURES	
-kiyere, -kyere	island
-kuya	extended part (of a river)
-nai	lake
-patawa	gorge
-numa(na)	mouth of river, also word, language
-pina	swampy area of a river or a lake
-pua	river, riverway
-pukuipe	turn (of river)
-taku	promontory, cape (of a river)
-thiwa	ravine-like waterway
OTHER ENVIRONMENTAL FEATURES	
-khay, khe	thick jungle
-peda	low bush, small heap
-pukuda	a bigger bush
-purikuda	mountain, small hill
-pusita	clearing

Table 4 Classifiers for means of procuring food, subsistence, and material culture

CLASSIFIER	SEMANTICS
IMPLEMENTS	
-(i)thepu	bow
-iwai, -wi	trap, wall, fence
PATCHES OF PLANTS	
-lima	patch of naturally growing plants
-liki	plantation
MANIOC	
-ki	manioc (staple)
-kuthe	manioc bread (staple starch)

The sheer number of these classifiers reflects the Tarianas' cultural preoccupation with the riverine environment—the backbone of their subsistence.

Table 4 features classifiers which reflect the common means of procuring food, material culture, and subsistence, including types of plantations, relevant for the Tariana as slash-and-burn agriculturalists.

Of these, the classifier *-iwai* (Traditional Tariana), *-(i)wi* (Innovative Tariana) refers to traps used for small rodents and fish. The classifier *-(i)thepu* 'bow' is specific to 'bow' as the main hunting instrument in the traditional times.

Two classifiers distinguish naturally growing patches, e.g. *yeka-lima* 'place where rubber trees grow', *puperi-lima* 'place where peach palm grows', *manaka-lima* 'place where açai grows' and man-made plantations, e.g. *abiu-liki* (abiu.fruit-CL:PLANTATION) 'plantation of abiu-fruit', *kainiki-liki* 'plantation of manioc'. This distinction reflects an essential feature of the Tariana subsistence— their dependence on slash-and-burn agriculture and thus on planted crops.

Manioc is the staple starch for the Tariana and other peoples of the region, so it appears to be appropriate for the language to have a special classifier for different types of *kaini* 'manioc (in general)', e.g. *kaini-ki* (manioc-CL:MANIOC) 'individual manioc plant', *da:pi-ki* (liana-CL:MANIOC) 'liana-like manioc', *de:ri-ki* (banana-CL:MANIOC) 'banana-like manioc', *kanali-ki* 'mirror-CL:MANIOC) 'mirror-like manioc'. Manioc bread (*pethe, paithe*) is the major type of starch consumed by the Tariana. No wonder it warrants a special classifier (*-kuthe*).

Where do specific classifiers come from? A number of classifiers which reflect environmental features and subsistence originate in nouns, e.g. *-kyere* 'CL:ISLAND' from *kewere* 'island', *-taku* 'CL:PROMONTORY' from *-taku* 'nose, extremity' and *-numana* 'CL:MOUTH.OF.RIVER', from *-numa-na* (mouth-POSS) 'someone's mouth'. The origin of others is unknown. For most of them, a corresponding noun is formed using the dummy root *maka-* followed by the classifier, e.g. *maka-pina* (GEN.ADJ-CL:SWAMPY.AREA) 'swamp', *maka-pukui* means 'stretch of a river', and *maka-thiwa* 'ravine' (the dummy root+classifier construction is a result of East Tucanoan influence: Aikhenvald 2002: 94–5).

The frequency of classifiers in Tariana narratives confirms their centrality in the grammar of the language (the ratio is 1/10 for nouns compared with classifiers in terms of token frequency). In casual conversations, especially when discussing environmental features and place-names on boat journeys, the frequency is 1/20: the object can be pointed at, and is anaphorically referred to with a classifier only.

Language endangerment does not appear to have any effect on the system of classifiers in Tariana, for two reasons. First, despite the slow advent of modern technologies, subsistence and living patterns remain the same as they have been for hundreds of years. Secondly, Tucano, the major language the Tariana are currently switching to, has a very similar system of multiple classifiers (its comprehensive analysis remains a matter for further investigation). In this instance, contact between peoples with similar life-styles reinforces the integration points in their languages.

5 Information source and access to knowledge

A salient feature of Tariana and the East Tucanoan languages from the Vaupés River Basin linguistic area is a complex and obligatory system of evidentiality, or grammaticalized marking of information source. The choice of evidentials reflects principles of interaction, attitudes to information, access to information, beliefs, spirits, and dreams. Evidentials are sensitive to social and technological changes. Speakers are aware of the reasons for their use and are prepared to discuss them. That is, as shown in §3.4 of Chapter 1, evidentials are typically indicative of the parameters in A, and C–F.

5.1 Evidentials in Tariana: Their meanings and their forms

Tariana has a five-term system of grammatical evidentials. Their main function is to express information source. Just like other evidential systems, they have nothing to do with 'truth', nor with having 'evidence' for what one says (as one would have 'evidence' in court). The major meaning of evidentials is how one knows things (and not whether this is true or whether one has 'proof'). If the audience doubts the speaker's information source, the speaker can add justification as 'evidence' for what they are saying—for instance, adding a lexical explanation 'I saw it' or 'I heard it'.

One can easily tell a lie by manipulating evidentials—all one has to be is smart enough. There are two options—to deliberately use the wrong evidential, and thus tell a lie about how one knows things. Or to use the correct evidential, and the wrong facts (examples are in Aikhenvald 2004: 98–9, 136). One can also make a wrong inference, or an incorrect assumption.

Tariana evidentials are used in main clauses only. A larger set of evidentials occurs in declarative clauses, and a reduced set is used in questions (see §5.5). Commands employ one evidential (reported, meaning 'do something on someone else's order'). This is consistent with many other languages of the world (see Aikhenvald 2004, 2018b).

Evidential markers in Tariana are fused with tense: present (zero-marked), recent past (marked with the suffix -ka), or remote past (suffix -na). The inferred and the assumed evidential have no present tense forms. The semantics of tenses correlates with the time of the happening and the time of when the information was first acquired (Aikhenvald 2003: 289–90). So, the remote past visual evidential will refer to something the speaker has seen a long time ago and can see right now as well. The markers themselves are 'floating clitics':

Table 5 Evidentials and tense in affirmative clauses in Tariana

Labels	present	recent past	remote past
Visual	*-naka*	*-ka*	*-na*
Nonvisual	*-mha*	*-mahka*	*-mhana*
Inferred	-	*-nihka*	*-nhina*
Assumed	-	*-sika*	*-sina*
Reported	*-pida*	*-pidaka*	*-pidana*

they tend to have the predicate as their host, but can attach to any focussed constituent. No evidentiality distinctions are made in the future (which is what one would expect).

The forms of evidentials in three tenses are listed in Table 5.

Evidentials as exponents of information source have the following meanings.

- VISUAL EVIDENTIALS are used if the speaker has seen the event or the state, or the event can be easily observed.
- NONVISUAL EVIDENTIALS refer to something heard, or smelt, or felt by touch (or something one can not quite discern).
- INFERRED EVIDENTIALS refer to something inferred based on visible results: for instance, that it has rained because one can see the puddles, or that someone has eaten chicken because their hands are greasy.
- ASSUMED EVIDENTIALS are used if a statement is based on reasonable assumption and general knowledge.
- REPORTED EVIDENTIALS are employed if the information comes from a speech report by someone else.

The following examples illustrate five real-life situations. Evidentials were straightforwardly used to express different information sources for the speaker (from author's fieldwork, 2012). (Chicken is expensive and is prized as 'prestige food', so the comments were made in the context of showing how rich and corrupt the uncle was). Evidentials are in bold throughout this section. Note that Tariana evidentials do not have any modal or epistemic overtones.

(12) Nu-nami   karaka   di-merita-**naka**
      1sg-father's.younger.brother   chicken   3sgnf-fry-**PRESENT.VISUAL**
      My younger uncle is frying chicken. (I (the speaker) see him)

(13)   Nu-nami   karaka
       1sg-father's.younger.brother   chicken
       di-merita-**mha**
       3sgnf-fry-**PRESENT.NONVISUAL**
       My younger uncle is frying chicken. (I can smell, but cannot see, the
       fried chicken)

(14)   Nu-nami   karaka
       1sg-father's.younger.brother   chicken
       di-merita-**nihka**
       3sgnf-fry-**INFERRED.RECENT.PAST**
       My younger uncle has fried chicken. (I see bits of grease stuck on his
       hands and he smells of fried chicken)

(15)   Nu-nami   karaka
       1sg-father's.younger.brother   chicken
       di-merita-**sika**
       3sgnf-fry-**ASSUMED.RECENT.PAST**
       My younger uncle has fried chicken. (I assume so: he gets so much
       money he can afford it, and he looks like he has had a nice meal)

(16)   Nu-nami   karaka
       1sg-father's.younger.brother   chicken
       di-merita-**pidaka**
       3sgnf-fry-**REPORTED.RECENT.PAST**
       My younger uncle has fried chicken. (I was told recently)

Just like members of any closed grammatical system, evidentials are semantically complex. They may combine reference to the information source of the
speaker and of the addressee (see also §3.4 of Chapter 1), along the following lines.

- FIRST, the use of evidentials may reflect access to knowledge (for which
  other languages may have a special category of egophoricity: see Aikhenvald
  2018b, for a summary). Access to knowledge expressed via evidentials
  may reflect established social relations, including kinship relations and
  speaker's status.
- SECONDLY, attitudes to information may underlie the way evidentials
  are used.

- THIRDLY, the cultural environment in the form of beliefs, religion, spiritual world, and dreams may correlate with conventionalized patterns of evidential use.

If the speaker has access to more than one information source (which is typically the case), visually obtained information, if available, is preferred over any other information source (Barnes 1984: 262 reported the same principle for Tuyuca, an East Tucanoan language spoken in the Colombian Vaupés; see also Aikhenvald 2004: 307–8). The next preferred choice will be nonvisual evidential, then inferred based on visible results, then reported, and only then the assumed. However, the actual choice of evidentials will vary depending on:

(a) what kind of access speaker has to information,
(b) the type of information, and
(c) the status of the speaker.

This is what we will see in §5.2–7. The issue of 'preferred' evidential is much more complex, and culturally embedded, than is assumed by superficial formalist approaches with their artificial focus on the 'best' evidential (see Aikhenvald 2018b). There is no 'best' or 'worst' evidential—to decide what is appropriate and what is not under what circumstances, one needs to have more than a one-dimensional 'hierarchy'.

Specific integration points in the use of evidentials concern access to information determined by established social relationships, and by religion and beliefs—this is what we turn to next.

5.2 Special access to information: Internal states

The nonvisual evidential in Tariana is used for what cannot be seen—one's physical and mental states, including illness, suffering, fever, and also thought, sadness, happiness. When talking about oneself, the speaker uses the nonvisual evidential.[6]

An example is in (17). Batista Brito is talking about his work for a white man on rubber extraction where he caught a fever (or rather, a fever 'got' him); he had almost died and was feeling weak.

---

[6] This phenomenon has been described as 'first person effect' (Aikhenvald 2004: 224–5), or as 'endophoric' meaning (Aikhenvald 2018b: 26; Sun 2018).

(17) Madali-da   i-pumina   nu-na   adaki
      three-CL:ROUND   INDEF-after   1sg-OBJ   fever
      dhipa-**mhana**   kaiperi.   Tuki
      3sgnf+get-**REM.P.NONVIS**   pain-COLL   little
      nu-yami-maya-**mhana**   nu-yena.
      1sg-die-ALMOST-**REM.P.NONVIS**   1sg-exceed
      Nhua   meyakude-**mhana**.
      I   lacking.strength-**REM.P.NONVIS**
      Three (days) later fever got me, painful (fever), I well and truly almost
      died (lit. to excess), I was lacking strength.

The choice of evidential can be considered tantamount to person marking.
Personal pronouns are often omitted, and in this instance the first person
reference is clear from the context. The rest of the story is cast in remote past
visual, as befits an autobiographic narrative (see §5.6).

Internal physical and mental states of someone other than oneself have to
be described using a different evidential. It can be visual, if the speaker can
see what happened to a third party (as in (18)). Or it can be inferred, if
one can see visual traces of the event. A further option would be to use the
assumed evidential, if the statement is based on reasoning (as in (19c)).

In (18), from the same story as (17), the speaker talks about his companions
whom he had seen being taken with fever. He uses visual evidential, as they
were visibly sick.

(18) Na-na-pita   adaki   dhipa-**na**-pita.
      3pl-OBJ-AGAIN   fever   3sgnf+get-**REM.P.VIS**-AGAIN
      Paita   di-yami-maya-**na**   di-yena
      one+CL:ANIM   3sgnf-die-ALMOST-**REM.P.NONVIS**   3sgnf-exceed
      Fever got them again. One well and truly almost died. (lit. to excess)

The evidentials used to talk about one's own feelings and physical and emotional states occur in statements about other people only if the speaker has a
close kinship relationship with the addressee or a third person. In (19), a
speaker comments on her own state of being dizzy (on a day of heavy drinking), using the nonvisual evidential.

(19) yali-**mha**-niki   nu-na
      be.dizzy-**PRES.NONVIS**-COMPL   1sg-OBJ
      I am dizzy. (lit. dizzy to me)

In (20), produced on the same occasion, the speaker comments about how others (whom we could not see at the moment) feel: one assumes that since they have all been drinking for a long time, they will be dizzy, hence the assumed evidential.

(20)   yali-**sina**   na-na
       be.dizzy-**REM.P.ASSUMED**   3sg-OBJ
       They are dizzy (assumed).

A comment in (21) was made by the same speaker about her younger brother—she used the nonvisual evidential to refer to his state of being dizzy as if she could feel what he felt.

(21)   di-yena   keru   yali-**mha**   di-na
       3sgnf-exceed   be.angry   be.dizzy-**PRES.NONVIS**   3sgnf-OBJ
       He is very angry (and) dizzy.

Someone who is not the speaker is treated as if they were: the speaker has intimate knowledge about his close family members and talks about them as if talking about their own self. This is what Sun (2018: 55–6) refers to as 'upgraded' access to intimate knowledge: in many Tibeto-Burman languages (including Taku and Japhug Rgalrong), an egophoric marker denoting 'personal access' is extended to cover someone closely associated with the speaker—in all examples quoted this far, to members of the speaker's family. Such 'epistemological rights'—to refer to other peoples' states and feelings as if they were one's own—are determined by the boundaries of the immediate, or core, family. In this way, the choice of an evidential correlates with kinship relations: it is a means of setting one's immediate family apart from a wider network of classificatory kin (as mentioned in §2).

5.3 'Reduced information access': Lack of control

A nonvisual evidential may refer to something that the speaker did accidentally, not being in control or aware of what was being done. In (22), the speaker broke the pot accidentally—as if not looking properly. The nonvisual evidential is used:

(22)   episi-aphi-nuku   nu-thuka-**mahka**
       iron-CL:POT-TOP.NON.A/S   1sg-break-**REC.P.NONVIS**
       I broke the pot accidentally.

In (23), the speaker broke the pot on purpose (it was cracked anyway, and of no use).

(23)   episi-aphi-nuku   nu-thuka-**ka**
       iron-CL:POT-TOP.NON.A/S   1sg-break-**REC.P.VIS**
       I broke the pot on purpose.

The nonvisual evidential can also be used to refer to aimless actions. A man—desperate because he couldn't get a wife and had no money—ran off into the jungle. There, he encountered a beautiful white woman—she turned out to be a dangerous Fish-woman who had come to lure him into her enchanted abode. In (24), the man tells the woman what he is doing in the jungle: his description of 'aimlessly walking around' is cast as 'I walk around-nonvisual'.

(24)   hiku   nu-ni   nu-emhani-**mha**   awakada-se
       like.this   1sg-do   1sg-walk.around-**PRES.NONVIS**   jungle-LOC
       I am walking aimlessly in the jungle like this.

The visual evidential effectively carries additional overtones of responsibility one takes for one's actions (one of the typical extensions of visual and direct evidentials across the world: Aikhenvald 2018b).

The distinction between accidental and purposeful action via evidentials is normally restricted to first person (this is part of the 'first person effect' in evidentials: see also Sun 2018: 57–8). A nonvisual evidential with second or third person usually implies that the speaker did not have access to visual information.

In addition, similar to what we saw in §5.2, a nonvisual evidential can be used to describe an accidental action by third (or second) person if the speaker talks about a close family member. Raimundo's little son badly cut his finger, and the boy was brought to me to help put a dressing on. Raimundo explained what had happened saying (25).

(25)   di-kapi-da-tiki-nuku   di-pisa-**mahka**
       3sgnf-hand-CL:ROUND-DIM-TOP.NON.A/S   3sgnf-cut-**REC.P.NONVIS**
       (a) He cut his finger. (I didn't see it happen)
       (b) He cut his finger accidentally.

This sentence can be interpreted in two ways. Reading (a), a straightforward nonvisual, would have been correct if Raimundo hadn't been there when the child had cut his finger playing with a knife. But Raimundo was there; so the reading (b) was the appropriate one.

The 'accidental action' overtone (referred to as 'reduced information access' by Sun 2018: 56–8) has only been attested when speaking about a close member of one's blood family—a child, a close sibling, or a parent. This is another means by which immediate family is singled out among classificatory relatives at large.[7]

5.4 What cannot be seen with human eye: Dreams, spirits, and shamans

The nonvisual evidential can be used to refer to something one cannot quite see. It is also the preferred choice in talking about one's own dreams. People rely on dreams in predicting the reality of the day; and yet the dreams by a common mortal without any special supernatural powers are treated as if they are not quite what one sees in reality. In (26), Olívia Brito describes the dream she had the night before her father, the late Cândido Brito, had passed away (see also example 14.37 in Aikhenvald 2003: 298).

(26) nu-haniri   di-ñami-karu   i-peya   nuhua-misini
      1sg-father   3sgnf-die-PURP   INDEF-before   I-too
      hi-nuku   tapulisa-**mhana**
      DEM.ANIM-TOP.A/S   dream-**REM.P.NONVIS**
      tapuli-se   paika   nu-kapi-se   dhita-**mhana**
      dream-LOC   father   1sg-hand-LOC   3sgnf+take-**REM.P.NONVIS**
      Before my father died, I too dreamt of this (nonvisual), in the dream
      Dad took me by the hand.

When I asked another speaker, Jovino, why he did not use the visual evidential in talking about a bad dream he had just had, his answer was (27):

---

[7] In traditional stories, talking about the actions or whereabouts of the members of one's immediate family tends to require visual or inferred evidential. When a character uses a reported evidential to talk about a spouse, this is recognized as either a means of distancing oneself from their relative, or as an instance of lying by using the wrong evidential (see examples in Aikhenvald 2004: 98, 136). At present, hardly any family can afford to live up to these expectations, since people often travel to faraway places and lose touch with one another for a long time. The relaxation of such a requirement may be seen as a 'disintegration' point.

(27) ma-ka-kade-**mha**   nhua   tapuli-se   mẽda
      NEG-see-NEG-**PRES.NONVIS**   I   dream-LOC   don't.you.know
      I didn't really see it in the dream, don't you know.

This is similar to the analysis of evidential use among the Kagwahiv (see Chapter 1, item D in §3.4 and further references there). When one recounts a dream by another person, one uses either a direct speech report or a reported evidential. No matter how close a person is to the speaker, the nonvisual evidential is not used to talk about the dreams of an ordinary human not endowed with shamanic powers.

A human is always in danger of being attacked by a malignant spirit, especially in the jungle or while fishing on the river (or if breaching a taboo—for instance, if one eats cold food at night-time, or has a bad dream before going hunting).[8] Spirit attacks and their consequences are described using the nonvisual evidential (see also Aikhenvald 2003: 299, 2019c). Similarly, something potentially dangerous and related with spirit activities is cast in the nonvisual evidential. In (28), Jovino Brito tells a story about how he and his elder brother went hunting and were attacked by a spirit *ñamu*. The hunters managed to thwart the attack by lighting fire and throwing hot tar on the ground. The visual evidential is used when the speaker recounts what he and his brothers did (their feelings are described using the nonvisual evidential, in agreement with §5.2). The actions of the spirit are cast in the nonvisual evidential.

(28) a. hĩ   nu-weri-nuku   nu-kalite-**na**
          DEM.ANIM   1sg-younger.brother-TOP.NON.A/S   1sg-tell-**REM.P.VIS**
          paita   yaphini-**mha**   diha   wa-na
          one+CL:ANIM   thing-**PRES.NONVIS**   he   1pl-OBJ
          I told my younger brother (visual), something different (contrary) it
          is for us (nonvisual).

      b. ai-nuku   nu-a-**na**
          then-TOP.NON.A/S   1sg-say-REM.P.VIS
          mhema-kade-**mha**   nhua   di-a-**na**
          NEG+hear-NEG-**PRES.NONVIS**   I   3sgnf-say-**REM.P.VIS**
          I told (him) then (visual), I haven't heard (nonvisual), he said (visual).

---

[8] A classification of Tariana spirits is in Aikhenvald (2003: 13–14). A number of taboos are outlined in Aikhenvald (2019c). There used to be several grades of shamans with varying degrees of power depending on the stage of initiation and the strength of snuff they employed in their healing and in shamanic travels. This 'vertical' classification of shamans is a feature Tariana shares with Baniwa of Içana and is part of its Arawak inheritance (Wright 2003; Aikhenvald 2003: 13–14).

c. wha   ñame   waka   wema   whema-**na**
   1pl   silent   1pl+look   1pl+try   1pl+hear-**REM.P.VIS**
   čo!   ñamu-**mha**   wa:-**na**   whameta
   oh!   evil.spirit-**PRES.NONVIS**   1pl+say-**REM.P.VIS**   1pl+think
   We got silent and tried to look and listen (visual), 'Oh! This is evil
   spirit (nonvisual), we said in our thoughts (visual).

d. apale   ha-hipita   di-ñupiru
   differently DEM:CL:GROUND   3sgnf-move.up.down
   dy-eku   di-a-**na**
   3sgnf-run   3sgnf-go-**REM.P.VIS**
   ihmeni-ka   wa-na   di-pitita-tha-**mhana**-niki
   say.ih-SEQ   1pl-OBJ   3sgnf-kick-FRUST-**REM.P.NONVIS**-FULLY
   wa-daki   wa-phina-pe
   1pl-body   1pl-thing-PL
   Ground moved up and down in a different way (visual), making
   sound of *ih*, the evil spirit almost kicked us, our bodies, our thighs
   (nonvisual).

After the attack by *ñamu*, the speaker summarizes what had happened:

e. wa-na   hī-kayu-**mhana**   di-ni   ñamu
   1pl-OBJ   this-like-**REM.P.NONVIS**   3sgnf-do   evil.spirit
   This is how the evil spirit acted on us (nonvisual).

The effect of evil spirit's actions cannot be seen by a human, but they can be
assumed. A man has not come back from hunting. His wife says (29), as it is
reasonable to assume that he was eaten up by the evil spirit.

(29) diha   ñamu   di-hña-**sika**-niki   di-na
      he   evil.spirit 3sgnf-eat-**REC.P.ASSUMED**-COMPL 3sgnf-OBJ
      The evil spirit has eaten him (one assumes).

   In talking about the actions and the practices of shamans and healers, the
nonvisual evidential is the preferred choice. In (30), Leonardo Brito describes
what a shaman does (more examples are in Aikhenvald 2019c). Dreams
which lead to the diagnosis of an illness are also described with the nonvisual
evidential.

(30) Diha-**mha**   maliĕri tsome maliĕri alite
      he-**PRES.NONVIS**   shaman a.lot   shaman be+CL:ANIM
      hiku-wani-naku
      appear-CL:ABSTR-TOP.NON.A/S
      nha na-mači-keta-mi-naku
      they 3pl-bad-THEM+CAUS-NOMZ-TOP.NON.A/S
      di-ka-**mha**   tapuli-se
      3sgnf-see-**PRES.NONVIS** dream-LOC
      The shaman sees in the dream the apparent damage made by a lot of
      shamans.

      Di-weni   nha   na-kamia-naku
      3sgnf-vengeance   they   3pl-fall.ill-TOP.NON.A/S
      di-yeneta-**mha**   ne-misini-naku
      3sgnf-pass+CAUS-**PRES.NONVIS**   then-also-TOP.NON.A/S
      Having snuffed snuff, he sees (it) then. Those who fall ill because of
      vengeance, he also makes (the illness) pass.

When I asked why the nonvisual evidential was used, the answer was (31):

(31) Dihmeta-nipe-ne   di-ni-**mha**
      3sgnf+think/feel/forbode-NOMZ-INST   3sgnf-do/act-**PRES.NONVIS**
      mĕda
      don't you know
      He does (it) with his thinking, don't you know.

The nonvisual evidential reflects access to information by those whose powers and thus actions lie beyond the realm of the human eye. We find many
analogies across the world. In traditional Wintu, the nonvisual evidential was
used to talk about the supernatural (Lee 1941). The Trio and the Wayana,
speakers of Carib languages with just two evidentials, witnessed and unwitnessed, describe shamanic attacks using the unwitnessed form (Carlin 2018).
The nonvisual evidential marker ŋa- in Dyirbal was used when talking about
spirits (Dixon 2014: 186–7). The 'auditive' evidential in Nenets (a Samoyedic
language) and in Yukaghir (a Palosiberian isolate) typically refers to something one had heard or felt (but not seen) (Skribnik and Kehayov 2018:
548–50). The same form is used when talking about shamanic activities in
Nenets (Ilyina 2017: 167–9).

    If a shaman talks about himself, he will have access to a different informa-
tion source—the topic of our next section.

5.5 What 'they' see and 'we' do not

A powerful shaman and an evil spirit can see what a common human does not. An account of a dream told by a powerful shaman usually will be cast in the visual evidential—in contrast to dreams by common mortals presented as 'nonvisual' (or to an account of a shamanic dream by a common person). In a story about a shaman who turned into a jaguar and took a man's heart away, the shaman says, about his own actions:

(32) hi)   matsite-nuku   di-kale
     this bad+NCL:ANIM-TOP.NON.A/S   3sgnf-heart
     nhuta-**na**   deikina   di-ñale-mhade
     1sg+take-**REM.P.VIS** afternoon   3sgnf-disappear-FUT
     I took the heart from this bad one, he will die in the afternoon.

An evil spirit has similar powers. A man goes hunting on Good Friday (a taboo in the culture of the modern Tariana). The evil spirit stops him in his tracks. The man pretends he does not have a calendar and does not know what day it is. The evil spirit 'sees' it all and says:

(33) kayka   nu-na   pi-mañe-ka-**naka**   phia
     in.vain 1sg-OBJ   2sg-lie-DECL-**PRES.VIS** you
     You are lying to me in vain.

The visual access to information by shamans can be a topic for discussion. Jesús, a powerful shaman of Wanano origin, visited us in the Tariana village of Santa Rosa. He told Jovino that our work will be fine—he had seen this in a dream. Jovino translated this as (34).

(34) Mača-mhade   i-hpani-nipe   tapuli-se   nu-ka-**na**
     good-FUT   2pl-work-NOMZ   dream-LOC   1sg-see-**REM.P.VIS**
     Your work will be good, I saw in a dream.

Jovino then added an explanatory comment—(35).

(35) mariĕri-pu-**naka**   diha thui di-ka-**naka**
     shaman-INTENS-**PRES.VIS**   he   all   3sgnf-see-**PRES.VIS**
     mĕda
     don't.you.know
     He is a real shaman (lit. very much a shaman, or big shaman), he sees everything.

A shaman and a spirit 'see' everything, and thus are entitled to use visual evidentials. But a common mortal who uses the visual evidential to talk about what others did or felt (unless they are a member of their close family) is likely to get into trouble. In one story, a widow whose child was taken by a shaman confronts him and says:

(36) phia   ma:čite   di-kale   phita-**ka**
      you   bad+NCL:ANIM   3sgnf-heart   2sg+take-**REC.P.VIS**
      You bad one took his heart away.

The shaman was not amused: it sounded like she was accusing him, or perhaps she could 'see' as much as he did. Subsequently, the woman went to her garden, tripped over and dropped dead: the shaman had been at work.

In a few Amazonian languages, a shaman will use a visual or a witnessed evidential when talking about their own shamanic revelations—as Carlin (2018) put it, they represent an 'alternative reality'. Among the Shipibo-Konibo, a shaman recounts their experiences obtained under the influence of the powerful hallucinogen *ayahuasca* using visual evidential. Those who use the visual evidential to talk about something others think they had not seen may be accused of being unreliable 'braggarts', or simply crazy (such an instance in Huallaga Quechua was described by Weber 1986: 142).

The correlation between the use of the visual evidential and the person's status finds its reflection in how questions are used among the Tariana. Across the languages of the world, evidentials in questions offer three options: they may presuppose the information source of the addressee, the information source of the speaker, or both of them, as well as the information source of the audience. In Tariana, evidentials in interrogative clauses contain reference to the information source of the addressee. In using the visual interrogative evidential, the speaker presupposes that the addressee had visual information.[9] Asking a question using a visual evidential may carry overtones of an accusation.

In the story about a man who had encountered a Fish-woman in the jungle (from the same story as (24)), the man receives money from the Fish-woman's father. As soon as he gets back to his village, the money turns into leaves, and he throws it away. The Fish-woman comes back and rebukes him for having thrown away the money her father had given him. She asks him a question couched in visual evidential.

---

[9] See Ramirez (1997: 144) on Tucano; Lee (1938: 92), for a similar phenomenon in Wintun, and Aikhenvald (2018b: 21–2) for a general perspective.

(37) Kwe-**nihka**   pi-a   pi-pe   phia
      How/why-**REC.P.VIS.INTER**   2sg-go   2sg-throw   you
      How did you throw (the money) away?

This implies that she had seen him do it—which she could only have done using her supernatural powers (as she was not with him when he went back to his village).

A shaman or someone with special knowledge (or authority) would be entitled to ask as many questions as they wish. If a common human does this, suspicion may arise—are we dealing with a hidden sorcerer? Or is this person imposing their authority on whoever is being questioned? In day-to-day interactions, asking too many questions is normally avoided.

5.6 Evidentials in varied genres and experiences

In Tariana, as in many other languages, established, or 'conventionalized', evidential choices come to be associated with particular genres. Autobiographical stories are cast in the visual evidential—as we saw in (28). Stories about shamanic practices and evil spirits are couched in nonvisual evidentials—we saw this in (30). The reported evidential is a conventional choice in stories based on gossip and what one has learnt from someone else, and tales about evil spirits, the Fish-people, and animals and birds. Such stories can be told by anyone, and are not considered particularly valued or serious.

The assumed evidential is the preferred choice for traditional stories. These include origin myths—such as the appearance of the Tariana and their ancestral travels, the origin of tobacco, fire, peach-palm, and manioc (examples are in (8)–(9); see also Aikhenvald 2003: 300). The same evidential is used in translations from Portuguese and in relating things one has read in a book, or in an announcements.

The correlation between evidential conventions and type of stories is shared with a few East Tucanoan languages of the area. In Desano, 'the assumed evidential with past tense is most often used for legends'; 'the hearsay evidential is also used, especially by the younger generation hearing the stories from other people' (Miller 1999: 67).[10] Along similar lines, speakers of Wanano use

---

[10] According to Kaye (1970: 33–5), traditional oral tales in Desano are told using the reported evidential, while non-traditional stories introduced from other cultures are marked with 'inferred' evidential. I suspect that his corpus and his exposure to the language were much less extensive than those of Miller.

the assumed evidential for traditional stories 'in which they take on the role of a narrator', 'being the conduit for shared, collective knowledge' (Stenzel and Gomez-Imbert 2018: 383).

This use of assumed evidential in Tariana and in other languages of the area is rooted in its correlations with access to knowledge. The assumed evidential is preferred if the speaker and the addressee share access to common knowledge— something accessible to both via prior knowledge or reasoning (as mentioned in §5.1). This is somewhat similar to the 'general knowledge' evidential translated as 'as everyone knows', described for Mamaindê and South Nambiquara, from the Nambiquara family (Eberhard 2018: 350–1, 353–5), Na (Mosuo), a Tibeto-Burman language (Lidz 2007: 60–3), and Kalmyk, a Mongolic language (Skribnik and Seesing 2014: 163), where a 'common knowledge' evidential often occurs in proverbs reflecting 'common wisdom'.

As Eberhard (2018: 353) put it, the general knowledge evidential in Nambiquara languages expresses 'knowledge that was passed down from one generation to the next for centuries, representing the accumulated learning of an entire people...that body of historical information that every normal adult in the community is expected to know'.[11]

The assumed evidential is used by representatives of all generations of speakers to talk about what they had read (all of the extant speakers, except for two elders, are functionally literate), and in translations. Only those elders who consider themselves well-versed in the centuries-old knowledge and lore (and are considered so by others) venture to tell traditional stories cast in assumed evidentials. There is thus a correlation between the status of a person within the community, their knowledgeability (acknowledged by them and by others), and the use of the assumed evidential referring to 'shared knowledge'— what all members of the community do, or ought to, know.

The use of evidentials correlates with the ways of accessing information. New means—phone, radio, television, and internet—require new conventions for the use of evidentials. In Tariana, as in many other languages, evidentials adjust to the new ways of acquiring knowledge.

In the early 1990s, a phone was a rarity. Since information acquired via a phone conversattion was heard, speakers used to relate it using the nonvisual evidential. Currently, those who do not have continuous access to mobile phone, still use the nonvisual evidential. Those who use a mobile phone on a day-to-day basis treat phone interactions on a par with face-to-face chat, and

---

[11] Special evidentials for 'mutual knowledge' have been described for South Conchucos Quechua (Hintz and Hintz 2017); a general perspective and further examples are in Aikhenvald (2018b: 25–6).

use the visual form. Short-wave radio has been the main means of communication with remote villages (including some of the Tariana villages), and partly remains so. Information obtained via the radio is treated as 'nonvisual'. Those Tariana who live in the mission centre Iauaretê and in the regional centre—the town of São Gabriel da Cachoeira—have access to Brazilian TV and watch it a lot. The information received is recounted as 'seen', with the visual evidential.

More and more Tariana—especially those who live in the mission and the regional centre—have internet, access social media, and employ 'WhatsApp'. The visual evidential is a normal choice in all these means of communication.

5.7 Evidentials, language awareness, and speakers' status

Obligatory use of evidentials correlates with the requirement to be precise in one's information source. This is related to a common belief that there is an explicit cause for everything, especially for adverse events. So as not to attract suspicions of having secret powers or knowledge, one needs to be careful in always saying how one knows things. 'White people's' language (Portuguese or Spanish) does not have to mark information source. Many Indians comment that White people are not to be trusted because they never tell you how they know things. They are thus suspected of having something to hide or perhaps of having some hidden malicious powers. Lexical expression of information source has grown to be a feature of the local variety of Portuguese spoken by most indigenous people within the Vaupés River Basin area: 'I saw' for 'visual', 'I didn't see' for nonvisual, 'I have proof' for inferred based on visual traces, 'it appears' for assumed, and 'it is said that' for the reported (expressed with *dizque*, a wide-spread feature of Amazonian Portuguese and Spanish on the whole: see Alcázar 2018; and also Aikhenvald 2020).

In many Amazonian societies, clear and precise expression is what defines a person's 'worth'. Among the Mamaindê, a Northern Nambiquara group from southern Amazonia, a typical way of referring to a 'good, trustworthy person' is to call them 'one who speaks well'. Someone who is 'untrustworthy or of a questionable moral reputation is labelled as one who does not speak well' (Eberhard 2009: 468). The correct use of evidentials is the 'token' of a good speaker and henceforth, a good, reliable, and trustworthy person.

The same principle applies to the Tariana (and also the East Tucanoan peoples in the Vaupés River Basin area: see Aikhenvald 2015: 267–76; and also 2002: 213–20, 2004: 336–7). Those who use the wrong evidentials are *mēda-peni* 'those good for nothing, useless'. So are those who do not know traditional lore.

Speakers are prepared to discuss why a particular evidential had been used. This is what we saw in metalinguistic comments such as (27), (31), and (35) where speakers explain why an evidential has been used. Metalinguistic awareness of evidentials sets them apart from other grammatical categories (see also Aikhenvald 2004: 360).

5.8 Evidentials as an integration point: To summarize

The main meaning of evidentials is information source. Their use reflects access to information and special experiences. Evidentials reflect kinship relations: one can talk about a close kin's physical or mental state, or a close kin's uncontrolled actions using the same evidentials as one would use for oneself (§§5.2–3). This use of evidentials sets apart one's core family from the classificatory family at large.

For the Tariana, as for their neighbours, nothing ever happens without a reason. Being precise in talking about how one knows things is a mark of a good speaker of language and also of a reliable and trustworthy person (similar attitudes have been described for the Tuyuca: Barnes 1984, Malone 1988, for Huallaga Quechua: Weber 1986, 1989, and for Nambiquara: Eberhard 2009; see also Aikhenvald 2013). The choice of an evidential also hinges on special access to information source—what one can see and the other cannot. Using an incorrect evidential may betray an incompetent fool, a liar, or someone with special dangerous powers.

Evidentials reflect special access to information source by shamans and spirits, as distinct from human mortal's observing what shamans and spirits do. Shamans perform their activities 'with their thinking'—hence the nonvisual evidential used to describe them. One can never see a spirit acting on a human.

Evidentials adjust to the changing social environment—new evidential choices come about to reflect new ways of acquiring information via radio, television, phone, and internet. Speakers are aware of how and why each evidential is used, and are prepared to explain these. The correct use of evidentials is what defines a person as a competent, trustworthy, and reliable member of the society.

Evidentials and their uses among the Tariana constitute an instance of grammatical elaboration of a cultural theme—precision in how you talk about the information source and who has access to it (along the lines of Ameka 2004: 25's approach to the logophoric marking in the West African context).

6 What can we conclude?

The three integration points relevant for the Tariana language and society reflect several parameters. We have seen that gender manipulation reflects the status of women in Tariana society (§4.2). Classifiers reflect the environment and subsistence practices (§4.3).

Evidentials (§5) reflect the requirement to be precise in stating how one knows things, and also the types of access to information. One can use non-visual evidentials to talk about the feelings, physical states, and uncontrolled actions of oneself and one's core family members. Common mortals cannot 'see' what a shaman or a spirit can: beliefs and supernatural powers are reflected in the use of evidentials. Speakers are aware of the meanings and the uses of evidentials; they are prepared to discuss and explain them. Evidentials are sensitive to technological changes, as they adjust to new ways of acquiring information. Evidentials constitute a focal point in speakers' language awareness and in evaluating one's language proficiency and status within the community.

Diagram 1 summarizes the integration points in Tariana and the parameters (A–F) reflected in them.

1. Reference classification: Gender manipulation ➜ traditional status of women and relationships between social genders = **A**

2. Reference classification: Multiple classifiers ➜ environment and subsistence = **E**

3. Evidentiality (grammatical marking of information source)

↓	↓	↓	↓
(i) requirement to be precise = **D**	(ii) kinship categorization = **A**	(iii) beliefs, spirits, supernatural powers = **C**	(iv) language awareness, sensitivity to changes = **F**

Diagram 1 The integration points in Tariana and the parameters (A–F) reflected in them

Integration points may apply beyond one language within an established linguistic area. In the case of Tariana, they definitely do. Evidentials and classifiers are shared across the Vaupés River Basin linguistic area. Their development in Tariana bears a strong imprint of its East-Tucanoan neighbours. The many similarities between Tariana and other languages of the region point towards the areal character of these integration points. Contact between speakers of adjacent languages appear to have shaped the speakers' interaction patterns and the language features which go with this—supporting the idea that the more impact a category has on cultural and environmental practices and conventions, the more diffusible it is expected to be (Aikhenvald 2006: 29). The prominence of the Vaupés-wide integration points goes hand-in-hand with attested contact-induced changes in Tariana. In contrast, gender manipulation has not been described for any of the other languages of the region.

Of the three integration points, only gender manipulation (§4.2) is on its way out. The reason for this may lie in societal changes concerning the status of women in the Vaupés society and the obsolescence of traditional stories about the Woman-Creator. This suggests that gender manipulation also reflects parameter F (as it is sensitive to societal changes). We can hypothesize that parameters reflecting the erstwhile co-dependence between language and society may undergo 'disintegration', if a practice falls out of use and the corresponding linguistic form becomes obsolete. This is what we see with specific classifiers in dying languages, such as Nivkh, and with Tariana gender switches, from feminine to non-feminine.

Linguistic categories of different kinds correlate with different groups of parameters. Gender and evidentials are closed grammatical systems. They are indicative of parameters A (relations within a community), C (principles and interactions and attitudes to information), D (beliefs), and also F (language awareness and sensitivity to societal changes).

Multiple classifiers as a grammatical integration point reflect parameters under E—environment and subsistence. Multiple classifiers are a large, semi-open system, where each choice can be considered lexical (many of them come from nouns). Nouns with specific subsistence-related meanings grammaticalize into classifiers. Is it the case that environmental and subsistence-related parameters (E) tend to be reflected in categories with obvious lexical origins? (Appendix to Chapter 1 discusses a recurrent exception). Other parameters (A–D, and F) are reflected in closed grammatical systems. The question of whether this principle holds in other languages remains open for now.

Acknowledgements

I am forever indebted to my Tariana adopted family for teaching me their remarkable language. Special thanks go to R. M. W. Dixon, for his suggestions and feedback. I am grateful to Luca Ciucci, Nerida Jarkey, and all the participants of the International Workshop 'The Integration of language and society', and to Brigitta Flick for careful proof-reading. This and all my other work throughout the tumultuous 2020 would not have been accomplished without ongoing support from Janice Wegner, against the evil winds across malicious lanes of adversity.

References

Aikhenvald, Alexandra Y. 2000. *Classifiers: A typology of noun categorization devices.* Oxford: Oxford University Press.

Aikhenvald, Alexandra Y. 2002. *Language contact in Amazonia.* Oxford: Oxford University Press.

Aikhenvald, Alexandra Y. 2003. *A grammar of Tariana, from northwest Amazonia.* Cambridge: Cambridge University Press.

Aikhenvald, Alexandra Y. 2004. *Evidentiality.* Oxford: Oxford University Press.

Aikhenvald, Alexandra Y. 2006. 'Grammars in contact: a cross-linguistic perspective', in Alexandra Y. Aikhenvald and R. M. W. Dixon (eds), *Grammars in contact: A cross-linguistic typology.* Oxford: Oxford University Press, 1–66.

Aikhenvald, Alexandra Y. 2013. 'The language of value and the value of language'. *Hau: a Journal of Ethnographic Theory* 3 (2): 55–73.

Aikhenvald, Alexandra Y. 2015. *The languages of the Amazon.* Oxford: Oxford University Press.

Aikhenvald, Alexandra Y. 2016. *How gender shapes the world.* Oxford: Oxford University Press.

Aikhenvald, Alexandra Y. 2018a. *Serial verbs.* Oxford: Oxford University Press.

Aikhenvald, Alexandra Y. 2018b. 'Evidentiality: the framework', in Alexandra Y. Aikhenvald (ed.), *The Oxford handbook of evidentiality.* Oxford: Oxford University Press, 1–46.

Aikhenvald, Alexandra Y. 2019a. 'A view from the North: Genders and classifiers in Arawak languages of north-west Amazonia', in Alexandra Y. Aikhenvald and Elena Mihas (eds), *Genders and classifiers: A cross-linguistic study.* Oxford: Oxford University Press, 103–43.

Aikhenvald, Alexandra Y. 2019b. 'Hidden from women's ears: Gender-based taboos in the Vaupés area'. *International Journal of Language and Culture* 6: 96–119.

Aikhenvald, Alexandra Y. 2019c. 'Tenets of the unseen: The preferred information source for the supernatural in Tariana', in Alexandra Y. Aikhenvald and Anne Storch (eds), *Taboo in language and discourse*. Special issue of *The Mouth* 4: 59–75.

Aikhenvald, Alexandra Y. 2020. 'Language loss and language gain in Amazonia: On newly emergent varieties of a national language, in Stefan Fafulas (ed.), *Amazonian Spanish. Language contact and evolution*. Amsterdam: John Benjamins, 7–34.

Aikhenvald, Alexandra Y. Forthcoming. 'The Amazon basin: linguistic areas and language contact', to appear in Salikoko S. Mufwene and Anna María Escobar (eds), *The Cambridge handbook of language contact*. Cambridge: Cambridge University Press.

Aikhenvald, Alexandra Y. and Diana Green. 2011. 'Palikur and the typology of classifiers', in Alexandra Y. Aikhenvald and R. M. W. Dixon (eds), *Language at large. Essays on syntax and semantics*. Leiden: Brill, 394–450.

Alcázar, Asier. 2018. '*Dizque* and other emergent evidential forms in Romance languages', in Alexandra Y. Aikhenvald (ed.), *The Oxford handbook of evidentiality*. Oxford: Oxford University Press, 725–40.

Ameka, Felix K. 2004. 'Grammar and cultural practices: The grammaticalization of triadic communication in West African languages'. *Journal of West African Languages* XXX.2: 5–28.

Barnes, Janet. 1984. 'Evidentials in the Tuyuca verb', *International Journal of American Linguistics* 50: 255–71.

Brüzzi, Alcionílio Alves da Silva. 1977. *A civilização indígena do Vaupés*. Roma: Las.

Carlin, Eithne B. 2018. 'Evidentiality and the Cariban languages', in Alexandra Y. Aikhenvald (ed.), *The Oxford handbook of evidentiality*. Oxford: Oxford University Press, 315–32.

Chernela, Janet M. 2003. 'Eastern Tukanoans', in C. R. Ember and M. Ember (eds), *Encyclopedia of Sex and Gender*. Boston, MA: Springer. (accessed electronically).

Chernela, Janet M. 2004. 'The politics of language acquisition: Language learning as social modeling in the Northwest Amazon'. *Women and Language* 27: 13–20.

Chernela, Janet M. 2011. 'The second world of Wanano women: Truth, lies, and back-talk in the Brazilian northwest Amazon'. *Journal of Linguistic Anthropology* 21: 193–210.

Cheshire, J. 2008. 'Still a gender-biased language? Updates on gender inequalities and the English language'. *English Today* 93: 7–10.

Christen, Helen. 1998. 'Die Mutti oder das Mutti, die Rita oder das Rita? Über Besonderheiten der Genuszuweisung bei Personen- und Verwandschaftsnamen in schweizerdeutschen Dialekten', in André Schnyder (ed.), *Ist mir getroumet mîn leben? Vom Träumen und vom Anderssein*. Göppingen: Kümmerle, 267–81.

Denny, J. P. 1979. 'The 'extendedness' variable in classifier semantics: Universal semantic features and cultural variation', in Madeleine Matthiot (ed.), *Ethnology: Boas, Sapir and Whorf revisited*, 97–119. The Hague: Mouton.

Dixon, R. M. W. 2004. *The Jarawara language of Southern Amazonia*. Oxford: Oxford University Press.

Dixon, R. M. W. 2014. 'The non-visible marker in Dyirbal', in Alexandra Y. Aikhenvald and R. M. W. Dixon (eds), *The grammar of knowledge: A cross-linguistic* typology. Oxford: Oxford University Press, 171–89.

Du Bois, John. 1985. 'Competing motivations', in John Haiman (ed.), *Iconicity in syntax*. Amsterdam: John Benjamins, 343–65.

Eberhard, David M. 2009. 'Mamaindê Grammar: A Northern Nambikwara language and its cultural context'. PhD dissertation, Vrije Universiteit Amsterdam.

Eberhard, David M. 2018. 'Evidentiality in Nambikwara languages', in Alexandra Y. Aikhenvald (ed.), *The Oxford handbook of evidentiality*. Oxford: Oxford University Press, 333–56.

Green, Diana. 2019. *Jungle gems*. Wycliffe Bible translators.

Hintz, Daniel J. and Diane M. Hintz. 2017. 'The evidential category of mutual knowledge in Quechua', *Lingua* 186-7: 88–107.

Hugh-Jones, Christine. 1979. *From the Milk River. Spatial and temporal processes in Northwest Amazonia*. Cambridge: Cambridge University Press.

Ilyina, L. A. 2017. 'On probable socio-cultural determinants of nonvisual sensory perception evidential grammemes in diachrony of Northern Asian languages'. *Sibirskij filologicheskij zhurnal* 2: 159–74.

Kaye, Jonathan D. 1970. 'The Desano verb: Problems in semantics, syntax and phonology'. PhD dissertation, Columbia University.

Lee, Dorothy D. 1938. 'Conceptual implications of an Indian language'. *Philosophy of Science* 5: 89–102.

Lee, Dorothy D. 1941. 'Some Indian texts dealing with the supernatural'. *The Review of Religion* 5: 403–11.

Lidz, Liberty. 2007. 'Evidentiality in Yongning Na (Mosuo)'. *Linguistics of the Tibeto-Burman Area* 30: 45–88.

Malone, Terrell A. 1988. 'The origin and development of Tuyuca evidentials'. *International Journal of American Linguistics* 54: 119–40.

Mihas, Elena. 2017. 'The Kampa subgroup of the Arawak language family', in Alexandra Y. Aikhenvald and R. M. W. Dixon (eds), *The Cambridge handbook of linguistic typology*. Cambridge: Cambridge University Press, 782–815.

Mihas, Elena. 2019. 'Gender-switching strategies in the activity of *tsinampantsi* 'joking' among Northern Kampa Arawaks of Peru'. *International Journal of Language and Culture* 6: 119–47.

Miller, Marion. 1999. *Desano grammar*. Arlington: Summer Institute of Linguistics and the University of Texas at Arlington.

Nübling, Damaris. 2017. 'Funktionen neutraler Genuszuwiesung bei Personen-namen und Personenbezeichnungen im germanischen Vergleich'. *Linguistische Berichte, Sonderheft* 23: 173–211.

Ramirez, Henri. 1997. *A Fala Tukano dos Yepâ-masa*. Tomo I. *Gramática*. Manaus: Inspetoria Salesiana Missionária da Amazônia CEDEM.

Skribnik, Elena and Petar Kehayov. 2018. 'Evidentials in Uralic languages', in Alexandra Y. Aikhenvald (ed.), *The Oxford handbook of evidentiality*. Oxford: Oxford University Press, 525–53.

Skribnik, Elena, and Olga Seesing. 2014. 'Evidentiality in Kalmyk', in Alexandra Y. Aikhenvald and R. M. W. Dixon (eds), *The grammar of knowledge: A cross-linguistic typology*. Oxford: Oxford University Press, 148–70.

Sorensen, A. P. Jr. 1967(1972). 'Multilingualism in the Northwest Amazon'. *American Anthropologist* 69: 670–84 (reprinted as pp. 78–93 of *Sociolinguistics*, edited by J. B. Pride and J. Holmes. Harmondsworth: Penguin Modern Linguistics readings, 1972).

Stenzel, Kristine and Elsa Gomez-Imbert. 2018. 'Evidentiality in Tukanoan languages', in Alexandra Y. Aikhenvald (ed.), *The Oxford handbook of evidentiality*. Oxford: Oxford University Press, 357–87.

Sun, Jackson T.-S. 2018. 'Evidentials and person', in Alexandra Y. Aikhenvald (ed.), *The Oxford handbook of evidentiality*. Oxford: Oxford University Press, 47–64.

Weber, David J. 1986. 'Information Perspective, Profile, and Patterns in Quechua', in Wallace L. Chafe and Johanna Nichols (eds), *Evidentiality: The linguistic coding of epistemology*. Norwood: Ablex Publishing, 137–55.

Weber, David J. 1989. *A grammar of Huallaga (Huánuco) Quechua*. Berkeley: University of California Press.

Wojtylak, Katarzyna I. 2020. *A grammar of Murui (Bue)—A Witotoan language from northwest Amazonia*. Leiden: Brill.

Wright, Robin M. 2003. *Mysteries of the Jaguar shamans of the Northwest Amazon*. Lincoln, NE: Nebraska University Press.

7

Links between language and society among the Murui of north-west Amazonia

Katarzyna I. Wojtylak

1 Introduction

The indigenous peoples of the Caquetá-Putumayo River Basins from north-west Amazonia inhabit vast territories of impenetrable rainforest delimited by large bodies of water, the Caquetá (known also as Japurá) and the Putumayo (Içá) Rivers. Besides sharing similar living conditions, these small-scale societies have related principles of social and cultural interaction in common, based on homogenous kinship structures (distinguishing parallel cousins and cross-cousins, etc.), collective taboos (regarding food consumption and preparation, tabooing one's name and death, etc.), and ceremonial organization and rituals (based mainly on ingesting pulverized coca and liquid tobacco) (see among others Echeverri 1997; Gasché 2009; Epps 2020; Aikhenvald forthcoming). The languages spoken by these north-western Amazonian groups, although unrelated (belonging to the Witotoan, Boran, and North Arawak language families, plus one language isolate—Andoke), share certain grammatical features, including classifiers and evidentiality markers. Arguably, these are examples of *integration (points)*—that is, linguistic features that are demonstrably associated with non-linguistic parameters such as physical environment (based on the forestal and riverine landscapes) and social relations within the community (established through particular societal hierarchies and kinship systems).[1] Take for instance classifiers which, as noun categorization devices, are known to mirror social, cultural, and environmental conditions (Aikhenvald 2000: 340–7). North Arawak, Boran, and Witotoan languages all have a classifier for a culturally important means of transportation, a canoe. (This is also the case in Tariana, another North

---

[1] For the full account of possible linguistic and non-linguistic parameters, see Aikhenvald, Dixon, and Jarkey, Chapter 1, this volume

Katarzyna I. Wojtylak, *Links between language and society among the Murui of north-west Amazonia*. In: *The Integration of Language and Society: A Cross-Linguistic Typology*. Edited by: Alexandra Y. Aikhenvald, R. M. W. Dixon, and Nerida Jarkey, Oxford University Press. © Katarzyna I. Wojtylak 2021. DOI: 10.1093/oso/9780192845924.003.0007

Arawak language spoken to the north of the Caquetá-Putumayo area: see Aikhenvald, Chapter 6, this volume). Prolonged language contact between speakers as well as the proximity to culturally and linguistically important centres in north-west Amazonia (such as the Vaupés River Basin; cf. Aikhenvald 2002, forthcoming) might have further facilitated adoption and usage of specific linguistic patterns that reflect culturally important principles.

Following violent contact with the Western world, the Amazonian population witnessed many dramatical changes and unprecedented sociolinguistic shifts. Many indigenous communities—and their languages—have disappeared. Others either resisted the change or combined their forces to create new indigenous nations. An example of the former are the Witotoan peoples, more specifically, the Murui-Muina from Colombia and Peru. Today, with a population of about 6,000, the Murui-Muina are one of the most powerful indigenous groups in southern Colombia. An example of the latter are the Yucuna, a North Arawak-speaking group from the same region. Today's Yucuna are an amalgam of different groups and languages (Aikhenvald 2012: 27).

When a language faces obsolescence and specific social practices are being lost, associations between the language and the society may undergo yet another process, that of *disintegration*. Disintegration may be accompanied by an influx of borrowed forms, as in the case of the decimated Resígaro (a North Arawak-speaking group from southern Colombia in contact with the Bora). Although the Resígaro language does not show many lexical borrowings from Bora, it did undergo a heavy structural and morphological change. As a result, it now has a specific 'Boran' flavour (cf. Aikhenvald 2001; Seifart 2011).

In this chapter, I offer an insight into the world of the Murui people of Colombia and Peru. I argue that a number of linguistic categories available in the Murui language can be explained by specific principles present in the Murui society. I begin by introducing the Murui people and the language in §2. In §3, I focus on what can be regarded as integration and disintegration points between the language and society. I take the following linguistic categories into consideration: reference classification—classifiers (§3.1), possession—possessive marking (§3.2), spatial distinctions—spatial adverbs (§3.3), and speech styles—linguistic avoidance (§3.4). In §4, I offer conclusions.

2 The Murui and their language

Murui (also known as Bue) is a dialect of the 'Murui-Muina language' (known previously as Witoto, Huitoto, or Uitoto) from the Witotoan language family, one of the smaller language families in Amazonia. Murui-Muina is in fact a dialect continuum. It comprises four different ethnolinguistic groups: the Murui, the Minɨka, the Mɨka, and the Nɨpode. The differences between the dialects are not significant; they are mainly found on the phonological level. In this chapter, I specifically focus on Murui. For an overview of all Murui-Muina dialects, see Echeverri, Fagua Rincón, and Wojtylak (forthcoming).

In terms of their geographical distribution, about 2,800 Murui inhabit the region spanning the middle sections of the Caquetá and Putumayo River Basins in southern Colombia. As the result of forced displacements in the Rubber Boom period at the beginning of the nineteenth century (see among others Hardenburg 1912; Echeverri 2011), nowadays there are also a handful of Murui communities on the Ampiyacú and Napo Rivers in northern Peru. Presently, the actual number of fluent Murui speakers will not exceed 1,000. Given the pervasive use of Spanish in almost all contexts of everyday life, Murui is rapidly shifting, with young people not showing language proficiency as strong as that of their parents and grandparents (see Wojtylak 2021 on Muruiñoz, a Spanish-Murui mixed language used by younger generations of the Murui).

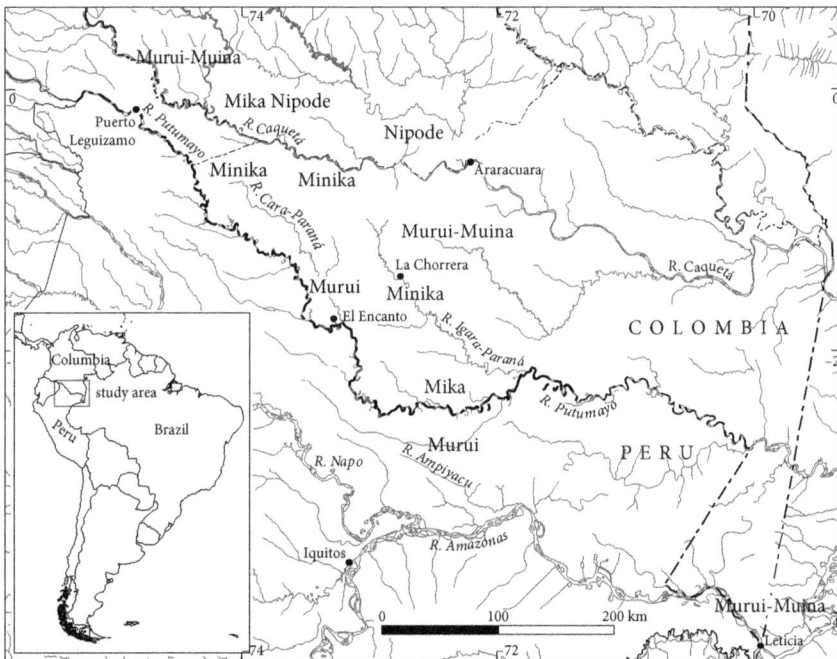

Map 1 The distribution of the Murui-Muina

Traditionally, the Murui-Muina peoples were slash-and-burn horticul-
turalists, fishers, hunter-gatherers, and inter-riverine dwellers, who lived between
smaller waterways and strayed away from major rivers (e.g. Echeverri 1997;
Wojtylak 2017, 2020a). Socially, they belong to a broader multicultural area of
the Caquetá-Putumayo region, called the 'People of the Centre (of the World)',
known in Spanish as *la Gente de Centro* (Echeverri 1997). Map 1 shows the
distribution of the Murui-Muina.

The religious worldview of the Murui-Muina peoples is traditionally based
on animism, although over the past two centuries, Christian missionaries
have significantly influenced the native belief system of the Murui-Muina.
According to their traditional world view, non-human entities (such as
animals, insects, plants, and rocks) are anthropomorphized (Echeverri 1997).
Today, much of the traditional knowledge appears to be lost, especially among
young people (see also Pereira 2012).[2]

Murui is a 'typical' Amazonian language (Wojtylak 2020a; Echeverri,
Fagua Rincón, and Wojtylak forthcoming). It has a relatively simple system of six
vowels: /i/, /ɛ/ written as <e>, /a/, /ɔ/ <o>, /u/, /ɨ/, and seventeen consonants:
/p/, /b/, /t/, /d/, /k/, /g/, /ɸ/ <f>, /β/ <v>, /h/, /s/, /θ/ <z>, /c/ <ch>,
/ɟ/ <y>, /n/, /ɲ/ <ñ>, /m/, /ɾ/ <r>. In terms of language structure, it is nominative-
accusative with head marking (on the verb) and elements of dependent marking
(case); it is also largely agglutinating and suffixing with some fusion. There are
no prefixes, which distinguishes it from other Witotoan languages (these are
Ocaina and Nonuya, see Echeverri, Fagua Rincón, and Wojtylak forthcoming).
There are three open lexical word classes: nouns, verbs, and adjectives.

Nouns can take up to three suffix slots that can be filled simultaneously
with: classifiers (up to three classifier positions), number (plural, kinship plural,
and collective, whereby the non-singularity of nouns is often determined by
context), and case marking (S/A subject, non-S/A subject in function of an
object, locative, ablative, instrumental, translative, and privative; S/A and
non-S/A subject markers are conditioned by principles of differential case
marking). The system of classifiers consists of large sets of classifier suffixes
that can occur in various morphological environments (so called 'multiple
classifier system', in agreement with Aikhenvald 2000: 204–41). In addition
to nouns, Murui classifiers can occur on verbs, adjectives, demonstratives,
interrogative words, pronouns, number words, and quantifiers. They

---

[2] The term 'young (Murui) people' refers to those speakers who are younger than thirty-five
years old.

characterize the noun referents in terms of e.g. their form, size, function, and quantification (see Wojtylak 2016 for details). Murui nouns are illustrated in (1): *kiifo* 'beehive' takes the classifier *-fo* for 'cavity-like forms' and the non-S/A case marker *-na*; *oima* 'sister's husband' takes the animate masculine classifier *-ma*:

(1) kii-fo-na$_o$ oi-ma$_A$
     honey-CL:CAVITY-N.S/A   sisters.husband-CL:M
     iba-oi-aka-d-e$_{PRED}$
     compensate-DUR-DESID-LINK-3
     The sister's husband is wanting to buy a beehive.

The system of Murui classifiers also includes so-called 'classifier-repeaters'. These are partially repeated nouns that occur in the classifier slot (cf. Aikhenvald 2000: 222–4). An example of this is *-mana* for 'week', from Spanish *semana* with the same meaning, e.g. *jifai-ya-mana* (get.intoxicated-EVENT.NOMZ-CL.REPET:WEEK) 'party week (lit. week of getting drunk)'.

The Murui possessive NP involves a simple juxtaposition of the Possessor and the Possessed, in this order. This is shown in (2):

(2) [Lusio$_{POSSESSOR}$ yoe-fai$_{POSSESSED}$]$_{NP}$
     Lucio   metal-CL:SHORT.THICKER
     Lucio's machete

With eighteen slots available, the structure of a Murui verb is more complex than that of a noun. In addition to one tense marker (future *-i*), we find numerous verbal categories. Example (1) illustrates the aspectual and attitudinal modality markers: durative *-oi* and desiderative *-aka*. Other categories include verbal classifiers (Wojtylak 2019a), directionality (andative, ventive), and plural participants markers. Pronominal verbal suffixes—like the 3-person *-e* in (1)—cross-reference S/A subjects and distinguish person (1, 2, 3) and number (singular, dual, and plural). They can be further followed by epistemic modality (certainty, uncertainty) and evidentiality (reported) enclitics (Wojtylak 2018). For a detailed description of the Murui language, see the reference grammar of Murui (Wojtylak 2020a). I now turn to the topic of this chapter, that is: what linguistic features of the Murui language (if any) can be shown to be motivated by non-linguistic traits specific to the Murui society?

3 Integration and disintegration of relations between Murui language and society

Four linguistic parameters show correlations with societal traits: classifiers (§3.1), possessive marking (§3.2), spatial adverbs (§3.3), and linguistic avoidance (§3.4). I discuss them in turn.

3.1 Classifiers

Perhaps one of the most salient areas where grammatical structures are found to give voice to the Murui society is in its extensive system of more than 110 classifiers. The classifiers are assigned to nouns on the basis of properties such as animacy, sex, shape, size, function, and arrangement. Many of these classifiers reflect the ways people live and their physical environment (cf. 'means of subsistence and physical environment', referred to as parameter E in Chapter 1 this volume); some are also motivated by the Murui belief system (cf. parameter D, 'beliefs, religion, spirits, and dreams').

Traditionally, the Murui used to settle along smaller rivers and streams separated by the mixed terrain of the rainforest. This is reflected in the language. We thus find special classifiers for different types of watercourses (such as -mani 'big river' and -tue 'small stream') and specific land formations (e.g. -du 'hill'). Other classifiers reflect the importance of the rainforest itself; they refer to forms of plants, trees, and bushes (e.g. -fu 'small young roundish plants', -rɨ 'bush, clump of trees'). Yet another type of classifiers refer to time, distinct ways in which objects are used, and the functions of those objects. The specificity of those semantic domains is thus indicative of what is salient (and important) for the Murui society. Table 1 gives examples of these classifiers.

The system of noun categorization shows a clear distinction between humans and non-humans (rather than between animates and inanimates). In Murui, human beings can be specified in terms of their natural gender: either feminine (-ño/-ñaiño) or masculine (-ma/-mɨe). That is, jimoma is a 'Yagua man', while 'jimoño is a 'Yagua woman'. Although the -ño vs -ma distinction does also apply to some non-human animates and also inanimates, the gender assignment is 'fixed' in these cases. For instance, the animal jigadɨma 'tapir' is always masculine. In order to talk about a female tapir, one has to add iñaiño 'female'; that is, jigadɨma iñaiño means 'female tapir'.

Gender marking on some animates appears to be based on the Murui belief system. Those animals that are considered dangerous take masculine gender

Table 1 Examples of semantic domains of Murui classifiers

Semantic domain	Form and gloss	Meaning of the classifier
Forest-related	-*bai* (CL:NODE.LEAF)	nodes with small leaves
	-*be* (CL:LEAF)	oval, oblong leaves
	-*bɨ* (CL:STEM.TUBER)	stem of certain trees, tuberous in form
	-*fu* (CL:SMALL.BUNCH)	small, roundish, young plants
	-*gai* (CL:NODE)	tree branch
	-*jɨ* (CL:TUBER)	specific form of roots with a tuber shape
	-*na* (CL:TREE)	(vertical) tree-like forms
	-*re* (CL:PLANT.PLACE)	location, opening in the jungle associated with certain plants, field
Land formations	-*du* (CL:HILL)	hill
	-*ba* (CL:WIDE.CAV)	underground cavity, hole
	-*fo* (CL:CAV)	cavity
Watercourses	-*kue* (CL:BIG.RIVER)	big river
	-*ye* (CL:RIVER)	river (general)
	-*kue* (CL:BIG.STREAM)	big stream, small river
	-*tue* (CL:RIVER)	small stream
Functions	-*fe* (CL:STRING.THICK)	line-like, used for transporting
	-*gai* (CL:BASKET)	basket-shaped, woven
	-*go* (CL:SKIN.SACK)	leather sack forms
	-*roi* (CL:CLOTHES)	clothes
	-*yai* (CL:TOGETHER)	heaped up, piled up together
Time-related	-*rui* (CL:DAY)	time cycle of one day
	-*vui* (CL:CYCLE)	time cycle of one moon (one month)
	-*mona* (CL:SEASON)	time cycle of a season, a year

marking (as it is the case with *jɨgadɨma* 'tapir' above); other animals are seen as harmless and take feminine gender marking (e.g. *ñeniño* 'armadillo').[3] Interestingly, the majority of sex differentiable animals are not marked for gender at all. Examples include *jiko* 'jaguar, dog', *janayari* 'jaguar (specific name)', *mero* 'peccary', *jemɨ* 'woolly monkey', including *kuita* and *guamɨ* 'types of monkeys'. Further, some non-sex differentiable animals and snakes, insects, some birds and some fish, are not considered to be animate. They are thus classified based on shape and form (similarly to most nouns with inanimate referents mentioned at the beginning of this section). Certain inanimates

---

[3] Note that this is not always the case, and many counterexamples can be found. For instance, the masculine *ma-* occurs with some fish and wasps, e.g. *kuegoma* (see §3.4), *jikodoma*, and *unema* are all different types of wasps. The same applies to the feminine -*ño*; it occurs on other fish types, frogs, ants, and wasps, e.g. *ueño* is a type of frog.

however, including important artefacts, are classified as animate. So, for instance, *dobeño* 'yuca squeezer' is feminine, possibly by association with gender-specific tasks (among the Murui-Muina peoples, women are responsible for squeezing yuca), and *yoema* 'axe', belonging to the realm of men, is masculine (cf. Aikhenvald 2016). The choice between the feminine and masculine ('Yagua man/woman') appears to be thus available for human referents only.

The distinction human vs non-human is also important for classifier-repeaters (see §2). An example of a classifier-repeater is *-to* in *nuikɨto* '(type of) fish'. It originates in the truncated noun *jito* 'son'. *Nuikɨto* is a derived form from the name of a mythological figure *Nuikɨ*, a primordial being with bird-like characteristics that was sent to kill *Agaro*, the anaconda (Agga Calderón 'Kaziya Buinaima', Wojtylak, and Echeverri 2019: 74). After an unsuccessful attempt at tramping *Agaro*, *Nuikɨ* transformed itself into the *nuikɨ-to* fish, meaning literally the *Nuikɨ*-son. As a fish, it is recognizable by a characteristic bird-like claw symbol on its back. The distinction human vs non-human is important for the classifier-repeater as their referents must be non-human. This principle appears to be different from that of other languages spoken in the neighbouring area of the Vaupés.[4]

The human vs non-human distinction evident in the Murui noun classification system can arguably be understood from the perspective of the Murui-Muina cosmology. Following Murui mythology, at the very beginning, many beings were perceived as both human and non-human at the same time (see also Ciucci, Chapter 8, this volume, who describes the mythological ancestors of the Ayoreo from Bolivia and Paraguay as entities who 'shared a primordial state of humanity'). They were able to communicate with each other and had certain physical or behavioural traits characteristic of human beings. They later transformed into the present-day species of animals, vegetables, artefacts, and other kinds of beings retaining the physical and behavioural characteristics of their original 'forms'. This can be interpreted as an instance of 'Amazonian perspectivism' wherein animism extends its 'human qualities' to other non-human beings (Viveiros de Castro 1996, 1998). An example is *Jimenakɨ* Possum Man, once a powerful mythological being who had a characteristic monkey-like speech (cf. 'possum speech' in Wojtylak 2017: 81). As a form of punishment for burning his children alive, *Jimenakɨ* transformed itself into today's species of possum, whose 'scientific' term in Murui is also

---

[4] For instance, in Tariana (North Arawak, spoken to the north of the Murui-Muina territories), the noun must have inanimate semantics to function as a repeater (Aikhenvald 2003b: 117). This is also the case in East Tucanoan languages from the same geographical area as Tariana (Aikhenvald 2000: 223).

jimenakɨ.[5] Many of such 'original' transformations may explain today's assignment of Murui (animate and inanimate) classifiers to nouns with non-human referents; *jimenakɨ* would be an example of this.

It is thus apparent that many of Murui classifiers reflect the ways people live, their physical environment, and their belief system.

3.2 Possessive marking

Further evidence of integration of linguistic and societal features can be found in the expression of Murui possessive marking. Its non-linguistic aspect lies in 'alienable possessibility' of certain noun types and the understanding of Murui communal possession. That is, in this respect, the language reflects certain 'relations within a community, social hierarchies, and kinship categorization' (cf. parameter A).

None of the Witotoan languages synchronically show a morphological distinction between alienably and inalienably possessed nouns. A few Murui terms however contain what appears to be an archaic first person singular possessive prefix fused with nouns and/or classifiers. Today, these nouns—a few kinship and part-whole terms, shown in (3a–d)—are lexicalized and can be further possessed. (3a) illustrates a kinship relation in the Mɨka dialect of Murui-Muina 'my mother'; Murui, Mɨnɨka, and Nɨpode do not have such forms, shown in (3b). Other Murui-Muina kinship terms—including non-consanguineal kin relations, illustrated in an example in (3c)—do not show lexicalized first person marking either. (3d) shows a lexicalized noun 'house' in all dialects of Murui-Muina. It historically contains the first person prefix; 'my house' expresses ownership.[6] The first person marker is in bold; prefixes in round brackets indicate an optional possessor in a possessive NP.

---

[5] Some of the names for species of animals and plants in Murui share the same roots, and are thus understood by the people to somehow 'belong to one another' (Wojtylak 2015: 555). The possum *jime-na-kɨ* shares the root *jime-* with *jime-na* 'a type of edible palm tree (*pijuayo* in Spanish)' (cf. *-na* is a classifier for 'tree-like forms'; *-kɨ* is a classifier meaning some kind of possession/inherent feature) (Wojtylak 2020a: 162, 164). The fruit of *jime-na* is called *jime-kɨ* (with the classifier *-kɨ* for 'round objects, like fruit'). Just like *jime-na-kɨ*, many of the Murui terms for 'lizards' end with the 'inherent/possession' classifier *-kɨ*, e.g. the *tura-kɨ* lizard (cf. *tura-o* 'type o vine'; *-o* is a classifier for 'long and flexible forms'). These are referred to as 'formal associations' in Wojtylak (2015). Some of these types of associations are used as substitution terms in the hunting speech style (§3.4). The ontological nature of such 'formal' animal-plant relations remains a topic for further study.

[6] To my knowledge, those are just two kinship terms: 'mother' and 'father-in-law'.

(3)   a. KINSHIP: CONSANGUINEAL
       In Mɨka, 'my (female) ancestor' lexicalized with 1sᴳ meaning 'mother':
       - historically: *k-ei-ño* (ARCHAIC.1SG-ancestor-CL:DR.F) '**my**
       (female) ancestor'
       - synchronically: *(oo) keiño* '(your) mother'

       b. KINSHIP: CONSANGUINEAL
       In Murui, Mɨnɨka, and Nɨpode, 'mother' did not lexicalize with 1sᴳ:
       - synchronically: *(oo) ei(-ño)* '(your) mother'

       c. KINSHIP: NON-CONSANGUINEAL
       In Murui, Mɨka, Mɨnɨka, and Nɨpode, 'father-in-law' did not
       lexicalize with 1sᴳ:
       - synchronically: *(kue) jɨfai* '(my) father-in-law'

       d. OWNERSHIP
       In Murui, Mɨka, Mɨnɨka, and Nɨpode, 'my inside' lexicalized with
       1sᴳ as 'house':
       - historically: *jo-foo* (ARCHAIC.1SG-inside)
       - synchronically: *(oo) jofo* '(your) house'

This phenomenon is shared with two other Witotoan languages (Echeverri,
Fagua Rincón, and Wojtylak forthcoming). In Ocaina and Nonuya, we find a
handful of forms shared with Murui-Muina; they are lexicalized and contain
the first person prefix. Compare examples (3a–d) above with (3e–f) below.
These examples also show, however, that some of Ocaina and Nonuya lexicalized forms do not coincide with the Murui-Muina ones. For instance, the
morphologically complex noun 'father (male parent)-in-law' in Ocaina shown
in (3e-i) and in Nonuya in (3f-i) does not have an archaic prefix in Murui-Muina,
cf. (3c). The situation is reversed in the case of 'house', cf. (3d) with (3e-iii) and
(3f-iii)—while 'house' is lexicalized in Murui-Muina, it is not in Ocaina and
Nonuya. The examples of words for 'mother' are also somewhat similar, cf. (3a–b)
with (3e-ii) and (3f-ii)—in the Mɨka dialect of Murui-Muina, in (3a), and in
Nonuya, in (3f-ii), it is an instance of lexicalization; this is not the case in other
Murui-Muina dialects however, shown in (3b), and in (3e-ii) for Ocaina.

(3)   e. In Ocaina:
          i.   'my (male) parent-in-law' lexicalized with 1sᴳ as '(male)
               parent-in-law':
               - historically: *x-oráá-ma* (ARCHAIC.1SG-parent.in.law-CL:M)
               '**my** (male) parent-in-law'

- synchronically: *(ja-)xoráá-ma* (1SG-parent.in.law-CL:M) '(my) father-in-law'

ii. 'mother' did not lexicalize with 1SG:
- synchronically: *(o)-ánjin-ko* (2SG-mother-CL:F) '(your) mother'

iii. 'house' did not lexicalize with 1SG:
- synchronically: *(o)-foojo* '(your) house'; cf. *foo* 'inside' in (3d)

f. In Nonuya:
i. '**my** father-in-law' lexicalized with 1SG as 'father-in-law':
- historically: *ju-po* (**ARCHAIC.1SG**-father.in.law) '**my** father-in-law'
- synchronically: *(jo-)jupo* (1SG-father.in.law) '(my) father-in-law'

ii. '**my** (female)' lexicalized with 1SG as 'mother':
- historically: *ju-ño* (**ARCHAIC.1SG**-CL:F) '**my** (female)'
- synchronically: *(jo-)-juño* (1SG-mother) '(my) mother'

iii. 'house' did not lexicalize with 1SG:
- synchronically: *(jo-)-foʼó* (1SG-house) '(my) house'; cf. *foo* in (3d, 3e-iii)

Given the scarcity of those lexicalized forms outlined above, it is difficult to speculate about their precise origin.[7] Wojtylak and Echeverri (ms) do not reconstruct inalienable-alienable possession for the proto-language. It is evident however that those words belong to very specific semantic domains: those of kinship and important possessions. This might indicate that at some point in the past, these domains must have been important for the Murui-Muina people.

Perhaps a clearer instance of how language reflects social values in terms of possession is manifested by the co-occurrence of first person singular and plural pronouns with certain culturally important concepts. The Murui-Muina have a number of restrictions on what can be owned by either an individual or by the community; this reflects people's attitudes to ownership (cf. 'togetherness' in Iraqw, see Mous, Chapter 10, this volume). Traditionally, there is a strong aversion to individualism among the Murui. The elders always stress that they should talk in collective terms, recognizing the contributions of 'all' the people:

---

[7] Constructions with alienable affixes are a feature of most Arawak and Carib languages, some of which (Karijona) were traditionally located in close proximity to the Murui-Muina (Aikhenvald 2012: 163–4).

(4)   kaɨ-kɨno=dɨ   'kaaɨ'   rei-t-e$_{\text{PRED}}$
      1PL-CL:NEWS=S/A.TOP   1PL.EMPH   say-LINK-3
      'kuue'   rei-ñe-d-e!$_{\text{PRED}}$
      1SG.EMPH   say-NEG-LINK-3
      Our tradition says 'we', it doesn't say 'I'!

For instance, *rafue naanɨ* 'the masters of the *rafue* ritual (the most important ritual for the Murui-Muina)' would never say *bee, *kue jiibie* '(look) **my** coca'; they
always say *bee, kaɨ yera, bee kaɨ jiibie* '(look) **our** tobacco paste, **our** coca' (Juan
Alvaro Echeverri, p.c.). The Mɨnɨka say that only the 'generation' of primordial
beings (called *jagagɨ urukɨ*), such as the Possum Man *Jimenakɨ* (mentioned in
§3.1), are 'qualified' to speak in individual terms. That is, only those beings are
allowed to say 'I'. They are referred to as *'kue' daaɨ-dɨ-no* (1sg say-LINK-CL:PR.
GROUP) 'those who say "I"' (Echeverri, p.c.). The existence of the archaic forms
as in (3a–f) above could perhaps be related with those specific social attitudes.

The idea of what can belong to an individual and what to the collective is
reflected in the language. The possession of certain objects has to be expressed
in relation to a group. That is, depending on the type of the noun referent,
singular and dual possessors are not allowed; only with plural referents, such
objects become 'possessable'. An illustrative example of this is a jungle garden
which traditionally could only belong to a clan. Such terms are grammatical
only with a plural possessor. Other communally possessable entities are given
in Table 2 (adapted from Wojtylak 2017: 263).

Interestingly, some concepts like these present semantic differences depending on whether the referents of the nouns are 'possessed' by an individual or a
group. This is the case with *uai* illustrated in Table 2. *Uai*, when possessed by
an individual (singular or dual), refers to 'voice, word', as in *kue/koko uai* 'my/
our (of us two) voice, my/our word(s)'. When possessed by a group, it means
'language', as in *kaɨ uai* 'our language (of us all)' (Wojtylak 2020b: 231–2).

Table 2 Possessibility of salient cultural entities in Murui

Ungrammatical use with singular and dual	Grammatical use with plural
*kue/koko iyɨ 'my/our (of us two) jungle garden'	*kaɨ iyɨ* 'our (of us all) jungle garden'
*kue/koko Yetarafue 'my/our (of us two) laws'	*kaɨ Yetarafue* 'our (of us all) laws'
*kue/koko jazikɨ 'my/our (of us two) forest'	*kaɨ jazikɨ* 'our (of us all) forest'
*kue/koko iye 'my/our (of us two) river'	*kaɨ iye* 'our (of us all) river'
*kue/koko komɨnɨ 'my/our (of us two) people'	*kaɨ komɨnɨ* 'our (of us all) people'
*kue/koko uai 'my/our (of us two) language'	*kaɨ uai* 'our (of us all) language'

Nowadays, with the integration of the local exchange system into the Colombian market economy, the ideas of what is culturally possessable have been changing. Many of the young Murui now own jungle gardens which are not shared with other members of their family or clan, as it was in the old days. Thus, instead of talking about 'our (of us all) jungle gardens', young people commonly refer to them with *kue* 'my' or with *koko* 'our (of us two, when owned by a couple, i.e. a husband and wife). This leads to the strong disapproval of the elders who openly say 'not only do Murui speak broken words now' (specifically referring to Muruiñoz, Wojtylak 2021) but that they also 'have lost their way of life'.

The currently 'negotiated' possessibility of the Murui jungle gardens clearly demonstrates the sensitivity of possessive pronouns to an ongoing societal change. This correlation between language and society can be seen in two ways, either as i) as either a case of disintegration (from the perspective of the elders, whose use of the language still reflects their traditional attitudes towards possession) or perhaps as ii) a case of 'reintegration' (from the perspective of the young people, whose innovative use of Murui reflects a certain degree of reinterpretation followed by a linguistic adaptation to the Colombian market economy).

3.3 Spatial adverbs

Some of the topographic terms available in Murui directly correlate with the physical environment the Murui-Muina live in (cf. parameter E). The river system is central not only for the navigation routes, but it is also fundamental in the origin myth of the people. In the story of creation, a jaguar called *Kuegoma*[8] cuts off the tails of the primordial monkey-beings as they leave the Cave of Humanity (cf. the 'Centre [of the World]', see §2) and they become people. As they go down the hill to bathe, their mythological forefathers, Muruima and Muinama[9], gaze in two directions: upriver and downriver. Those lands would later become the territories of the Murui-Muina peoples (Agga Calderón 'Kaziya Buinaima', Wojtylak, and Echeverri 2019). Spatial adverbs include two central direction points: *afai* 'upriver' and *fuiri* 'downriver'. They are associated with the river that passes through the Murui-Muina land

---

[8] In the myth of creation of the Murui-Muina, the jaguar *Kuegoma* appears in the form of a wasp (see *kuegoma* 'wasp' discussed in §3.1; cf. the masculine classifier -*ma*).

[9] The names of the Murui-Muina language and its dialects originally derive from the names of these two forefathers: Muruima and Muinama.

and for these peoples, they are thus intimately linked to their topographic environment.

In addition to the 'upriver' and 'downriver' directions, there are also two other locational terms related to river, *ruika*, which is inherently related to watercourse, and *ari*, which is describes land surface. *Ruika* 'across river' is used deictically, and it is relative to the speaker's view (for instance, my house across the river from you is *ruika*, so is your house across the river from me).[10] *Ari* refers to any terrain which is away from the level of the water (e.g. my house can be referred as *ari* if it is located above the area which gets flooded if the water level rises to a particular elevation). These two terms are however not as 'central' as the 'upriver'-'downriver' ones.

In the past, the Murui used the terms *afai* 'upriver' and *fuiri* 'downriver' as an absolute frame of reference that relied on arbitrary fixed bearings (in terms of Levinson 2004).[11] An elder once told me that going in the direction towards somebody's house located away from the speaker used to be described as 'downstream'. Although today this practice has long been forgotten, it can serve as an illustrative example of disintegration, regardless of the speaker's age. Today, four cardinal directions borrowed from Spanish are used to refer to the locations of villages and landmarks: *sur* 'south' (sometimes referred to by the elders with *fuiri*), *norte* 'north' (called sometimes *afai*), *este* 'east', and *oeste* 'west'. In addition, there are a few semi-lexicalized nominalizations referring to 'sun rising' (east) and 'sun going down' (west) but they are not used to indicate directions.

The Murui upriver-downriver system appears to be no different from those found among other north-west Amazonian groups, such as the Tariana of the Vaupés. To describe navigation routes, the Tariana traditionally relied on landmarks, namely rivers and secret places (Aikhenvald 1996). The inter-riverine dwellers, the Murui-Muina, also relied on established landmarks and trade routes that existed throughout the territory of the Caquetá-Putumayo River Basins. Just like the Murui, the Tariana also once used the upriver-downriver distinctions as the absolute frame of reference—'going downstream' would be used to describe going in the direction towards an object located away from the speaker (Alexandra Aikhenvald, p.c.).

---

[10] Note that the spatial adverbs 'upriver' (*afai*) and '(land) uphill' (*ari*) contain the element *a-*. Arguably, *a-* could be related to the adverb *aa* meaning 'up, above'. Perhaps this may explain why *ari* and *afai* share some vertical dimension relating to 'up' ('upriver'/'uphill') (cf. Wojtylak and Echeverri ms consider *a-* to be an archaic 'dummy' demonstrative root which is also present in the Boran languages spoken in the area).

[11] Murui does not rely on body-centred relative terms 'left' and 'right'. The words for 'left hand' and 'right hand' do exist but they do not express spatial relations of any sorts (Wojtylak 2017).

In conclusion, the Murui spatial adverbs demonstrate that the system of orientation which the language has at its disposal reflects the physical environment in which people live.

3.4 Linguistic avoidance

The final argument for the correlation between the Murui language and the society revolves around two special avoidance speech styles: the hunting and the jungle-at-night speech registers (Wojtylak 2015, 2019b). Those speech styles are examples of linguistic avoidance and thus reflect the integration of the language with those societal features that are characterized by people's 'beliefs, religion, spirits and dreams' (cf. parameter D). I briefly discuss those two speech styles in turn.

The Murui hunting speech register is based on the principle of indirect communication. Its usage is determined by social taboos, identified with the realm of spirits, that restrict the appropriateness of particular linguistic forms in a very specific context. When preparing for a hunt, the Murui men employ a special vocabulary meant to 'disguise' the true names of animals that they will hunt. It is a system of lexical substitution to 'deceive' animal spirits; pronouncing actual names of the animals would result in an unsuccessful hunt, as those beings would 'overhear' that they are to be hunted and would escape. Animal names are thus substituted with (mostly) plant-related terms. For instance, when intending to hunt a peccary, one would 'collect the *obedo* fruit'. The peccary-*obedo* fruit relation is based on an impressionistic association between the peccary and this particular fruit: the *obedo* has a specific scent which, like peccaries, attracts mosquitoes (Wojtylak 2015: 554). The hunting of game animals goes beyond the simple acquisition of food for the Murui. The actual 'hunting' takes place in an alternative reality, which is an inherent part of the Amazonian existence (cf. the human vs non-human opposition discussed in §3.1; the right of the primordial beings to say 'I' in §2). In what you and I (as non-indigenous people) perceive as dreams, 'the animals have to be defeated first, before they are defeated in the physical world of the everyday life' (Wojtylak 2015: 557). That is, the hunter has to slaughter the animal's 'soul' first, before he can kill its actual body. The vast majority of the hunting avoidance terms are little known to the young Murui who do not hunt and so do not have to know the principles of the hunting register or how to follow them. This is a case of disintegration of the relation between language and culture.

The use of the Murui jungle-at-night register is also solely based on the Murui understanding of the spiritual world; those beliefs, as it were, determine a specific linguistic behaviour. The jungle is seen by the Murui as extremely dangerous and full of threats. Especially at night, when one is away from the safety of their own settlements, it is imperative to employ a certain way of speaking when conversing at a distance with those who cannot be seen. By changing prosodic patterns of speech (simply by rising intonation which is accompanied by high pitch and slow tempo, Wojtylak 2019b: 82), the speakers disguise their voices and rid themselves of an indefinable threat. Breaking this taboo would result in being recognized by malevolent spirits who then would be able to seriously harm the person. Unlike the hunting speech style, the jungle-at-night register is vigorously used by all the people equally, regardless of their age.

The hunting and the jungle-at-night registers in Murui assert specific mental links that spiritually connect the people to their land and reality (cf. Dyirbal, Dixon 2013). The use of these registers is thus guided by societal principles within the context of perceived danger.

4 Conclusions

In this chapter, I argue that the Murui language has at its disposal a number of linguistic features that show firm integration with the society of the Murui people, a Witotoan-speaking group from southern Colombia and northern Peru. I examined four linguistic parameters that reflect this integration: i) classifiers, ii) possessive marking, iii) spatial adverbs, and iv) linguistic avoidance styles. All are inherently (and demonstrably) associated with the non-linguistic parameters related to: a) the subsistence, b) the surrounding physical environment, c) the realm of spirits and dreams, perceived through the existence of an alternative 'Amazonian' reality, and d) relations within a community which manifest themselves in the people's attitudes to ownership and kinship categorization.

The consequences of language and culture shift resulting from the increased prestige of the Spanish language and the Western lifestyle onto the Murui language and society are two-fold:

i) On one hand, some of the linguistic features described in this chapter—possession (by shifting ideas of what is 'possessable'), topographic orientation (by not relying on the traditional absolute frames of reference), and the hunting avoidance speech style (by discontinuing the use

Table 3 (Dis)integration of relations between Murui language and Murui society

Linguistic parameters	Linguistic category	Societal parameters	Existing correlations and their approximate degree of (dis)integration	
			Young people	Elders
referent categorization	classifiers	means of subsistence and physical environment (parameter E)	total integration	
		beliefs, religion, spirits, and dreams (parameter D)	total integration	
possession	possessive marking in form of an archaic first person prefix	relations within a community, social hierarchies, and kinship categorization (parameter A)	total integration	
	possessive marking on 'unpossessable' objects		partial disintegration	total integration
topographic distinctions	spatial adverbs	means of subsistence and physical environment (parameter E)	partial disintegration	
special speech styles	hunting avoidance terms	beliefs, religion, spirits, and dreams (parameter D)	full disintegration	full integration
	voice modulation used in the jungle at night		full integration	

of the hunting substitution terms)—show high sensitivity to societal changes. Those language-culture 'links' disintegrate and fade away as relevant cultural practices are gradually abandoned and are no longer in place.

ii) On the other hand, other language-society correlations—referent categorization (by employing culturally-important classifiers), possession (by using highly lexicalized nouns with meanings relating to kinship and ownership), and the jungle-at-night speech style (by modulating voice when speaking at a distance in the jungle at night)—remain strong.

The language-society links are less prone to decay with regard to the latter (and perhaps 'tighter') correlation types. They remain important even for those young speakers who live less traditionally and are much less proficient in Murui than their parents and grandparents. A brief summary of the integration and disintegration points discussed in this chapter is given in Table 3.

Acknowledgements

Many thanks to the participants of the Integration of language and society Workshop (James Cook University, August 2019), especially to Alexandra Aikhenvald, R.M.W. Dixon, and Nerida Jarkey for their comments on the first drafts of this chapter. Special thanks to David Felipe Guerrero-Beltran for additional suggestions of the material.

References

Agga Calderón 'Kaziya Buinaima' Lucio, Katarzyna I. Wojtylak, and Juan Alvaro Echeverri. 2019. 'Murui: Naie jiyakɨno. El lugar de origen. The place of origin', in Kristine Stenzel and Bruna Franchetto (eds), Special issue *Línguas indígenas: Artes da palavra / Indigenous Languages: verbal arts* 15(1): 50–87.

Aikhenvald, Alexandra Y. 1996. 'Placenames in Tariana', *Names: A Journal of Onomastics* 44(4): 272–90.

Aikhenvald, Alexandra Y. 2000. *Classifiers: A typology of noun categorization devices*. Oxford: Oxford University Press.

Aikhenvald, Alexandra Y. 2001. 'Areal diffusion, genetic inheritance, and problems of subgrouping: A North Arawak case study', in Alexandra Y. Aikhenvald and R. M. W. Dixon (eds), *Areal diffusion and genetic inheritance. Problems in comparative linguistics*. Oxford: Oxford University Press, 167–94.

Aikhenvald, Alexandra Y. 2002. *Language contact in Amazonia*. Oxford: Oxford University Press.

Aikhenvald, Alexandra Y. 2003a. 'Evidentiality in typological perspective', in Alexandra Y. Aikhenvald and R. M. W. Dixon (eds), *Studies in evidentiality*. Amsterdam: John Benjamins, 1–33.

Aikhenvald, Alexandra Y. 2003b. *A grammar of Tariana, from Northwest Amazonia*. Cambridge: Cambridge University Press.

Aikhenvald, Alexandra Y. 2012. *The languages of the Amazon*. Oxford: Oxford University Press.

Aikhenvald, Alexandra Y. 2016. *How gender shapes the world*. Oxford: Oxford University Press.

Aikhenvald, Alexandra Y. Forthcoming. 'The Amazon basin: Linguistic areas and language contact' in Salikoko S. Mufwene and Anna María Escobar (eds), *The Cambridge Handbook of Language Contact*. Cambridge: Cambridge University Press.

Dixon, R. M. W. 2013. 'Possession and also ownership – vignettes', in Alexandra Y. Aikhenvald and R. M. W. Dixon (eds), *Possession and ownership: A cross-linguistic typology*. Oxford: Oxford University Press, 291–308.

Echeverri, Juan Alvaro. 1997. *The people of the center of the world. A study in culture, history and orality in the Colombian Amazon*. PhD dissertation, New School for Social Research.

Echeverri, Juan Alvaro. 2011. 'The Putumayo Indians and the Rubber Boom'. *Irish Journal of Anthropology* 14(2): 13–18.

Echeverri, Juan Alvaro, Doris Fagua Rincón, and Katarzyna I. Wojtylak, Forthcoming. 'The Witotoan language family', in Patience Epps and Lev Michael (eds), *International handbook of Amazonian languages*. Berlin: De Gruyter Mouton.

Epps, Patience. 2020. 'Amazonian linguistic diversity and its sociocultural correlates' in Mily Crevels and Pieter Muysken (eds), *Language dispersal, diversification, and contact: A global perspective*. Oxford: Oxford University Press, 275–90.

Gasché, Jürg. 2009. 'La sociedad de la "Gente del Centro"', in Frank Seifart, Doris Fagua Rincón, Jürg Gasché, and Juan Alvaro Echeverri (eds), *A multimedia documentation of the languages of the People of the Center*. Nijmegen: DOBES-MPI, 1–32.

Hardenburg, Walter E. 1912. *The Putumayo: The Devil's Paradise. Travels in the Peruvian Amazon region and an account of the atrocities committed upon the Indians therein*. London: T. Fisher Unwin.

Levinson, Stephen C. 2004. *Space in language and cognition: Explorations in cognitive diversity*. Cambridge: Cambridge University Press.

Pereira, Edmundo. 2012. *Um povo sábio, um povo aconselhado: Ritual e política entre os Uitoto-murui*. Brasilia: Paralelo 15.

Seifart, Frank. 2011. 'Bora loans in Resígaro: Massive morphological and little lexical borrowing in a moribund Arawakan language'. *Cadernos de Etnolingüística* (Série Monografias, 2). Available at: http://hdl.handle.net/11858/00-001M-0000-0012-1A14-A.

Viveiros de Castro, Eduardo. 1996. 'Os pronomes cosmológicos e o perspectivismo ameríndio'. *Mana* 2(2): 115–44.

Viveiros de Castro, Eduardo. 1998. 'Cosmological deixis and Amerindian perspectivism'. *Journal of the Royal Anthropological Institute* 4(3): 469–88.

Wojtylak, Katarzyna I. 2015. 'Fruits for animals: Hunting avoidance speech Style in Murui (Witoto, Northwest Amazonia)'. *Proceedings of the 41st Annual Meeting of the Berkeley Linguistic Society. University of California at Berkeley*, 545–61.

Wojtylak, Katarzyna I. 2016. 'Classifiers as derivational markers in Murui (Northwest Amazonia)', in Livia Körtvélyessy, Pavol Štekauer, and Salvador Valera (eds), *Word-formation across languages*. London/Newcastle-upon-Tyne: Cambridge Scholars Publishing, 393–425.

Wojtylak, Katarzyna I. 2017. *A grammar of Murui (Bue), a Witotoan language of Northwest Amazonia*. PhD dissertation (unpublished), James Cook University.

Wojtylak, Katarzyna I. 2018. 'Evidentiality in Boran and Witotoan languages', in Alexandra Y. Aikhenvald (ed.), *The Oxford handbook of evidentiality*. Oxford: Oxford University Press, 388–408.

Wojtylak, Katarzyna I. 2019a. 'The elusive verbal classifiers in "Witoto"', in Alexandra Y. Aikhenvald and Elena Mihas (eds), *Genders and classifiers: A cross-linguistic study*. Oxford: Oxford University Press, 176–95.

Wojtylak, Katarzyna I. 2019b. 'Talking to the spirits: A jungle-at-night register of the Murui people from Northwest Amazon', in Alexandra Y. Aikhenvald and Anne Storch (eds), *Taboo in language and discourse* (A special issue of *Mouth*, 4), 78–90.

Wojtylak, Katarzyna I. 2020a. *A grammar of Murui (Bue), a Witotoan language from Northwest Amazonia*. Leiden: Brill.

Wojtylak, Katarzyna I. 2020b. 'The phonological and grammatical status of Murui "word"' in Alexandra Y. Aikhenvald, R. M. W. Dixon, and Nathan M. White (eds), *The phonological and grammatical Word: A cross-linguistic typology*. Oxford: Oxford University Press.

Wojtylak, Katarzyna I. 2021. 'Language contact and change: the case of Muruiñoz from northwest Amazonia'. A Special Issue of *Italian Journal of Linguistics*, edited by Alexandra Y. Aikhenvald and P. Maitz, 33(1): 135–56.

Wojtylak, Katarzyna I. and Juan Avaro Echeverri. Ms. 'Towards a reconstruction of the pronominal system of Proto-Witotoan from the Northwest Amazon'.

8

How grammar and culture interact
in Zamucoan

Luca Ciucci

1 Introduction

This chapter investigates the integration of language and society in Zamucoan, a family consisting of three languages traditionally spoken in the Boreal Chaco of South America: †Old Zamuco, Ayoreo, and Chamacoco. Zamucoan is characterized by a split which crucially affects the reciprocal interaction of language and society: Old Zamuco and Ayoreo share the same cultural background (although relatively little is known about the Old Zamuco culture), while Chamacoco shows both cultural and linguistic innovations (Ciucci 2019).

Following this brief introduction, §2 will introduce the language family and its main typological features (§2.1). Zamucoan displays a rare system of nominal suffixation, which comprises gender marking (masculine vs feminine), number, and the category of 'form'. I will first analyse the Ayoreo origin stories, in order to show a connection between the grammatical gender of nouns for non-humans and a poetic metaphor for their personification (§3). This kind of connection is found in many languages with grammatical gender (Aikhenvald 2016), but the peculiarity of Ayoreo is the pervasive character of this association, which involves almost everything known to the Ayoreo traditional culture. By contrast, Chamacoco has lost most origin stories, where a non-human is linked to a mythological character (§4). This correlates with one morphological innovation of Chamacoco. In Zamucoan, terms for humans usually have gender switch, that is, they morphologically differentiate between masculine and feminine following the natural gender of the referent. Chamacoco has extended gender switch to animal nouns, and one can see the effect of this innovation in some Chamacoco stories (§4.1). The presence of a teknonymic suffix in Ayoreo may have to do with the importance of the relationship between the father and the first legitimate child, which in the past often led to extreme acts (§5). In §6, I will show that the morphological

Luca Ciucci, *How grammar and culture interact in Zamucoan*. In: *The Integration of Language and Society: A Cross-Linguistic Typology*. Edited by: Alexandra Y. Aikhenvald, R. M. W. Dixon, and Nerida Jarkey, Oxford University Press.
© Luca Ciucci 2021. DOI: 10.1093/oso/9780192845924.003.0008

difference between direct vs indirect possession and the fact that animals and plants cannot be directly possessed may reflect the attitude of the Zamucoan peoples towards consumable resources and their environment. Old Zamuco, the most conservative Zamucoan language, shows traces of a situation in which there were originally no specific comparative structures: this is characteristic of egalitarian societies and corresponds to what is known about the Old Zamuco/Ayoreo peoples (§7). Equality in Old Zamuco/Ayoreo society also involves gender balance, and some mismatches between linguistic and natural gender appear to be indicative of the important role occupied by women (§8). Section 9 will mention the secret register used by the Chamacoco speakers, a consequence of cultural and linguistic change which occurred after contact with Western society. Section 10 concludes the discussion.[1]

2 The Zamucoan family

The Zamucoan family consists of three languages spoken in the northern Chaco: †Old Zamuco, Ayoreo (ca. 4,500 speakers), and Chamacoco (ca. 2,000 speakers). Old Zamuco was spoken in the eighteenth century in the Jesuit mission of *San Ignacio de Zamucos*, one of the Jesuit missions of Chiquitos. The family-internal comparison shows that Old Zamuco is the most conservative language (Ciucci 2016 [2013]; Ciucci and Bertinetto 2015, 2017, 2019; Bertinetto and Ciucci 2019). Most of the documentation available so far consists of a grammar by the Jesuit Ignace Chomé (1958 [ante 1745]), but the recent discovery of Chomé's dictionary (see Ciucci 2018 for details) will soon make available the most important source of data for this language (Ciucci forthcoming a). Zamucoan is genetically isolated, as confirmed by biological studies on Native American populations (Demarchi and García Ministro 2008; Rickards et al. 1994). At the same time, traces of contact with other Chaco languages have emerged (Ciucci 2014): in particular, comparison with Mataguayan and Guaycuruan shows several morphological borrowings in and from Zamucoan.

---

[1] Data are reported in the orthography of each language (for a detailed discussion, see Ciucci 2016). In the Ayoreo myths, the name of human characters always coincide with common nouns for non-humans (§3), so that it can often be challenging to disambiguate between the two: I will use the initial capital letter to refer to the proper noun of the mythological figure, and initial lowercase to indicate the common noun. Even though in this chapter I often use the present tense to refer to the traditional Ayoreo and Chamacoco culture, the way of life of both populations had undergone dramatic changes, particularly in the last decades, and many of their cultural features are disappearing or have been lost. Linguistic data for Old Zamuco come from Chomé (1958) and Ciucci (forthcoming a). Data for Chamacoco come from my fieldwork, while for Ayoreo I used data from fieldwork by Pier Marco Bertinetto and me, as well as lexicographical sources such as Barrios et al. (1995), Higham et al. (2000), Morarie (2011), and an anonymous dictionary by evangelical missionaries (SIM 1967).

```
                        *Proto-Zamucoan


                                                Chamacoco
        Old Zamuco      Ayoreo
                                          Ebitoso       Tomaraho
```

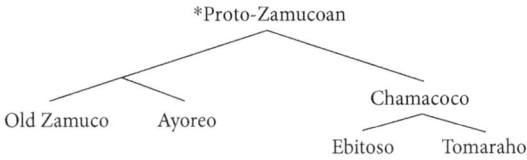

Figure 1 The internal classification of the Zamucoan family

As I will demonstrate, linguistic proximity goes hand in hand with cultural proximity in the languages discussed in these chapters. Figure 1 shows the internal classification of the Zamucoan family. Old Zamuco and Ayoreo are very close to each other from both a morphological and lexical point of view (Kelm 1964; Ciucci 2016), while they only share 30% of the lexicon with Chamacoco. Diachronic studies show that Ayoreo does not directly stem from Old Zamuco, but from one or more sister languages, already spoken at the time of the Jesuits (Ciucci 2016; Ciucci and Bertinetto 2015, 2017). Since Old Zamuco and Ayoreo are two distinct languages, it sometimes happens that only one of the two shares archaic morphological features with Chamacoco: this is mostly the case in Old Zamuco, but it can also happen for Ayoreo (Bertinetto and Ciucci 2019).

There is little information about the Old Zamuco culture (see Combès 2009 for the available historical sources), but there is some evidence that the Old Zamuco ethnic population had the same cultural background as the ancestors of the Ayoreo (Ciucci 2019), so that considerations on the Ayoreo culture presented in this chapter very likely also apply to Old Zamuco. The Ayoreo had the first stable contacts with Western culture in 1947, but they had largely been affected by eighteenth-century contact with Jesuits, and at least some of their ancestors had lived for a while in the Jesuit missions (Fischermann 1988, 1996; Combès 2009). In conclusion, although there is no language continuity, one can speak of cultural continuity between Old Zamuco and Ayoreo, and in this chapter, I will discuss some historical and linguistic evidence concerning mythology (§3.4), naming practices (§5), the lack of a strict societal hierarchy (§7), and the status of women (§8).

Chamacoco is, by contrast, the most innovative language of the family, and this correlates with cultural innovation. While both the Ayoreo and the Chamacoco are traditionally semi-nomadic populations with a similar material culture, the Chamacoco religious view is reasonably different from that of other Chaco populations, including the Ayoreo. The cultural and linguistic change was due to contact with surrounding ethnicities (Cordeu

1997). Cordeu (1989–92; 1997) points out the influence of Jê groups on the Chamacoco, but cultural similarities with the Chiquitano (unclassified) (Sušnik 1969) and the Kadiwéu (Guaycuruan) (Cordeu 1989–92) also emerge. Recent studies have found shared linguistic elements with Kadiwéu (Ciucci 2014; Aikhenvald 2018) and Tupí-Guaraní (Ciucci and Bertinetto 2015), among others (cf. Ciucci 2014). Besides, after the first contact with Western society, in 1885, Chamacoco was profoundly affected by Spanish. In this chapter, I will primarily refer to the pre-contact Chamacoco culture, but in §9 will discuss a recent development in the interaction between the language, heavily influenced by Spanish, and Paraguayan society, where the Chamacoco now live.

The Chamacoco are now divided into two groups, corresponding to two dialects: Ebitoso (or Ybytoso, *Ɨbitoso* in proper Chamacoco spelling) and Tomaraho. According to DGEEC (2014), there were 1,915 Ebitoso and 152 Tomaraho in 2012. In this chapter, I will use the term 'Chamacoco' to refer only to the Ebitoso (or *Ɨbitoso*) people, among whom I have done my fieldwork. Although the two groups used to share the same culture, the present-day situation is very different: the Ebitoso have lost many elements of their cultural tradition, which are still preserved among the Tomaraho, who have lived in isolation from Western society for a more extended period (on Tomaraho, see Sequera 2006 and Escobar 2007).

2.1 Main features of Zamucoan

Zamucoan languages are fusional. The main constituent order is A-V-O or S-V. The possessor precedes the possessum, and adjectives follow the head of the NP. The three major word classes are verbs, nouns, and adjectives. They are generally open, and their morphology will be dealt with throughout the chapter. Minor word classes common to all Zamucoan languages include adpositions, adverbs, connectives, demonstratives, interrogatives, negators, pronouns, number words, possessive classifiers, and interjections. All have possessive classifiers (Ciucci and Bertinetto 2019), addressed in §6. Verbs have prefixes marking subject (A/S) and mood (realis vs irrealis), with plural number usually expressed by verb suffixes. Realis and irrealis are frequently neutralized, in which case, I will not indicate the mood in the glosses. Most verbs are strictly transitive or intransitive. There is also a group of extended transitives and a few positional verbs (overlapping with existential verbs and, in Ayoreo, the copula). Nouns are divided into inflected and uninflected for possessor, with the former having pertensive prefixes to mark the possessor (see §6).

Bertinetto and Ciucci (2015) point out several rare or unusual features found in Zamucoan, such as para-hypotaxis (Bertinetto and Ciucci 2012), the presence of voiceless nasals (Bertinetto, Ricci, and Zhi 2010), the radical tenselessness of verbs (Bertinetto 2014b) and gender marking on possessive classifiers (Ciucci and Bertinetto 2019; see §6). A unique feature of Zamucoan needs to be introduced here, in order to make the glosses of this chapter intelligible. Nouns and adjectives have one suffix which obligatorily expresses gender (masculine or feminine), number (singular or plural), and nominal form. As far as the last feature is concerned, Zamucoan nominals distinguish between a PREDICATIVE FORM, an ARGUMENT FORM, and an INDETER-MINATE FORM. This very tripartition is a peculiar feature of Zamucoan. Table 1 offers a synopsis of nominal suffixation in the three Zamucoan languages.

Table 1 The Zamucoan threefold system of nominal suffixation (cf. Ciucci 2016; Ciucci and Bertinetto 2019)

	Old Zamuco		Ayoreo		Chamacoco	
	Singular	Plural	Singular	Plural	Singular	Plural
Masculine Predicative Form	-Ø	-(y)o, -ño	-Ø	-(y)o, -ño	-Ø, -k, -(y)ak	-(y/w)o, -(y)e, -tso, -cho, -lo, -no
Masculine Argument Form	-(i)tie (-re)	-oddoe, -onnoe	-i	-ode, -one	-(i)t, -(i)ch	
Masculine Indeterminate Form	-nic, -ric, -tic	-nigo, -rigo, -tigo	-nic, -ric, -tic	-ningo, -rigo, -ringo, -tigo	-ĩrk, -tik,	-tiyo, -ĩr
Feminine Predicative Form	-Ø	-(y)i, -ñi	-Ø, (-e)	-i	-Ø, -aʔ, -eʔ, -oʔ, -ĩʔ	-(y/w)e
Feminine Argument Form	-(i)tae	-(i)yie, -(i)ñie	-Ø, -(i)a, (-e)	-(i)die, -(i)nie	-(i)ta, -(i)cha	
Feminine Indeterminate Form	-nac, -rac, -tac	-rigui	-nac, -rac, -tac	-ningui, -rigui, -ringui, tigui	-rã(k), -tã(k)	-ĩr

The PREDICATIVE FORM carries out nominal predication in the absence of a copula, while the ARGUMENT and INDETERMINATE FORMS are used in argument position, as is evident in the contrast between the PREDICATIVE (1) and the ARGUMENT FORM (2) of 'jaguar'. At the core of the Zamucoan nominal tripartition, there is a contrast between the predicative vs argument function. What makes the system unique is the presence of the INDETERMINATE FORM, differing from the ARGUMENT FORM because it conveys non-specific reference, as in (3). For a typological comparison of Zamucoan nominal tripartition, see Bertinetto, Ciucci, and Farina (2019).

(1)   Ayoreo
      ¡[Carataque]_{INTRANSITIVE.PREDICATE}   que   don   Pedro   a!
      jaguar.m.sg.PF   RETR   don   Pedro   MOD
      It was a jaguar, don Pedro! (Briggs 1972, II: 35; cit. in Bertinetto 2014a)

(2)   Ayoreo
      Ch-uninga   mu   [carata-i]   t-õraja   guesi
      3-be_surprised   but   jaguar-m.sg.AF   3-throw_into   outside
      He was surprised but the jaguar came out. (Briggs 1972, II: 36)

(3)   Ayoreo
      A   ore   ch-ajna   [ajarame-tique].   [Aramoro-raque]
      MOD   3pl   3-follow   armadillo-m.sg.IF   brown_brocket-f.sg.IF
      a   deji
      MOD   3.EXIST
      They are following an armadillo, or perhaps a brocket. (Briggs 1972, II: 28)

Examples (1–3) show the primary uses of the nominal forms. In Zamucoan, adjectival modifiers follow the head of the NP. Noun and adjective(s) always agree in gender. As far as number and form are concerned, there are two different configurations within the NP. In Ayoreo and Old Zamuco, the form and number required by the context, such as the plural ARGUMENT FORM, are only marked on the last element of the NP (4), while all preceding nominals are in singular PREDICATIVE FORM. This occurs even though the referent is plural, as in (4), where 'jaguar' and 'two' are morphologically singular PREDICATIVE FORMS, while the final adjective is in plural ARGUMENT FORM.

(4) Ayoreo
Ch-imo [carataque   gare   querujn-ane]   iji   ta
3-see   jaguar.**m.sg.PF** two.**m.sg.PF** very_big-**m.pl.AF** LOC   there
He saw two big jaguars right there. (Briggs 1972, I: 31; cit. in Bertinetto 2014a)

In Chamacoco, there is generally agreement, not only in gender, but also in number and form, between the head and its adjectival modifiers (5).

(5) Chamacoco
Esee=ni   hno   o-ch-ichew   [jotsɨ-t
DM=RETR   3.REAL.go   pl-3.REAL-dig hole-**m.sg.AF**
bahlu-t]=ni
big-**m.sg.AF**=RETR
Then, they went to dig the deep hole.

Since one has to report nominals in one of the three forms, nominals will be cited in singular ARGUMENT FORM, which is also the citation form most frequently used by the Ayoreo and Chamacoco speakers when they are asked for a word.

3 How grammatical gender shaped Ayoreo mythology

As is known, linguistic gender can exert an influence on culture (Aikhenvald 2016; Chapter 1). In Ayoreo, grammatical gender has deeply influenced mythology, and such a pervasive connection is hardly found in any other language in the world. In this section, I will expand on several points raised in Ciucci (2019), showing how linguistic gender has systematically shaped Ayoreo mythology.

As already mentioned, Zamucoan has a small gender system distinguishing masculine and feminine. Gender is overtly marked on nouns. Human nouns follow their natural gender, and most of them have gender switch depending on the referent's natural gender. In the case of non-human nouns, one can identify some tendencies: for instance, in the whole family, plant and tree names are mostly feminine, but the exact rules for gender assignment have not been identified so far (Ciucci and Bertinetto 2019). In Zamucoan, adjectives, demonstratives, and possessive classifiers agree in gender with nouns.

In Chamacoco, where articles exist, they too agree in gender with the head of the NP. The Chamacoco nouns for animals usually show gender switch depending on the (often alleged) natural gender of the animal. This is an innovation of Chamacoco, which is discussed in §4.1.

3.1 On Ayoreo myths

In the traditional Ayoreo culture, myths, called *adode* (3.m.pl.AF), are sacred texts. The act of telling myths (*adode*), independently of the narrator's intention, can have magic consequences. These are often nefarious (see the examples in Idoyaga Molina 2000: 69–98), but can be positive in some cases: for instance, telling the story of *Guebi* 'small rain' is a way of calling the rain (Pia 2018: 83). Some myths are only known by shamans, and the degree of secrecy depends on each myth or even on single parts. The shaman proper is called *daijnai/naijnai* (m.sg.AF). Similar to a shaman, although at a much lower level, is the *igasitai* (m.sg.AF), he who knows myths and magic formulas (Pia 2016: 37–8). Telling a myth considered taboo, or even a tabooed a part of a story, is very dangerous for both the narrator and the listener. For instance, the taboo part of the story of *Pamoi* (GF.m.sg.AF) 'woven belt used by elderly people to sit with' will cause the death of a pregnant woman close to childbirth (Bórmida 2005, II: 27). This can also have repercussions in the community where something secret has been revealed, and this is another factor which prevents people from telling sacred stories: the narrator could be accused by the community of having caused adverse events. Some years ago, the Ayoreo of Jesudi (Paraguay) attributed a series of divorces occurring at around the same time to the fact that a myth had just been recounted on a local radio (Otaegui 2014: 81–2).

As Otaegui (2014) points out, the motivation for secrecy in the Ayoreo culture has to do with the centrality of language in traditional religious beliefs. Some particular stories or formulas exert power on reality; it is not the person who pronounces some words, or the spirits listening to them, but the words themselves which can have magic power. This has significant consequences for the available documentation of myths: in Bórmida (2005 [1973–9]) and Fischermann (1988), many myths are incomplete or interrupted because, according to the informants, it was dangerous to tell the rest of the story. The same picture emerges if one compares the recompilations of the Ayoreo and Chamacoco myths published at UCLA (Wilbert and Simoneau 1989 for Ayoreo; Wilbert and Simoneau 1987 for Chamacoco):

owing to the taboo, the Ayoreo myths are usually shorter than the Chamacoco ones.

The brilliant young anthropologist Lucien Sebag committed suicide in 1965. According to the Ayoreo, this was because he had been told prohibited stories by a shaman, who allegedly suffered from mental disorders as a consequence of telling narratives that he was not supposed to tell (Bórmida 2005, I: 106). Pia (2016: 41) reports that Sebag brought another informant to Sucre, far from the Ayoreo communities, so that the dangerous consequences following his revelations could not manifest themselves in the Ayoreo territory. Telling a prohibited myth can have consequences going much beyond a single unlucky event: Rosadé, one of the informants who had worked with Sebag and Bórmida, had to face social disapproval for having told myths and ritual formulas and ultimately abandon his village, because, according to the people of his community, his doing so had caused accidents (Idoyaga Molina 2000: 89–91).

Gabriella Erica Pia spent many years living with the Ayoreo, in order to document myths and other sacred texts. She could get access to most of them only after having been adopted by the clan *Etacõri* (Pia 2014: 48). Since the degree of prohibition varies according to each myth, she could then collect those stories which are taboo for the non-Ayoreo, but which can be recounted to the members of the community. She continued the documentation, but it took her some years before she was able to record one particular story which was considered extremely dangerous (Pia 2014: 54–6). In many cases, her informants wanted to remain anonymous and only shared with her fragments of stories, or stories in a concise form, in order to avoid unpleasant consequences (Bertinetto, Ciucci, and Pia 2010: 112–13).

3.2 The Ayoreo origin stories and their characters

A great deal of Ayoreo myths explain the origin of non-human entities (animals, plants, natural phenomena, traditional objects, etc.). I will show in §3.3 that linguistic gender plays a fundamental role in these origin (or etiological) narrations. For the Ayoreo, almost all non-human entities are the result of a transformation of an Ayoreo who, for different reasons, decided to turn into a given entity.[2] The ethnonym *Ayoreo* in the homonymous language

---

[2] There can be some degree of variation, mostly depending on the informant, concerning whether some entities, particularly objects, were originally people or not. See for instance the comparison of data by different informants done by Bórmida (2005, I: 44–6). But here one has to keep in mind the

is properly the masculine plural PREDICATIVE FORM of *Ayorei* (m.sg.AF), which means 'human being, real person'. The people who gave rise to the entities of this world in a mythological past are the ancestors of the Ayoreo and are the 'first men' (*jnani bajade*, m.pl.AF) and 'the first women' (*cheque bajedie*, f.pl.AF) (Pia 2014: 49).[3] They are also called *cuchade quicujaidie*, lit. 'the ancestors of the things', or *quicujaidie* (3.f.pl.AF) 'the ancestors' (singular *quicujadia* 3.f.sg.AF, see §8, ex. 23b). For reasons of simplicity, I will refer to them as 'the ancestors'.[4] Data on a sample of mythological ancestors are reported in Table 3 in the Appendix.

One can see here a possibly universal cultural feature of the Lowland South American peoples, which is also found in other hunter-gatherer societies across the world: the idea that in the past humans and animals shared a primordial state of humanity. While mythology explains how animals have lost the original human bodily form, human and animal consciousness have remained identical. This cultural trait, termed 'Amerindian perspectivism', and theorized by Viveiros de Castro (1998, 2004), mostly applies to certain species of animals considered important for cultural or practical reasons. However, it can also extend to all animals, plants, and even include virtually all non-human entities, as in Campa cosmology (Viveiros de Castro 2004: 465), which in this respect is very similar to that of the Ayoreo: Indeed, the mythological ancestors of today's Campa were 'the primal substance out of which many if not all of the categories of beings and things in the universe arose' (Weiss 1972: 170).

In Ayoreo origin myths, non-human entities are generally named after the ancestors who turned into them. Given the systematicity with which this scheme occurs in Ayoreo stories, the few exceptions are noteworthy: *Sumajningai* (m.sg.AF) 'courage' never underwent any transformation (see Table 3). Similarly, *Guebi* (DIM.m.sg.AF) 'small rain' is the personification of a sudden and short downpour. He did not transform into the atmospheric event he impersonates, but is described as a non-Ayoreo boy who fell from the sky; he was adopted by an Ayoreo and then went back to the sky (see Table 3 and Pia 2018: 83–97). Even without metamorphosis, *Sumajningai* 'courage' and

---

above-mentioned limits in the analysis of Ayoreo mythology and the fact that not all informants have the same knowledge of the stories.

[3] *Jnani bajade* 'the first men' and *cheque bajedie* 'the first women' are adjectival phrases inflected in ARGUMENT FORM; as seen in §2.1, in adjectival phrases the first element is always in singular PREDICATIVE FORM, while the final element is in the number and form required by referent and context.

[4] As pointed out by Bórmida (2005, II: 13–4), the word *quicujaidia* (3.f.sg.AF), *quicujaidie* (3.f.pl.AF) is a compound. It is an exception, because while in Ayoreo the unmarked gender is masculine, 'ancestor' is a feminine noun which is also used for men. This will be discussed in §8.

Guebi 'small rain' are, however, relevant to the present discussion on gender, because they personify non-humans.

There are also some stories, i.e. those of *Dacatereato* 'red rope', *Gase* 'pitchfork', and *Pibotai* 'drinking tube' (Table 3), where an object is mentioned before the metamorphosis. For instance, *Pibotai* (m.sg.AF) 'drinking tube' was a young man who was able to hunt in places where water is scarce. He invented a drinking tube to drink the water contained in tree hollows. At the end of the story, he turned into a drinking tube (Pia 2018: 60–1). In order to explain such chronological inconsistencies, Pia (2018: 52) hypothesizes that the object can be interpreted as the soul of the person who later transforms themself into it.

Like the present-day Ayoreo, the ancestors also belong to one of the seven Ayoreo clans (cf. Bórmida 2005, II: 187–205 and Fischermann 1988); all entities are assigned to the clan of the ancestor from whom they transformed, and there is a distinction between strong and weak clans depending on whether the number of entities that they symbolically own is high or low. For a list of entities and the respective clans, see Fischermann (1988). Even though the reason for the transformation is often a conflict between the ancestors and the rest of the community of the time, just before their transformation into entities, the ancestors are asked to leave something useful, and give the Ayoreo a ritual formula or song, used to perform some magic, mostly healing a specific disease.

Each mythological ancestor usually has at least one ritual formula, or *sari* (m.sg.AF).[5] These formulas, *sarode* (m.pl.AF) in the plural ARGUMENT FORM, can be used by everybody and are also the most common healing technique in the Ayoreo traditional culture, so that their importance strengthens the interdependency between mythological ancestors, the non-human entities they transformed into, and today's people. In myths, the ancestors explain the specific use of *sarode* (m.pl.AF) 'magic formulas' and the taboo concerning the narration of their stories (Idoyaga Molina 2000: 84).

3.3 The role of grammatical gender in Ayoreo origin myths

The ancestors turning into non-human entities in Ayoreo origin stories always have a well-defined natural (and social) gender, about which speakers are never confused (Pia 2016), although the Ayoreo are not aware of the reason why an ancestor belongs to one or the other gender (Bórmida 2005). The

---

[5] There are only a few ancestors who did not leave any ritual formula; see Table 3 in the Appendix.

mythological characters not involved in a metamorphosis, such as *Guebi* (DIM.m.sg.AF) 'small rain' and *Sumajningai* (m.sg.AF) 'courage' (§3.2), also have a well-defined gender (Table 3).

I have analysed a sample of Ayoreo origin myths in order to see whether there is an identity between the natural gender of the ancestor who turned into a non-human and the grammatical gender of the Ayoreo noun for that entity. The data are reported in Table 3 in the Appendix. The stories examined come mostly from Pia's Ayoreo anthropological dictionary (*Diccionario antropológico ayoreo*; Pia 2014, 2015, 2016, 2018).[6] Owing to the secrecy involving myths, Pia sometimes had to assemble, like pieces of a mosaic, many fragments of Ayoreo myths, often narrated at different times by different informants over years of work. Another problem for the documentation of these stories is that only shamans have access to complete information (§3.1), but shamans are now disappearing owing to cultural change, so that the older people interviewed form the last generation to have lived a part of their life according to their traditional culture. Other sources of myths used in compiling Table 3 were Bórmida (2005 [1973–9]), Fischermann (1988), and Idoyaga Molina (1998). Wilbert and Simoneau (1989) is a recompilation of stories which also includes those collected by Bórmida and Fischermann. I only considered stories for which there is enough information on the natural gender of the character, the name assigned to the character by the Ayoreo themselves, and the transformation they have undergone. Such data are often lacking, since many texts are very short for the reasons explained in (§3.1), or the transcription of nouns is not accurate (an exception are nouns reported in Pia or Fischermann's works).

As one can see from Table 3 (in the Appendix), the gender of the ancestor always coincides with the morphological gender of the common noun. There is only one apparent exception to the identity between the natural gender of the ancestor and the linguistic gender of the entity they originated. I will discuss this exception in §3.4. In Table 3, the names of the ancestors always appear in singular ARGUMENT FORM (§2.1): this form has a higher frequency than the PREDICATIVE and the INDETERMINATE FORM, and, as already mentioned, is the citation form generally used by speakers. Nouns for objects can inflect for possessor (see also §6). While gender, number, and

---

[6] This is an unprecedented work for the quantity of the materials collected. It is the outcome of an investigation which began in 1984 and lasted over thirty years. The first four volumes have more than 400 pages and only cover part of the letter A. The fact that the author suddenly passed away in 2019 has put an abrupt end to this work. Gabriella Erica Pia has left over 10,000 pages of field notes containing, among many other things, a huge amount of otherwise undocumented myths and ritual formulas.

nominal form are marked at the right periphery of a nominal, possession instead involves the left periphery of a noun. If the noun for an object inflects for possessor, the name of the ancestor is in third-person possessor form or, whenever available, in the so-called 'generic form' (GF), which indicates an unspecified possessor.

In the plot of each story, the entity concerned is named after an ancestor. However, in the ontogenesis of that story, the grammatical gender of an Ayoreo common noun has actually determined the natural gender of the character associated with it, and, consequently, many aspects of the narration.[7] This is an example of how grammatical gender affects cognition, providing a source of metaphors, whereby the linguistic gender of an entity turns into its natural and social gender (Aikhenvald 2016). The grammatical gender of the name of the entity has been projected onto its personification through the mediation of shamans. Indeed, the role of the shaman is central to Amerindian perspectivism: only shamans can see the internal human form of non-human entities, enter into a relationship with them and share their message with the rest of the tribe (Viveiros de Castro 1998, 2004). The Ayoreo myths have been elaborated by shamans through the visions they have when they are in a trance (on Ayoreo shamanism and how trance is provoked, see Sebag 1965). When the Ayoreo shamans are in a trance, they communicate with natural entities, which appear in the form of the ancestors who turned into them. For this reason, the Ayoreo shamans can provide descriptions of the human being associated with each entity (there are several examples in Idoyaga Molina 1998).

The Ayoreo myths would be very different if the Ayoreo language had no linguistic gender. For instance, in the stories, the natural gender of the ancestor (emanating from the linguistic gender of the entity concerned) correlates with its social gender and gender-specific roles or activities. In both Ayoreo society and narratives, men are military leaders, warriors, hunters, and honey gatherers; they fight and kill people. Women, by contrast, wear makeup, produce woven fabrics, or make skirts, an activity prohibited for men. The ancestor *Dacatereato* (f.sg.PF/AF) 'red rope', for instance, was a woman who continued to wear makeup after her marriage, thus breaking a traditional taboo and turning into a red rope (Pia 2016: 100). In some myths, overcoming social gender differences actually causes the loss of human nature: *Durujnai* (m.sg.AF), a young male, was transformed into a palm, because he

---

[7] For the other factors which have played a role in the creation of the mythological characters associated with each entity, see Bórmida (2005).

performed some activities which are only allowed for women, such as picking the caraguata plant (Pia 2014: 59). This story is iconic; most plant nouns are grammatically feminine, but *durujnai* (m.sg.AF) 'type of palm' (*Trithrinax schizophylla*) is masculine. There are also stories concerning attractive women who turned into non-human entities because of the problems caused by their beauty. Female characters can get pregnant, such as *Cuco* (f.sg.PF/AF) 'type of tree', who, having no partner, secretly gave birth to a child, and then married *Tobejnai* (m.sg.AF) 'hook-billed kite'. *Carujnanguejna* (f.sg.PF/AF) 'purpleheart', a plant whose wood is purplish, lost too much blood during menstruation. However, she managed to heal herself and even to give birth to a child. Her history serves to help women during childbirth (Pia 2016: 40–1).

Ancestors of opposite sex formed a couple and turned into different entities (see Bórmida 2005, I: 50–1): *Doridi* (m.sg.AF) and *Bujote* (f.sg.PF/AF) or *Choyo* (f.sg.PF/AF) were partners who turned into birds. *Chibisidi* (m.sg.AF) and *Chibiside* (f.sg.PF/AF) were also a couple and turned together into plants. Another couple were *Pugutadi* (GF.m.sg.AF) 'mortar' and *Parangue* (GF.f.sg.PF/AF) 'pestle'. *Potaquero* (f.sg.PF/AF) 'rufous nightjar' fell in love with *Potatai* (m.sg.AF) 'scissor-tailed nightjar'. Love can also have harmful consequences: *Ajacaratai* (m.sg.AF), a plant (*Jatropha grossidentata*), fell in love with the wife of his brother *Chicŏri* (m.sg.AF) 'tuber plant', who subsequently killed him. *Erejnai* (m.sg.AF) was unsuccessful with women, became evil, and transformed himself into a climbing plant.

All of these stories have been shaped by the arbitrarily assigned grammatical gender of common nouns and its influence on the shamanic vision of the world.[8] Before gender could affect stories, the assignment of grammatical gender may have been influenced by cultural factors (see the possible example of *Guede* 'sun', below), but such cases are very hard, if possible at all, to identify, because they took place a long time ago. For this reason, the only possibility is to consider the Ayoreo grammatical gender as the starting point for the interaction between gender and mythological metaphors.

Two examples in which gender assignment is based exclusively on grammatical principles are *dequeyutiguei* (m.sg.AF) 'smallpox' and *pitijinaquei* (GF.m.sg.AF) 'joy'. They are derived via the suffixes *-tiguei* and *-quei*, respectively, which form abstract nouns and are always masculine (see Ciucci 2016). Consequently, 'smallpox' and 'joy' are represented as men. Similarly, *guebi* (DIM.m.sg.AF) 'small rain' and *cuguebi* (DIM.m.sg.AF) 'buff-throated

---

[8] I use the adjective 'arbitrary', because the exact principles of gender assignment in Ayoreo have not been identified so far (§3), and remain a topic for further research.

woodcreeper' (a bird) are diminutives of two masculine nouns (see Table 3), and inherit the gender of their bases. The name can also shape characters in other ways: e.g. the already mentioned *cuguebi* (DIM.m.sg.AF) 'buff-throated woodcreeper' is the diminutive of *cuguei* (m.sg.AF) 'bean'. The semantic association between *cuguei* and *cuguebi* is not straightforward. The myth explains that *Cuguebi* (DIM.m.sg.AF) was a young man who devoted himself to agriculture and liked to grow beans. Then, since too many people wanted a part of his harvest, he decided to transform himself into a woodcreeper.

In some languages, the linguistic gender of some nouns is assigned on the basis of legend and beliefs, as in Dyirbal, an Australian language from North Queensland (Dixon 2015: 19–43), and in Manambu, a Ndu language of Papua New Guinea (see Aikhenvald 2016: 120–1 for more examples). In Ayoreo, the opposite occurs: it is the overtly marked gender which has affected mythology. As already mentioned, one cannot exclude the possibility that myths might occasionally have influenced linguistic gender, but this is far from certain, and could only have happened in the case of a few, culturally significant words. Besides, the secrecy of many Ayoreo stories could have made it harder for these stories to produce systematic changes in the language.

An example in which cosmovision may have affected grammatical gender is the case of *Guede* (m.sg.PF/AF), the sun. *Guede* used to be the most important figure of Ayoreo mythology, and during the contact with the Jesuits it was associated with *Dupade* (m.sg.AF), the Christian God (Fischermann 1988; Idoyaga Molina 1998: 55). Morphologically, the Ayoreo word for 'sun' *guede* (m.sg.PF/AF) is irregular, because it is the only masculine noun whose singular ARGUMENT FORM lacks the suffix *-i* and is identical with the PREDICATIVE FORM (unmarked for gender), two features found instead in feminine nouns. A similar irregularity existed in Old Zamuco: *guiede* (m.sg.PF) 'sun' is properly a singular masculine PREDICATIVE FORM (also unmarked for gender), but it is generally used instead of the ARGUMENT FORM *guiedetie* (m.sg.AF), in which gender is overtly marked by *-tie*. The form *guiedetie* (m.sg.AF) 'sun', which is seldom used, is possibly an Old Zamuco innovation caused by regularization. If this is so, the salience of the sun in traditional religious beliefs and the original lack of overt gender marking on 'sun' in Ayoreo and Old Zamuco may suggest that here linguistic gender has been assigned by mythological representation.

One has to exclude that Ayoreo non-human entities are named after dead people who may have had some particular connection with them during their lifetime. Although there are stories in which an Ayoreo makes or invents an object before turning into it, they are not the general rule. The hypothesis that ancestors (or at least some of them) may be eponyms is not supported by what we know of Ayoreo naming practices. The Ayoreo people are named with common nouns, often related to a significant event that happened to them at the time of their birth or before, to someone in their family. There is no set of lexical units specialized as proper nouns, as, for example, in Indo-European languages (Ciucci and Pia 2019: 45–7).[9] All traditional Ayoreo names for men include the teknonymic suffix *-de/-ne* after the birth of their first legitimate child (see §6), but never do the names for mythological male ancestors show such an ending. In Table 3, there are only two apparent exceptions: *Guede* 'sun' and *Guedoside* 'moon'. While in 'sun' *guede* (m.sg.PF/AF) coincides with the root, 'moon', in *guedosi-de* (m.sg.AF) 'moon', the final *-de* is the relic of a suffix which is no longer used to mark the singular ARGUMENT FORM (see Ciucci 2016: 454). Finally, the names of dead people are a linguistic taboo (Ciucci and Pia 2019: 47); once someone is dead, people try to avoid mentioning them to protect themselves from grief and sorrow. Such a habit makes it very hard to preserve the memory of the dead in stories.

To sum up, many Ayoreo myths explain the origin of the world's entities, and the linguistic gender of the common noun for each entity, masculine or feminine, has characterized the protagonists of the story and its plot. The Ayoreo have stories dealing with almost everything belonging to their traditional culture, since almost everything used to be an Ayoreo, so that linguistic gender has shaped stories to an unusually large extent.

3.4 Cultural continuity and innovations in origin stories

Ayoreo and Old Zamuco have the same cultural background (Ciucci 2019), so that it is very likely that what is explained in §3.3 on the role of grammatical gender in the Ayoreo origin myths also applies to Old Zamuco, although no stories of the Old Zamuco-speaking people were recorded. The high percentage of lexical similarity between Ayoreo and Old Zamuco, as well as traces of the contact with the Jesuits in the Ayoreo culture, indirectly suggest that also many, if not most stories, date back at least to the split between the Old Zamuco/Ayoreo and the Chamacoco branches of the family. However, one could even hypothesize that many stories come from the *Proto-Zamucoan culture, considering that the Chamacoco cosmovision is innovative, owing to contact with other populations (Cordeu 1989–92).

---

[9] Along with cultural changes, naming practices are also changing. For instance, my Ayoreo informants in Colonia Peralta told me that they no longer use teknonyms.

In Table 3, there is one exception to the otherwise consistent identity between the natural gender of the ancestor and the linguistic gender of the entity from which they originated. *Cucujna* was a boy who turned into the Bolivian tuco-tuco (*Ctenomys boliviensis*), a type of rodent. The word *cucujna* (f.sg.PF/AF) is feminine in Ayoreo, but its Old Zamuco cognate *cucudda* (m.sg.PF), *cucuddatie* (m.sg.AF) is masculine. Since Old Zamuco is more conservative than Ayoreo, linguistic gender shift has possibly occurred in the latter language, and the myth originated before this change. If this is so, Old Zamuco still preserves the exact correspondence between the linguistic gender of the noun and the natural gender of the mythological ancestor.

There are also myths which may be relatively recent, meaning that shamans have continued to elaborate stories in which linguistic gender plays a role. A very dangerous myth is the one of *Chunguperedatei* (m.sg.AF), the jabiru (*Jabiru mycteria*), a large stork. Anthropologists such as Sebag and Bórmida could only collect parts of this story, and even then, the narrators were considered responsible for the death of some Ayoreo who had listened to those parts (Fischermann 1988: §3.2.2). In the version reported by Fischermann, *Chunguperedatei* (m.sg.AF) 'jabiru' was a mighty chief and the husband of *Queneguete* (f.sg.PF/AF) 'spider' (see Table 3). Since this stork is mostly white, he was a white man, which is unusual in the Ayoreo stories, but this is a first sign that the myth developed at least after the first contacts with Spaniards. At some point, *Chunguperedatei* became the owner of most iron objects and was killed for that by the Ayoreo. This is another hint that contact with Spaniards is the *terminus post quem* for the origin of the story, since the Ayoreo only learned about iron objects after the first contacts with Spaniards. Until the recent sedentarization of the Ayoreo, they only had iron objects that they had stolen or found in the jungle among abandoned war materials from the Chaco war.

Another example of a fairly recent story is that of *Dequeyutiguei* (m.sg.AF) 'smallpox', who used to be a powerful Ayoreo leader (only men can be leaders). Smallpox is a disease brought after the first contacts with the Spaniards. The epidemics in the Jesuit missions, which ultimately led to the abandonment of the mission of *San Ignacio de Zamucos* in 1745 (Combès 2009: 83), still remain in the memory of the Ayoreo (Fischermann 1988: myth number 65). Contact with missionaries in the twentieth century also caused epidemics (Pia 2014: 43–4). Apart from these historical points, one has to note that *Dequeyutiguei* 'smallpox' derives from *eyutiguei* (m.sg.AF) 'weariness, fatigue, tiredness, emptiness, destruction' (Higham et al. 2000: 309). This noun does not inflect for possessor, yet *dequeyutiguei* (m.sg.AF) 'smallpox' shows the prefix /dek-/. This is the prefix for the unspecified possessor of possessable nouns (the 'generic form', §3.3), but here /dek-/ is used for derivation. This irregularity suggests that *dequeyutiguei* 'smallpox' is an innovation, and so must be its mythological association with a former Ayoreo leader. Besides, this term is not documented in Old Zamuco, which lacks a specific lexeme for 'smallpox'.

In conclusion, as Aikhenvald (2016: 121) puts it: 'Linguistic Genders influence beliefs, superstitions, and poetic metaphors revolved around an inanimate referent, which is then promoted to the status of an "honorary" human, or "anthropomorphized"'. This is precisely what has happened, but, unlike the many cases in which linguistic gender has been a mere source of poetic inspiration (Aikhenvald 2016), in the Ayoreo cosmovision, anthropomorphized entities have turned into the real characters who gave rise to almost all non-human entities. In other words, in the religious belief, the actual mythopoetic process (grammatical gender of the non-human entity > natural gender of the mythological ancestor) has been reinterpreted in the reversed order (natural gender of the mythological ancestor > grammatical gender of the non-human entity). Next to psycholinguistic experiments to assess the influence of linguistic gender on cognition (Aikhenvald 2016: 126–7), one might consider the genesis of the Ayoreo origin myths an unusual and systemic phenomenon in which linguistic gender has subconsciously affected human cognition, thus influencing the culture of a whole population.

4 Cultural change and linguistic change in Chamacoco

The Chamacoco traditional religious culture is very different from the Old Zamuco/Ayoreo one. This was possibly due to extended contact with other indigenous populations (Cordeu 1989–92), and coincides with the loss of a high percentage of the original Zamucoan lexicon. Like the Ayoreo, the Chamacoco have stories where a human being, owing to discomfort, unease or conflict, originates a new entity by turning into it. However, while this kind of narration dominates the Ayoreo cosmovision, it plays a less important role in the Chamacoco one (Cordeu 1989–92). Indeed, the Chamacoco stories concerning the metamorphosis of a human into a non-human entity are few compared to Ayoreo mythology, and only concern animals and celestial bodies. So far, I have found no plant, traditional object, or any other inanimate entity with a human origin, as in the Ayoreo stories.

Wilbert and Simoneau (1987) is a collection of all traditional stories docu-mented by the Chamacoco ethnographers up to the time of its publication.[10] In this corpus, one can find only a few animals whose origin is due to the metamorphosis of a human. Reading the Chamacoco stories, one has the impression that, in the Chamacoco cosmovision, the explanatory purpose of the origin myths plays a secondary role when compared with the Ayoreo cosmovision. In the Chamacoco narratives, it can sometimes be a matter of interpretation whether or not a transformation originates a new non-human entity. This is in stark contrast to the countless Ayoreo origin myths, which serve to explain the origin of almost everything (see §3.2).

There is another difference between the Ayoreo and Chamacoco stories: before metamorphosis, each Ayoreo mythological character leaves a specific magic formula/song, the so-called *sarode* (m.pl.AF) (§3.2). The Ayoreo have a massive inventory of *sarode*, whose words are considered powerful and taboo. Through these formulas, the power of the Ayoreo ancestors, from whom the entities of the world originated, still manifests itself. This creates a strong linkage between the Ayoreo mythological characters and the entities they turned into. By contrast, such magic formulas are absent from Chamacoco origin stories, which thus do not have the same importance they have for the Ayoreo.

In conclusion, the comparison between Ayoreo and Chamacoco myth-ology shows that a significant change has occurred in the Chamacoco cosmo-vision: the systematicity of the association between mythological human beings and non-human entities (originated by the former) has disappeared. In the following section, I show that such cultural change has a relation with a Chamacoco morphological innovation: the gender switch characterizing ani-mal nouns.

4.1 Myths and gender switch for animal terms: A reciprocal interaction

Both Ayoreo and Old Zamuco have gender switch for nouns referring to humans, but not for animal nouns. If needs be, the natural gender of the ani-mal can be specified by adding the words 'animal male' or 'female, woman', as in example (6) for Old Zamuco and (7) for Ayoreo (see Kelm 1964: 475).

---

[10] Most stories in Wilbert and Simoneau (1987) were collected by the Argentinian anthropologist Edgardo Cordeu, and some of them were later published, in Spanish, in Cordeu (1989–92).

(6)   Old Zamuco (Chomé 1958: 132)
   a.   ibohi (monkey.f.sg.PF) → ibohi (monkey.f.sg.PF) choqui-tie
        (male-m.sg.AF) 'male monkey'

   b.   potit (dog.m.sg.PF) → potit (dog.m.sg.PF) cheque-tae
        (female-f.sg.AF) 'female dog'

(7)   Ayoreo (Morarie 2011)
   a.   carata-i (jaguar-m.sg.AF) → carataque (jaguar.m.sg.PF) cheque
        (female.f.sg.PF/AF) 'female jaguar'

   b.   arapujnangue (fox.f.sg.PF/AF) → arapujnangue (fox.f.sg.PF/AF)
        choqui (male.m.sg.PF/AF) 'male fox'

By contrast, most animal nouns in Chamacoco have gender switch, which
expresses the natural, or sometimes supposed, gender of the animal (8) (see
Ciucci 2016: 567–83 for more examples; this work also explains the criteria
for morphological segmentation).

(8)   Chamacoco (Ciucci 2016)
   a.   'armadillo' ahmurmɨ-t (m.sg.AF), ahmurm-o (m.pl), ahmurmɨ-k
        (m.sg.PF)
        → ahmurmɨ-ta (f.sg.AF), ahmurm-e (f.pl), ahmurmeʼ (f.sg.PF)

   b.   'dog' poho-ch / pohi-ch (m.sg.AF) 'dog', poyt-o (m.pl)
        → poytii-ta (f.sg.AF) 'dog', poytii (f.pl), poytiiʼ (f.sg.PF)

   c.   'capybara' kerpish-t (m.sg.AF), kerpish-o (m.pl), [no m.sg.PF]
        → kerpish-ta (f.sg.AF), kerpish-e (f.pl), kerpish-ɨʼ (f.sg.PF), from
        Spanish carpincho

   d.   'jaguar' ɨlpiyo-t (m.sg.AF), ɨlpiyo (m/f.pl), ɨlpiyoʼ (m.sg.PF)
        → ɨlpiyo-ta (f.sg.AF), ɨlpiyo (m/f.pl), ɨlpiyoʼ (m/f.sg.PF)

Gender switch for animal terms seems an innovation correlated to the
changes that occurred in the Chamacoco culture. In the Ayoreo cosmovision,
animals are associated with the person who originated them, whose natural
gender is rigidly associated with the grammatical gender of the animal noun.
This was most likely a cultural block to the development of gender switch for
animal nouns. By contrast, the loss of the systematic association between person and animal in Chamacoco origin myths has enabled the gender switch

mechanism, which exists for human nouns in all Zamucoan languages, to spread to Chamacoco animal nouns.

Since, as seen for Ayoreo, grammatical gender shapes culture, the gender switch in Chamacoco animal nouns correlates with, and has most likely caused, considerable gender-related changes in the few Chamacoco stories in which the metamorphosis of a person originates an animal. Indeed, in Chamacoco myths both a man and a woman can turn into the same animal species. This does not happen in the Ayoreo narratives, where the ancestor of each non-human entity is either a man or a woman.

In one Chamacoco story, for example, the alligator was a young man who felt tired of his married life, so that he jumped into the water and became an alligator. His wife then followed him, turning into an alligator as well, supposedly into a female alligator (Wilbert and Simoneau 1987: 223–30). Similarly, the red woodpeckers were generated by the transformation of both a young man and his grandmother, who fled from their group members (Wilbert and Simoneau 1987: 234–42).

There are two different stories for the origin of the capybara: in one, it used to be a woman, in the other a young man (Wilbert and Simoneau 1987: 232–3, 242–7). The term currently in use for 'capybara', *kerpisht* (m.sg.AF), has gender switch (8c). *Kerpisht* (m.sg.AF) is a loanword from Spanish *carpincho* 'capybara', which shows that gender switch is not only still productive, but may even have been reinforced by the similar mechanism of gender switch in Spanish. Note also that the archaic Chamacoco term for 'capybara' has gender switch: *olokɨhlt* (m.sg.AF) ~ *olokɨhlta* (f.sg.AF).

The jaguar (8d), a culturally significant animal, is the most compelling case. This story, for which Wilbert and Simoneau (1987: 186–220) report several versions, can be seen as iconic of the spread of gender switch to animal terms: the first part explains the origin of *ɨlpiyot* (m.sg.AF), the male jaguar, the second the origin of *ɨlpiyota* (f.sg.AF), the female jaguar, a Chamacoco linguistic innovation (assuming that the word was initially masculine).

In conclusion, in the Chamacoco cosmovision, animals have lost their systematic association with the human beings who originated them, and whose natural gender was always well-defined. This loss of primordial humanity has allowed Chamacoco animal nouns to acquire gender switch, a morphological feature restricted to human nouns in Ayoreo and Old Zamuco. If cultural change has first affected grammar, then the Chamacoco innovative gender switch for animal terms has made it possible to use both grammatical genders as a source of poetic metaphor for some characters who brought animals into being in origin stories.

5 The Ayoreo teknonymic suffix -de/-ne

The birth of the first legitimate child is an important moment for the Ayoreo. After this child is born, family members are referred to as the father, mother, grandfather, and grandmother of the firstborn. This practice is known as 'teknonymy'. For the father, the language has a specific teknonymic suffix -de, with allomorph -ne, depending on the variety of Ayoreo and on the occurrence of nasal harmony. The suffix -de stems from dai (3.m.sg.PF) 'father' (9), from Proto-Zamucoan *daj (3.m.sg.PF), through the process ai/aj > e.[11]

(9)   a.   Old Zamuco: dai (3.m.sg.PF), daitie (3.m.sg.AF)

　　 b.   Ayoreo: dai (3.m.sg.PF/AF), daye (3.m.sg.PF/AF)

Children are named after an object or a natural entity connected with something that has happened in the period of their birth, or in the past to someone of the family. A common noun thus turns into a proper noun (§3.3). The linguistic gender of the noun chosen generally corresponds to the natural gender of the child (for examples, see Ciucci and Pia 2019: 45–7). After the first child has been born and accepted as legitimate, they receive a name, and the marriage turns into a permanent union (Fischermann 1988: §2.5.3). The new name of the father is the name of the child, plus the teknonymic suffix: *Caitabi* (the proper name of the child) + - de → *Caitabide* lit. 'the father of Caitabi'; *Ejei* + -ne → *Ejeine* lit. 'the father of Ejei'; *Sama* + -ne → *Samane* lit. 'the father of Sama'.

The father can also be referred to with a possessive NP which is equivalent to the teknonym: e.g. *Caitabi daye* 'the father (*daye*) of Caitabi', *Ejei daye* 'the father of Ejei', *Sama daye* 'the father of Sama', etc. The other kinship relationships have no specific teknonymic suffix; they are expressed by a possessive NP consisting of two phonological words, so that one can say *Caitabi date* 'the mother (*date*) of Caitabi', *Caitabi daquide* 'the grandfather (*daquide*) of Caitabi', *Caitabi dacode* 'the grandmother (*dacode*) of Caitabi'. Note that this practice occurs regardless of whether the first child is a boy or a girl; no sexual discrimination is made.

The development of a teknonymic suffix for the father has to do not only with the importance of the first legitimate child for the couple, but also with: (i) the importance of the father in order to feed the family; (ii) the need for

---

[11] See Ciucci and Bertinetto (2015: 50–1) for a similar development (*ai > e*) in the Ayoreo verb *-ise* 'to find, to meet, to reach'.

the father to be sure that he is the biological father of the child. From a social and practical point of view, a mother cannot have a child if she has no husband, because a man who hunts is absolutely needed. The child of a woman without a husband is considered a child without value. They are called *emi abi* 'child of the wind' (*em-i* wind-m.sg.AF; *ab-i* 3.child-m.sg.AF) and telling someone that they have no father is a severe offence (Ciucci and Pia 2019: 45). In the past, if a woman had a child and she was not married, or if the husband died during her pregnancy, the child was buried alive immediately after birth.

At the same time, the father needs to be sure about the baby's biological paternity. This has to do with the remarkable sexual freedom enjoyed by men and women before marriage (Ciucci and Pia 2019: 41). Since the woman is free to have sexual intercourse with whomever she wants to, until she marries, it is assumed that the paternity of the first child is uncertain and that the child has all defects of the previous partners of the woman. In pre-contact times, burying the child alive was considered the only option (Pia 2015: 16).[12] By contrast, the second child of a married woman is considered the real child of her husband and the legitimate firstborn child, so that their father is named after them.

The practice of burying children alive was prohibited by missionaries, so that it has stopped among sedentarized Ayoreo, but one can see a connection between the cultural motivations leading to infanticide and those yielding the teknonymic suffix for the father. In the Ayoreo culture, the names of the dead people are no longer pronounced, in order to avoid the grief for the loss of a loved one (§3.3). For this reason, if the first legitimate son or daughter dies, the father changes his name, adding the teknonymic suffix to the name of his next living son or daughter (Ciucci and Pia 2019: 46–7). To sum up, the development of a teknonymic suffix correlates with the importance of the connection between the firstborn child and the father in the Ayoreo culture.

No teknonymic suffix is found in Chamacoco, whose traditional culture was very different in this respect. For the Chamacoco, the relationship between father and children was less important. Having a small child, but not a husband, did not preclude women from getting married (many family stories I have heard prove this). Infanticide was not unknown in the past, but happened for other reasons than ensuring that the child was legitimate (Sušnik 1969: 139, 167). Apart from the father, other family figures were also

---

[12] Maria Paz was an 'illegitimate' firstborn child who was supposed to be killed. In order to avoid this, her mother escaped to a Catholic mission. Other Ayoreo of her group reached the mission, asking for the child, whom they wanted to kill. The child was saved by missionaries. For her story, see Paz (1966).

important for the child: 'the Chamacoco think in terms of "grandfathers-grandchildren" and not directly in terms of "fathers-children" [relationship] when it comes to a domestic and residential group' (Sušnik 1969: 170, my translation). By contrast, within society, the paternal uncle (who did not live in the same domestic group) was the central figure and the main authority for the children, since he represented their clan. He was seen as a second father, and the Chamacoco traditionally used to say that the children listened to the words of their father, but understood and retained the teaching of their paternal uncle (Sušnik 1969: 176, 181).

One may wonder whether the teknonymic suffix is an Ayoreo innovation or if it was found in Old Zamuco (or its dialects), whose speakers had a similar culture. According to Tomichá Charupá (2002: 325), in the *Missions of Chiquitos*, the Jesuits used to prepose the Spanish name given in the Baptism to the indigenous proper names. This led to the disappearance of the original proper names of the Chiquitano and other ethnicities of the missions, including the tribes speaking Old Zamuco and its dialects. The outcome of this practice of the Jesuits is evident in Chomé's grammar and dictionary of Old Zamuco (Chomé 1958; Ciucci forthcoming a), where no indigenous proper names are reported; in the examples, there are Spanish proper names such as *Pedro, Pablo, Diego*, or *Juan* (also adapted as *Yuan*). The only possible exception is the proper name *Paticu*, translated as 'Pedro', although it does not seem to be an Old Zamuco form of this Spanish name. Old Zamuco *Paticu* corresponds to the eighteenth-century Chiquitano proper name *Paticus*, translated into Spanish as 'Francisco' (and possible an early adaptation of the latter). Indigenous names are reported in other historical documents, including a letter by Chomé (Tomichá Charupá 2003).

Tomichá Charupá (2002: 317, 326) provides two lists of indigenous proper names found in historical documents from the Missions of Chiquitos. Among them, he lists seventeen indigenous names of men speaking Old Zamuco and its dialects. He also reports *Paticú*, but from another source than Chomé. More interestingly, five Old Zamuco names end in *-de/-ne*: *Dioné, Gofoiidé, Gozocoerade, Sofiade*, and *Tapaiuene*. One cannot be entirely sure that they are all teknonyms, although in Ayoreo this is the general rule for men's proper names. However, the fact that the Old Zamuco names are the only ones in the list which end in *-de/-ne* (there is only one exception) may be indirect evidence that they are teknonyms. Also, one can surmise that the Old Zamuco-speaking people, like the Ayoreo, used masculine and feminine common nouns as proper names for men and women, respectively. This seems to be confirmed by the proper name *Nupe*, which is the masculine singular PREDICATIVE FORM of 'earth, ground'.[13] The forms in -de/-ne do not look like common nouns used as proper names for men, since the endings -de/-ne are not very frequent in the masculine singular PREDICATIVE FORM of common nouns. They often characterize the feminine singular PREDICATIVE FORM in both Old Zamuco and Ayoreo (cf. the feminine nouns in Table 3, Appendix). Indeed, the only proper name for an Old Zamuco-speaking woman reported by Tomichá Charupá is *Assoné*. For this reason, *Dioné, Gofoiidé, Gozocoerade, Sofiade*, and *Tapaiuene* suggest that in the Zamucoan varieties spoken in the Missions of Chiquitos there was the same teknonymic suffix -de/-ne as in Ayoreo, which would confirm the similarity between the Old Zamuco and the Ayoreo culture in this as well as many other respects.

6 Possession

Some features of possession in Zamucoan reflect the cultural context in which these languages are spoken. By 'possession', I refer here to both 'association' and 'ownership'. The head of the possessive NP, the possessed, can generally be any noun, except for proper nouns. However, one has to distinguish between nouns that can be directly possessed and those that can be indirectly possessed. As in Oceanic languages, this distinction can have iconic motivation (Aikhenvald 2019: 11). In Zamucoan, as well as in most Chaco languages (Fabre 2007), nouns which are directly possessed have pertensive prefixes (term from Dixon 2010: 268). By contrast, the other nouns can be possessed through a possessive classifier or via simple apposition of possessor and possessed. The latter strategy is particularly frequent in Chamacoco. Indeed, this language shows many innovations owing to contact with Spanish: many Chamacoco nouns, for instance, have lost their pertensive prefixes, and only one classifier is regularly used, while two other classifiers are now rare. For this reason, Old Zamuco and Ayoreo better represent the traditional cultural situation.

In Zamucoan, the distinction between nouns inflected for possessor (that is, directly possessed) and those uninflected for possessor (that is, indirectly possessed) is more salient than the distinction between alienable and inalienable nouns. Indeed, some nouns inflected for possessor also have a

---

[13] The form itself is *nup*. Final [e] is a vowel often added to words ending with consonant in order to recreate the preferred syllable structure CV. In the available sources on the language, it is not possible to find the meaning of the other proper names listed by Tomichá Charupá (2002).

form (here called 'generic form') for unspecified possessor, so that they are alienable, while the rest of nouns inflected for possessor are inalienable, in that they necessarily mark a possessor. In other words, inalienability is subordinate to the distinction between direct and indirect possession. Kinship terms, for instance, have pertensive prefixes, but no form for unspecified possessor, so that they are always treated as inalienably possessed. In Zamucoan, direct possession can be an association such as: (i) whole-part relationship (parts of human and non-humans); (ii) kinship relation (with kinship terms); (iii) attribution (for abstract nouns, such as 'courage', 'excellence'); (iv) orientation or location (mostly for nouns used as postpositions or referring to places); (v) other general associations (mostly with abstract nouns, such as 'life', 'death', 'courage', 'word', or non-kinship terms referring to humans, such as 'friend'). If the possessed noun does not fit in one of the previously mentioned categories, the possessive relationship will most likely be one of ownership, as for 'food', 'house', and 'stick'. These have to be understood as general rules, as there are exceptions, such as 'lance', which cannot inflect for possessor in Old Zamuco and Chamacoco, but it does in Ayoreo: cf. Old Zamuco *azoretae* (f.sg.AF), Chamacoco *asōrrza* (f.sg.AF) vs Ayoreo *asōre* (3.f.sg.PF/AF) 'lance'.

The lack of direct possession in Zamucoan is a property of those items which cannot be owned for pragmatic reasons, such as 'day', 'night', and 'spring'. However, one can express association through a possessive classifier, as in the following example from Old Zamuco.

(10) Old Zamuco
      [**Chugupêre**   deha-tie   g-anec]
      bird.m.sg.PF   night-m.sg.AF   3-PCLF:general.m.sg.PF
      Night bird. (lit. 'bird of the night')

There are two groups of terms which cannot be directly possessed: nouns for animals and plants. The fact that they cannot be directly possessed may reveal a cultural practice. Animals, plants, and fruits (which are derived from plants) can only be possessed with a classifier. As I will show, this reflects the speakers' attitude towards consumable resources, and the need to protect their environment. The list of documented classifiers in Zamucoan is presented in Table 2. Classifiers are given in the third person. Like nominals, they also inflect for gender, number, and nominal form (the citation form is also here the singular ARGUMENT FORM). The classifier's inflection depends on the different configurations within the possessive NP. The reader interested in more details on the morphology and morphosyntax of classifiers in Zamucoan can consult Ciucci and Bertinetto (2019), the source of these data.[14]

Table 2 Zamucoan classifiers (Ciucci and Bertinetto 2019).

Semantics	Old Zamuco	Ayoreo	Chamacoco
general	*ganetie*	*gajnei, (yui, aniri)*	-
domesticated animal	*gachitie*	*gachidi*	*echit*
prey, haul	*yutie*	*yui*	-
fellow	-	*ujoi*	*uhut*
vehicles	-	*pi, gachidi*	-
plants	-	*acai* (also for fruits)	*ihyõrta*
long objects	*ohotae*	-	-

The use of a classifier for animals specifies the kind of relationship between possessor and possessed. In Old Zamuco and Ayoreo, the classifier indicates whether the animal was captured (11) or is a domestic animal (12). In the first case, Old Zamuco uses *yutie* (3.m.sg.AF), Ayoreo *yui* (3.m.sg.AF). Since this classifier has an irregular inflection in both languages, the inflected form in (11) cannot be immediately associated with its third person in Table 2. The classifier for domesticated animals (12) is the only one found in all Zamucoan languages. In Old Zamuco and Ayoreo, it is also a deverbal noun derived from 'to rear, to breed' (whose stem is *-achia* in both languages). The Ayoreo classifier for plants (and fruits) is also a deverbal noun from the verb stem *-aca* 'to plant'. It is employed to talk about the ownership of cultivated plants or fruits (13–14).

(11)   Old Zamuco
       Ch-ic   amitac
       1sg-PCLF:prey.m.sg.PF   turtle.m.sg.PF
       My turtle.

(12)   Old Zamuco
       G-achide   cucu
       3-PCLF:pet.m/f.sg.PF   dove.m.sg.PF
       His/her/their dove.

---

[14] Only Old Zamuco *ohotae* and Chamacoco *ihyõrta* are in the feminine, since no masculine form is attested.

(13)   Ayoreo
       B-aca-de   guejna
       2sg-PCLF:plant-m.pl.AF   plant_of_corn.m.pl.PF
       Your plants of corn.

(14)   Ayoreo
       Y-agu   y-aca-die   a-die
       1sg-eat 1sg-PCLF:plant-f.pl.AF   fruit-f.pl.AF
       I eat my fruits. (the fruit I have cultivated)

Classifiers for animals and plants can also be used as independent nouns. Chamacoco *echɨt* (3.m.sg.AF) 'domestic animal' and *ihyõrta* (3.f.sg.AF) 'plant' are nouns with general meaning also used as classifiers (15). For this reason, they are the only nouns for animals and plants showing pertensive prefixes. In Chamacoco, classifiers have mostly disappeared, and also *echɨt* 'domestic animal' and *ihyõrta* 'plant' are now rarely used with such a function, so that the most common strategy to express possession and ownership of plants and animals is the mere juxtaposition of possessor and possessed (16).

(15)   Chamacoco
       Wɨchɨ   [p-echɨ-t   poho-ch]
       3.m.sg   1sg-pet-**m.sg.AF** dog-**m.sg.AF**
       This is my dog.

(16)   Chamacoco
       [Yok   poho-ch]
       1sg   dog-m.sg.AF
       My dog.

Fruits are not directly possessed, and one of the reasons is that, when there is a specific term for a given fruit, it is mostly derived from the name of the plant. Gender here can have a derivational function, as in (17b–c), where plants are feminine and their fruits masculine:

(17)   a. Old Zamuco: cuco (f.sg.PF) 'species of tree' (*Ceiba ventricosa, Ceiba speciosa*) → cuca (f.sg.PF) 'fruit of *cuco*' (Ciucci forthcoming a)

       b. Ayoreo: cuya (f.sg.PF/AF) 'plant' (*Capparis retusa*) → cuya-i (m.sg.AF) 'fruit of *cuya*' (Pia 2014: 58; Morarie 2011: 98).

       c. Chamacoco: hnɨmɨ-ta (f.sg.AF), hnɨmɨʔ (f.sg.PF) 'cactus' → hnɨm-oʔ (m) 'cactus fruit' (Ciucci 2016: 587)

To sum up, nouns for plants, fruits, and animals can only be indirectly possessed, and a classifier specifies the kind of possessive relationship. A reason for this is that the Zamucoan people were traditionally semi-nomadic, and had to move in order to make the most of the few resources available in the northern Chaco. Hence the impossibility of owning animals and plants. Most Chaco languages have possessive classifiers, which is a possible areal feature, and, if they have classifiers, they have one for (domestic) animals (Ciucci 2020). This also occurs in Bororo (Macro-Jê) (Crowell 1979), not a Chaco language, but close enough to the Chaco. From a cultural point of view, animals are considered autonomous entities which are not owned by Chaco populations (Comrie et al. 2010: 113). The fact that the relationship with animals does not involve 'ownership' has to do with the management of the resources. Indeed, a 'distant' relationship, in which the people do not own the animal, gives them no right for excessive exploitation of the fauna. This would not just endanger the animals, but also threaten the survival of the indigenous people.[15]

According to Renshaw (1988), indirect possession depends instead on the attitude of the indigenous people towards consumable items (which include fruits, plants, and animals) rather than on ecological reasons. Among the Chaco indigenous peoples, equality is a moral value, which implies the obligation to share (in particular) consumable resources with the rest of the community. The idea of equality and the practice of semi-nomadism make it impossible for the individual to accumulate possessions, and this is a necessary survival strategy for the group in traditional hunter-gatherer societies with little agriculture. Since consumable items are not regarded as personal property, they are only indirectly possessed. By contrast, the indigenous concern for the preservation of natural resources is, according to Renshaw (1988: 344), 'perhaps more of an ideal than a historical fact'. Indeed, he claims that individual hunter-gatherers tend to exploit all available resources in an environment which is seen as inexhaustible. However, at a collective level, the impossibility to accumulate resources (for both practical reasons and to maintain social harmony) has counterbalanced the rational, short-term, impulse of the individual to get the maximum of consumable goods out of the environment (Renshaw 1988).

---

[15] One of my Chamacoco informants pointed out to me that hunting requires a particular knowledge in order to kill animals without compromising the reproduction of the local fauna. He compared the indigenous management of natural resources, which is sustainable, to the attitude of the Western people, who kill animals without any concern for their preservation. He found it contradictory that the Western world also manifests itself with the presence of ecologists, who tell indigenous people not to hunt in their traditional territory, because some species are endangered. This made him angry, because hunting is still necessary for the economic survival of the community.

Renshaw's compelling arguments do not exclude the suggestion that the need to protect natural resources can also play a role in the non-possessability of animals and plants. Particularly for animals, there is another factor, not considered by Renshaw, which at a societal level contributes to the long-term preservation of the environment: traditional religious beliefs.

In the Chamacoco culture, several species of animals have their own spirit master (see Cordeu 1989–92; Blaser 2010: 214), often referred to by the animal species plus *bahlut* (m.sg.AF) which means 'chief, leader', but also 'big': e.g. *ilpiyot* (m.sg.AF) 'jaguar' → *ilpiyot bahlut* 'chief of the jaguars, big jaguar'; *inermitit* (m.sg.AF) 'turtle' → *inermitit bahlut* 'chief of the turtles, big turtle'. Chamacoco also has a general term which can refer to any spirit master: *yoniit* (3.m.sg.AF) 'spirit master; spirit, ghost'. Spirit masters protect animals and take care of them. They are regarded with respect by hunters, because they can be dangerous, and do not allow hunters to kill too many animals. If this or other rules for the preservation of the fauna are broken, the respective *yoniit* 'spirit master' will make the responsible people sick.

Spirit masters frequently occur in the culture of the Lowland South American peoples (Viveiros de Castro 1998, 2004), including other neighbouring Chaco populations. For instance, among the Toba (Guaycuruan), each species has its animal spirit master (aka *dueño de los animales*, literally 'animals' owner') (Cordeu 1969–70). These are very similar to the Chamacoco spirit masters: in both cases, they are imagined as big representatives of the respective species. The Chiquitano (nowadays also called Monkóka) also have a spirit master who rears the animals, protects them, and punishes those who kill more animals than they need for their families (Arrien 2008: 34). These functions are similar to the animal spirit masters of the Wichi, who also have spirit masters for plants and substances (Montani 2017: 57–61).

Apart from cultural influence of neighbours, the presence of animal spirit masters in the Chamacoco culture may have to do with the weakening of the linkage between humans and non-humans that occurred in the Chamacoco cosmovision. In comparison, in the Ayoreo cosmovision, I have found no reference to spirit masters. Indeed, when the single animal specimens are denied a spiritual essence common to humans, spirit masters, representing an animal species, typically serve to establish a connection with humans, with whom spirit masters share the same subjectivity or consciousness (Viveiros de Castro 1998: 471, 2004: 470–1).

In Zamucoan, there is only one animal which inflects for possessor: the louse. Indeed, in both Old Zamuco and Ayoreo, it takes pertensive prefixes. Pediculosis (infestation with lice) was frequent in traditional societies characterized by poor hygienic conditions, so that 'louse' can actually be 'possessed'. Also in neighboring Chiquitano (aka Bésɨro, unclassified), animals do not inflect for possessor, but here also *napáx* (GF.sg) 'louse' is an exception and takes pertensive prefixes.[16] By contrast, in Chamacoco, *hnatsɨkɨta* (f.sg.AF) 'louse' does not inflect for possessor (Ciucci 2013: 13). This has possibly to do with the fact that many Chamacoco words have lost the possessive inflection, which is also no longer productive.

(18) a. Old Zamuco 'louse' y-unnar (1sg.m.sg.PF), a-nnar (2sg.m.sg.PF), unnar (3.m.sg.PF), ay-unnar (1/2pl.m.sg.PF), nar (GF.m.sg.PF)

     b. Ayoreo 'louse' ñ-ujnari (1sg.m.sg.AF), ma-jnari (2sg.m.sg.AF), ujnari (3.m.sg.AF), jnari (GF.m.sg.AF)

Finally, in today's Chaco indigenous societies, money, which is an impersonal and transient means of exchange, is considered a property that the owner is not obliged to share with their family and community, unlike consumable items (Renshaw 1988). For this reason, *iplata* (3.f.sg.PF/AF) 'money', a borrowing from South American Spanish *plata* 'money', has possessive inflection in Ayoreo (Ciucci 2016: 360). The term for 'money' is uninflected for possessor in Chamacoco, since the mechanism is no longer productive. Among the items which cannot be directly possessed in Zamucoan, there are 'sun', 'moon', 'earth', and 'jungle, forest'. This has pragmatic reasons, possibly intertwined with cultural reasons. The same items cannot be owned in a number of Tupí-Guaraní languages and in Waujá (Arawak) (Aikhenvald 2019: 21–2). Here one cannot identify specific cultural reasons for Zamucoan, but the fact that these items cannot be possessed has generic cultural motivations common in many traditional societies.

7 Comparative structures and egalitarian values

The Zamucoan people traditionally lived in small, egalitarian societies. In this section, I will explore a possible correlation between the expression of comparison and the egalitarian nature of the Old Zamuco and Ayoreo societies.

---

[16] This is the form of the Lomeriano dialect of Chiquitano. In the Ignaciano dialect, 'louse' is *oiñapáx* (□.GF.sg) / *ñapáx* (□.GF.sg), with a difference according to male and female speech. Like Zamucoan and most Chaco languages, Chiquitano also has a form for unspecified possessor (GF) (Ciucci and Macoñó 2018: 49). In Chiquitano there is also another animal which can take possessive inflection: the horse. Something similar occurs in Dakota (Siouan), in which animals cannot be possessed, with the exception of the horse (Aikhenvald 2019: 22).

All Zamucoan languages have dedicated comparative constructions. In Old Zamuco, the index of comparison is the verb *ch-iozochêre* (3.REAL), or *no gai* (3). Both mean 'to outdo, to surpass, to exceed'. The only difference is that *no gai* is a complex predicate consisting of the verb *no* (3) 'to go' and the adposition *gai* 'over', which follows the object.[17] In the simplest comparative structure, the parameter of comparison involves dimension and it is implicitly expressed by the verb; the comparee and the standard are the transitive subject (A) and the object (O) shown in (19).

(19) Old Zamuco

Z-uti-tie	ch-iozochere	a-uti-tie
1sg-field-m.sg.AF	3.REAL-exceed	2sg-field-m.sg.AF
COMPAREE	INDEX-PARAMETER	STANDARD

My field is bigger than yours. (Chomé 1958: 134)

However, when the parameter is specified, it appears both as head of the transitive subject (A), and as the object (O). The comparee is the possessor of A, and the standard of comparison the possessor of O, as in example (20). When expressed, the parameter can only be an abstract noun. In Old Zamuco, abstract nouns are often derived from past participle-like nouns, adjectives, and verbs. For instance, *gonigatie* (3.m.sg.AF) 'excellence' is derived from the verb *gom* (3) 'be worthy, be right, be good' through the derivational suffix *-niga*. In other words, this complex construction requires the availability of a derivational mechanism.

(20) Old Zamuco

[Azote_Santa_Maria]	goniga-tie,			no
Holy_virgin_Mary	3.excellence-m.sg.AF			3.exceed
COMPAREE	PARAMETER			INDEX
[angeles-oddoe	nez	ore]	goniga-tie	gai
angel-m.pl.AF	all	3pl	3.excellence-m.sg.AF	exceed
STANDARD			PARAMETER	INDEX

The Holy Virgin Mary is more excellent than all angels. (lit. 'the excellence of the Holy Virgin Mary is superior to the excellence of all angels') (Ciucci forthcoming a)

---

[17] Alternatively, one could interpret this not as a complex predicate, but just as a verb followed by the adposition. This would just increase the complexity of the comparative construction.

Chomé notes that there is another, simpler, although less elegant, way to express comparison in Old Zamuco, that is, by the juxtaposition of two clauses shown in (21).

(21) Old Zamuco
    a. A-igueda-ré   amâ;   y-igueda-re   dieda
        2sg-house-m.sg.AF little 1sg-house-m.sg.AF big.m/f.sg.PF
        My house is little, your house is big, i.e. my house is bigger
        than yours.

    b. Da-raha   amâ; uyu a-iraha=puz
        2sg-know little 1sg 1sg-know=AUG
        You know little, I know much, i.e. I know more than you.
        (Chomé 1958: 134)

This is the strategy employed by languages which do not have proper comparative constructions, such as Warekena, an Arawak language of Brazil (Aikhenvald 2015: 232). On comparative constructions, see also Chapter 1 and Chapter 10, present volume. The fact that specific comparative constructions were not always used suggests that they were an innovation and that the starting point was a situation where the only option was juxtaposing two clauses, as in (21). Chamacoco does have comparative constructions, but they were borrowed from Spanish (22), so that it is unknown whether pre-contact Chamacoco had comparative constructions (Ciucci 2021).

(22) P.   **ma**   ɨlaroˀ   **je**   S.
      P.   more old.m/f.sg.PF than S.
      COMPAREE INDEX PARAMETER MARK STANDARD
      P. is older than S.; cf. Spanish: *P. es **más*** (INDEX) ***viejo que*** (MARK) *S.*

As pointed out by Dixon (2008: 814), the lack of dedicated comparative constructions characterizes small tribes with an egalitarian social system, where there is little or no emphasis on competition. Such a situation fits Chaco societies, which place particular emphasis on the value of equality. Indeed 'equality here is not merely the absence of any kind of social stratification, but is a positively affirmed moral principle' (Renshaw 1988: 339). As Renshaw (1988: 338–9) points out, this can be noted in the 'remarkable uniformity in the material conditions of life' of today's Chaco indigenous communities, which is not observed among the Paraguayan population with comparable economic situation. As already noted (§6), the ethics of equality prevented the indigenous individual from accumulating material possessions and obliged them to share consumable items.

Equality can be observed in many aspects of Ayoreo society. The Ayoreo live in small local groups which can unite in case of war. Each group has a leader, the *dacasute* (GF.f.sg.AF/PF, see §8), who is someone who has killed a certain number of enemies or jaguars, but also has the appropriate mental and moral qualities to be a leader. In each local group, next to the proper leader, there are a number of men who have qualities and merits similar to those of the leader, and who are also called *dacasute*. Even though only one person can be the actual leader, almost all adult men reach the same social rank of *dacasutedie* (f.pl.AF) 'chiefs' (Fischermann 1988: §2.1.2).

The leader of a local group has much power in wartime, but limited authority during peacetime; he mostly has the same obligations and rights as the other men of the group. Decisions are taken by the men in meetings chaired by the leader, whose role is to sanction the dominant opinion (Fischermann 1988: §2.1.4). As I will show in §8, in Ayoreo society there is an equilibrium between men and women, and the latter substantially influence community decisions. Finally, once a decision is taken, according to Fischermann, there is no obligation to agree with the decisions and, 'people who do not follow the decisions cannot be obliged to do this, nor can they be publicly criticized' (my translation). Indeed, in Chaco societies, equality goes together with the autonomy of the individual (Renshaw 1988).

The education of Ayoreo children is also anti-authoritarian (Fishermann 1988: §2.5.2); children, for instance, are never hit, because it is believed that this would result in the soul abandoning the body of the child. In general, the young people have no obligations until they marry (Pia 2016: 116).

The general equality and respect for individual freedom could be related to the fact that neither in Old Zamuco nor in Ayoreo are there specific terms for 'must' 'to have to', 'to oblige', 'obligation', echoed by the lack of other verbs with deontic meaning such as 'can' or 'may'. In Old Zamuco, the only exception could be the verb *chiroc* (3.REAL), which is also translated as 'to oblige'. However, it is not clear whether the verb really implied an obligation. This was possibly the translation of a missionary who needed to express 'to oblige'. Indeed, the verb *chiroc* (3.REAL) seems to properly mean 'to command, to order', like Ayoreo *chiroque* (3) 'to command' (but also 'to send'), which does not necessarily include the obligation to obey. The corresponding Old Zamuco deverbal noun, *iroique* (3.m.sg.PF), is translated as 'order', not as 'obligation', and the same applies to Ayoreo *iroque* (3.m.sg.PF) 'command'. The lack of a feature or lexeme is often hard to correlate with any cultural feature.

For instance, many languages lack a verb meaning 'must' or 'to have to', but this does not imply that a culture lacks obligations or prohibitions. Indeed, the Ayoreo culture has obligations, although they may be fewer than in many other societies.

At the same time, the Ayoreo refuse obligations which are felt as imposed by someone else, unless there is an actual need for them, as in wartime. Such a notion of individual freedom has contributed to the voluntary isolation of the Ayoreo from the eighteenth century until the second half of the twentieth century. Indeed, the Ayoreo partly descend from people who spent some time in the Jesuit mission of *San Ignacio de Zamucos* (abandoned in 1745), before going back into the forest, because they did not like the new lifestyle imposed by the Jesuits. In the oral memories of the Ayoreo, the Jesuits gave them orders, obliged them to work and punished those who dared to disobey (Fischermann 1996). All of this is in stark contrast with traditional Ayoreo values.

8 The importance of women: Mismatches between linguistic and social gender

The notion of equality in traditional Zamucoan society goes together with a search for gender balance, notwithstanding the gender-specific roles considered proper for each sex (see §3.2). Some morphological exceptions reflect this. Example (23) shows three Ayoreo feminine nouns which can refer to men.

(23) a. ero (3.f.sg.PF/AF) 'leader' (man or woman)

 b. quicujadia (3.f.sg.AF), quicujat (3.f.sg.PF) 'ancestor, forefather' (man or woman)

 c. dacasute (GF.f.sg.PF/AF), asute (3.f.sg.PF/AF) 'chief, leader' (only men)

Ero 'leader' (23a) and *quicujadia* 'ancestor' (23b) refer to both men and women, while *dacasute* 'chief, leader' (23c) only refers to men. Indeed, in the traditional Ayoreo culture, the *dacasute* is the leader of a group (§7), a role reserved only for men (Pia 2014: 21). Traditionally, in order to be a leader, one had to show courage and kill; the type of victims who gave the most prestige to a future *dacasute* 'chief, leader' were jaguars or white men (Pia 2016: 4). Women could not become leaders because they had no military role.

The word *dacasute* 'chief, leader' (23c) has an interesting etymology. Its root is *asute*, which coincides with the form for third-person possessor (23c).

The original meaning of *asute* is possibly 'our mother'. Indeed, the word is similar to Old Zamuco *azote* 'our mother', and the old Chamacoco form *aset* 'our mother'. In both cases, initial *as-* is a Proto-Zamucoan prefix for the first-person plural possessor (Ciucci and Bertinetto 2017). The prefix *as-* is lost in Ayoreo, but it is fossilized in the root of this word for 'leader'. Pia (2014: 20) also documents *dacasutei* (GF.m.sg.AF), but notes that it is only found in some local groups and rarely used.[18]

Quicujadia 'ancestor' (23b) is a key term in Ayoreo mythology, since, as mentioned above, it can refer to the first Ayoreo people who turned into the entities of the world (§3.2). In Ayoreo, the unmarked gender of nouns is usually the masculine, but the fact that *quicujadia* and the two terms expressing leadership shown in (23) are feminine, while also referring to men, may have to do with the traditionally important position of women in Ayoreo society.

Ayoreo society is characterized by rigid gender distinctions, with specific activities only allowed to either men or women, and this is reflected in many myths (see §3.2 and Table 3 in the Appendix). At the same time, the important role of women is clearly recognized. There is a striking historical testimony regarding a Zamucoan group of the early eighteenth century, related to the Old Zamuco-speaking people and to the present-day Ayoreo: 'They honor women with the title of Ladies, and truly they (f) are, because they command their husbands, and by their (f) whim they (m) move from one place to another; they (f) never do their (f) housework, but they employ their husbands, even for the humblest chores'. (Fernández 1726, apud Combès 2009: 49; my translation).[19] Such claims are surely excessive, but the missionary who wrote them correctly grasped that the women's position in that Zamucoan society was unusual, particularly for someone more familiar with the eighteenth-century Spanish culture.[20]

In Ayoreo society, both men and women enjoy great sexual freedom before marriage. One of the few restrictions is that women are allowed to woo men, but not vice-versa. In the family, the man has no dominant role, also because the complementary and gender-specific activities of both partners are considered equally important for survival (Fischermann 1988: §2.5.3). The Ayoreo are

---

[18] An Old Zamuco term for 'leader', *date-tie* (m.sg.AF), is masculine, but still comes from 'mother', *date-tae* (f.sg.AF). In all Zamucoan languages the root for 'mother', *date*, was also converted into the adjective for 'big', which as an adjective could take masculine and feminine suffixes. In Old Zamuco the masculine forms of 'big' were used to refer to the 'leader'.

[19] Original version: 'Honran a las mujeres con el título de señoras, y verdaderamente lo son, porque ellas mandan a sus maridos, y por su capricho se mudan de un lugar a otro; jamás ponen mano en las haciendas domésticas, sino que se sirven de sus maridos, aun para los ministerios más humildes'.

[20] It was also unusual from the point of view of the Chiquitano, the dominant ethnic group of the *Missions of Chiquitos*, whose traditional society was dominated by men.

divided into seven clans, with clan exogamy being the main rule for marriage. Clan membership is inherited from the father. A balance between genders, can, however, be seen in the fact that women maintain their clan membership after marriage, which is characterized by uxorilocal residence: the married couple lives with the extended family of the wife (Fischermann 1988: §2.6.4).

The Ayoreo take decisions in meetings chaired by the *dacasute* 'chief, leader' (23c). Although women do not participate in these meetings, they still play an essential role in the decisions of the community, because issues are discussed at home before official community meetings, and 'most men frankly admit that in home discussion, women have the last word and conclusively influence their position' (Fischermann 1988; §2.1.4, my translation). The importance of women also has to do with the fact that they establish the allocation of resources (Fischermann, p.c.). During fieldwork in Bolivia, Pier Marco Bertinetto and I had the occasion to see that the Ayoreo men were very respectful and even gave the impression of having a certain reverential fear while talking to women, including their own wives.

The Ayoreo women are allowed access to religious knowledge; they can be shamans, as shown in the gender switch of the word for 'shaman': *daijnai/naijnai* (m.sg.AF) → *daijne/naijne* (f.sg.PF/AF). Similar considerations applied in the past to Old Zamuco-speaking women; indeed, in Old Zamuco *naina* (m.sg.PF) 'shaman' has the feminine *naine* (f.sg.PF). By contrast, the Chamacoco women cannot be shamans and a large amount of religious secrets were traditionally reserved to initiated men. As a consequence, the Chamacoco term for 'shaman', *konsehet* (M.SG.AF), has no gender shift. Finally, also another component of religion, mythology, illustrates the high status of Ayoreo women: *Asojna* (see Table 3), one of the key figures in the Ayoreo religious beliefs, was a woman and a mighty shaman.

9 The Chamacoco secret register: A short note

The integration points of language and society analysed so far concern the traditional culture, and even though Chamacoco often shows innovations, these took place long before contact with Western society. Nowadays, most aspects of the Chamacoco (Ebitoso) traditional culture have disappeared, and the language is the main factor in the Chamacoco identity. Here, I will briefly mention another integration point which only has to do with present-day Chamacoco society and is a direct result of the influence exerted by Spanish on the language: the emergence of a secret register.

An indigenous language spoken by a minority of people is useful as a secret language, and Chamacoco can be used in order not to be understood by the other Paraguayan people (who speak Spanish and/or Paraguayan Guaraní). However, Chamacoco has introduced a high number of borrowings from Spanish. This is problematic, because Spanish loans are potentially recognizable by the Spanish-speaking people, who could thus partly 'crack' the code. For this reason, Chamacoco has developed a secret register. This register consists in a number of strategies aimed at avoiding seemingly recognizable borrowings from Spanish (Ciucci forthcoming b). They involve:

(i)   use of archaic words, which in the everyday language are usually replaced by Spanish borrowings;
(ii) phonological manipulation of Spanish loanwords;
(iii) extension to non-adapted Spanish borrowings of Chamacoco inflectional elements which are weakening elsewhere in the language;
(iv) use of periphrases instead of Spanish lexicon.

Two chapters in this volume (Chapter 5 by Dixon and Chapter 10 by Mous) address a different kind of avoidance registers, used to deal with in-laws (on special speech styles, see also Chapter 1). Unlike in the languages discussed by Dixon and Mous, the Chamacoco secret register is not restricted to uses related to kinship or any other category, and it is a recent innovation as a consequence of prolonged and intense contact with Spanish. By contrast, the Ayoreo were contacted later than the Chamacoco, and their language has a much lower number of Spanish borrowings than Chamacoco. Spanish borrowings are, however, increasing in Ayoreo and, correspondingly, cases of linguistics purism in order to avoid Spanish lexicon are documented, at least in older generations (Ciucci and Pia 2019: 47–50). It is hard to say whether, in the early phases of contact, Chamacoco was also characterized by the avoidance of Spanish borrowings, because we do not have enough historical data on the language at an earlier stage of contact comparable with that of present-day Ayoreo.

10 Conclusions

In this chapter, I have dealt with the interaction of language and society in the Zamucoan languages (†Old Zamuco, Ayoreo, and Chamacoco). Zamucoan has a peculiar system of nominal suffixation, which expresses, among other features, gender (§2.1). This grammatical category has exerted a remarkable influence on Ayoreo mythology: the metamorphosis of humans generated almost all non-human entities, and the grammatical gender of each entity became the social gender of the mythical figure who impersonated it (§3). While the Ayoreo and Old Zamuco speakers share the same cultural background, Chamacoco society has multiple innovations, owing to contact with neighbouring populations. In the Chamacoco cosmovision, for instance, the association between humans and non-humans plays a reduced role, and this has had consequences for inflectional morphology (§4). Chamacoco animal terms have developed gender switch, and this, in turn, has affected some mythological stories (§4.1). A further point of integration between language and society is the presence of a teknonymic suffix for the father in Ayoreo (§5). Such a suffix is not present in Chamacoco, but, despite little data, one can surmise that it was also found in Old Zamuco. A feature common to all three languages is the use of possessive classifiers for items which cannot directly be owned (§6). The inventory of classifiers can reflect some aspects of the society where the language is spoken (see Chapter 1, and Chapter 6 by Aikhenvald, present volume). Zamucoan possessive classifiers for animals and plants have to do with the distribution of consumable resources and the management of the environment providing them. There are hints of a possible lack of dedicated comparative constructions in the past (§7), and this correlates with small, egalitarian groups, which still today constitute Ayoreo society. Ayoreo women have high social status, as reflected by some mismatches between linguistic and natural gender (§8). Finally, progressive disruption of traditional societies in the contemporary world redefines the interaction between language and culture (as far as the former is preserved): the use of a secret register in Chamacoco (§9) is an example of how the language reflects and adapts to a new societal context.

Acknowledgements

I would like to express my gratitude to Alexandra Y. Aikhenvald, Pier Marco Bertinetto, R. M. W. Dixon, Brigitta Flick, Sonja Gipper, Nerida Jarkey, †Gabriella Erica Pia, Dineke Schokkin, Nathan M. White, and Katarzyna I. Wojtylak. This work is dedicated to the memory of the late Gabriella Erica Pia.

Appendix. An analysis of the Ayoreo mythological characters

Table 3 The grammatical, natural, and social gender of the Ayoreo mythological characters.

Mythological figure and grammatical glosses	Meaning	Gender of the character	Source and other information on the story
Abujei (m.sg.AF)	type of fish (*Hoplerythrinus unitaeniatus*)	male	Pia (2015: 25–6). If the story is told, people will fight with each other.
Acherangori (m.sg.AF)	tempest	male	Pia (2014: 127–9).
Ajacaratai (m.sg.AF)	type of plant (*Jatropha grossidentata*)	male	Pia (2014: 74–6; 2016: 115–16). See *Chicōri*.
Aramato (f.sg.PF/AF)	big coleopteron	female	Pia (2018: 54–6).
Aramui (m.sg.AF)	sickle	male	Pia (2018: 18). He was a young man who was always bowed and cultivated the land.
Asojna (f.sg.PF/AF)	night hawk (*Caprimulgus parvulus*)	female	Pia (2014: 96–8, 2016: 46–7); see also Fischermann (1988). *Asojna* was the first female shaman. She is one of the most important figures of Ayoreo mythology. Her stories and formulas can be very powerful and dangerous.
Asōre (3.f.sg.PF/AF)	lance	female	Bórmida (2005, II: 112–13). No generic form for this word is documented in any Zamucoan language.
Bujote (f.sg.PF/AF)	type of bird (*Cacicus solitarius*)	female	Pia (field notes); Fischermann (1988, myth number 42). She was the wife of *Doridi*.
Cadua (f.sg.AF)	type of tree (*Amburana cearensis*)	female	Bórmida (2005, II: 125–6); Pia (field notes).
Cani(r)ojnai (m.sg.AF)	type of plant (*Jatropha grossidentata*)	male	Pia (2014: 74–6). Like *Chicōri*, he kills *Ajacaratai* in another version of the story.
Carai (m.sg.AF)	toco toucan (*Ramphastos toco*)	male	Pia (2016: 106). *Carai* was a honey hunter.
Caratai (m.sg.AF)	jaguar	male	Pia (2015: 34). *Caratai* was a chief.

Mythological figure and grammatical glosses	Meaning	Gender of the character	Source and other information on the story
Carujnanguejna (f.sg.PF/AF)	violet wood, purpleheart (*Peltogyne confertiflora*)	female	(Pia 2016: 40–1). She was a woman with menstruation problems.
Catague (f.sg.PF/AF)	bristly starbur (*Acanthospermum hispidum*)	female	Pia (2018: 18). She was a solitary girl who had quarrels with the other girls and scared them with a needle.
Chibiside (m.sg.PF/AF)	type of plant (*Moya spinosa*)	female	Pia (field notes). The scientific name of the plant is in Fischermann (1988). She is the wife of *Chibisidi*.
Chibisidi (m.sg.AF)	type of plant (*Mandevilla angustiflora*)	male	Pia (field notes). He is the husband of *Chibiside*.
Chicōri (m.sg.AF)	tuber plant that holds water (*Jacaratia corumbensis*)	male	Pia (2014: 74–5, 2016: 115–16). *Chicōri* killed his brother *Ajacaratai*, who had an adulterous relationship with his wife.
Choyo (f.sg.PF/AF)	blue-crowned trogon (*Trogon curucui*)	female	Pia (2016: 96). *Choyo* was the partner of *Doridi*. They turned into birds together.
Chume (f.sg.PF/AF)	type of thorny shrub	female	Fischermann (1988: §7.1).
Chunguperedatei (m.sg.AF)	jabiru (*Jabiru mycteria*)	male	Fischermann (1988: §3.2.2). He was a powerful chief and the owner of iron objects. Since the jabiru is mostly white, it is considered a white man, and this explains his association with iron objects. His myth is very taboo.
Corangarāi (m.sg.AF)	shovel	male	Pia (2018: 32). He was a man who liked to cultivate the land and had a good harvest, which caused the envy of the other people.
Corodi (m.sg.AF)	type of palm (*Acrocomia totai*)	male	Pia (2018: 51). He was a young man, tall and slim. This plant is also called *picadei* (m.sg.AF) in Ayoreo.
Cucarane (f.sg.PF/AF)	stone	female	Bórmida (2005, II: 117–18).
Cuco (f.sg.PF/AF)	type of tree (*Ceiba ventricosa*, *Ceiba speciosa*)	female	Pia (2014: 87–8, 2015: 19, 2018: 113–14). She was the wife of *Tobejnai* and had a child from him.

(Continued)

Table 3 (Continued)

Mythological figure and grammatical glosses	Meaning	Gender of the character	Source and other information on the story
Cucoi (m.sg.AF)	type of tree (*Ceiba insignis*)	male	Pia (2018: 79–80). He was a tall man.
Cucujna (f.sg.PF/AF)	Bolivian tuco-tuco (*Ctenomys boliviensis*)	male	Fischermann (1988, myth number 22). In Old Zamuco the noun was masculine: *cucudda* (m.sg.PF), *cucuddatie* (m.sg.AF), 'small animal, like a rabbit, whose teeth were used as a knife' (Ciucci forthcoming a; translated from Spanish).[a]
Cucujui (m.sg.AF)	pigeon (*Patagioenas picazuro*)	male	Pia (2016: 42–3). As a man, *Cucujui* told prohibited stories and magic formulas which killed many Ayoreo, until he turned into a bird not to be killed. Nobody asked him any *sari* (or *sarode*, the Ayoreo magic formulas, see §3.2).
Cuguebi (DIM.m.sg.AF), from *cuguei* (m.sg.AF) 'bean'	buff-throated woodcreeper (*Xiphorhynchus guttatus*)	male	Pia (2018: 31). According to Fischermann (1988), this bird is the *Pseudoleistes virescens*.
Curude (f.sg.PF/AF)	red stone used for makeup	female	Pia (2016: 93–4, 108–9). This red stone is used mostly by single women, but also by men, to apply as makeup in order to attract a partner. *Curude* was an attractive woman with wonderful makeup. Her *sari* is used to let people fall in love.
Cusi (m.sg.AF)	cassava, manioc (*Manihot esculenta*)	male	Pia (2016: 68–9, 2018: 58). It is *Manihot heterophylla* according to Fischermann (1988).
Cuya (f.sg.PF/AF)	type of plant (*Cynophalla retusa*)	female	Pia (2016: 71). *Cuya* was an evil female shaman.
Dacatereato (f.sg.PF/AF)	red rope used by men to tie up the hair	female	Pia (2016: 100). *Dacatereato* was a woman who used this very object as adornment and turned into it because she wore makeup after having married. For this reason, the object is now only used by men.

[a] Original version: 'animalito, como conejo, cuyos dientes les servian de cuchillo'.

Mythological figure and grammatical glosses	Meaning	Gender of the character	Source and other information on the story
Dequeyutiguei (m.sg.AF)	smallpox, serious illness	male	Fischermann (1988, §7.1). He was a powerful Ayoreo leader.
Dibe (f.sg.PF/AF)	fox	female	Fischermann (1988: §3.2.2). She was the sister of *Putugutoi* (the jaguar).
Dicacuei (m.sg.PF/AF)	black-collared hawk (*Busarellus nigricollis*)	male	Pia (2018: 111). He was a man who burned parts of the forest to hunt.
Diguiriquia (f.sg.PF/AF)	bare-faced curassow (*Crax fasciolata*)	female	Pia (2016: 95–6). *Diguiriquia* was a woman who made wonderful adornments. She left no *sari*, but technical suggestions.
Direjna (f.sg.PF/AF)	big cricket (*Gryllotalpa gryllotalpa*)	female	Pia (2016: 21–2, 2018: 35); Idoyaga Molina (1998: 41). She was the grandmother of water birds and other animals. Among them is *Chunguperedatei* (the jabiru).
Docoji (GF.m.sg.AF)	bow	male	Bórmida (2005, I: 26).
Doria (f.sg.AF)	type of plant (*Bromelia balansae*)	female	Idoyaga Molina (1998: 67). She was a beautiful woman, but she had been cursed so that men did not fall in love with her.
Doridi (m.sg.AF)	crested oropendola (*Psarocolius decumanus*)	male	Pia (2016: 96; field notes); Fischermann (1988, myth number 42). In one version, *Doridi* was the husband of *Bujote*, in another the partner of *Choyo*. In both cases, they turned into birds together.
Ducayoi (GF.m.sg.AF)	headband worn by the Ayoreo men	male	Pia (2016: 110). The Ayoreo chiefs wear a headband of jaguar skin, and *Ducayoi* was a leader. The form recorded by Pia is *docayoi* or *dacayoi*. Higham et al. (2000) and Bertinetto (p.c.) document *ducayoi*. The difference depends on the vowel of the generic form prefix *dVc-*, for which some variability was described (Ciucci 2016).

(Continued)

Table 3 (Continued)

Mythological figure and grammatical glosses	Meaning	Gender of the character	Source and other information on the story
Durujnai (m.sg.AF)	type of palm (*Trithrinax schizophylla*)	male	Pia (2014: 59). *Durujnai* was a boy who did activities traditionally reserved for women. For this reason, he did not grow up and turned into a plant. This story was very likely inspired by the fact that most plant nouns are feminine, but this noun is masculine.
Echoi (m.sg.AF)	salt	male	Idoyaga Molina (1998: 41–2).
Erejnai (m.sg.AF)	climbing plant with violet flowers (*Fridericia pubescens*)	male	Bórmida (2005, I: 34); Pia (2018: 3, 26). He was a shaman who became evil, because women did not like him. He looked for women and he hugged them with much strength.
Gajño (f.sg.PF/AF)	lake	female	Pia (2014: 92).
Gase (GF.f.sg.PF/AF)	stick with a hook, pitchfork for collecting the plant of caraguata	female	Pia (2018: 52–5, 74). She was an evil female shaman.
Goyide (f.sg.PF/AF)	Venezuelan troupial (*Icterus icterus*)	female	Pia (2016: 97–8). *Goyide* was a beautiful woman who turned into a bird, because too many men fell in love with her, and she did not want to be sexually immoral. Her *sari* gives the power to let husbands fall in love again with their wives.
Gueaye (f.sg.PF/AF)	drop of rain	female	Pia (2018: 61). She was a woman who liked to bathe in the river.
Guebi (DIM.m.sg.AF) from *guei* (m.sg.AF) 'rain', lit. 'small rain'	a sudden and short downpour	male	Pia (2018: 83–97); Idoyaga Molina (1998: 40–1). He was the son of the rain, a non-Ayoreo boy fallen from the sky. The gender of the character depends on the fact that its name is the diminutive of 'rain'. No transformation occurs in the story.
Guede (m.sg.PF/AF)	sun	male	Pia (2015: 5). The inflection of this word is irregular.

Mythological figure and grammatical glosses	Meaning	Gender of the character	Source and other information on the story
Guedoside (m.sg.AF)	moon	male	Pia (2015: 5); Fischermann (1988: §3.2.2). He was a big leader, and the son of the sun. The inflection of this word is irregular.
Guetõrai (m.sg.AF)	storm, tempest	male	Pia (2018: 69). He was an irritable man.
Ijmose (f.sg.PF/AF)	type of plant (*Spathicarpa hastifolia*)	female	Pia (2018: 50). She was a woman who was able to collect plants, but was unpopular, because she only wanted to share her plants with her relatives.
Imichacua (f.sg.AF)	Ayoreo game	female	Pia (2018: 82).
Jesabia (f.sg.AF)	spider	female	Bórmida (2005, I: 55–6).
Jiriria (or *Iriria*) (f.sg.AF)	brushland tinamou (*Nothoprocta cinerascens*)	female	Pia (2016: 46). *Iriria* or *Jiriria* was a powerful female shaman.
Jmajugunori (m.sg.AF)	grey-bellied hawk (*Accipiter poliogaster*)	male	Pia (2018: 100–2). There are different versions of his story.
Jmiacacai (m.sg.AF)	white-tailed hawk (*Buteo albicaudatus*)	male	Pia (2016: 69–70, 2018: 106–8). He was a leader who had two wives.
Jnumi (m.sg.AF)	earth	male	Pia (2014: 116); Idoyaga Molina (1998: 48); Wilbert and Simoneau (1989: 27–30).
Jubi (m.sg.AF)	fly	male	Bórmida (2005, I: 61–2)
Judui (m.sg.AF)	Amazonian motmot (*Momotus momota*)	male	Pia (2018: 65). He was a young man who was able to find spring water.
Juticai (m.sg.AF)	deerfly	male	Pia (2016: 112); Fischermann (1988, myth number 54). *Juticai* was both a leader and an evil shaman.
Narujna (f.sg.PF/AF)	type of cactus (*Cereus stenogosus*)	female	Pia (2016: 59–60).
Ojnai (3.m.sg.AF)	needle	male	Pia (2018: 115).
Ojnate (f.sg.PF/AF)	plant with thorns	female	Pia (2015: 34–5).

(Continued)

Table 3 (Continued)

Mythological figure and grammatical glosses	Meaning	Gender of the character	Source and other information on the story
Pamoi (GF.m.sg.AF)	belt used by elderly people to sit with	male	Bórmida (2005, II: 100–1). Telling this myth is very dangerous. There are also different versions concerning the origin of this object, whose production and use is not allowed to all Ayoreo people.
Parangue (GF.f.sg.PF/AF)	pestle used for grinding	female	Bórmida (2005, I: 92–3). *Parangue* was the wife of *Pugutadi* (see below).
Petarugai (m.sg.AF)	night butterfly, moth	male	Pia (2018: 22–3). He was envied, because he was a great hunter (a typical male activity).
Pibotai (GF.m.sg.AF)	drinking tube	male	Pia (2018: 60). He was a young man who invented the drinking tube. At the end of the story, he decided to turn into a drinking tube.
Picadei (m.sg.AF)	type of palm (*Acrocomia totai*)	male	Pia (2018: 118–19). He was a tall and thin young man.
Piogoto (f.sg.PF/AF)	broad-winged hawk (*Buteo platypterus*)	female	Pia (2018: 108–9). She was a woman who caused a fire in the forest.
Pitijinaquei (GF.m.sg.AF)	joy	male	Bórmida (2005, I: 36).
Poji (m.sg.PF/AF)	black tegu (*Tupinambis teguixin*)	male	Pia (2014: 113–4, 2016: 43, 2018: 20–2); Ciucci and Pia (2019). He was a powerful shaman. It is the red tegu (*Salvator rufescens*) in the southern part of the Chaco area where the Ayoreo live.
Porai (m.sg.AF)	centipede (*Scolopendra cingulata*)	male	Pia (2018: 6). He was a boy who was too light and weak to play sport with the other children.
Potajnarua (f.sg.AF)	type of leaf cactus (*Pereskia sacharosa*)	female	Pia (2018: 119). She was a girl who used to make wooden needles.
Potaquero (f.sg.PF/AF)	rufous nightjar (*Caprimulgus rufus*)	female	Pia (2014: 98). She fell in love with *Potatai*.
Potatai (m.sg.AF)	scissor-tailed nightjar (*Hydropsalis torquata*)	male	Pia (2018: 20–2). He was a good shaman who helped *Poji* to become a shaman. He is considered the husband of *Asojna* (Pia 2014: 58) or simply her helper (Pia 2014: 96).

Mythological figure and grammatical glosses	Meaning	Gender of the character	Source and other information on the story
Pugutadi (GF.m.sg.AF)	mortar used for milling	male	Bórmida (2005, I: 92–3). *Pugutadi* was the husband of *Parangue* (see above).
Queneguete (f.sg.PF/AF)	spider	female	Pia (2015: 6). She was a woman who weaved and made better skirts and fans than the other women, who hated her for that. In Fischermann (1988: §3.2.2), she is the wife of *Chunguperedatei*. She produced woven objects characteristic of Western culture.
Quiraquirai (m.sg.AF)	southern crested caracara (*Caracara plancus*)	male	Pia (2014: 71–2). He was a big shaman.
Sidejnai (m.sg.AF)	(*Nicotiana rustica*)	male	Pia (2014: 61); Fischermann (1988, myth number 26); Idoyaga Molina (1998: 41).
Simijnai (m.sg.PF/AF)	spring water	male	Pia (2018: 65–6). He was a man who liked to bathe in pools.
Sorei / Sori (m.sg.AF)	harpy eagle (*Harpia harpyja*)	male	Pia (2018: 102–4). He was a powerful but evil leader, feared by his people.
Sumajningai (m.sg.AF)	courage	male	Pia (2014: 79, 2016: 89); Idoyaga Molina (1998: 46–8). He is represented as a man who lives in the sky and gives courage to leaders. He did not undergo any process of transformation.
Suaria (f.sg.AF)	parrot	female	Bórmida (2005, I: 57).
Tibide (f.sg.PF/AF)	red stone	female	Bórmida (2005, II: 145–6).
Tiegaito (f.sg.PF/AF)	Blue-throated piping guan (*Pipile cumanensis*)	female	Pia (2018: 70). She was a woman who specialized in looking for water. The scientific name comes from Rocha et al. (2012: 34).
Tirite (f.sg.PF/AF)	blue-tufted starthroat (*Heliomaster furcifer*)	female	Pia (2018: 118). She was a woman who used a needle to weave every day.
Tiroi (m.sg.PF/AF)	savanna hawk (*Buteogallus meridionalis*)	male	Pia (2018: 111). He was a young man and a good honey hunter.

(Continued)

Table 3 (Continued)

Mythological figure and grammatical glosses	Meaning	Gender of the character	Source and other information on the story
Ti(r)oti (m.sg.AF)	feather ornament of shamans and military leaders	male	Pia (2018: 113). He was a handsome boy, who invented the feather ornament named after him. No information on metamorphosis is reported.
Tobejnai (m.sg.AF)	hook-billed kite (*Chondrohierax uncinatus*)	male	Pia (2018: 113–14). He was *Cuco*'s husband.
Tobi (m.sg.AF)	sharp-shinned hawk (*Accipiter striatus*)	male	Pia (2018: 109). He is described as a man who was small but good at killing the enemy, because he was strong and fast.
Toje (f.sg.PF/AF)	southern screamer (*Chauna torquata*)	female	Pia (2016: 25, 2018: 63). She was a woman who did not want to share her belongings with the other women.
Usere (f.sg.PF/AF)	type of plant (*Dioscorea alata*)	female	Pia (2015: 27). *Usere* was a woman who made skirts. She decided to turn into a plant after having being criticized by other women who did not appreciate her skirts. *Usere* has left no *sari*.
Yajogue (f.sg.PF/AF)	anteater (*Myrmecophaga tridactyla*)	female	Fischermann (1988, myth number 22).
Yame (f.sg.PF/AF)[b]	type of monkey (*Aotus trivirgatus*)	female	Pia (field notes). She was a beautiful woman, envied by the other women.
Yame puye (f.sg.PF/AF), lit. 'taboo monkey'	*yame puye* (*Aotus azarae*)	female	Pia (2016: 78). She was a female shaman who turned into a monkey after a dispute with another woman. The adjective *puye*, feminine of *puyac* (m.sg.PF) 'holy, taboo', is considered part of the character's name.

[b] As seen in §4.1, Ayoreo has no gender switch for animal terms. However, in Fischermann (1998, myth number 22) there is an exception, because in one version of the story of *Yajogue* 'anteater' (above) her husband is a monkey called *Yamei*. *Yamei* (m.sg.AF) is the masculine of *yame* (f.sg.AF/ PF). This monkey is always feminine in all other sources available, including all other citations by Fischermann. Pia (p.c.), who tried to check this piece of information, was not able to find the masculine form *yamei*. If *yamei* is correct, it could be an unusual local variation of *yame*. This is, however, an exception which confirms the rule. Indeed, if the grammatical gender of the noun changes, the social gender of the mythological character also changes.

Mythological figure and grammatical glosses	Meaning	Gender of the character	Source and other information on the story
Yiquiqui (m.sg.PF/AF)	solitary eagle (*Harpyhaliaetus solitarius*)	male	Pia (2018: 105–6). He was a singer. For Fischermann (1988), this bird is *Spizaetus ornatus*.
Yojnai (m.sg.AF)	plant of the bromeliads (*Aechmea bromeliifolia*)	male	Pia (2018: 62–3). He was a hunter. He turned into a plant because he did not want to share water with his group. For Fischermann (1988), the plant is *Aechmea distichanta*.

References

Aikhenvald, Alexandra Y. 2015. *The art of grammar: A practical guide*. Oxford: Oxford University Press.

Aikhenvald, Alexandra Y. 2016. *How gender shapes the world*. Oxford: Oxford University Press.

Aikhenvald, Alexandra Y. 2018. *Serial verbs*. Oxford: Oxford University Press.

Aikhenvald, Alexandra Y. 2019. 'Expressing "possession" motivations, meanings, and forms', in Lars Johanson, Lidia Federica Mazzitelli, and Irina Nevskaya (eds), *Possession in languages of Europe and North and Central Asia*. Amsterdam: John Benjamins, 7–25.

Arrien, Mario. 2008. *Sistemas de subsistencia y cosmovisión de los chiquitanos*. Santa Cruz de la Sierra: CLWR.

Barrios, Armindo, Domingo Bulfe, and José Zanardini. 1995. *Ecos de la selva. Ayoreode uruode*. Asunción: CEADUC.

Bertinetto, Pier Marco. 2014a [2009]. 'Ayoreo', in Mily Crevels and Pieter Muysken (eds), *Lenguas de Bolivia*, Vol. 3, *Oriente*. La Paz: Plural Editores, 369–413. [English version: 'Ayoreo (Zamuco). A grammatical sketch', *Quaderni del Laboratorio di Linguistica* 9 n.s.]

Bertinetto, Pier Marco. 2014b. 'Tenselessness in South American indigenous languages with focus on Ayoreo (Zamuco)', *LIAMES* 14: 149–71.

Bertinetto, Pier Marco and Luca Ciucci. 2012. 'Parataxis, hypotaxis and para-hypotaxis in the Zamucoan languages', *Linguistic Discovery* 10, 1: 89–111.

Bertinetto, Pier Marco and Luca Ciucci. 2015. 'On rare typological features of the Zamucoan languages, in the framework of the Chaco linguistic area', paper presented at *Diversity Linguistics: Retrospect and Prospect*. Max Planck Institute for Evolutionary Anthropology, Leipzig. 1–3 May 2015 / *Quaderni del Laboratorio di Linguistica* 14 n.s.

Bertinetto, Pier Marco and Luca Ciucci. 2019. 'Reconstructing Proto-Zamucoan. Evidence (mostly) from verb inflection', in Paola Cotticelli Kurras and Sabine Ziegler (eds), *Tra semantica e sintassi: il ruolo della linguistica storica - Zwischen Semantik und Syntax: die Rolle der historischen Sprachwissenschaft*. Rome: Il Calamo, 1–20.

Bertinetto, Pier Marco, Luca Ciucci, and Margherita Farina. 2019. 'Two types of morphologically expressed non-verbal predication', *Studies in Language* 43, 1: 120–94.

Bertinetto, Pier Marco, Luca Ciucci, and Gabriella Erica Pia. 2010. 'Inquadramento storico, etnografico e linguistico degli Ayoreo del Chaco' in Roberto Ajello, Pierangiolo Berrettoni, Franco Fanciullo, Giovanna Marotta, and Filippo Motta (eds), *Quae omnia bella devoratis. Studi in memoria di Edoardo Vineis*. Pisa: Edizioni ETS, 109–46.

Bertinetto, Pier Marco, Irene Ricci, and Na Zhi. 2010. 'Le nasali sorde dell'ayoreo: prime prospezioni', *Quaderni del Laboratorio di Linguistica* 9, 1 n.s.

Blaser, Mario. 2010. *Storytelling globalization from the Chaco and beyond.* Durham/London: Duke University Press.

Bórmida, Marcelo. 2005 [1973–9]. 'Ergon y mito. Una hermenéutica de la cultura material de los Ayoreo del Chaco Boreal', *Archivos del Departamento de Antropología Cultural* 3, 1–2.

Briggs, Janet. 1972. *Quiero contarles unos casos del Beni.* Cochabamba: Instituto Lingüístico de Verano/Ministerio de Educación y Cultura, Dirección Nacional de Antropología. 2 vols.

Chomé, Ignace. 1958 [1745 ca.]. 'Arte de la lengua zamuca', (Présentation de Suzanne Lussagnet', *Journal de la Société des Américanistes de Paris* 47: 121–78.

Ciucci, Luca. 2013. 'Chamacoco lexicographical supplement I', *Quaderni del Laboratorio di Linguistica* 12 n.s.

Ciucci, Luca. 2014. 'Tracce di contatto tra la famiglia zamuco (ayoreo, chamacoco) e altre lingue del Chaco: prime prospezioni', *Quaderni del Laboratorio di Linguistica della Scuola Normale Superiore di Pisa* 13 n.s.

Ciucci, Luca. 2016 [2013]. *Inflectional morphology in the Zamucoan languages.* Asunción: CEADUC.

Ciucci, Luca. 2018. 'Lexicography in the eighteenth-century Gran Chaco: The Old Zamuco Dictionary by Ignace Chomé', in Jaka Čibej, Vojko Gorjanc, Iztok Kosem, and Simon Krek (eds), *Proceedings of the XVIII EURALEX International Congress: Lexicography in global contexts*. Ljubljana: Ljubljana University Press, 439–51.

Ciucci, Luca. 2019. 'A culture of secrecy: The hidden narratives of the Ayoreo', in Anne Storch, Andrea Hollington, Nico Nassenstein, and Alexandra Y. Aikhenvald (eds), *Creativity in language: Secret codes and special styles*, 175–94. A special issue of the *International Journal of Language and Culture* 6, 1.

Ciucci, Luca. 2020. 'Matter borrowing, pattern borrowing and typological rarities in the Gran Chaco of South America', in Francesco Gardani (ed.), *Borrowing matter and pattern in morphology*, 283–310. A special issue of *Morphology* 30, 4.

Ciucci, Luca. 2021. 'The hispanization of Chamacoco syntax'. *Italian Journal of Linguistics* 32,1: 111–34.

Ciucci, Luca. Forthcoming a. Editor of *Ignace Chomé: Vocabulario de la lengua zamuca – Edición crítica y comentario lingüístico*. Madrid/Frankfurt: Iberoamericana Vervuert Verlag.

Ciucci, Luca. Forthcoming b. Language secrecy in Chamacoco (Zamucoan).

Ciucci, Luca and Pier Marco Bertinetto. 2015. 'A diachronic view of the Zamucoan verb inflection', *Folia Linguistica Historica* 36, 1: 19–87.

Ciucci, Luca and Pier Marco Bertinetto. 2017. 'Possessive inflection in Proto-Zamucoan: A reconstruction', *Diachronica* 34, 3: 283–330.

Ciucci, Luca and Pier Marco Bertinetto. 2019. 'Possessive classifiers in Zamucoan', in Alexandra Y. Aikhenvald and Elena Mihas (eds), *Genders and classifiers: A cross-linguistic typology*. Oxford: Oxford University Press, 144–75.

Ciucci, Luca and José T. Macoñó. 2018. *Diccionario básico del chiquitano del Municipio de San Ignacio de Velasco*. Santa Cruz de la Sierra: Ind. Maderera San Luis SRL/Museo de Historia UAGRM.

Ciucci, Luca and Gabriella Erica Pia. 2019. 'Linguistic taboos in Ayoreo', *The Mouth* 4: 31–54.

Combès, Isabelle. 2009. *Zamucos*. Cochabamba: Instituto de Misionerología.

Comrie, Bernard, Lucía A. Golluscio, Hebe A. González, and Alejandra Vidal. 2010. 'El Chaco como área lingüística', in Zarina Estrada Fernández and Ramón Arzápalo Marín (eds), *Estudios de lenguas amerindias 2: contribuciones al estudio de las lenguas originarias de América*. Hermosillo, Sonora (Mexico): Editorial Unison, 85–130.

Cordeu, Edgardo J. 1969–70. 'Aproximación al horizonte mítico de los Tobas', *Runa* 12, 1–2: 67–176.

Cordeu, Edgardo J. 1989–92 [1980]. 'Aishnuwéhrta. Las ideas de deidad en la religiosidad chamacoco', *Suplemento Antropológico* 24, 1–27, 2.

Cordeu, Edgardo J. 1997. 'La religione degli indios chamacoco', in Lawrence E. Sullivan (ed.), *Trattato di antropologia del sacro*, Vol. 6, *Culture e religioni indigene in America centrale e meridionale*. Milan: Jaca Book-Massimo, 231–51.

Crowell, Thomas Harris. 1979. *A grammar of Bororo*. PhD thesis. Ithaca, New York: Cornell University.

Demarchi, Darío A. and Angelina García Ministro. 2008. 'Genetic structure of native populations from the Gran Chaco region, South America', *International Journal of Human Genetics* 8, 1–2: 131–41.

DGEEC = Dirección General de Estadística, Encuestas y Censos. 2014. *Pueblos Indígenas en el Paraguay. Resultados Finales de Población y Viviendas 2012.* Fernando de la Mora, Paraguay.

Dixon, R. M. W. 2008. 'Comparative constructions: A cross-linguistic typology', *Studies in Language* 32: 787–817.

Dixon, R. M. W. 2010. *Basic linguistic theory*, Vol. 2: *Grammatical topics*. Oxford: Oxford University Press.

Dixon, R. M. W. 2015. *Edible gender, mother-in-law style, and other grammatical wonders: Studies in Dyirbal, Yidiñ, and Warrgamay.* Oxford: Oxford University Press.

Escobar, Ticio. 2007. *The curse of Nemur: In search of the art, myth, and ritual of the Ishir.* Pittsburgh: University of Pittsburgh Press.

Fabre, Alain. 2007. 'Morfosintaxis de los clasificadores posesivos en las lenguas del Gran Chaco (Argentina, Bolivia y Paraguay)', *UniverSOS* 4: 67–85.

Fischermann, Bernd. 1988. *Zur Weltsicht der Ayoréode Ostboliviens.* PhD thesis. Bonn: Rheinische Friedrich-Wilhelm-Universität. [Spanish translation: *La cosmovisión de los ayoréode del Chaco Boreal*, manuscript]

Fischermann, Bernd. 1996. 'Viviendo con los Pai. Las experiencias ayoreode con los jesuitas', in Eckart Kühne (ed.), *Martin Schmid 1694-1772. Las misiones jesuíticas de Bolivia.* Santa Cruz de la Sierra: Pro Helvetia, 47–54.

Higham, Alice, Maxine E. Morarie, and Greta Paul. 2000. *Ayoré-English dictionary.* Sanford, FL: New Tribes Mission. 3 vols.

Idoyaga Molina, Anatilde. 1998. 'Cosmología y mito. La representación del mundo entre los ayoreo del Chaco Boreal', *Scripta Ethnologica* 20: 31–72.

Idoyaga Molina, Anatilde. 2000. *Shamanismo, brujería y poder en América Latina.* Buenos Aires: CAEA-CONICET.

Kelm, Heinz. 1964. 'Das Zamuco: eine lebende Sprache', *Anthropos* 59: 457–516, 770–842.

Montani, Rodrigo. 2017. *El mundo de las cosas entre los wichís del Gran Chaco. Un estudio etnolingüístico.* Cochabamba: Instituto Latinoamericano de Misionología/ Itinerarios Editorial.

Morarie, Maxine E. 2011. *Diccionario Ayoré – Español.* Manuscript.

Otaegui, Alfonso. 2014. *Les chants de nostalgie et de tristesse ayoreo du Chaco Boreal paraguayen (une ethnographie des liens coupés).* PhD thesis. Paris: École de Hautes Études en Sciences Sociales.

Paz, María. 1966. 'Apuntes sobre la lengua ayorea', *Revista de la Universidad Autónoma Gabriel René Moreno* 3, 25–6: 29–44.

Pia, Gabriella Erica. 2014. *Diccionario antropológico ayoreo. Parte primera: Ensayo introductivo.* Pisa: Laboratorio di Linguistica della Scuola Normale Superiore.

Pia, Gabriella Erica. 2015. *Diccionario antropológico ayoreo. Parte segunda: Abalanzarse - Achuma.* Pisa: Laboratorio di Linguistica della Scuola Normale Superiore.

Pia, Gabriella Erica. 2016. *Diccionario antropológico ayoreo. Parte tercera: Adecuado - Adulto casado.* Pisa: Laboratorio di Linguistica della Scuola Normale Superiore.

Pia, Gabriella Erica. 2018. *Diccionario antropológico ayoreo. Parte cuarta: Aéreo - Agujero.* Pisa: Laboratorio di Linguistica della Scuola Normale Superiore.

Renshaw, John. 1988. 'Property, resources and equality among the Indians of the Paraguayan Chaco', *Man*, new series 23, 2: 334–52.

Rickards, Olga, Marco Tartaglia, Cristina Martínez-Labarga, and G. F. De Stefano. 1994. 'Genetic relationships among the Native American populations', *Anthropologischer Anzeiger* 52, 3: 193–213.

Rocha, Omar O., Sol A. Aguilar, Carmen O. Quiroga, and Omar Martínez. 2012. *Guía fotográfica de las aves de Bolivia.* La Paz: Industrias Gráficas SIRENA.

Sebag, Lucien. 1965. 'Le chamanisme Ayoreo', *L'Homme* 5, 1: 5–32 and 5, 2: 92–122.

Sequera, Guillermo. 2006. *Tomáraho. La resistencia anticipada.* Asunción: CEADUC. 2 vols.

SIM = South-American Indian Mission. 1967. *Diccionario ayoré-castellano.* Yoquiday/Poza Verde: SIM.

Sušnik, Branislava. 1969. *Chamacoco I. Cambio cultural.* Asunción: Museo Etnográfico Andrés Barbero.

Tomichá Charupá, Roberto. 2002. *La primera evangelización en las Reducciones de Chiquitos, Bolivia (1691–1767).* Cochabamba: Verbo Divino.

Tomichá Charupá, Roberto. 2003. 'Carta inédita del P. Ignacio Chomé desde San Ignacio de los Zamucos (15 de Octobre de 1745)', *Anuario de la Academia Boliviana de Historia Eclesiástica* 9: 159–75.

Viveiros de Castro, Eduardo. 1998. 'Cosmological deixis and Amerindian perspectivism', *Journal of the Royal Anthropological Institute* 4, 3: 469–88.

Viveiros de Castro, Eduardo. 2004. 'Exchanging perspectives: The transformation of objects into subjects in Amerindian cosmologies', *Common Knowledge* 10, 3: 463–84.

Weiss, Gerald. 1972. 'Campa cosmology', *Ethnology* 11, 2: 157–72.

Wilbert, Johannes and Karin Simoneau. 1987. Editors of *Folk Literature of the Chamacoco Indians.* Los Angeles: UCLA, Latin American Centre Publications.

Wilbert, Johannes and Karin Simoneau. 1989. Editors of *Folk Literature of the Ayoreo Indians.* Los Angeles: UCLA, Latin American Centre Publications.

9

The integration of languages and society

A view from multilingual Southern New Guinea

Dineke Schokkin

1 Introduction

This chapter discusses practices of traditional small-scale multilingualism (Lüpke 2016) in southern New Guinea (SNG), specifically linking these to the expression of possession in one of the languages spoken here: the variety of Idi spoken in Dimsisi village and its two satellites, Birem and Iblamnd. New Guinea is one of the most linguistically diverse parts of the globe, and SNG is arguably its third most diverse region, after the north coast and the Sepik (Evans et al. 2017). SNG is a flat, alluvial region, stretching from the Maro River in the west (in Indonesian Papua) to the Fly River in the east (in Papua New Guinea), and mostly consists of low-lying savannah, rainforest, or swamp bounded to the north by the two aforementioned rivers and to the south by the Torres Strait. Map 1 shows the major language families of the area. Of these, the Morehead-Maro or Yam family is the one covering the largest geographical area, and also the best-studied one. It comprises three main subgroups: the Tonda/Kanum and Yei branches to the west, and the Nambu branch to the east. Immediately adjacent, further eastwards we find the Pahoturi River family, of which Idi is a member. The easternmost Yam language, Nen, is spoken only in one village, Bimadbn, about twenty-five kilometres from Dimsisi, and Nen and Idi are in close and stable contact through intermarriage, based on symmetrical sister exchange. Many endonyms for the Yam and Pahoturi River languages, for instance *Nen*, *Nmbo*, *Idi*, or *Ende*, are based on the word for 'what' in the respective language. Still further east towards the mouth of the Fly River we find a number of further smaller families. On its western, northern, and eastern fringes the region contains languages classified as Trans-New Guinea: Marind, Suki-Gogodala, and Kiwai, and to the south we find the Australian language Kalau Kawau Ya. For more detailed discussion, see the surveys in Evans (2012) and Evans et al. (2017).

Dineke Schokkin, *The integration of languages and society: A view from multilingual Southern New Guinea*. In: *The Integration of Language and Society: A Cross-Linguistic Typology*. Edited by: Alexandra Y. Aikhenvald, R. M. W. Dixon, and Nerida Jarkey, Oxford University Press. © Dineke Schokkin 2021. DOI: 10.1093/oso/9780192845924.003.0009

Until recently, very little was known about any of the languages of this area. The last few years have seen the publication of a number of PhD theses, either comprehensive descriptive grammars or containing a sketch grammar section (Carroll 2017; Döhler 2018; Kashima 2020; Lindsey 2019; Olsson 2017), and journal articles on specific linguistic problems (Evans 2014, 2015a,b, 2017, 2019; Evans and Miller 2016; Schokkin and Lindsey in preparation; Siegel 2014, 2017). Most languages are small—ranging from a few hundred to a few thousand speakers, and population density is very low. In the Papua New Guinean part of the region the languages remain secure, still being learned by children. On the Indonesian side they are starting to give way to Indonesian.

Across the region, groups are self-sufficient to a large extent, practising subsistence agriculture by the slash-and-burn method. Important staples include cassava, taro, sweet potato, and particularly yams, which are traditionally highly valued. In the swampier areas nearer to the Fly River, we find a relatively greater dependence on sago. There are no established practices of animal husbandry, although young pigs, crocodiles, and cassowaries are occasionally caught and held in pens until they are ready to be butchered. The main sources of protein are hunting and fishing. Only limited trade of material goods takes place across the region, although this is probably increasing as of recent years. The main relations between groups consist of exchange of social capital in the form of marriage practices, as will be discussed below.

2 Social organization

Throughout the region, patterns of language contact are grounded in established cultural practices of intermarriage, via a system of *symmetrical sister exchange*. A significant proportion of marriages is linguistically exogamous and produces bilingual households. Before discussing multilingualism on an ideological level and linguistic outcomes of intermarriage in following sections, I will first provide a brief sketch of social organization across the region more generally. At least three levels of social organization can be recognized that are relevant for the Dimsisi community: tribe, section, and clan. Clans form the lowest level and most clearly show the characteristics of descent groups based on common ancestry.

A tripartite system of non-local sections (cf. Ayres 1983), which form exogamous groups, functions as the basis for sister exchange. Particularly in the western area where Tonda/Kanum and many Nambu languages are spoken,

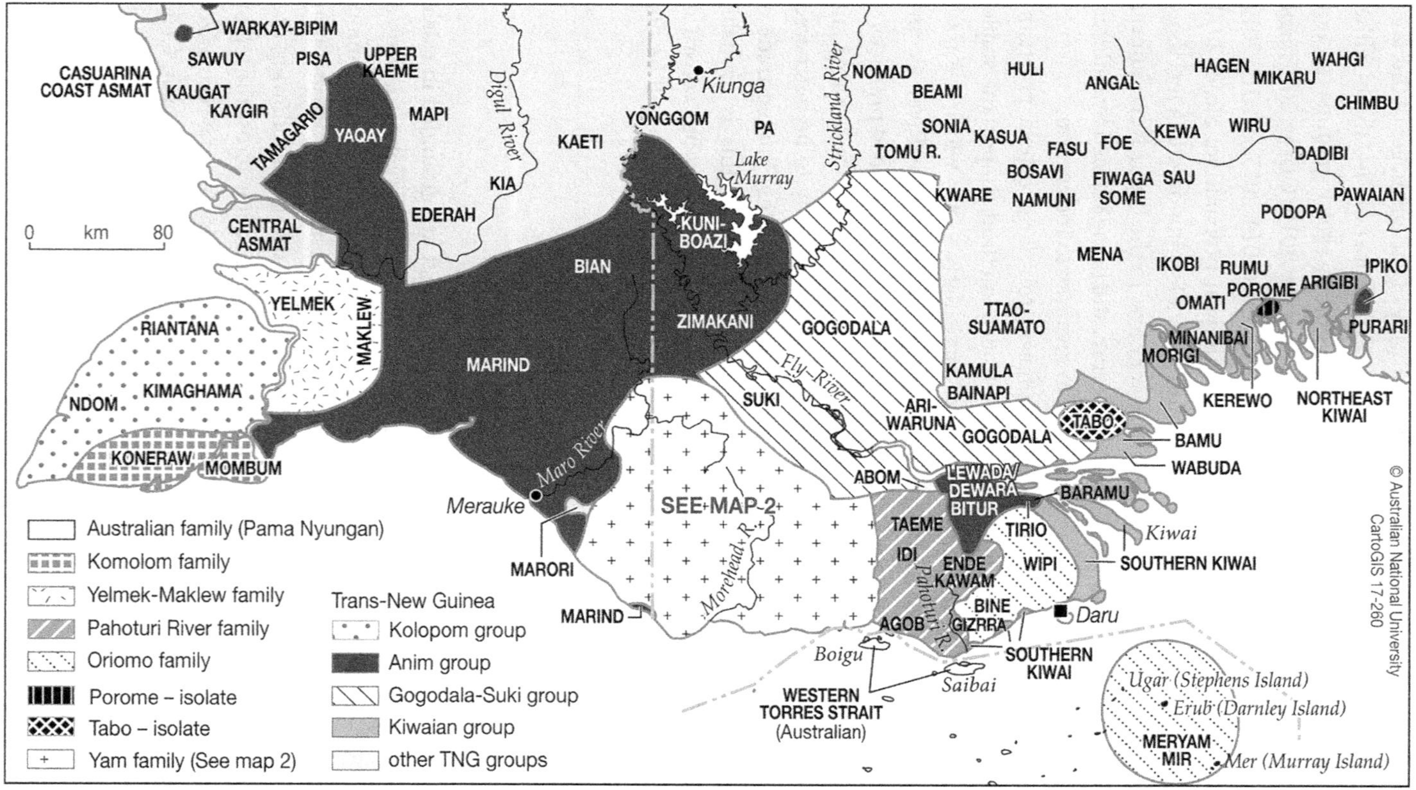

Map 1 Language families of the southern New Guinea area

Map labels and legend:

© Australian National University
CartoGIS 17-260

Legend:

- Australian family (Pama Nyungan)
- Komolom family
- Yelmek-Maklew family
- Pahoturi River family
- Oriomo family
- Porome – isolate
- Tabo – isolate
- Yam family (See map 2)

Trans-New Guinea
- Kolopom group
- Anim group
- Gogodala-Suki group
- Kiwaian group
- other TNG groups

0 km 80

this is the most prominent form of social organization (Döhler 2018; Kashima 2020), and in some places sections are not further divided into clans. Section boundaries run across language boundaries, and thus the linguistic exogamy that is observed can be regarded as an epiphenomenon of the marriage system, rather than a direct prescription.

Moving further east into Pahoturi River territory, the tripartite section system gradually gives way to a different one in which clans take a more prominent position, with the Nen-Idi contact zone appearing to be a 'transition zone'. In Dimsisi, most people primarily identify as members of a particular clan, in a system comprising about a dozen descent groups in total. Members of each clan consider themselves as descending from a common apical ancestor; descent is patrilineal. Clans appear to be closely tied to place, all belonging to a certain tract of land and believed to stem from the same origin place or 'story place'. Most clan names consist of a place name plus one of the attributive suffixes: -äg or -ang ~ -ong.

Dimsisi clans, in turn, belong to either one of two sections: *Banggu* and *Sanggara*. 'Section' only appears to exist as a rather abstract notion. From what I could gather, it is not associated with a particular place, or considered a descent group based on common ancestry, in contrast to the clans. The section names overlap with those in Nen-speaking Bimadbn (and presumably serve as the rationale for determining who can marry whom across village boundaries). Marriage is exogamous on the section level, and consequently also on the clan level: people from different sections can intermarry, but not people from the same clan, or from different clans within the same section. While a third section, *Mayawa*, is clearly recognized across the Yam-speaking area (and complicating patterns of intermarriage here), this third section was never mentioned to me in Dimsisi.

While other Pahoturi River groups also practise sister exchange, there are no indications of a tripartite section system being in use here. The Ende-speaking village of Limol, further east, has a clan system very similar to the one in Dimsisi. Although clans belong to either one of two moieties, there is no indication that these form exogamous groups. Lindsey (2019: 273) mentions that nowadays the moieties are used e.g. to divide the village into teams when games are played, and that marriage is exogamous on the clan level. It appears that the tripartite section system from further west was 'imported' into Dimsisi when people started to intermarry with Nen speakers, and may have been partially superimposed on an earlier moiety system. As mentioned, it is still not a very distinct social grouping in the present-day community. While some people will volunteer either of the section names when asked to which clan they belong, most people's primary orientation with regard to intra-village social identity seems to be towards the smaller clan units.

The most general overarching level of social organization across the Nambu and Idi heartland is that of groups referred to as 'tribes'. In contrast to sections, these do appear to coincide with language boundaries: over on the Yam side, the *Kerake* tribe speaks the Nmbo language, whereas the *Äkämer* tribe speaks the Nen language, and so forth. Tribal identity is strongly intertwined with language identity and with place: in the Idi corpus, *Nen yeka* 'Nen language' is equally often referred to with *Äkämer yeka* 'Äkämer tribe language' or *Bimadbn yeka* 'Bimadbn village language'. It is unlikely that tribes are regarded as descent groups, as one and the same tribe will comprise different sections, members of which can intermarry. However, since every clan belongs exclusively to one tribe, one result of this system of organization is that a person's patriclan determines their primary linguistic identity. For instance, a person whose father is of the *Nänggbläg* clan, belonging to the Idi-speaking *Dibläg* tribe, will identify as an Idi speaker (and be identified as such by everyone else), even when they have lived in Bimadbn village their whole life.

In the Dimsisi area, historical events have brought together multiple tribes. Members of the *Dibläg* tribe consider themselves the traditional owners of the land where Dimsisi village is now located, and the rightful speakers of Idi. In addition, a large proportion of the population of Dimsisi and its satellite Birem belongs to the *Wärubi* tribe. Their ancestors used to speak a closely related Pahoturi River variety called *Idzuwe*, but according to traditional lore they were displaced by Suki headhunting raids into Idi-speaking territory, and subsequently shifted to Idi. Iblamnd settlement is the home of a group of people referring to themselves as the *Bug*, who claim they were displaced and consequently shifted to Idi, previously speaking a Yam language (probably Len).

Tribal conflicts, particularly land disputes, are a source of ongoing tensions between and within Dimsisi and the satellite communities, causing rifts between individuals and families and occasionally leading to violence. These issues, brought on by historical events that saw large displacements of people, were probably exacerbated through a decision by the Australian colonial government to bring all people in the area together in one location, the current village of Dimsisi. Customarily, people would reside in smaller hamlets usually consisting of only one extended family, scattered throughout the area. Due to erupting tensions, around two decades ago the clans belonging to the Wärubi and the Bug tribes made a decision to relocate to their own tribal grounds, and settled into what are currently known as Birem and Iblamnd. Putting physical distance between oneself and an opponent by relocating is an important strategy, used throughout the region, to avoid and mitigate conflict, and may be an important driving factor in language diversification (see Kashima 2020 for more discussion).

3 Multilingual ideologies

As discussed, intermarriage leads to a general high incidence of multilingualism throughout the region. In addition to their father's language, which is their primary or 'emblematic' (Grace 1975; Laycock 1982; Ross 1996) language of identification, children from multilingual marriages acquire their mother's language. Sometimes, the family lives in a village where a third language is spoken and children will also acquire that one, in addition to languages that more distant family members such as aunts or grandmothers may speak. Even more languages are picked up across the life span as people travel within the region or further afield for education, work or church activities. While every person has their own emblematic language, preferentially used when they are in their home village, it is seen as good manners to address others in their local language when visiting different villages, particularly with frequently used formulae such as greetings. Practices of 'receptive multilingualism' (Rehbein, ten Thije, and Verschik 2011; Singer 2018 for Australian examples) are also widely reported throughout the region. This term describes the scenario where one person speaks their own language, while the interlocutor speaks another language. Since both parties are fluent in both languages, the use of two languages in one conversation presents no obstacle to mutual understanding. An example comes from a travelling court held in Dimsisi in 2015, in which the magistrates spoke Taeme, and the accused and commentators spoke Idi. Similarly to what has been observed in Australia and the Amazon, receptive multilingualism 'may scaffold a minimization of code-switching' (Vaughan and Singer 2018: 84). Indeed, speakers in the SNG region do not code-switch between local languages, and doing so would potentially attract criticism and ridicule.

These observations are in line with what can be called practices of *egalitarian multilingualism* (Haudricourt 1961; François 2012) or *small-scale multilingualism* (Lüpke 2016). The term 'egalitarian multilingualism' refers to a language contact situation in which there is 'virtually no relationship of dominance or prestige of one community over the others' (François 2012: 93).

'Small-scale multilingualism' designates 'communicative practices in hetero-glossic societies in which multilingual interaction is not governed by domain specialization and hierarchical relationships of the different named languages and lects used in them, but by deeply rooted social practices within a meaningful geographic setting' (Lüpke 2016: 35). The SNG situation has commonalities with various types of traditional multilingualism observed and documented elsewhere, e.g. in indigenous Australia (Singer 2018), the Amazon (Aikhenvald 2002; Epps 2018), Vanuatu (François 2012), and West Africa (Lüpke 2016), and it is likely that this has been the most common way for neighbouring language groups to coexist since the earliest evolution of language (Evans 2018).

The PNG side of SNG is unusual, however, in the present day and age, because these traditional practices are not yet superimposed (or at least barely) by an 'outsider' language that came in during colonial times. While many people have added English, Motu, or Tok Pisin to their repertoire, these are not generally used for communication with speakers of adjacent language groups. Note also that Tok Pisin came late to the area, perhaps one or two decades ago. This stands in sharp contrast to various other parts of PNG, where Tok Pisin sometimes has been around for more than a century, and where it is now firmly established for intergroup (and often also intragroup) communication. The documented cases elsewhere, mentioned above, also seem to have in common a relatively dominating presence of a lingua franca such as English, Portuguese, French, or Bislama. While these can be absorbed into language ecologies without necessarily leading to language shift or loss, it seems to be a common denominator that they 'change [language ecologies] in *some* way' (Vaughan and Singer 2018: 84, emphasis in original). This makes SNG one of the last vestiges where a traditional form of multilingualism may still resemble as closely as possible the practices of pre-colonial times.

For numerically larger groups like the population of Dimsisi and its satel-lites, there tend to be more marriages within the speech community, and thus the community contains more monolingual households compared to other villages in the area (Evans, Kashima, and Schokkin 2018). Still, many Idi people, particularly the middle-aged and elderly, report speaking upwards of five languages, and being multilingual is widely seen as a positive trait and something to aspire to. As mentioned, there is no pronounced hierarchical relationship between the languages involved in a system of egalitarian or small-scale multilingualism, and the languages or lects are held in equilib-rium through their mutual, culturally prescribed presence. Language use is often sanctioned by specific myths. One such example is a widespread myth in which the first human being hears speech issuing from a palm (*Caryota rumphiana*; Idi *wiäwiä*, Nen *sakr*) or fig tree and releases the people one by one as he seeks his own people. Earlier descriptions of this myth can be found in Williams (1936: 299) and Ayres (1983: 87); a recent version was recorded by Hoenigmann, Evans, and Johnson (2016) in Nen-speaking Bimadbn village.

Importantly, by using the term 'egalitarian' I do not mean to imply that in any one village, all languages are regarded as completely equal. On the contrary, there is an intrinsic connection between a particular place and a language, which is mediated through clan and tribe membership. In this respect, the SNG region shows similarities to the linguistic ideologies in Australian Aboriginal communities, especially in Arnhem Land (Merlan 1981) and Cape York (Sutton 1978). Furthermore, language purism plays an important role in most, if not all communities, and people are quick to point out mistakes or accuse other groups (e.g. in-marrying women, or younger speakers) of 'ruining' the language. One's own immediate circle of intimates, and particularly the elderly speakers within it, are usually seen as adhering most closely to an idealized, 'pure' version of the associated emblematic language. The system of multilingualism is egalitarian in the sense that no speech community has much more power or status as compared to any other (society as a whole is acephalous), and (as Lüpke 2016 points out) there is no domain specification and associated power dynamics for any of the languages involved. Particularly on the personal affective and attitudinal level, this does not mean that individuals regard every language or variety as fundamentally equal, as we will see below.

4 The Idi language

We will now further zoom in on Pahoturi River (PR) and on Idi, first introducing the language family in more general terms and then providing some discussion of the expression of possession in Idi. Typologically, SNG languages show many unique characteristics, such as a system of verbal morphology in which information is distributed, constructive, and cumulative, and complex tense, aspect, and number systems, and PR is no exception to this. PR-speaking communities have extensive social relationships with speakers of the Yam language family to the west, the Anim and Gogodala-Suki (Trans-New Guinea) groups to the north, the Oriomo family to the east, and the Pama-Nyungan family to the south. Evans et al. (2017: 641–3) deem the evidence used for earlier classifications of PR as part of a bigger language family to be tenuous, and propose five maximal clades (currently unrelatable families) for the entire region: Pahoturi River, Komolom, Yelmek-Maklew, Tabo, and Yam.

PR currently consists of at least six named varieties. As shown in Map 2, these are spoken in an area between Idi-speaking Sibidiri, Taeme-speaking Kondobol, Agob-speaking Sigabaduru, and Em-speaking Kibuli. The most commonly used names for the PR varieties are those shown in the map. Most endonyms are based on the word for 'what' in each language (*enda* [Ende], *agobda* [Agob], *emdag* [Em], *kada* [Kawam], *yiden* [Taeme], and *idi* [Idi]). Alternative names reference the geographical location of the language; a clan,

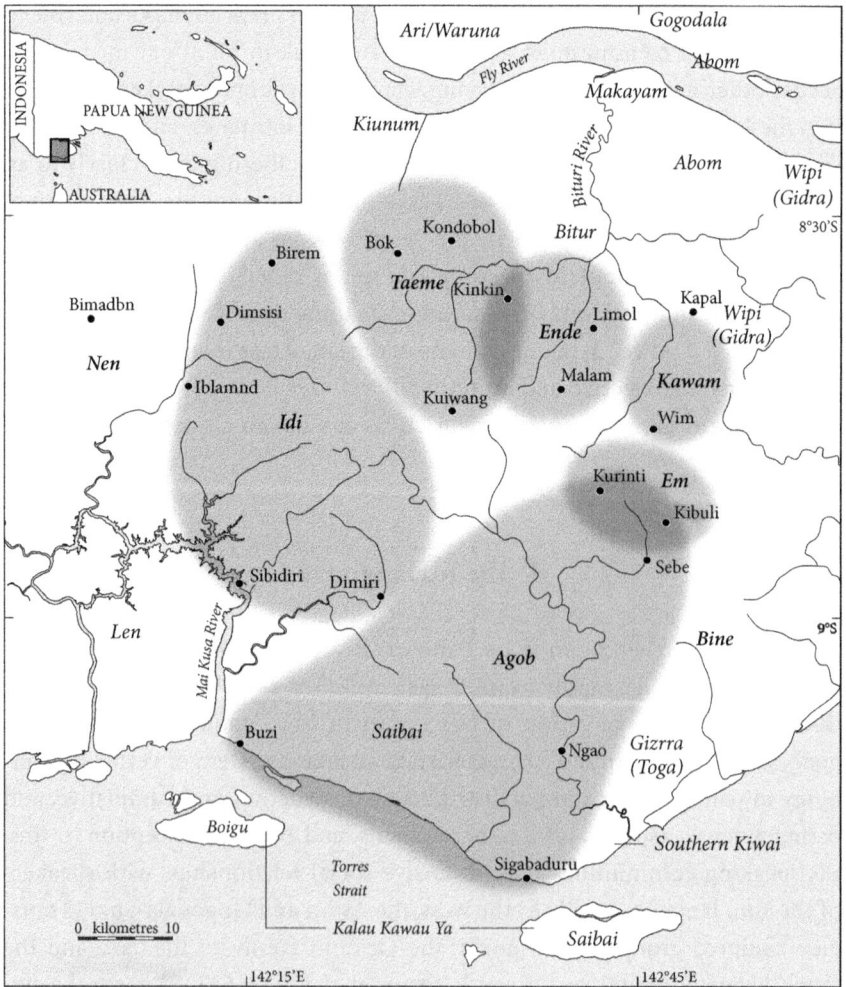

Map 2 Languages of the Pahoturi River family

tribe, or village associated with the language; or even the word for 'no' in the language (Lindsey 2019: 229). PR has been treated as a dialect continuum with Idi and Taeme at one end and Agob and Ende on the other (Eberhard, Simons, and Fennig 2019).

5 Existing work on PR

Of the PR varieties, we know the most about Idi and Ende; for an overview of existing work on Ende, see Lindsey (2019). Idi is spoken in Dimsisi, its two satellite villages Birem and Iblamnd, Dimiri, and Sibidiri by approximately 1,600 people. We have the best coverage on the Dimsisi variety through field-work and publications by Dineke Schokkin (e.g. Schokkin 2015a,b, 2016, 2017, 2018), with an archived corpus in Paradisec (Schokkin 2014). Additional data are available on the Sibidiri variety from the work of Volker Gast (e.g. Gast 2013, 2014, 2015a,b, 2017a,b). A comparison of the Dimsisi and Sibidiri varieties reveals some dialectal variation: phonological, lexical, and perhaps morphological. There exists an anonymous sketch grammar based on data gathered in Dimsisi, probably by the missionaries Tom and Robin Coleman (Unknown 1988). No data are available on the Dimiri variety. The most detailed discussion to date of grammatical phenomena pertaining to PR lan-guages, with a focus on Idi and Ende verbal morphology, can be found in Schokkin and Lindsey (in preparation).

6 Multilingualism in Dimsisi

All data in this chapter, both linguistic and sociolinguistic, are obtained from a corpus of naturalistic speech (Schokkin 2014), supplemented by observations of interactions during field stays. The corpus mostly consists of narratives accompanied by so-called 'sociolinguistic questionnaires'. Dimsisi residents were interviewed by their peers, and asked a set of questions including self-reports on the languages they speak. Nearly everyone in Dimsisi speaks Idi, with a small number of exceptions such as some women who recently mar-ried in from somewhere else, or school teachers who were recently stationed in the village. The most frequently spoken other languages are Nen (Yam fam-ily), Taeme (also PR, and closely related to Idi), and English (since about the 1960s, through the school system). Taeme and particularly Nen are commonly spoken and understood because of the established system of intermarriage discussed above. Other, less frequently mentioned languages in people's port-folios include Agob, Tok Pisin, Suki, and Yam languages further afield such as Nmbo and Nama. In Idi, as in other languages of the region, there exists a range of established ways of describing one's competence in a range of lan-guages, for example: *dndr dabe* (*lit.* 'only hearing'), referring to only having receptive command of a particular language, or *näplä yeka qéth* (*lit.* 'soft words') to refer to the ability to get by with a few common phrases, but not having full command of the language.

For in-married women, the expectation is that they will speak or learn to speak Idi. While in the idealized system, sister exchange occurs directly (i.e. a woman marries a man, whose sister in turn marries her brother), in practice the exchange often occurs with classificatory sisters, and sometimes in a tri-angular fashion.[1] This means exchange patterns usually include several gen-erations, and many in-marrying women will have a certain command of their husband's language, having been exposed in childhood because of an Idi-speaking mother or grandmother. In Figure 1, an example is given of such a repeated pattern of linguistic exogamy across two generations within one Dimsisi family, descending from the same union in the first generation between an Idi-speaking man and a Nen-speaking woman. 'Speaking', in this context, has the sense of primary, emblematic language affiliation, inherited through the father: all children from the union have Idi as their emblematic language. Note that not all descendants in the second and third generations are shown, Nen-speaking individuals are circled, and the places of residence of the individuals shown are distributed between Bimadbn and Dimsisi villages.

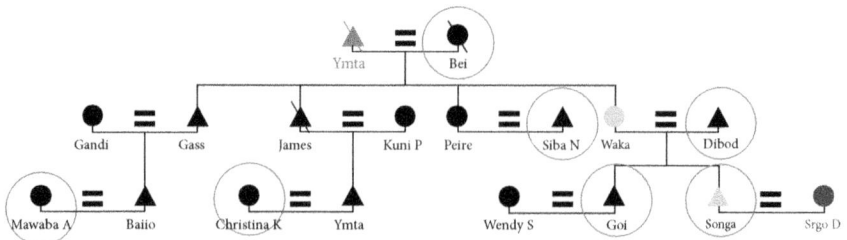

Figure 1 An example of a repeated pattern of linguistic exogamy across two generations within one Dimsisi family

---

[1] If a marriage happens and a man does not immediately have a sister to exchange, usually a clans-woman from the next generation will be 'fed back' into the exchange system when she is ready to marry. Sometimes this occurs in a roundabout way: a woman from clan A marries a man from clan B, and a woman from clan B in turn marries a man from clan C. The exchange is completed when a woman from clan C marries a man from clan A.

The two sisters shown in the second generation both married Nen-speaking men, while their brothers did not marry Nen-speaking women. In the third generation, however, all marriages shown are linguistically exogamous: the Idi-speaking sons from the two brothers' marriages both married Nen-speaking women, while the Nen-speaking sons from one sister's marriage both married Idi-speaking women (the other sister's children are not yet married). While the exact exchange mechanisms are not deducible from this graph (the clan affiliations for the affines are not shown, for instance) it does give an idea of the complexity of intergenerational intermarriage patterns.

Despite this frequently occurring intermarriage and the concomitant patterns of multilingualism, due in part to the size of the Dimsisi speech community there is also a relatively large number of individuals who report that they don't really have command of any other language besides Idi. Speakers usually ascribe this to 1) the fact that both their parents are Idi speakers and 2) they didn't go and live anywhere else, particularly during their childhood. Place of origin appears to be less pronounced within the Dimsisi community than it is in some other villages in the area (as reported by e.g. Christian Döhler (p.c.)), and there is no prohibition against marrying someone from the same village as long as it happens across section boundaries. Marrying someone from another clan but within the same section is frowned upon, but seems to occasionally happen.

Because data about multilingual portfolios are based on people's self-reports, the actual practices of mixed language use within households, and people's actual competence in the reported languages, are not well understood. It is quite likely that there are individual differences in how people will judge their own competence in a particular language. And while, as mentioned, there is the expectation that in-marrying women, particularly after relocating to their husbands' villages, will speak only their husband's language, in practice this is not followed through. Particularly when there is a sizeable group of women in a village who have the same language background, they tend to continue speaking their own language amongst themselves. When their numbers are getting large enough, this may give rise to a language shift. It seems this is currently occurring in some villages over in the Yam area, which are shifting from Yarne Nambo to the very closely related Kerake Nmbo (see Kashima [2020: 88–90] for details).

7 Idi phoneme inventory

In Table 1 the Idi consonant inventory is shown, with (between brackets) the symbols used by the practical orthography when these do not coincide with

Table 1 Idi consonant inventory

	Bilabial	Alveolar	Post-alveolar	Retroflex	Palatal	Velar	(Labialized velar)
Plosive	p b	t d		ʈ ɖ (th dh)		k g	k͡pʷ g͡bʷ (q ḡ)
Affricate		d͡ʒ ~ z (dz)					
Nasal	m	n			ɲ (ny)	ŋ (ng)	
Fricative		s					
Tap or flap		r ~ ɾ					
Approximant					j		w
Lateral approximant		l			ʎ (ly)		

IPA symbols. There are six full vowels /i e æ a o u/ and two 'reduced' vowels of short duration /ɪ ə/. /æ/ is represented by *ä* in the orthography, while /ɪ/ is represented by *é* and /ə/ is not written. Retroflex plosives often exhibit a significant amount of affrication, and the affricate /d͡ʒ/ is variably realized as a fricative. See Schokkin et al. (2021) for more details on Idi phonetics and phonology.

8 Possession in Idi

Idi has two different sets of possessive pronouns. The first set, termed 'close possessive', can occur as a free pronoun or as an enclitic on a full NP. The second set, termed 'distant possessive', can do both these things, but additionally can substitute a full NP to form a constituent by itself. Paradigms for the two sets are shown in the tables below.

Table 2 Paradigms for close and distant set of possessive pronouns

	Free form:close	Enclitic			Free form:distant	Enclitic
1sg	bo			1sg	bänä	
2sg	bnä			2sg	bnänä	
3sg	obo	=bo		3sg	obänä	=bänä
1nsg.inc	ba			1nsg.inc	bana	
1nsg.exc	yba			1nsg.exc	ybana	
2nsg	bna			2nsg	bnana	
3nsg	oba	=(ya)ba		3nsg	obana	=(ya)bana
inter	amo			inter	ämänä	

Below, examples are given of the use of the close and distant sets, respect-ively, as possessive pronoun (1a,b) and enclitic (2a,b). In all Idi possessive constructions the possessor (Po) is preposed to the Possessee (Pe).

(1) a. obo   yaya   b. obänä   ngi=ä
         3sg.CL.POSS   father   3sg.DIST.POSS   coconut=CORE
         his father   his coconut

(2) a. Rocky=bo   yaya   b. Rocky=bänä
         person.name=CL.POSS   father   person.name=DIST.POSS
         Rocky's father   ngi=ä
                                                coconut=CORE
                                                Rocky's coconut

The first set has close similarities to the personal pronoun paradigm. It seems that possessive enclitics of either set are most often used on NPs with human reference. When the NP has nonhuman reference, possessor and possessee are usually juxtaposed with the order Po Pe, e.g. in *thmngg bena* 'garden name' or *tn bena* 'clan name'. However, these are tendencies only: sometimes juxta-position happens with NPs that have human reference too, and NPs with nonhuman reference can bear possessive enclitics: *gta ngi=bo thonthona* 'the coconut's story'. There may be a relation between specificity and/or definite-ness of the possessor NP and whether juxtaposition or an enclitic is found. This remains an area for further research.

There is a clearly recognizable semantic and pragmatic distinction in the use of the two sets of possessive markers. While notions of alienability definitely play a role, use of either the one or the other set appears to be context-dependent rather than highly grammaticalized. Idi does not have obligatory possession of any noun, in which it contrasts with many Oceanic languages spoken in Papua New Guinea, where certain nouns with inalienable semantics cannot occur without a possessive marker. Typically, this encompasses at least the majority of body part terms and kinship terms. In Idi, such nouns are allowed to occur without a possessive marker, but there is a clear tendency for them to occur with a possessive pronoun or enclitic. In contrast, nouns referring to ani-mals or inanimate objects that are still typically someone's possession, like *gäl* 'canoe' or *bgly* 'bow', occur more often without a possessive marker than with.

For this chapter, a study was made of a selection of frequent nouns that fall into semantic classes associated in the literature with an alienability dis-tinction (see e.g. Aikhenvald and Dixon 2013; Chappell and McGregor 1996;

McGregor 2009): kinship terms, body parts, and important assets or characteristics of a person such as name, clan, village, and language. To compare, a further look was taken at important artefacts or material possessions in daily life, and at abstract concepts that in Idi are expressed as possessed nouns (examples investigated are *umläng* 'knowledge' and *kämä* 'ignorance'). As the corpus contains a large collection of 'coconut tree stories', and these are important assets to people, lastly I looked at *ngi* 'coconut tree'.[2]

From the study it turns out that semantically, the first paradigm is associated with a closer relationship between possessor and possessee than the second, and the labels 'close' and 'distant' are chosen accordingly. A number of kinship terms, many terms for body parts, and important characteristics or assets of a person such as clan, totem, and name, are found with the close possessive marker exclusively. The distant possessive is associated with a more distant relationship, and its use appears to be more context-dependent: past or future possession, in reference to people who have passed away (in the case of some kinship terms), sickness or injury (in the case of body parts), temporary possession or association, and people or objects that are physically at a distance from the speaker. In Table 3, an overview is given of some typical patterns of usage encountered for different semantic classes of nouns.

Below, usage of the two sets of pronouns within sentences is exemplified.[3] In (3a) and (3b), use of the two possessive markers with the kinship term *gäd* 'child' is compared. In (3a), the speaker refers to her children in general, marked with the close possessive, indicating that she planted her coconut tree to feed them. In (3b), she specifically refers to those of her children who work in jobs elsewhere, and she uses the distant possessive.

(3)   a.   ngn   ngi=ä   gta   y/bäny\in   glä
           1sg.NOM   coconut=CORE this   plant/1sg>3sg.RMPST   FOC
           bo   gäd   mit=mä
           1sg.CL.POSS   child   reason=LOC
           I planted this coconut for my children. (20150902_DIM_CI_F09_12)

      b.   bänä   gäd=ä   kaly   may   wangen
           1sg.DIST.POSS   child=CORE   work   place   PL.PRES.COP
           I have children in jobs. (20150902_DIM_CI_F09_51)

---

[2] Throughout the SNG region, coconut trees are planted to mark important occasions. Within the ARC Laureate project *The Wellsprings of Linguistic Diversity*, for which the data was collected, telling the story of one's coconut tree was chosen as an interview topic, in order to achieve comparability of data across field sites (similar genre and topics) as much as possible.

[3] Only a rudimentary gloss is used, indicating person/number of core arguments indexed on the verb plus tense. Fully glossing all inflected verbs takes up a lot of space and would detract from the overall argument made in this chapter. For more on Idi verbal inflection, see Schokkin and Lindsey (forthcoming).

Table 3 Usage of the two possessive sets for different noun classes

Semantic class	Examples	Use of possessive markers
Kinship I: close kin	*yaya* 'father', *mle* 'mother', *kak* 'grandparent', *yerang* 'exchange', *mlbä* 'sister (ms), daughter', *baba* 'uncle'	Only close possessive found.
Kinship II: more distant kin	*gäd* 'child, son', *thithim* 'female child, girl', *mangg* 'brother (fs)', *mosn* 'older sibling, same sex', *mndzn* 'younger sibling, same sex', *mnde* 'husband', *mla* 'wife'	Usually close possessive, but occasionally distant possessive, e.g. when talking about a dead person or about future generations.
Body parts	*bén* 'head', *thängg* 'hand, arm', *nyngg* 'foot, leg', *pth* 'body', *kthäm* 'liver', *qam* 'hair'	Usually close possessive, but distant possessive is used when the context is about disease, injury, or death, or when there is a metaphorical use of a body part term.
Assets and characteristics of individuals or groups	*bén* 'clan', *tn* 'clan', *meybn* 'totem', *ben* 'name', *thmngg* 'garden', *yeka* 'language', *may* 'house, village', *mätu* 'land'	The first five are found with close possessive only (interestingly, 'name' is used with the distant one with reference to God). The latter three are found with either type of possessive.
Artefacts and material possessions	*gäl* 'canoe', *bgly* 'bow', *sémbl* 'pig', *ngi* 'coconut'	These often occur without possessive marking; when they are possessed they occur with the close marker except when they are located at a physical distance.
Abstract concepts	*umläng* 'knowledge', *kämä* 'ignorance'	Only close possessive found.
Other	*pa* 'bird', *yeka* 'remark, speech', bodily actions	Distant possessive is usually found when talking about temporary possession or association: a bird someone just shot, a scream, a remark.

In (4a) and (4b), *may* 'house' is used with the close and distant possessive, respectively. These are two consecutive questions from the same coconut interview. The interviewer is asking about the owner of the property where the coconut tree is located. In (4a), she enquires whether this man is still living here, or has moved away. *May* is used with the close possessive. When the answer is affirmative that the man has indeed since moved away, the interviewer is asking in (4b) who is now living in the house that used to belong to him. This time she uses the distant possessive.

(4) a. **obo**   may=a   ydi   sisiri   gämä
     3sg.CL.POSS   house=CORE   Q   now   here
     wlan
     3sg.PRES.INTR.AUX

o   bo   gwa/klyme\n
or   3sg.NOM   shift/3sg.RMPST
Is his house still here now [i.e. does he live here], or did he move
away? (20150921_BIM_CI_F22_1_85)

b. a   sisiri   ako   yaka=yä   **obänä**   may
   and now   again who=EMP   **3sg.DIST.POSS** house
   qét=mä   gämä   gädl wlan
   abandoned=LOC   here   stay 3sg.PRES.INTR.AUX
   And who is now living here in his former house?
   (20150921_BIM_CI_F22_1_87)

While providing just a small vignette of the ways in which the two possessive systems in Idi can be used, these examples make clear that particularly the
distant possessive is highly context-dependent. The same noun, indeed with
the very same referential entity, can be used with either possessive marker
depending on the context. This seems to apply to the majority of nouns. The
only exceptions found in the corpus have strong inalienable semantics: close
kin, central inherited attributes such as clan or totem, and abstract 'possessions' such as knowledge. These are attested only with a close possessive marker.

9 Referring to the languages you speak

Against this background, the final section of this chapter zooms in on how
speakers of Idi refer to the languages they speak. In what ways is there fluidity
in the use of possessives when it comes to languages spoken? *Yeka* 'language'
belongs to the class of personal assets that can be used with either possessive marker. Most often, people refer to languages they speak or know with
the close possessive forms, particularly when these are the language they are
licensed speakers of (father's language) and other languages of close association (mother's language, spouse's language). People typically refer to their
father's language with *bo yeka mg* 'my true language'. The distant possessive
forms are often used when referring to languages one only learned in passing,
those that are literally spoken at a further distance; ones that the speaker
doesn't have close ties to. Examples are given of this distinction. In (5a), the
interviewer asks the interviewee, who is married to a Nen-speaking woman,
whether his wife speaks Idi. He uses the close possessive, first person inclusive
form to refer to the language, as both interviewer and interviewee are licensed
Idi speakers.

(5) a. **yba**   yeka   yeka   wlan
     1nsg.inc.CL.POSS language   speak   3sg.PRES.INTR.AUX
     Does she speak our language? (20150808_DIM_CI_M16_62)

In (5b), from a different interview, the interviewee had just been asked to list all the places he travelled to in his life, and he mentioned a number of villages further away towards the Fly River and the coast. Asking the interviewee whether he has learned any of the languages there, the interviewer uses the distant possessive to refer to these languages further afield:

(5) b. yau   bä   **obana**   yeka   dhob
     NEG   2.NOM **3nsg.DIST.POSS** language   some
     g/ngglbe\ä
     pick.up.PL/3sg>3pl.RMPST
     Did you learn any of their languages? (20141012_BIR_CI_M02_54)

Note also the use of the verb 'pick up, collect' (plural root: -*ngglb*-). This verb in its literal sense can be used to describe picking up items such as sticks in a distributed fashion, e.g. when collecting firewood, and is quite frequently used to metaphorically refer to adding languages to one's 'collection' as one travels.

Perhaps unexpectedly, it also appears that speakers can use the distant possessive for a language that they have actually been speaking from infancy. To illustrate these interesting dynamics, the following excerpt is given. It comes from an interview recorded in Birem settlement in 2015. In order to be able to interpret the use of possessives here, a bit of historical context, already discussed above (§2), will be repeated. The interviewer is a member of the *Nänggbläg* clan (*Dibläg* tribe), who consider themselves the traditional owners of the land where Dimsisi village is now located. The interviewed man belongs to the *Mikdäg* clan (*Wärubi* tribe). *Wärubi* tribe members used to speak a closely related variety called *Idzuwe*, but were displaced by Suki headhunting raids into Idi-speaking territory, and subsequently shifted to Idi. When asked about the languages he speaks, the interviewee first mentions Idi and Idzuwe, but note how he uses the possessive forms.

Interviewed man:

(6) a. Idi   yeka=nda
     language.name   language=INST
     (I speak) in Idi language.

b. gta   **ba**   yeka   mg=a
   PROX.DEM   **1nsg.exc.CL.POSS**   language   real=CORE
   Idzuwe
   language.name
   But our [close possessive] true language (is) Idzuwe.

c. uh   Dibläg=**bo**   Idi
   uh   tribe.name=**sg.CL.POSS**   language.name
   da=nd
   INT.DEM=1|3sg.PRES.COP
   Digbläg's [close possessive] (language) is Idi.

Interviewer:

(7) bä   sisiri gta   yeka   yeka   wlälä
     2.NOM   now   PROX.DEM   language   speak   2SG.PRES.INTR.AUX
     Are you (sg) speaking this language now?

Interviewed man:

(8) yau   yau   mn   **bnana**   yeka=nda   be
     NEG   NEG   just   **2nsg.CL.POSS**   language=INST   NOMPRT
     yeka   wlan
     speak   1SG.PRES.INTR.AUX
     No, I am speaking only in your [distant possessive, nonsingular]
     language. (20150816_BIR_CI_M36_55–61)

It is possible to interpret the interviewee's somewhat puzzling use of the distant possessive form in (8) as a means to emphasize the distant relationship he has with Idi, even though the language shift may have already happened before he was born, or during his very early childhood at the latest. Thus, people seem to hold on to their linguistic affiliations for quite a long time, even when no one actively speaks the language anymore and only a handful of words are remembered by elderly people. This excerpt offers an interesting insight into how speakers can relate to each other, and each other's languages, in everyday conversation.

10 Conclusion and discussion

This chapter provided a general discussion of traditional multilingual practices in the southern New Guinea region, followed by an analysis of possessive marking in Idi and how this relates to people's multilingual profiles. The linguistic landscape of the region appears to be reflected in Idi, in the ways that possessive forms are used to refer to the different languages people acquire during their lifetime. This shows the close integration of language and society, also when 'language', in this case, almost by default refers to multiple codes. The chapter has also shown that a language can remain a badge of identity for groups and individuals even long after that language has ceased to be actively spoken.

The chapter is a poignant reminder that more detailed studies of small-scale and egalitarian multilingual practices around the world remain vital to the study of language contact and multilingualism more generally. Terms often used in the literature without any qualification, such as 'native speaker' or 'first language' make little sense in a context such as the SNG one. People can be native speakers of a language that they nevertheless feel does not belong to them, and conversely, a person could be ascribed an emblematic language (based on descent) that they may not actively speak.

Another issue when multilingual practices are culturally prescribed and sanctioned is where to draw the boundaries between different speech communities, and indeed, whether this is possible and appropriate. The Bimadbn and Dimsisi communities are integrated to a much larger extent than, for instance, the Dimsisi and Sibidiri ones, despite the fact that the former clearly have two distinct codes, while the latter nominally speak the same language, although the two varieties of Idi may be drifting apart because of a decreasing degree of interaction between their speech communities. Certainly there are many smaller-scale communities of practice, like nuclear families or church groups, in the area that comprise emblematic speakers of both Nen and Idi. Nevertheless, both Nen and Idi speakers are at pains to point out their different tribal and linguistic identities, and would certainly resist being classified overall as a single society. The more we learn about dynamics like these, the better we are able to understand the intricate connections between languages and societies.

Acknowledgements

I owe a debt of gratitude to the many Idi speakers in Dimsisi, Iblamnd, Birem, and Bimadbn without whose efforts this research would not have been possible. Particular thanks are due to Puli Ämädu, Simon Bagi, Birke Eka, Carls Gana, Kaune Gana, Masa Gegera, Kmonde Gigu, Magham Greh, Judy James, Qandro Kaeko, Titi Masa, Pastor Deba Masro, Paul Mikuku, and Bess Purge, all of whom assisted with conducting the interviews, making audio and video recordings, and transcription. Fieldwork on which this study is based was funded by the Australian Research Council (Grant # FL130100111). I wish to thank Sasha, Bob, and Nerida for inviting me to take part in the workshop *The Integration of Language and Society* held in Cairns in August 2019, and workshop participants for their helpful feedback. Lastly, I owe much of what is said here to insightful discussions with Eri Kashima, Mark Ellison, Nick Evans, and other team members of the *Wellsprings of Linguistic Diversity* project, and other colleagues working in the southern New Guinea area.

References

Aikhenvald, Alexandra. 2002. *Language contact in Amazonia*. Oxford: Oxford University Press.

Aikhenvald, Alexandra Y. and R. M. W. Dixon. 2013. *Possession and ownership: A cross-linguistic perspective*. Oxford: Oxford University Press.

Ayres, Mary C. 1983. 'This side, that side: Locality and exogamous group definition in Morehead area, Southwestern Papua'. PhD thesis, University of Chicago.

Carroll, Matthew. 2017. 'The Ngkolmpu language, with special reference to distributed exponence'. PhD thesis, The Australian National University, Canberra.

Chappell, Hillary and William McGregor. 1996. *The grammar of inalienability: A typological perspective on body part terms and the part-whole relation*. Berlin/ New York: Walter de Gruyter.

Döhler, Christian. 2018. *A grammar of Komnzo*. Berlin: Language Science Press.

Eberhard, David M., Gary F. Simons, and Charles D. Fennig (eds). 2019. *Ethnologue: Languages of the world*. 22nd edn. Dallas, Texas: SIL International.

Epps, Patience. 2018. 'Contrasting linguistic ecologies: Indigenous and colonially mediated language contact in northwest Amazonia', in Ruth Singer and Jill Vaughan (eds), *Indigenous multilingualisms. Language and communication* 62(B): 156–69.

Evans, Nicholas. 2012. 'Even more diverse than we thought: The multiplicity of Trans-Fly languages', in Nicholas Evans and Marian Klamer (eds), *Melanesian Languages on the Edge of Asia: Challenges for the 21st Century. Language Documentation and Conservation* Special Publication 5: 109–49.

Evans, Nicholas. 2014. 'Positional verbs in Nen'. *Oceanic Linguistics* 53(2): 225–55.

Evans, Nicholas. 2015a. 'Valency in Nen', in Andrej Malchukov and Bernard Comrie (eds), *Valency classes in the world's languages*. Berlin: Mouton de Gruyter, 1069–116.

Evans, Nicholas. 2015b. 'Inflection in Nen', in Matthew Baerman (ed.), *The Oxford handbook of inflection*. Oxford: Oxford University Press, 543–75.

Evans, Nicholas. 2017. 'Quantification in Nen', in Edward Keenan and Denis Paperno (eds), *Handbook of quantifiers in natural language*, Volume 2. Dordrecht: Springer, 573–607.

Evans, Nicholas. 2018. 'Did language evolve in multilingual settings?' *Biology and Philosophy* 32.10.1007/s10539-018-9609-3.

Evans, Nicholas. 2019. 'Waiting for the word: Distributed deponency and the semantic interpretation of number in the Nen verb', in Matthew Baerman, Andrew Hippisley, and Oliver Bond (eds), *Morphological Perspectives. Papers Honours of Greville G. Corbett*. Edinburgh: Edinburgh University Press, 100–23.

Evans, Nicholas, Wayan Arka, Matthew Carroll, Yun Jung Choi, Christian Döhler, Volker Gast, Eri Kashima, Emil Mittag, Bruno Olsson, Kyla Quinn, Dineke Schokkin, Philip Tama, Charlotte van Tongeren, and Jeff Siegel. 2017. 'The languages of Southern New Guinea', in Bill Palmer (ed.), *The languages and linguistics of New Guinea: A comprehensive guide*. Berlin: Walter de Gruyter, 641–74.

Evans, Nicholas, Eri Kashima, and Dineke Schokkin. 2018. 'Emic views on having multiple languages in Southern New Guinea: A qualitative description of stable multilingualism across generations'. Paper presented at the Workshop on Intergenerational Multilingualism, *International Congress of Linguists*, Cape Town.

Evans, Nicholas and Julia Colleen Miller. 2016. 'Nen'. *Journal of the International Phonetic Association* 46(3): 331–49.

François, Alexandre. 2012. 'The dynamics of linguistic diversity: Egalitarian multilingualism and power imbalance among northern Vanuatu languages'. *International Journal of the Sociology of Language* 2012(214): 85–110.

Gast, Volker. 2013. 'Issues in Idi Verb Morphology'. Unpublished ms.

Gast, Volker. 2014. 'Verbmorphology'. Unpublished ms.

Gast, Volker. 2015a. 'The vowels of Idi as spoken in Sibidiri'. Unpublished ms.

Gast, Volker. 2015b. 'Advanced tongue root harmony in Sibidiri Idi, a language of Southern New Guinea'. Paper presented at the eleventh *Biennial Meeting of the Association for Linguistic Typology*, Albuquerque, NM.

Gast, Volker. 2017a. 'Associated motion in Sibidiri Idi (Pahoturi River family, Southern PNG)'. Paper presented at the *Workshop on the Languages of Papua* 4, Manokwari, West Papua, Indonesia.

Gast, Volker. 2017b. 'Directional inflection in Sibidiri Idi (Southern PNG)'. Unpublished ms.

Grace, George W. 1975. 'Linguistic diversity in the Pacific: On the sources of diversity'. Paper presented at the thirteenth *Pacific Science Congress*, Vancouver.

Haudricourt, André-Georges. 1961. 'Richesse en phonèmes et richesse en locu-
teurs'. *L'Homme* 1(1): 5–10.

Hoenigman, Darja, Nicholas Evans, and Penelope Johnson. 2016. *Sakr:
Re-enactment of the local myth of origin in Bimadbn, Western Province, Papua
New Guinea*. (Film)

Kashima, Eri. 2020. 'Language in my mouth: Linguistic variation in the Nmbo
speech community of southern New Guinea'. PhD thesis, The Australian
National University, Canberra.

Laycock, Donald C. 1982. 'Melanesian linguistic diversity: A Melanesian choice?',
in R. J. May and H. Nelson, *Melanesia beyond diversity*. Canberra: Research
School of Pacific Studies, Pacific Linguistics, 33–8.

Lindsey, Kate L. 2019. 'Ghost elements in Ende phonology'. PhD thesis, Stanford
University.

Lüpke, Friederike. 2016. 'Uncovering small-scale multilingualism'. *Critical
Multilingualism Studies* 4(2): 35–74.

McGregor, William (ed.). 2009. *The expression of possession*. Berlin: Mouton de
Gruyter.

Merlan, Francesca. 1981. 'Land, language and social identity in Aboriginal
Australia'. *Mankind Quarterly* 13: 133–48.

Olsson, Bruno. 2017. 'The Coastal Marind Language'. PhD thesis, Nanyang
Technological University.

Rehbein, Jochen, Jan D. ten Thije, and Anna Verschik. 2011. 'Lingua receptiva
(LaRa)—remarks on the quintessence of receptive multilingualism'.
International Journal of Bilingualism 16(3): 248–64.

Ross, Malcolm D. 1996. 'Contact-induced change and the comparative method:
Cases from Papua New Guinea', in Mark Durie and Malcolm D. Ross (eds), *The
Comparative Method reviewed: Regularity and irregularity in language change*.
Oxford: Oxford University Press, 180–217.

Schokkin, Dineke. 2014. Recordings of the Idi language (WSDS1). Digital collection managed by PARADISEC. [Open Access]. doi:10.4225/72/56E97A18E14F3.

Schokkin, Dineke. 2015a. 'Variation in Idi nominal case marking'. Paper presented at the *Workshop on the Languages of Melanesia*, ANU Kioloa Campus.

Schokkin, Dineke. 2015b. 'Idi verbs: Morphological and periphrastic options'.
Paper presented at the *Languages of Southern New Guinea Workshop*, Canberra.

Schokkin, Dineke. 2016. 'Irrealis and past habitual: Snapshots from the fringes of
Papua New Guinea'. Paper presented at the eighth *Austronesian and Papuan
Languages and Linguistics Conference*, London.

Schokkin, Dineke. 2017. 'Capturing inherent variability while doing language
description: The case of the Idi auxiliary'. Paper presented at the twelfth *Biennial
Meeting of the Association for Linguistic Typology*, Canberra.

Schokkin, Dineke. 2018. 'Towards a sociogrammar of Idi: Exploring final nasal deletion in verbs'. Paper presented at *New Ways of Analysing Variation (NWAV) Asia-Pacific* 4, Brisbane.

Schokkin, Dineke and Kate L. Lindsey. In preparation. 'The Pahoturi River language family, with special reference to its verbal puzzles'.

Schokkin, Dineke, Volker Gast, Nicholas Evans, and Christian Döhler. 2021. 'Idi phonetics and phonology', in Kate L. Lindsey and Dineke Schokkin (eds), *Phonetic fieldwork. Language Documentation and Conservations*. Special publication 24: 76–107.

Siegel, Jeff. 2014. 'The morphology of tense and aspect in Nama, a Papuan language of southern New Guinea'. *Open Linguistics* 1(1): 211–31.

Siegel, Jeff. 2017. 'Transitive and intransitive verbs in Nama, a Papuan language of Southern New Guinea'. *Oceanic Linguistics* 56(1): 123–42.

Singer, Ruth. 2018. 'A small speech community with many small languages: The role of receptive multilingualism in supporting linguistic diversity at Warruwi Community (Australia)', in Ruth Singer and Jill Vaughan (eds), *Indigenous multilingualisms. Language and communication* 62(B): 102–18.

Sutton, Peter. 1978. 'Wik: Aboriginal society, territory and language at Cape Keerweer, Cape York Peninsula'. PhD thesis, University of Queensland, Brisbane.

Unknown. 1988. 'The Dibla:g language/Idi: Statement of the grammar'. (Possibly by Coleman, Tom and Robin Coleman.) Unpublished ms.

Vaughan, Jill and Ruth Singer. 2018. 'Indigenous multilingualisms past and present', in Ruth Singer and Jill Vaughan (eds), *Indigenous multilingualisms. Language and communication* 62(B): 83–90.

Williams, F. E. 1936. *Papuans of the Trans-Fly*. Oxford: Clarendon.

10

The Iraqw society reflected in their language

Maarten Mous

1 Introduction

1.1 Iraqw language and society

The Iraqw live on a high plateau of over 2,000 metres between Lake Manyara and Lake Eyasi in Northern Tanzania. There are roughly half a million speakers in Northern Tanzania and some in big cities. Everybody also speaks Swahili. Iraqw is widely used in villages and towns in the Iraqw area but not for official business and not in education. Children do learn Iraqw but less so in the cities. Swahili influence is gradually getting stronger amongst the younger generations. English has also become a factor in recent years. People from other language backgrounds who settle in the Iraqw area learn Iraqw. It is the main Cushitic language of Tanzania, and forms with its three sister languages: Gorwaa, Alagwa, and Burunge the group of surviving South Cushitic languages. Currently Swahili (Bantu, the national language and the language of wider communication) is dominant; earlier Datooga (Nilotic, spoken mainly by semi-nomadic cattle herders) was most influential. In fact, whether Iraqw or Datooga was dominant shifted through the centuries (Kießling 1998).

Iraqw are predominantly and traditionally farmers growing maize, millet, sorghum, pearl millet, wheat, barley, beans, pumpkins, etc. The soil is fertile; there is enough sun and rainfall. They also keep cows, goats and sheep, pigs, and chickens. The domestic animals are kept in the house (nowadays often a separate house) and there is an elaborate daily procedure to make cow dung into a fertilizer. Herds are small and the care of cattle is distributed through a system of cattle loans.

Within the society, there is little formalized hierarchy. Traditional leaders are *waawutmo* 'chief, king'; *kaahamusmo*, literally 'speaker', who decides on

Maarten Mous, *The Iraqw society reflected in their language*. In: *The Integration of Language and Society: A Cross-Linguistic Typology*. Edited by: Alexandra Y. Aikhenvald, R. M. W. Dixon, and Nerida Jarkey, Oxford University Press.
© Maarten Mous 2021. DOI: 10.1093/oso/9780192845924.003.0010

land issues; and *qwaslaarmo* 'doctor', with supernatural powers, the power of prophecy and of healing. Such doctors may acquire political power through high numbers of followers. At the level of the neighbourhood there is a leader who needs to be present at local gatherings.

In order to investigate to what extent Iraqw society has influenced its language, the point of departure should be the analysis of Iraqw society. The anthropological literature on Iraqw is rich, with at least four PhD theses having been written: Thornton (1980), Snyder (1993), Rekdal (1999), and Hagborg (2001). The image that emerges from this literature is that local community is central in Iraqw social relations, more so than kinship. Snyder (1993) remarks, 'In Iraqw moral ideology, harmony and consensus are necessary for the fertility and prosperity of the community' and 'Ideally, residents in Iraqw communities should get along together "like water and honey'" (Snyder 2005: 33). Thornton (1980: 254–5) states in his conclusions that a community ritual, the *masay*, creates a political and social space which is essential for the Iraqw, whereas the 'genealogical group, the *tlah-hay*, is spatially dispersed and is never the focus of ritual activity, is rarely mentioned in oral texts of any sort, and never serves to mobilize either wealth or labor for any purpose'. Thornton (1980) also argues that the Iraqw concept of time differs from that in many other societies in that there is no chronology of time, no positioning on a time-line; this is further elaborated upon in §6.

The purpose of the chapter is to find indications in the Iraqw language for these two non-linguistic traits in society: the centrality of a local community, of 'togetherness' and the non-chronological concept of time. After a brief overview of the grammar (§1.2), I first discuss the centrality of 'togetherness' in special-purpose language use such as verbal art and ritual in §2. 'Togetherness' is also expressed by an adverb *al* which is often lexicalized with the verb, described in §3, where other manifestations of 'togetherness' in lexical semantics are also presented. I argue in §4 that the subject marker *ta* expresses, among other things, togetherness of a plural human subject. In §5, I show how only core kinship terminology is used as terms of address obligatorily distinguishing masculine and feminine gender. In this section, I also argue that Iraqw shows the remnants of a father-in-law name avoidance system. Next, in §6, I discuss the second central cultural trait, the nature of the concept of time not being absolute and being linked to space. I discuss how this is entrenched in the Iraqw lexicon and in the use of demonstratives, where I also address some structural properties of the Iraqw language that point to this concept.

1.2 Grammar overview

Iraqw is agglutinating with elements of fusion.[1] The verb tends to be clause final and is marked for subject, mood, and tense. There is a second clause constitutional element that precedes the main verb and that is termed 'selector' in Iraqw studies. This inflectional complex expresses aspect, tense, mood, gender, and person of subject and object. Subject and object constituents usually precede this selector and do not show case marking. The object constituent can also be positioned for backgrounding between selector and main verb, in which case it is marked with construct case, that is the high tone and gender linker that nouns receive when modified by any modifier. The subject marker *ta* for collective subject (see §4) belongs to the selector category.

My corpus mainly consists of narratives (c. one million words) and of metalinguistic discussions based on the stories within the corpus. The corpus was collected during fourteen periods of fieldwork, ranging between two weeks and nine months, beginning from 1987. The corpus is being continually expanded with cooperation from the community.

2 Community nature of genres of verbal art and ritual

The centrality of 'togetherness' in Iraqw culture and language is evident in the verbal art. Verbal art is primarily community art and is typically performed when people get together for a party after communal building of a house or clearing of a field, for a ritual in order to lift a curse, etc. On these occasions the leader of the neighbourhood should be present and should open the meeting with a few words in which he urges everyone to have a peaceful gathering. Songs, poetry, and stories can be performed (see www.verbafricana.org/iraqw). I briefly discuss the communal structure of the society as reflected in some of these genres.

2.1 Communal elements of *slufay* and *fiiro*

The *slufay*, literally 'blessing', is introduced by an evaluation of the well-being of the community present interspersed with spells (positive and negative) with all present joining in. This part is called *fiiro*, literally 'requesting': One man stands and discusses the state of the community as present on the

---

[1] Orthography: / = voiced pharyngeal fricative; hh = voiceless pharyngeal fricative; sl = voiceless lateral fricative, tl = ejective voiceless lateral palatal affricate, ts = ejective voiceless alveolar affricate; ' = glottal stop, not written but present word initially and between vowels of different quality, double vowels = long vowels; only high tone is marked with acute accent.

occasion. During the *fiiro*, strong wishes are chanted at high speed and in a high-pitched voice to express the hope that thieves should disappear and so should sickness. All people present join in these wishes. Then the poetic prayer starts with the performer canting short lines that are acknowledged and endorsed by all present saying *haya*. The community are a crucial part of the deliverance of the poem/prayer, establishing its rhythm and providing its power. The *slufay* has to end with fixed pairs, kind of coordinated compounds, of items that are intrinsically linked together and that express eternal connectedness: hand and mouth, sandal and heel, coat and back, eye and head, water and razor, pestle and mortar. The message of the *slufay* is one of peace and prosperity. It calls for good relations with the neighbours, who should become Iraqw. See Beck and Mous (2014) for a detailed discussion of the *slufay*.

2.2 Structure of songs and *girayda*

Most songs have a similar structure, with one (or alternate) lead singer(s) and an audience that sings a fixed refrain (*haylahilohee*, or the like). The same is true for the *girayda* poetic duel which requires a strong low toned 'refrain' which provides the atmosphere of the occasion. The two poets may represent the younger and the older generation. Poetic language is used to emphasize the cohesiveness of the groups, using metaphorical expressions such as *kintú basooro* '[we are like] a basket of very fine pearl millet'.

2.3 Cursing and lifting a curse

In cases of conflict, an individual can proclaim a curse, *lo'oo* 'curse, oath'. This is referred to as 'eating an oath' *lo'oo /ayma* which entails that justice is put in the hands of God. Typical words of a curse could be 'God you are my witness. If I am guilty, let this honey destroy me. If you prove my innocence, let it destroy him for what he has done to my reputation.' In this example the curse was executed by both parties together on an anthill, drinking honey together, but curses can be done in all kinds of places, at the river side for example, on a small hillock. They can also be done individually. If the wrongdoer is indeed wrong, punishment will follow in the form of sudden death or some other misfortune. This may be immediately or generations later (Kamera 1986: 138; see also Thornton 1980: 177–8). This is why the lifting of the curse, *lo'oo amohhu'uum,* is so important. This involves a long ceremony in which the relevant families and others must be present. It can take all night and may

nowadays involve the participation of a Christian priest. The ceremony of lifting the curse involves sharing beer on the same spot, and sucking each other's
blood. It contains a lot of long chants that are sung by all present, and in the
end 'the two opponents, who symbolize the opposing social forces, go through
the rite of reconciliation, with the society watching, and emerge cleansed. At
the end of the ceremony, the entire assembly is dismissed with peace and con-
solation since tragedy has been averted through a ritual release of tensions
and passions. Hence the society turns its energies to more down-to-earth
problems like droughts, epidemics' (Kamera 1986: 149). An excerpt from a
lifting of a curse ceremony, as reported in Kamera (1986: 144), is presented
here. The lifting of the curse was asked for by Amsi, who had several children
but no son; this was blamed on a curse that her companion Da/ati uttered
when she was a child. Note the emphasis on 'together' in the text.

(1)   Excerpt of lifting of the curse (Kamera 1986)
      Aako:

án	ham	Looa	a	di/i-t-i	kwaáhh
1sg	now	sun/God	of	fat-F-DIR	throw:1sg

      I now throw ghee to Looa.

nee	Amsi	nee	Da/ati	al	/ayayine
with	Amsi	with	Da/ati	togethere	at:IMPERV:3M:SUBJ

      Let Amsi and Da/ati eat together!

looa	di/i-t-óg	hanos
sun	fat-F-POSS.2sg	here (presenting)

      God, here is your ghee.

Amsi	laqwal.
Amsi	give.birth:IMP

      Amsi give birth!

Da/ati	sleemee	laqwal.
Da/ati	also	give.birth:IMP

      Da/ati also give birth.

dambay	ti	doog-i
other	RECIP	meet-SUBJ

      Let them meet each other!

ti	doog-iye	a-qo	ti	doog-iye.
RECIP	meet-3pl:SUBJ	COP-EMPH	RECIP	meet-3pl.SUBJ

      Let them meet, let them meet!

Assembly:

xayse	ala	gár		tlakw!	raqay[2]	gimse	dasu,	gimse!
well	but	thing:F:CON		bad:F	come	come.on	girls	come.on

Well what bad thing! Come on girls!

Da/ati:

Amsi	nao	garma	ng-u	laqwal.
Amsi	too	boy	DEP3-O.M	give.birth:3F

And Amsi, let her give birth to a boy.

Amsi:

nee	Da/ati	ni	al	/ayayima
with	Da/ati	HITH	together	eat:IMPERV:1sg-SUBJ

And let me eat with Da/ati together!

The language used in this ceremony is somewhat archaic, using subjunctives that are no longer in use. This adds to the solemnity of the occasion and gives extra power to the words. The content of the text emphasizes *togetherness* as a crucial and necessary element of the lifting. This is also clear from the setting and the participation of the large audience who represent both families (*lo'oo* 'curse, oath' is inherited!) and the community in which the lifting takes place. The locations are ideally both the place where the curse was administered and the home of the one who initiated the plea for lifting (see Snyder 2005: 114–21 and Hagborg 2001: 111–19 for more on Iraqw cursing).

The fact that Iraqw culture puts community first is evident from its indigenous juridical system. The highest penalty is *bayni* 'ostracism' and this can be applied if an individual consistently refuses to participate in communal activities. The nature of indigenous law, the views on what constitutes a crime, the manner of dealing with misbehaviour, and the wording used in that process, all assign a central role to the community.

3 Lexical properties reflecting centrality of togetherness

The cultural centrality of the concept of togetherness among the Iraqw is reflected in the Iraqw language. This is not only evident in language use in verbal art and ritual, as argued in §2, but it can also be seen in properties of

---

[2] *Raqay* is archaic; currently no Iraqw word can start with *r*.

Iraqw lexicon and grammar where the recurrent need to express togetherness has left its influence. In this section, I discuss the lexical expression of togetherness. In §4, I argue that the central system of selectors has been influenced by the need to express togetherness in the semantic expansion of the impersonal subject marker *ta*.

In several instances of lexicalization we can recognize the centrality of togetherness. This is evident at three levels: (i) togetherness lexically expressed (§3.1); (ii) the adverb *al* lexicalized in combination with several verbs (§3.2); and (iii) togetherness playing a role in lexical semantics and the evaluative overtone of the meaning of the verb (§3.3). In §3.4, I show that, although Iraqw seems to have a lexical verb for the concept 'to have', closer inspection shows that this verb has the semantic scheme at its base of 'be with', as in so many African languages in which possession is expressed with a comitative (Heine 1997).

3.1 Direct lexical expression of togetherness

As in many other languages, there are several lexical items referring to a group of people or animals, as shown in (2).

(2) *daqa* (f)   group, flock, herd, plenty
     doqoori (f)   group
     boohha (f)   bundle, heap
     xooroo (f)   crowd, people as a nation, people in a unit
     qari (f)   generation, age-group, age mate

The following basic lexical units shown in (3) denote specific groups of people that are often together as one unit. Some of these are typical terms to address all members of a group at once: *barisee, daaqaay, laqwloo*.

(3) *batlay* (m)   a group of boys
     daaqaay (m)   young boys
     barisee (f)   elders, set of senior men leading the village
     tlawaay (m)   wives
     laqwloo (f)   children (boys and girls of the age of 5–6 years)

In the area of nominal number marking, it is interesting to mention that Iraqw has among its many lexically determined plural formations a suffix that is predominantly used for collections, -*aay*, as in *batlay, daaqaay,* and *tla-waay* in (3).

In the case of a number of verbs and nouns, togetherness is one aspect of the meaning of the lexical item, exemplified in (4).

(4) *harawahh* (v)   join people in work
     tlaxuus (v)   work in turn on each other's plot
     bara/ (v)   march, walk with a group, sing while walking or
                             working, dance together to show pride
     fiyahhee (f)   mother of many children
     wangahheetsáy (m)   mother of many children (*poetic*)
     gixsa (f)   town, village, place with many houses like beads
                             sewn to a garment
     slaqwee (f)   directive for communal work, co-operative
                             endeavour

Iraqw also expresses collectivity of a plural object or subject in a number of verbs, which can be seen as supplecting pluractionals, as in (5).

(5) Lexical pluractional verbs
     fitsaahh (v) pursue (by many)
     tsuu/ (v)   kill (many people)
     qaatl (v)   die, break (of many)

3.2 The adverb *al* '(do something) together' in lexical compounds

There is a verbal adverb *al* that expresses 'together' in the meaning of '(do something) together', as in (6).

(6) atén   a-ga   al   Imború   kaw-áan
     1pl   1/2-per   together   Mbulu:CON   go-1pl
     We went to Mbulu together.

In compounds, *al* conveys the meaning of togetherness, but in the lexicaliza-tions of such compounds the cognitively related meanings of doing again, or of completeness can be discerned, as seen in Table 1.

Table 1 Compounds with *al*

base	meaning	al-compound	meaning
/aa/	'to cry'	al/aa/iim	'to pay tribute, express sorrow' [cry-together with]
axwees	'to talk'	al'axwees	'to plan' [talk together]
daakw	'to sharpen'	aldaakw	'to rethink' [sharpen again by thinking again]
gaas	'to kill'	algaas	'to return cattle to the group' [together > mix]
hhe'ees	'to finish'	alhhe'ees	'to complete fully' [completeness]
kii/	'to return'	alkii/	'to repeat, go against sb. in secret' [do again]
		alkii/iit	'to narrate'
qoom	'to be all right'	alqoom	'to be equal in comparison' [together > comparing]
qwaar	'to be lost'	alqwaarees	'to set (of sun)' [complete]
--	--	alqaad	'to give last instructions'

3.3 Words for PRIDE: Positive if group, negative if individual

In discussing basic cultural values of the Iraqw, the concept of 'pride' was mentioned as a most central one. Considering the several lexical items in the domain of pride, it becomes obvious that pride is evaluated positively when referring to the group and negatively when referring to an individual.

The most general term for showing pride is *daar/aam* (v) 'to boast', and this is met with disdain; it is seen as a negative character trait to boast about wealth, beauty, power. A specific type of pride which is considered positive is *gooranga* (f), *gooranguus* (v) which is a state of pride not of a specific person but a general state of the community after killing a dangerous animal. A verb like *durbiim* refers to showing happiness, contentment. This is considered positive, unless it is used for a single person. The verb *waahh* (v), and its noun *wahhay* (m), is a negative version of 'showing off (by a person)'. Even more negative is *diidúus* (v), and its noun *diida* (p) for 'the pride to make others jealous'.

The well-being of the community is crucial in these attitudes to the concept of 'pride' and to the lexical meaning of these words for 'pride'.

3.4 A possessive verb which marks 'companionship'

Iraqw has no special constructions for inalienable possession, nor a special construction for communal property such as cattle, house, etc. It differs from many other languages of Tanzania (and Africa in general) in that it has a lexical verb 'to have'. In many African languages the translation of 'to have' is a construction BE WITH. At first glance, this difference would suggest a dominant concept of individual possession for Iraqw. I argue, however, that this verb *koom* 'to have' has TOGETHERNESS at its core.

The verb *koom* 'to have' takes a wide range of possessed entities including property, family relations, and parts. Some examples from my corpus of possessed items with a person as possessor are flute, bow, gourd, instruments, cattle, meat, milk, ashes, information, nothing, wisdom, pregnancy, colour, mother, nose. When animals are possessors the possessed items that are attested are body parts: ears, horns, wings, tail. Non-animate possessors are attested to 'have' poison, sweetness, sand, people (land), bees (tree), blood (place). The entry for *koom* in our dictionary (Mous et al. 2002) is (7).

(7)   Dictionary entry of *koom*
       koom (v) possess
          kooma (f), *koomaakoom* hold, *komkaakoom* HAB. *komtis* CAUS
       follow, *komti* (f)
       following, having. *komtaangw* (m) being together, following each other.
          koomi (f) cattle loan, deposit SG: *koomuuso'oo*. PL: *koomay* (m) cows
       for paying debt.
       Derivations:
          alkoom (v) accompany, chase after, follow up sth. *ti alkoomaan* Let's
       go together.
          kuúng nee dahaaymowí ti alkoondá' You and this guest are together.
          alkomti (f) procession, going together.
             adkoom (v) complete, whole.

The details of the dictionary entry and of its derived entries suggest a wider concept than 'possession'. The middle-derived *komiit* or *kumiit* that developed the meaning of 'continue' is difficult to link to the meaning of possession and is easier to link to the root *koom* if the latter would have 'together with' as its core meaning from which the middle developed the meaning 'to follow, continue'. The sense of 'to follow' is present in the nominalizations *komti* (f) 'following, having' and *komtaangw* (m) 'being together, following each other'. The causative *komtis* is a transitive verb 'to follow'. The meaning 'together with' is present in the compound *alkoom* together+*koom* 'accompany, chase after'.[3]

---

[3] Denis Creissels pointed out to me that in the language Sara the verb 'to have' has similar extended meanings. In the Démé variety of Sar the verb *èmbè* means 'avoir, posséder, trouver, rencontrer' (Palayer 2006: 202).

Concluding, an important sense of the meaning of this verb *koom* 'to have' turns out to be the expression of a companion relation rather than location, action, existence, following Heine's comitative scheme (Heine 1997).

4 A collective third person subject marker?

In this section I argue that the centrality of 'togetherness' in Iraqw culture has resulted in it being incorporated in the expression of one of the selectors that is most commonly used in narratives, the subject marker *ta*. This subject marker is used for an unspecified and vague subject and in this usage it functions as an impersonal subject marker, being used as translation equivalent of passive sentences and with adjectives as complement (see §4.1). It developed the additional function of expressing a collective human subject (§4.2). This may be an innovative development of Iraqw within South Cushitic.

4.1 Properties of IMPERSONAL *ta*

Subject in Iraqw is marked on the verb and in the selector. The general marking of subject in the selector is speech act participant, 1/2 person, versus third person, with third person generally marked by *i*. There is another third person selector, and this is *ta*. A clause with *ta* as selector has the 3M form of the verb. The clauses with *i* can occur with 3M, 3F, or 3P verb inflections.

The third person subject marker *ta* is used with nominal and verbal complements. This subject marker may have a locative nominal complement, as in (8, 9), but cannot be used in an equation, for which the general copula *a* is used, as in (10).

(8) inoín   ta   do'
     3pl   IMPERS   house
     They are at home.

(9) inoín   ta   gawá   tlom'i
     3pl   IMPERS   on:CON   mountains
     They [the Yambi people] were in the mountains. (Berger and
     Kießling 1988: 192)

(10) inoín   a   daqa   NOT: ta   daqa
      3pl   COP   crowd   IMPERS   crowd
      They form a crowd.

The same *ta* can also be used with verbal complements, i.e. as selector in verbal clauses, (11).

(11) bálgeeraawo   ta   kaahi:
      once   IMPERS   say:3M
      Once upon a time, they say:

If an explicit pronoun is present in the sentence, it is the general third person plural pronoun *inoin* 'they', which is otherwise used with a third person plural verb form.

The subject marker *ta* is also used for sentences that translate as passives, as in (12):

(12) waawutumo-ín   ku-dá'   ta   babay   Haymú,...
      king:M-POSS.3pl   M-DEM4   IMPERS   call:3m   haymú
      That king of theirs, who was called Haymú,...

The selector *ta* shows up hidden in the amalgamated complex forms *ku, ka, ki* like *ku* in (13). The form *ku* is a contraction of *g-ta-u* in which *g-* is a marker of subject and object being a third person, and *u* is a masculine object pronoun.

(13) k-u-ri   báy   nee   mu-k-ós
      O3:IMPERS-O.M-CSEC   tell:3M   with/by   people-M-POSS.3sg
      So he was told by his people.

There is strong evidence for such an analysis. Example (12) is comparable to (13) but has *ta* where (13) has *ku* and this is because relative clauses (underlined in 12) do not contain object pronouns. Hence (12) and (13) both contain *ta* and (13) has *g-* and *-u* added to it. The same *g-* and *-u* are used in other independent clauses with subject and object being third person and an object pronoun *u* but without the *ta* selector and they show the voiced *g* in the absence of devoicing by *ta*, (14).

(14) do'   g-u   tleehhiit
      house   O3-O.M   build:3M
      He is building a house.

The same *ta* is used for sentences with adjectives as predicates. The forms *ku* (13), *ka*, and *ki* that are used in impersonal (passive translation) clauses are used with adjectives in the predicate slot and agree in gender with the noun. These copula consist of *k* (from *g-ta-*) and a pronoun *u*, *a*, and *i*. In (15a) the pronoun *u* refers to the masculine (intransitive) subject, in (15b) the pronoun *a* refers to the feminine, and in (15c) the pronoun *i* refers to the plural. These forms function as object pronouns in verbal clauses and hence are glossed as O.M, O.F, O.P.

(15) a. inós   k-u   hhóo'   tluway k-u   hhéer
          3sg   O3-O.M   nice:M/P   rain. M   O3-O.M   insufficient:M
          He is nice.   Rain is insufficient.

      b. inós   k-a   hhoo'   fa/a   k-a   hheer
          3sg   O3-O.F   nice:F   food. F O3-O.F   insufficient:F
          She is nice.   Food is insufficient.

      c. inoín   k-i   hhóo'   hhayso k-i   ququmaar
          3pl   O3-O.P   nice:M/P   tail   O3-O.P   short: P
          They are nice.   The tail is short.[4]

Ta functions as an impersonal. For example, it is often used with a verb 'to say' including situations where the subject is fully unspecified as in the first sentence of a story, as in (11). And with an object, it may translate as a passive, as in (16).

(16) idigu-w-í   k-ú-n   alkí/áa/iit
      news-M-DEM1   O.3:IMPERS-O.M-EXPEC   recount:IMPV:3M
      This news is being told.

This can have the usual discourse function of putting the object (us) central, as in (17) (where *ta* is part of *ta-i*), but that is not the only reason why it is used. In the following sentence, (18), the cows are not central but the milking and the subject is backgrounded by use of *ta*.

(17) ta-y   óo'   ti   faak
      IMPERS-CSEC   say:3m IMPERS:O1pl   finish:3M
      And they said: 'Now we are finished off.'

---

[4] This plural form may come as a surprise but some nouns are 'plural' in gender even if they refer to singular concepts and the agreement is purely with gender, see Mous (2008).

(18)   hikwa   k-áy   lotatín.
       hikwa   g-ta-i-áy   lot~at-iim-i
       cattle   O3-IMPERS-O.P-CSEC   milk~IMPERV-3M
       They used to milk the cows.

The impersonal comes very close to a grammaticalized passive construction.
The subject is no longer really impersonal when it is specified in the by-phrase
which we already saw in (13). Furthermore, this specified subject in the by-
phrase can even be singular as we see in (19).

(19)   ar   adoo-dá'   ku-wa   hara'ayín
       with   manner-F:DEM4   O3:IMPERS:O.M-BGND   command:3M
       nee   kwasleemuusmo
       by   judge
       Just the way that he was told by the judge.

The by-phrase for a specified subject is possible in an intransitive clause too, (20).

(20)   kw-a-i   burumburíit   nee
       O3:IMPERS:O.M-PER-DIR   be.gathered.together:3M   with(by)
       Sarwáat
       Darorajeeg-Datooga
       The Darorajeega have gathered. (Berger and Kießling 1988)

4.2 Function of *ta*: Collective subject

The impersonal subject marker *ta* 'they' has created constructions that are the
functional equivalent of a passive, allowing for expressing a specific and possibly singular subject in the by-phrase. The same marker has also developed
in another direction, expressing a collective subject as we can see in the collective subject, the Gisamjanga people in (21). The sentence leaves it open
who exactly killed the woman, but puts the blame on the Gisamjanga people
in general, as a collective subject. The subject can be specific but vague, as
in (22).

(21)   hare   ka-y   gáas
       wife   O3:IMPERS:O.F-CSEC   kill:3M
       They [the Gisamjanga people] killed a woman.

(22)   ta-y   wa~wáatl
       IMPERS-CSEC   DISTR~return.home:3M
       And everybody went home.

The pronoun *ta* is very common in stories. In the story of Geeso Duqa, the
clan of the cannibals is consistently referred to with *ta*. There are many of
them, but they act as a group (23). *Ta* is often used for large groups that act as
one but also for small groups that act together:

(23)   kú-ngú-rí   leehh   nee
       O3:IMPERS:O.M-HITH:O.M-CSEC   carry:3M   with
       múk   aako-dáa   ya/áw.
       people:M1:CON   old.man-DEM4:3:PER   send:3M
       They will carry it together with the people that the old man has sent.
       (Berger and Kießling 1988)

In the story of the half-brothers Booboo/ and /Awawaki, *ta* is used every time
it is emphasized that the two brothers are together as they want to be, eating
and drinking together, (24, 25, 26).

(24)   Amór   ta-qo   kay,   oo   wák   i
       place:F:CON   IMPERS-EMPH   go:3M   CON:M   one   3
       /aymár   ayká,   a   qo   ta-n
       eating:F:CON   go:NEG   COP   EMPH   IMPERS-EXPEC
       al-/ayín.
       together-eat:IMPERV1:3M
       Wherever they go, a single one does not eat; they are to eat together.

(25)   Maá   laatí   tsaraaw-o   ka-na   wáh,
       but   SURPRISE   two-PRED   O3:IMPERS:O.F-PAST   drink.3M
       ta   xwaantér   al-/aa~/aay
       IMPERS   porridge:F:CON   together-DISTR~eat
       But they drink it together. They eat porridge together.

(26)   Kár   supu-ín   kwí   k-u-na
       well   soup:M-POSS.3pl   M:DEM1   O3:IMPERS-O.M-PAST
       al-/aay~/aáy, al/aay/aáy, al/aay/aáy.
       together-DISTR~eat
       Their soup was eaten, eaten, eaten together.

Ta is used very often in stories for a collective protagonist (27). The functions of impersonal and collective subject are not always easily to separate. Example (17) can be taken as an instance of a collective protagonist as well.

(27) tookaaro /Arí nee dasú   aya   ta   hhekiit.
      some.day /Arí and girls:M:CON land IMPERS   draw.water:3M
      One day, /Arí and the girls of the neighbourhood were drawing water.

Note the switch in this story from *ta* to common third person *i* when an opposition between protagonists is made, (28).

(28) dasu   i   tlaa/ár   gwangwara'án   inós   i
      girls.M 3   rock:F:CON   roll:IMPERV2:3M   3sg   3
      ma'áa   í-hhekít
      water:P:CON   APPLIC-draw.water:3F
      The girls were rolling a rock, while she [/Arí] was drawing water.

Thus, the referent is often definite and specific in these stories and we cannot say that *ta* always expresses indefinite or nonspecific referents. In fact, *ta* seems to express a collective human subject. Clearly *ta* has a number of different functions. While it is impersonal in many of its usages, it is no longer impersonal when it expresses a collective subject.

The collective nature of *ta* is clear from the fact that when the adverb *al* 'together' is used with a plural third person subject, *ta* is nearly always used, rather than the common third person *i*. Nearly all (43 of 48) of the clauses with *al* in third person in our stories had *ta* rather than *i* as selector.

4.3 Related languages and a wider Cushitic perspective

The related language Burunge has *da* as equivalent to Iraqw *ta*. Anna Badman's (2010) MA thesis on this topic concludes that *da* is an indefinite subject marker used to form an impersonal passive in the absence of a canonical passive, while a subject may still be explicitly given post-verbally via the agentive phrase *ha*. The construction with *da* functions as a passive, promoting the object, demoting the subject. The subject of *da* may be a specific person, or even be non-human. It can also be used with intransitive verbs, such as 'to awaken', (29). In these instances *da* indicates that the subject is implicit rather than indefinite.

(29)   Ruuti   daa   pisi
       ruth   IMPERS:PAST   awake:3M:PER
       Ruth awoke. (Badman 2010: 11)

The use of the subject indefinite can keep a character in the syntactic subject position even if actions are being done to them and not by them. As
a discourse strategy, it lessens the overt mention of several characters over
a short space of time and maintains the thematic prominence of one
character.

It is also used for situations in which things simply exist and for spontaneous action. No instances have been reported in Burunge in which *da*
expresses a collective subject.

The Burunge *da* and Iraqw *ta* are related to Somali impersonal *la* which
can be used in generic sentences (Cabredo Hofherr 2008) but it does not have
the collective subject function. The collective nature of *ta* in Iraqw seems to
be an innovation.

Local community showing cohesion and peace is considered of paramount
importance to the Iraqw. This is reflected in their world view, beliefs, and legal
practices and is an underlying organizing principle of their verbal art.
'Togetherness' is a recurrent additional element in various lexical terms.
Adverbs for 'together' are often compounded with verbs which lexicalize,
showing that it is considered important for 'togetherness' to be expressed as a
component of a range of activities. 'Togetherness' is expressed in verbs with
inherent pluractional meaning. In the morphosyntax of Iraqw, the impersonal
pronoun *ta* is used to refer to plural collective subject and very often used for
such a protagonist in stories.

5 Kinship

An obvious area of language to reflect societal structure is in kinship terminology and its usage. The following discussion is a first attempt at this
for Iraqw. I look at which kinship terms can be used as term of address and
by whom and to whom, in order to check if that correlates with important
social organization (§5.1). The Iraqw neighbours, the Datooga, have/had a
well-developed register of respect to father-in-law and related kin,
(Mitchell 2015; Tramutoli 2012). There are rudiments of such a register
among the Iraqw too. The little information that I have on this is presented
in §5.2.

5.1 Terms of address

When addressing people, Iraqw, like many other people, use terms for family relations also to those with whom the family relation does not hold. Only some of the terms for family relations are used for addressing other people. To a woman one might say *aayi* or *aayo* 'mother', *aama* 'grandmother'. The difference between *aayi* and *aayo* is that the former expresses more endearment and is mostly used for one's own mother, while both are used out of respect to a married woman or a woman of that age; *aama* which is the equivalent to grandmother is used for an elderly lady.

Some general words are also used in addressing, including addressing family members. For example, the word *deena* 'young woman of marrying age' does not indicate a family relationship as such. It can be used to address a sister-in-law, elder sister, or an unmarried woman who is close to the age of the speaker. Only the basic meanings are given here. The word *dasi* 'girl' is used by parents to a daughter of any age, or for a girl of the age of one's daughter, or a girl too young to be married. Male kinship terms used as term of address are *baaba* 'father', *aako* 'grandfather', and also terms that are not strictly relational such as *garma* 'boy', *daaqaay* 'boys', and *barisee* 'elders'. Of course, one can also use the actual kinship terms as term of address to members of the family. For example, one may call the younger sister of one's mother *aayi* 'mother', which she technically is (according to the classificatory kinship system), even when she is much younger than oneself.

There is a gender symmetry in the sense that a man and woman of comparable age are addressed by terms at the same level. The term *aako* 'grandfather', originally used for an old man, is now used as respect term including to not so old men. This is considered to be a recent influence of Swahili, in which the use of the Swahili term *mzee*, originally 'old man', is similarly inflated in age.

The word *na/ay* 'child' can be used as a term of address. But generally the use of terms that do not refer to family relations as terms of address is uncommon. Thus words like *waawutmo* 'king' or 'chief', *kaahamusmo* 'speaker' or 'spokesperson', *qwaslaarmo* 'traditional doctor' are not used as terms of address, unless possibly within the context of a formal meeting or court case. The only terms of address that do not primarily refer to family relationships are *garma* 'boy', *daaqaay* 'boys', *dasi* 'girl', *dasu* 'girls', *deena* 'woman ready to be married', and *barisee* 'elders'.

Swahili terms are seldom used as terms of address, except possibly for the word *mama* 'mother'. Though it is common practice in (East-) Africa to call a woman after her eldest child, e.g. in Swahili *mama Lucy*, or, for a man, *baba Tausi*, this is not a tradition among the Iraqw when speaking Iraqw.

A number of kinship terms can only be used fictively as terms of address if the addressee is considered close enough to be family: *maamáy* 'uncle' (mother's brother), *ayishiga* or *ayisaga* 'aunt' (father's sister, literally mother head), *baabuú niiná* 'father's younger brother, literally little father), *aayí niína* 'mother's younger sister; daughter of father's sister', literally 'little mother', and also *kumbá* 'male-in-law, *hare* 'wife', and *hhawaata* 'husband'. This last term can be used in the plural *hhawaate*, to greet a group of men in a casual way.

I now turn to kinship terms that can only be used as term of address within the family. These include the compound terms that start with *hat* 'daughter' or with *nangw* 'son' as shown in the terms of address and responses to them in the following list, (30). These terms of address with a generational difference are thus not used fictively and only for the actual kinship relation.

(30)   Family internal terms of address

Term of address by EGO	Term of address to EGO
hat'aay: daughter of father's nephew	*hat'aay* to *f* and *nangw'aay* to *m* addressee
hat'hho'o: daughter of sister	*aayi niina* to *f* and *maamay* to *m* addressee
hat'ama: daughter of mother's sister	*hat'ama* to *f* and *nang'ama* to *m* addressee
hat'hato': daughter of daughter	*aama* to *f* and *aako* to *m* addressee
hat'nango': daughter of son	*aama* to f and *aako* to *m* addressee
hat'maamay: daughter of mother's brother	*aayi niina* (only applicable to *f* addressee)
hat'hhiyawo: daughter of brother	*aayishiga* (only applicable to *f* addressee)
har'maamay: wife of maternal uncle	*dasi* to *f* and *garma* to *m* addressee
nango': son	*aayi*, or *aayo* to f and *baaba* to *m* addressee
nangw'nango': son of son	*aama* to *f* and *aako* to *m* addressee
nangw'hato': son of daughter	*aama* to *f* and *aako* to *m* addressee
nangw'aay: son of father's cousin	*hat'aay* (only applicable to *f* addressee)
nangw'ama: son of mother's sister	*hat'ama* (only applicable to *f* addressee)
nanu maamay: son of mother's brother	*aayi niina* (only applicable to *m* addressee)
aayi niina: mother's younger sister or paternal aunt's daughter	*hat'hho'o* or *dasi* respectively

A group of people that are younger than yourself can be addressed as *haywa*. *Laqwlo* is used for addressing a group of children (can be mixed sex) and *barísee* for a group of elders or of a group of people with some power (also if women are among them).

Terms of address to individuals are always sex specified. This is clear from the terms mentioned above. But also very general and familiar attention-getting terms like *xáygan* 'hey, you there' are sex specific, with the often-heard *xaygán* to address men. The term used towards women is *xáysiri* but this is not so often used.

We can relate this to the sex distinction in the 2SG pronoun, *kúung* 2sg.M versus *kíing* 2sg.F; but no sex distinction in 3sg *inós*. But the 3sg pronoun is not used in addressing, and sex or actually grammatical gender is always distinguished in referring via subject and object agreement on the verb (subject) and in the selector (object).

Gender is always distinguished in addressing individuals, not only for the terms of address whether basically relational or fictive, but also for interjections calling for attention, and in the second person personal pronouns in all uses. The importance of gender distinctions is reflected in its obligatory expression in address. There is no indication that gender plays a more prominent role in Iraqw society compared to other societies, but Iraqw has used its linguistic potential to incorporate it into its linguistic system.

In conclusion, only the ascending kinship terms for parents and grandparents are used as more general respectful terms of address. Some terms can be used for non-kin to signal close relationship and these include the cross-uncle and cross-aunt which are considered to have a close personal bond with ego. It is only these closest kinship terms that are used as a more general term of address and these are expanded by more general non-relational terms. The extension of kinship terms to other functions is relatively limited, which may reflect the fact that kinship plays less of a role in daily dealings in Iraqw society than 'togetherness' (Thornton 1980: 255). The descending kinship terms of (30) which show remarkably detailed distinctions are never used fictively, possibly relating to the dependence on the older generation within the family bond.

5.2 Iraqw in-law respect practice *wakaari*

The Iraqw in-law respect practice is called *wakaari* (f) or *wakti* (f) derived from the verb *waak* '1. not to like each other, 2. not to use the name of husband's father or son's wife.' The practice is asymmetrical in gender, applying only to newly-wed women talking to male in-laws. Snyder (2005: 113ff) has a long section on *wakaari* as an enmity involving conventional behaviour that occurs when two people, or two families, have a serious and irreconcilable disagreement arising from conflicts involving land, debts (in livestock) incurred but not repaid, accusations of witchcraft. Hagborg (2001: 87) defined *wakaari* in similar fashion. The anthropological literature does not take the in-law avoidance aspect of *wakaari* into account.

For example, Basilisa's husband is called Buura and his father is called Amsí. Basilisa is not supposed to use the name Amsí, nor the word *amsi* 'midnight', nor *amsatsa* which is a wish for good night. This practice extends to all his brothers but not his grandfather. Instead of *amsi* she will say *tla/ang xweera* 'middle evening' and instead of *amsatsa* she will say *xweera hhooá* 'good night'. In other words, she will use descriptions for avoidance. The avoidance does not systematically extend to all words resembling the name to avoid, or its base, as it does in so many other similar avoidance systems in Africa, including the neighbouring Datooga. The woman's father-in-law will give her a cow at marriage as compensation for not using his name. This restriction is valid from the time of the wedding onwards and does not end. In case of emergency, she will ask someone else to use the name, or use *xweera* 'evening' instead of the name. There is no formal training in this. People know how to avoid traditional names and the avoidance choices are standard. The custom does not apply to other (Christian) names and is disappearing or has disappeared, though it was once common in *Irqwár da/aw*, the core area of Iraqw culture. In Table 2 some example names are presented with their replacements. The data are too scant to know whether these replacement terms are conventionalized or ad hoc; nor whether a more elaborate replacement vocabulary once existed.

In an attempt to get more avoidance forms I elicited the following expressions; speakers were, however, very hesitant about these. See Table 3.

It is interesting to report that this in-law name avoidance system existed among the Iraqw. Such systems have been reported for Nguni and Sotho languages in Southern Africa, *hlonipha*, for Oromo and Kambaata in Ethiopia, *laguu* and *ballisha*, and in Tanzania for the Nyakyusa (Bantu) (Kolbusa 2000), the Datooga (Nilotic), and now also for the Iraqw (Cushitic). It is likely that it once existed in more societies in Africa. More on honorific registers can be found in the chapters by Dixon and Jarkey in this volume.

Table 2 Examples of avoidance

Name	Base for name	Meaning	Replacement	Meaning	Explanation
Tsino	tsiino	fine dust from trashing or winnowing millet	teeri	dust	
Buura	buura	beer	slaqwe	communal work	refers to beer prepared for communal work
			kilaabu	club	English > Kiswahili loan to mean a place where beer is sold
			baafa	blessing or offering	refers to beer prepared as offering to ancestors
/Ayto'o	/ayto'o	maize	balangw /awak	white cereal	description of maize
Daaffi	daaf	bring cattle home	watliis	bring home	causative derivation of *waatl* come home
/Amsi	/amsi	night	tla/ang xweera	middle of night	description

Table 3 Elicited examples

Name	Sex	Base for name	Meaning	Avoidance term	Meaning
Maasay		maasáy	medicine	maʻaay	water
Laantá	F	Laanta	name for God	umuú looa oo hatláʻ	different name of God
Genda	M/F	genda	tree	xaʻanoodáʻloo/orós ta seepát hamtlaatliti	that tree its leaves clean the small gourd
tsangwalí	M	tsangwali	plant (vitus cyyphostemmanie)	loo/odár maʻaay	those leaves of water
or/ondí	M	or/ondi	plant (cucumis aculeatus)	loo/odár maʻaay	those leaves of water
Hhawú		hhawú	name for hyena	umuduú hatláʻ oo baha	that other name of hyena
Baha		baha	hyena	umuduú hatláʻ oo hhawú	that other name of hhawú
/Awakí	F	/awaak	white	looʻa	God
Da/atí		da/aat	red	looʻa	God
Kwa/angw	M	kwa/angw	hare	umuduú Lách	that name of Lách
Gwareehhí	M/F	gwareehhi	dikdik	adór leei	like goat
Ba/asá	M	ba/asa	bushbuck	gurtuú sla/a	goat of forest
Samtí	F	samti	porcupine	makitoʻór laqayaʻ	animal of thorns
Bee/í	M/F	bee/i	sheep	makitoʻór gár ya/aá ququmád	animal of short legs
Koonkí	M/F	koonki	hen	gár hayóh doʻo	the thing one takes home
Hhookí	M/F	hhooki	dove	tsirʻír wayda	bird of peace
Naanagi	M	naanagi	insect larvae in maize stalk	gadádáʻ tseegamisi hiʻinooro	the thing that walks slowly

6 The concept of time

As is evident from the title of his book, *Space, Time and Culture among the Iraqw of Tanzania*, for Thornton (1980) the Iraqw concept of time is of particular interest. This is so because events are put in sequence but not pinned to an absolute point in time. In history the emphasis is on continuity.

> Chief characteristics of Iraqw narratives are (a) the lack of chronology;[5]
> (b) the importance of oral performance and ritual; (c) the conservation of
> quality, place, and objects; and (d) the prominence of spatial relationships of
> events systematically related to one another in a topological way.
>
> (Thornton 1980: 171)

My reading of Iraqw oral history and verbal art confirms this. But can we find correlates of this insight in the Iraqw language? Thornton (1980: 171) remarks that the units such as 'hour', 'week', 'month', 'year' are not used as standards of measurement and indeed we find these temporal units are seldom counted.[6]

Iraqw has a large number of expressions for relative time but the only absolute time reference that is lexically expressed is 'now' (31a). The most general words for time refer to a period of time (31b). There are several ways to express succession in time (31c). Relative time can be expressed by a number of verbs for being late, (31d), and by adverbials for several parts of the day, some related to customary events (31e). Relative days from today go back two days and ahead five days, (31f). There are traditional names for months which refer to typical weather situations; it is unclear whether these are used to refer to actual months or more general periods (31g), but there are other terms for the main seasons (31h). The periodization of time has original Iraqw terms for the larger units 'year', 'month', and 'day' but Swahili loans for 'hour' and smaller units, (31i).

(31)   Time expressions in Iraqw
   a.   now (point in time): *daxa* 'now', and 'then, thus'; *hamí* 'now, present'; *sang* 'now, just, already'; *aleerí* 'nowadays'.
   b.   time (period): *de'ema* 'time, duration'; *siiwa* 'time, some time, a while'; *qoomaa* 'period'; *daqi* 'time, period'; *saga wa* 'time, turn'.

---

[5] *Chronology* refers to a link to external events; *sequence* of events is expressed in these narratives.

[6] In response to questions about how far away a certain place was, I did receive answers in terms of number of hours. However, those did not represent the time period needed for travel, but the point in time when one would arrive at that place, assuming a start just before dawn. Hence, hour is used for a point in time rather than a period in time.

c. sequence: *daqaní* 'then, afterwards'; *aluwo* 'afterwards, later, then';
aluudá' then, after that'; *looitleer* 'next day, afterwards'. (literally, the
sun has come up)

d. late: *adaa/* (v) 'be late, delayed'; *laala'aat* (v) 'to be late'; *tliig* (v) 'to
be late'; *kwaahhaas* (v) 'to be late'; *hhaaw* (v) 'to be late, pass time,
waste time, be idle'.

e. early: *tseewa* 'early'; *matlee* 'morning, tomorrow; *tsiindi* 'sunset';
wiririit (v) 'to fall (of night)'; *xweeraa* 'night'; *alxwayaangw* 'early
evening'; *axweesoo* 'evening, night (8–10 p.m.)'; *amsi* 'midnight,
night'; *dakiingw* 'time in the night before the cock's crow (3 a.m.)';
pinsliit 'dawn'; *looitleemu* 'sunrise'; *matlaatlee* 'morning'; *matlee*
'tomorrow, morning'; */ameetleemu* 'midday'; *tlatla/aangw* 'midday';
/aymadu 'midday, lunch time'; *furaai* 'late afternoon (4.30–6 p.m.)';
daafi 'bringing home the cattle, time of sunset (6 p.m.); *irambu*
'dusk, evening time (6–6.30 p.m.)'; *tsiindoo* 'evening (before dark)'.

f. days as counted from today: *lat'áangw* 'day before yesterday
(day-past)'; */isá* 'yesterday'; *laa* 'today'; *laarí* 'today' /day-DEM1/;
matloo 'tomorrow'; *baloqa* 'day after tomorrow' /day:DEM3/;
baldani 'two days after tomorrow /day:DEM4:?/; *toqani* 'three days
after tomorrow' /this-DEM3-?/; *tidanee ~ tadanee* 'four days after
tomorrow' /this:DEM4:?:PRED/.

g. month periods: *axwaarír hhoo'* /season.of.hunger-good/ (roughly
December); *axwaarír tlaakw* /~-bad/; *tlufqa* 'rain with large drop;
talaali; *huyaa'aa* 'constellation of five stars in March'; *doomú bóo/*
/rainy.season-black/; *doomú /awáak* /~-white/; *quua* 'misty';
tsaaqutumo 'cold'; *tlamboo/amo* 'wind of this period'; *tarqway* 'hot
period'; *qadóo kaháar* /dry.period-dry/; *qadoó maár* /~-folded/.

h. seasons: *doomu* 'continuous long rain, period of rains'; *buhaaree*
'rainy season (February–April)'; *agee* 'dry season (August–
September)'; */ido* 'dry season (for maize)'; *saxi* 'short period of rains
(September–October)'; *qadaay* 'end of the year, dry period'; *axwaari*
'season of hardship and food shortage (December–January)'.

i. periodization of time: *kuru* 'year'; *slahhaangw* 'moon, month,
waxing moon, period of waxing moon'; *wiiki* 'week' (Swahili loan);
dominika 'week' (Latin loan via Swahili); *baalaa* 'day (in
expressions)'; *lal'i* 'days'; *dakiika* 'minute' (Swahili loan); *hoomaa*
'first night after full moon'; */oona* 'period of old moon, the
waning moon'.

There is no straightforward lexical unit for 'time in general' in Iraqw. Thornton claims that:

> time words *qoma, xayla, siwa,* and *kiima* imply discrete and definite periods of time or duration, in contradistinction to an undifferentiated flow of time.... Both *qoma* and *xayla* appear to designate a discrete moment of time; *qoma* nearly always refers to a time in the past, while *xayla* nearly always refers to a time near, or during the present and in the future. *Siwa* designates a duration or period of time... All of these words presuppose a discrete topological structure on the abstract (and to the lraqw, irrelevant) notion of time as a continuous flow. Of course, we must do this to talk of time at all, but what is different for the Iraqw is that there is no 'axis' of time, a measuring stick with which to compare one moment to another.
>
> (Thornton 1980: 174)

Ki/ima 'turn', a verbal noun from the verb *kii/* 'turn, return' (parallel to English), does indeed refer to a unit of time. *Xayla* is the general question word for 'when', different from *daqamá* 'at what time?, when?-within a period'. *Siiwa* is used to position an event in time as a point or as period. *Qooma* refers to a period of time (not a point). Indeed all these words suppose a discrete notion of time and the only Iraqw word that comes close to 'time in general' is *iimi*, for example, *iimi a matle* 'the time is morning'. It is, however, not so clear that this refers to time since the word is also used to refer to 'people' and the first Swahili translation I got for the word was 'watu wengi = many people', Hence the word refers to more than time. It is probably conflated with the Datooga loan *eemeé(t)* 'people'. Indeed there is no straightforward lexical unit for 'time in general' in Iraqw.

I agree with Thornton that Iraqw uses some of the temporal words in (36c) to group events together and in sequence in a story. And indeed, Iraqw is rich in having three different inflectional sequential markers, *-ri, -ay,* and *-wa* on the selector, and only one for absolute tense (past tense).

The above discussion centres around Thornton's point a) Lack of chronology. His characteristics b) and c), though very valid, cannot be linked to properties of the Iraqw language.

> Chief characteristics of Iraqw narratives are (a) the lack of chronology; (b) the importance of oral performance and ritual; (c) the conservation of quality, place, and objects; and (d) the prominence of spatial relationships of events systematically related to one another in a topological way.
>
> (Thornton 1980: 171)

His fourth point, d), regarding how time is structured by mentioning places is confirmed by my reading of Iraqw songs. For example, a song about the events of Iraqw men going to join the King's African Rifles during World War II to serve in Asia refers to places (Misri, Bama [Burma], and back at the cattle market in Geendi for those who survived) indicating the various events that song preserves for memory.

> ... there is an ordering of narrative about the past that is not based on time. It is based on the relations of space.
>
> (Thornton 1980: 182)

More structurally in Iraqw grammar there seems to be a grammaticalized use of demonstratives that parallels this usage of places for temporal organization. There is a four-way distinction in demonstratives in Iraqw. When used for spatial deixis, the first degree is near the deictic centre, the speaker, the second near the addressee, the third one further away, and the fourth one for far away. The demonstratives are often used for temporal deixis. The most proximal is used for now, e.g. *laa-r-í* /day-F-DEM1/ for 'today'; the most distal demonstrative is used for events in the past. The demonstratives *-dá'* DEM4 and *-qá'* DEM3 are often used in an anaphoric function indicating that the nouns in question are already mentioned earlier: *-qá'* with present tense (33) and *-dá'* with past tense (32). The difference in deixis in anaphoric usage expresses the textual distance: *dá'* for entities mentioned longer ago and permanent in presence in the story; *qá'* for entities introduced rather recently. Demonstratives 3 and 4 are often doubled in that anaphoric function, *mu-k-dá-dá'* /people-M1-DEM4-DEM4/ 'those people mentioned before'.

(32) xa'i   i-na   túu...
      trees   O.P-PAST   uproot:3M:PAST
      xa'i-dá'   ka   kwáahh
      trees-DEM4   O.3:IMPERS:O.P:PERF   throw:PAST
      He uprooted trees... Those trees were thrown away.

(33) gwara-r-qá'   hhiya-ée'   i-r   gwâai ?
      death-f-dem3   brother-POSS.1sg   3-INST   die:INFIN:INTER:3M
      Is that a death for my brother to die?
      (after a sentence about the way he died.) (Mous 1993: 91)

In conclusion, Thornton's elaborate discussion on the concept of time among the Iraqw is supported by my data and can be shown to have some correlates in the language: in the lack of general word for 'time', and in the demonstratives extending from spatial to temporal and anaphoric deixis.

7 Summary and conclusions

Language is a social construct. The expected diversity in social and natural contexts and behaviour will lead to the emergence of different structures in different languages. It is likely that societal structure has an influence on linguistic structure over time. Due to the necessity of time for conventions to develop, influence from society on language is not likely to be instantaneous. Moreover, such an influence is ideally studied within an historical approach, which also entails that we are not looking for predictive statements but rather possible correlations of phenomena. In this study of the possible influence of the characteristics of Iraqw society on its language, I have taken the anthropological studies on Iraqw as a point of departure. The central concept of harmony in the local community can be recognized in the centrality of the expression of togetherness both in lexicon and in the common selector *ta* which has developed collectivity in the subject as part of its meaning. The Iraqw analysis of Time by the anthropologist Thornton has close correlates in lexicon (few absolute time indications and no general time expressions) and in the link between time and space in the temporal use of Iraqw demonstratives. The social organization of Iraqw society is reflected in the kinship system, the system of address. The in-law name avoidance that once existed is a reflection of the precarious relations of a newly-wed woman within the family and clan of the husband where she moves to.

References

Badman, Anna. 2010. 'Defining the Subject Indefinite in Burunge'. MA thesis, Leiden University.

Beck, Rose-Marie and Maarten Mous. 2014. 'Iraqw slufay and the power of voice', in Hannelore Vogele, Uta Reuster-Jahn, Raimund Kastenholz, and Lutz Diegner (eds), *From the Tana River to Lake Chad, Research in African oratures and literatures. In memoriam Thomas Geider*. Cologne: Rüdiger Köppe, 357–71.

Berger, Paul and Roland Kießling. 1988. *Iraqw texts.* Cologne: Rüdiger Köppe.

Cabredo Hofherr, Patricia. 2008. 'Les pronoms impersonnels humains - syntaxe et interprétation', *Modèles linguistiques* 57: 35–56.

Carlin, Eithne B. and Maarten Mous 1995. 'The back in Iraqw: Extensions of meaning in space', *Dutch Studies-NELL* 2: 121–33.

Hagborg, Lars. 2001. 'Silence: Disputes on the ground and in the mind among the Iraqw in Karatu District, Tanzania'. PhD thesis, Department of Cultural Anthropology and Ethnology, Uppsala University.

Heine, Bernd. 1997. *Possession. Cognitive sources, forces, and grammaticalization.* Cambridge: Cambridge University Press.

Kamera, W. D. 1986. 'Loo Ammohhuuma An Iraqw Reconciliation Rite', *Anthropos* 81: 137–49.

Kießling, Roland. 1990. 'Preverbal position as a cradle of grammatical innovation in Iraqw', *Afrikanistische Arbeits Papiere* 21: 67–86.

Kießling, Roland. 1998. 'Reconstructing the sociohistorical background of the Iraqw language', *Afrika und Übersee* 81,2: 167–25.

Kolbusa, Stefanie. 2000. 'Ingamwana Nyakyusa Schwiegermeidung'. MA thesis, University of Bayreuth.

Kruijt, Anne. 2017. 'Straight from the source: The semantics and functions of the ablative case clitic of Iraqw'. MA thesis, Leiden University.

Kruijt, Anne. 2019. 'The use of the ablative clitic in locative phrases in Iraqw, a Cushitic language of Tanzania', *Journal of African Languages and Linguistics* 39,2: 241–65.

Lawi, Y. Q. 2000. 'May the spider web blind witches and wild animals: Local knowledge and the political ecology of natural resource use in the Iraqwland, Northern Tanzania, 1900–1985'. PhD thesis, Boston University.

Mitchell, Alice. 2015. 'Linguistic avoidance and social relations in Datooga'. PhD thesis, University at Buffalo.

Mous, Maarten. 1993. *A Grammar of Iraqw.* Hamburg: Helmut Buske.

Mous, Maarten. 2008. 'Number as exponent of gender in Cushitic', in Zygmunt Frajzynger and Erin Shay (eds), *Interaction of morphology and syntax: Case studies in Afroasiatic.* (Typological Studies in Language, 75.). Amsterdam: John Benjamins, 137–60.

Mous, Maarten, Sandra Bleeker, and Amy Catling. 2018. *Iraqw Oral literature* (Verba Africana 6) <http://verbafricana.org/iraqw/>.

Mous, Maarten and Martha Qorro. 2010. 'The syntactic function of a scope marking suffix in Iraqw', *Journal of African Languages and Linguistics* 31: 47–78.

Mous, Maarten, Martha Qorro, and Roland Kießling. 2002. *An Iraqw - English Dictionary* (Cushitic Language Studies, 15). Cologne: Rüdiger Köppe.

Palayer, Pierre. 2006. *Dictionnaire démé (Tchad); précédé de notes grammaticales.* (Afrique et langage, 10.) Leuven: Peeters.

Peters, Twan H. M. 2016. 'Towards a grammar of space of Iraqw, a Cushitic language of Tanzania'. MA thesis, Leiden University.

Qorro, Martha P. S. 1982. 'Tense and aspect of the English and Iraqw verb'. MA thesis, University of Wales, Bangor.

Rekdal, Ole-Bjørn, 1999. 'The invention by tradition: Creativity and change among the Iraqw of northern Tanzania'. PhD thesis, Bergen University.

Snyder, Katherine A. 1993. '"Like water and honey": Moral ideology and the construction of community among the Iraqw of northern Tanzania'. PhD thesis, Yale University.

Snyder, Katherine A. 2005. *The Iraqw of Tanzania: Negotiating rural development.* (Westview Case Studies in Anthropology). Cambridge, MA: Westview Press Perseus Books.

Thornton, Robert J. 1980. *Space, time, and culture among the Iraqw of Tanzania.* New York: Academic Press.

Tramutoli, Rosanna. 2012. 'Giing'aweakshooda: A register of respect among Barbaig speakers of Tanzania'. MA thesis, Leiden University.

11

Waiting

On language and hospitality

Anne Storch

1 Introduction

In this chapter, I want to take a look at what lies 'in-between'. I want to think
about wasted time, interrupted journey, progress that has come to a halt, and
explore language in such transitional settings, where speech is interrupted by
attempts of translation, and where the ideology and imagination of a linguistic wholeness, of language as something that exists in a certain form at a certain place, fail us while opportunities abound. This chapter is not, in other
words, on language used in ways considered 'appropriate' or even 'correct' by
a community of speakers, or language described as a system or as a complete
text, but language that remains *processual*, *emergent*, and *incomplete*. The gap
and the disruption, I want to argue, are precisely where language can acquire
the power to integrate and to be integrated. Unlike its codified and fixed, stand-
ardized form, or its conceptualization as register, variety, lect, jargon, and so on,
disrupted language and language in disruption resist categorization to a larger
extent; terms such as 'broken' or 'improvised' seem to be what is offered most in
an attempt for order. And of course, they suggest lacking and insignificant
speech rather than noteworthy communicative practice (Faraclas 2012).

Yet, from the perspective of a poetics of culture, language is an outcome of
improvisation and creativity, of reassembling linguistic items as spoils amidst
all sorts of materials rather than recreating recurrent monochrome patterns.
In *Cultural Mobility*, Stephen Greenblatt reminds us of the 'restless process
through which texts, images, artifacts, and ideas are moved, disguised, translated, transformed, adapted, and reimagined in the ceaseless, resourceful
work of culture' (2010: 4), which 'obviously long preceded the internet [...] or
the spread of English on the wings of international capitalism. [...] The apparent fixity and stability of cultures is, in Montaigne's words, "nothing but a

Anne Storch, *Waiting: On language and hospitality*. In: *The Integration of Language and Society: A Cross-Linguistic Typology*. Edited by: Alexandra Y. Aikhenvald, R. M. W. Dixon, and Nerida Jarkey, Oxford University Press.
© Anne Storch 2021. DOI: 10.1093/oso/9780192845924.003.0011

more languid motion"' (2010: 5). Culture, and language, here are nothing but transgression: moving words, things, practices, and stories across the imaginary boundaries between different regimes, orders, and territories. This is, of course, a very hospitable way of looking at language, as it suggests that because the transgression of boundaries and borders is the normal situation and not the exception, we are in constant need of hospitality.

In order to explore what such linguistic generosity might actually be, this chapter focuses on waiting: time spent precariously, uselessly, angrily, leisurely.

But what precisely happens when we have to inconveniently stop over on a journey or when emigration is difficult, in a hostile environment? To the philosopher, poet, and literary critic Édouard Glissant, the crossing of borders was crucial. In Manthia Diawara's film *Un Monde en Relation* (2010), he mentions that he likes crossing borders and boundaries and enjoys moving from one environment into another. Borders should be permeable, he concludes, and not violent. An alternative form of thinking about borders is, as Glissant suggested much earlier in *Caribbean Discourse* (1996 [1981]) and then, more prominently, in *Poetics of Relation* (2010 [1990]), *antillanité*, 'Antillean thought', or 'Caribbeanness', which could be used as a method to deal with difference in history, language, culture, society, and so on: '*Antillanité* is grounded concretely in affirmation of a place, the Antilles, and would link cultures across language barriers' (Wing 2010: XXI). The unexpected and the potentially confusing experience of diversity is conceived here as a productive activity and an opportunity. Such ideas about language and culture are also expressed by many West African philosophers (e.g. Mbembe 2017) as being at the base for the construction of humanity.

In the light of the constant work of moving across barriers, of cultural mobility and linguistic fluidity, disruption is a salient and focal moment. This is where improvisation and ad hoc communicative interaction not only are instrumental for one's well-being (asking for water, a place to sleep), but fundamentally base on the creative and transgressive power of language to turn into something new that exists outside its own boundaries. Often, there is enjoyment and hilarity in these liminal moments of creativity, but there equally are notions of horror: what seeps through the cracks of order also resonates trauma and destruction.

Waiting, I want to suggest, is a method rather than a state, as it exposes us to unforeseen developments, to what we have not intended to experience, and it leaves us in settings where we are confronted with difference, in terms of power relations, emotions, and communication, which we are required to turn into hospitable practice. In many societies, the communicative creativity that emanates out of unpredictability, like the language of liminality and epiphany, is rationalized as being of particular meaning and spatial specificity. Waiting, in the examples I refer to in the following sections, has the potential to bring to light the 'deep' in language: that what we cannot understand if we have not shared any hospitality and conviviality with those who speak, and that what emerges out of the unforeseeable, the disruptive in life that brings out the essence of conviviality. Creativity and complexity in language are what can happen in the liminal (Turner 1969), subversive, marginal context of waiting when there is opportunity for playfulness. The following sections deal with the ways in which play and creativity in language do precisely what is meant by 'integration of language and culture' in the introduction to this volume: express the specificity of the moorings of language and offer a translation. They do so by dealing with Twelvetide, love songs, sweets, and gardens, based on the reflection of my own interactions and soliloquies that took place in the various liminal and transitional settings in question.

2 Twelvetide

While I write this text, I move into the 'lost nights'. Christmas is over, and New Year's Eve lies ahead. No lectures, no emails. Even though these nights increasingly tend to be seen as 'gained' rather than 'lost'—finally there is time to read and write, without any interruption—they always were the nights *zwischen den Jahren* 'in-between years', lost for work and efficiency. Not long ago, in my childhood days I should say, this time of the year still also had another name: *Rauhnächte* 'Twelvetide'. This name is so old that it sounds odd: why are these nights 'rough'? Or does the first part of the compound have a different etymology altogether? Hoffmann-Krayer and Bächthold-Stäubli (1935–6: 530) suggest *Rauch* 'smoke' rather than *rauh* 'rough' as the source, which makes sense as it was common in past centuries to burn frankincense during these nights in order to protect the home and the stables from the ghosts and evil powers that rode across the winter skies. This practice was based on the assumption that whatever was under control during other times of the year broke loose during *Rauhnacht*, when the most impossible creatures could be seen. Old fears of the return of 'lost' ghosts and spirits into a world now under control through the observation of the laws of religion resonated in play. In the small towns and villages of southern Hesse, there were not only folktales about undead warlords (Hoffmann-Krayer and

Bächthold-Stäubli 1934–5) riding on nocturnal winds, but masqueraded figures roaming about that were called *Bolischbock*, *Strohniggel*, *Mehlweibscher*, and *Stobbelgans*—'stubborn ram', 'straw lad', 'flour maiden', and 'juvenile goose' (Seebach 2002). While I am able to translate their names, as I am able to translate the name for their season, I fail to make sense of them. The *Stobbelgans*, a beheaded goose walking around, might remind us that geese are eaten around Christmas, but it has deeper meanings. Visions of beheaded persons and animals moving around at night were interpreted as sightings of revenant beings and pagan ghosts (Kremer 2003). The goose masquerade—a child wearing a white pillow slip—interprets such narratives in playful ways as funny and superstitious, but does not fully erase them: a beheaded animal (the goose) walks among the living. The other masks and names remain more enigmatic. They were part of a time that had been 'lost' so often that they represent sheer disruption, in themselves and in the discourse that is what now mostly remains of them. This is what we see in Figure 1.

Time was first documented to have been 'lost' through inconsistencies between calendars based either on the lunar month or on the solar year.

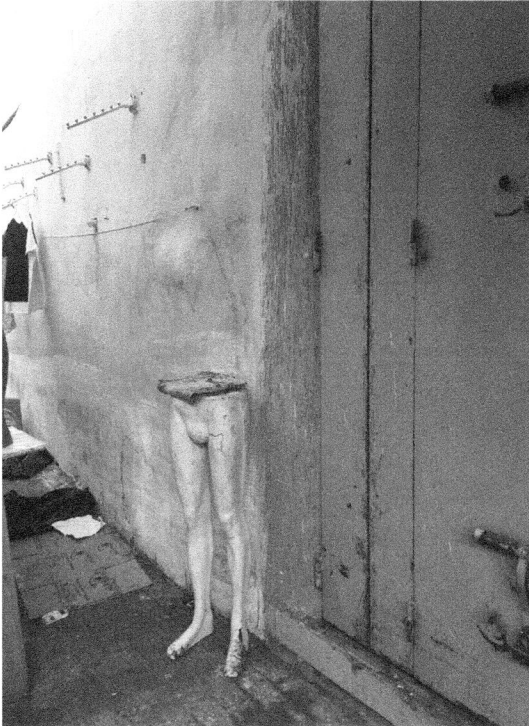

Figure 1 Headless revenant

Between these two calendars there is a gap of eleven days (or twelve nights) which required the addition of supplementary days, the 'epagomenal' days, to the shorter lunar year. Proclaimed as a sacred and festive season in the early middle ages, the added nights remained time apart, nights outside the lunar calendar that were dead and 'lost' (Groschwitz 2008). The creatures that roamed about during these nights were often explained in the same vein: fallen out of time, a remainder of a distant past when the lunar year provided the main basis for the organization of spiritual activities. Another notion of loss: the historian Carlo Ginzburg (2005 [1989]), writing about bedevilment and the social history of nocturnal transgression, argues that the mythological and religious concepts on which early modern discourse about witches and sorcerers were based are largely pre-Christian shamanic religions that remained meaningful to common people in Europe well into the renaissance (also Ginzburg 1990 [1976]). And so the figure of the *Mehlweibsche* does not represent a 'flour maiden'. The German term has different connotations than expressing ideas about domestic bakery and carries with it disturbing notions of horror. This very local name for a more widespread phenomenon actually refers euphemistically to the *Kornmuhme*, a female ghost that emerged out of barley fields (on which she fed) and that in many ways resembled the witches described in the early modern sources Ginzburg refers to. Both noun phrases, regardless of a hearer's capacity to make sense of them, to analyse them etymologically and so on, bear undertones of horror and repressed trauma, something that cannot easily be grasped but can be expressed as shared emotional reaction. The history of prosecution and torture, oppression and fear resonates in such rare yet prominent names for masks and legendary figures, as it does in material culture (Genesis 2018). The past that is never over seeps through the cracks of the festive season's calendar.

Ginzburg uses archive material to explore accounts of trance, of spiritual travel and its complex narratives which base on the capacity of language to refer to the unknown. His data speak of the repressed history of pre-Christian, marginalized religious practice, like the costumes once in use around where I grew up might have done in the past. And while I search for meaning, my language constantly asks me to cross borders. Not so much between past and present beliefs, but between words and places: like a trance, language, in my language (in the language which I make use of in my work of memory making), is motion across space and categories. Georges Arthur Goldschmidt, as he reflects on the translation of the language of philosophy, observes something in German that brings the conversation across different languages and space into a relation with each other:

Tout, d'une certaine manière, est ramené à une figuration spatiale, on peut en donner d'innombrables exemples, rien que dans le vocabulaire de Freud, ainsi « rapport » ou « relation » qui en français n'évoquent rien de précis, à moins de passer par le latin, deviennent en allemand un objet de représentation précis *Zusammenhang*, ce qui est accroché ensemble, ou *Beziehung*, ce qui tire vers. Traduire c'est *übersetzen* « faire passer par-dessus, sur l'autre rive » ou *übertragen*, « porter par-dessus », réfléchir c'est *überlegen*, « mettre dessus ».

(Goldschmidt 2016: 28)

Everything that is about making connections between words and meanings in different languages involves moving them across space; not time, not difference (as in the difference of cultures), but simply space. In order to reach an interlocutor in a conversation, to arrive at conclusions, come to a result, one needs to be mobile in this metalanguage of translation, which bases on motion verbs and spatial adjectives and nouns.[1] Like the masks and ghosts of old moved in and out the homes of people (Seebach 2002), words that come with their memory transgress time and space alike.

3 Love songs

Other times of the year seem to require less explanation. During summer, real travel takes place, for example to the Mediterranean. The Spanish island of Mallorca is one of the most often visited tourist destinations in Europe, and especially its beaches and their adjacent party zones are now considered to count among the continent's places that are threatened most by destruction through overtourism. El Arenal, a town near the island's airport, is particularly affected by the problem, as it has become the preferred resort of—mostly German—party tourists. A place dedicated to consumerism and intoxication, its architecture mimics pre-modern architecture that evokes faint memories of what the masks of the *Rauhnacht* once must have expressed: transgression and trance. Most notably, the *Megapark*, a discotheque where alcoholic beverage is served in two-litre vessels and table dancers move to the tunes of

---

[1] Yet, the difference between of motion and intellectual activity is indicated by stress, e.g. '*über-setzen* 'to cross' vs *über'setzen* 'to translate'.

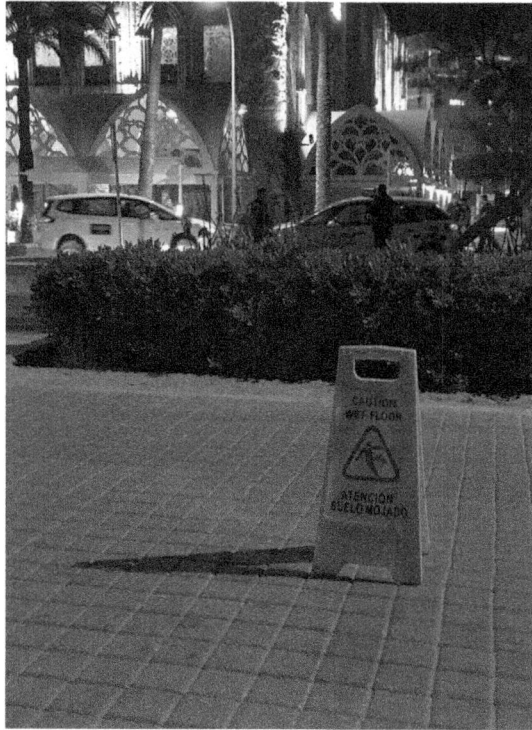

Figure 2 *Megapark*

old-fashioned *schlager* music, exhibits decorations that are reminiscent of Gothic cathedrals and medieval castles. The reference to historical form and practice is fake. There is no mooring to any form of memory-making beyond consumerism and extraction in this non-place. Figure 2 features a picture of a Megapark.

The songs played and performed in the *Megapark* mostly are about love and belonging. They ask audiences to celebrate the theme park in which they spend their leisurely time as their 'true home', where they can achieve self-actualization and be their true selves. A successful song published by the German singer Steffen Peter Hass, who performs under the name of *Peter Wackel* ('Shakin' Peter'), presents not only a construction of Mallorcan beaches as the homeland of Germans, but also asks these visitors to reclaim what is theirs, against the ownership of Mallorcans who protest against over-tourism and excessive partying of the tourists. The song makes use of specific phrases that are largely absent from standard German discourse on this place and are used to create a style that indexes a strong connection between par-ticular local cultural and social practices and a particular form of German (Rötgens, Weßling, and Wackel 2018):

(1) Solang   auf   Malle   der   Zapfhahn
     as long as.ADV   on.LOC   Mallorca.COLLOQ   DEF.MASC   beer tap
     noch   läuft
     still   run.PRES.3SG
     As long as the beer tap runs on Mallorca,

     Solang   der   Helmut   noch
     as long as.ADV   DEF.MASC   Senegalese.PEJ.COLLOQ   still
     Uhr-en   ver-käuft
     watch-PL   EGR-buy.PRES.3SG.COLLOQ
     as long as the Senegalese street vendor still sells watches,

     Solang   das   Bier   hier   noch   schmeckt,
     as long as.ADV   DEF.NEUT   beer   DEM.near   still   taste.INTR.3SG
     solang   geh-en   wir   nicht   weg
     that long   go-INF   1PL   NEG   away
     as long as the beer tastes good we will not leave.

     Malle   ist   einfach   perfekt
     Mallorca.COLLOQ   is.3SG   simply   perfect
     Mallorca simply is perfect.

     I   love   Malle
     1SG   love   Mallorca.COLLOQ
     I love Mallorca!

While the toponym *Malle* has gained currency well beyond language used by German audiences residing in Mallorca, the term *Helmut* has not. In German, it is usually conceived as a proper noun that incipiently falls out of use unless it denotes historical personalities, as only very few children are today given this name. Furthermore, it most likely is not used as a nickname beyond German party tourism spots in Mallorca. There, it denotes street vendors of West African, mostly Senegalese origin, both as a form of address and as reference (Storch 2020; Storch and Nassenstein 2020). While *Helmut* has the connotation of an excluding nickname when used as a form of address by speakers who claim ownership over the place, its referential use bears much stronger racist undertones and indexicalizes a whole bundle of social ascriptions, namely 'undocumented, poor, uneducated, illiterate, criminal, infantile, Black, African,' which are also referred to in New Right and current racist discourse in Germany (e.g. Wodak 2015).

   A register often referred to as 'German youth language' is used here to construct not so much membership of a certain age group or subculture, but to a liminal community dwelling in a southern colony. Most members reside in this liminality only for a certain period of time, but on a regular basis. One commentator to *Peter Wackel*'s video remarked:[2]

(2) War   auch   erst   2   Wochen   wieder   mal
     be.PAST.SG   also   recently 2   week-PL again   once
     DAHEIM   dort.
     at home   DEM.DIST
     Also recently again was [for/since] 2 weeks AT HOME there.

     War   wie   immer   fett und   freut   man
     be.PAST.SG   as   always fat   and   look forward.SG one
     sich   schon   auf   nächstes   Jahr.
     REFL   already   for   next.NEUT   year
     As always it was enjoyable and one looks forward to next year.

Love songs that are not about the singer's and audience's love of the place, but about romantic love among couples exhibit similar strategies in constructing ownership, overtones of liminality and particularity, as well as exclusion of others. Andreas Gabalier, an Austrian folk singer, has written one of the most popular love songs played at Mallorca's German party destinations, *Hula Palu* (Gabalier 2015). The title refers to incomprehensible conversation, and even though the chorus of the song expresses, in Austrian German, the singer's hapless reaction to what he could not understand, it has since been made part of a repertoire that is linked to transgression and excluding group membership practices:

(3) Wos   is   denn Hula Palu,   wos   ghert
     what.INTER   is.3SG   FOC   H.   what.INTER   belong.3SG
     denn   da   dazu?
     FOC   DEM.REF   to it
     What is this *Hula Palu*, what goes together with it?

The staged liminality of the club and its environments is performed with the help of heteroglossic language: not German is used to construct this German place of the 'in-between', but specific non-hegemonic, subcultural forms of German as well as its dialects, snippets of English and Spanish. While such

---

[2] EyAlter dumichauch, <https://www.youtube.com/watch?v=hyW8KW7WJXs>.

performances express ideas of German ownership of the site, they fundamentally negate the presences of much more liminal communities at this place.

Behind the *Megapark*, there is a Moroccan shisha bar. It looks like a tent, similar to the Amazigh tents found in southern Morocco at the fringe of the desert, but made of rubber tarp. From afar, the setting resembles a scene in Tarkovsky's film *Nostalghia* (1983) where a Russian farm house stands amidst the ruins of an Italian cathedral.

Inside the tent, the decoration consists of Oriental divans and cushions, on which clients, mostly migrants from North Africa, lounge while they operate their smartphones underneath a TV set. The tourism business attracts large numbers of young men and women from various parts of Africa (mostly Morocco, Senegal, Gambia, and Nigeria), who work as street vendors, lavatory attendants, sex workers, household help, and so on. Unlike their German (and other European) contemporaries, most of the African migrants stay much longer on the island than initially intended and very often do not achieve what they had been sent for or came for (Badaseraye 2018 & ms.). David Block (2014: 124–5) points at the continuities that characterize such experience in Europe's history and political economy of migrant labour:

> The more skilled the migrant and the job sought, the more likely he/she was to enter into open competition for work, factory assembly line work being a good example. By contrast, a good proportion of migrants took unskilled, low-level and poorly paid manual jobs (e.g. cleaning and serving) and therefore entered into no such conflict with the established local working class. The extent to which migrants were racialised in such contexts further complicated matters. [...] This is not to say that southern Europeans did not face discrimination and racism of a sort; however, their stories did not contain the feelings of rejection and the violence that sometimes accompanied it, to the degree found in the accounts provided by migrants who were darker skinned.

While the migrants wait for jobs and papers, linguistic practices from West Africa are newly introduced and implemented in the neighbourhoods around the party space. In the Moroccan rubber tarp tent, a colleague and myself wait for a meeting with a Senegalese migrant who has offered us a walk to places he favours during his own leisure time. As we wait, I mention that it was remarkable how little Catalan, Mallorquin, or German we had heard in the back streets of El Arenal, even though these languages were continuously presented as the languages of the competing owners of this place. Instead, we had encountered Darija, Wolof, Naija, and Castilian: languages spoken by marginalized immigrants from Africa and Andalusia. The colleague asks how I could be so sure about Catalan and Mallorquin, languages I did not know or speak. I switch on my smartphone, like the other customers, in order to play music by Maria del Mar Bonet to her: *Nova Canco*, mostly sung in Mallorquin by this artist whom I occasionally enjoy listening to. As the colleague nods, my fingertip accidentally runs across the glass surface of the phone and a new song is started: *Lamma Bada*. A beautiful tune, and very old. It is a song based on a *muwaššah*, a form of poetry that was created in al-Ándalus around the ninth century (Jones and Hitchcock 1991). As a secular genre, the *muwaššah* was dedicated to erotic and romantic topics as well as to descriptions of the beauty of nature. The *muwaššah* consists of several stanzas that are connected by a specific rhyme that appears in the last two verses of each stanza. As Zwartjes (1997) shows, the *muwaššah* is characterized by its multilingual composition: in numerous examples, the end of a *muwaššah*, the *ḫarǧa,* is in a different language than the rest of the song—Hebrew, Spanish, or other linguistic material.

Maria del Mar Bonet's version of *Lamma Bada* is sung in Catalan and based on a text by Albert Garcia, who has written songs for numerous musicians specializing in folk and protest music. The melody is based on a composition attributed to Sheikh Muhammad 'Abd ar-Rahim al-Maslub (1786–1895), and the first stanza begins with the words:

(4)   amat   amat   que   espero   cada   jorn
       beloved.FEM   beloved.FEM   how   desire.1SG   each   day
       Beloved, beloved, how I look forward to each day,

The subsequent lines speak about the pain felt over love that finds no response. The Andalusian Arabic text differs considerably, even though it equally tells of desire and pain that result from unfulfilled love. But while del Mar Bonet's and many other interpretations of the song are about the beauty of a desirable woman (*amat*), the medieval text, which presumably hails from the twelfth century, tells of the beholder's gaze at a desirable beautiful man.

(5)   لما بدا يتثنى
       lammā   badā   ya-ta-t̠anna
       when   it was   3SG-V-sway.IMPERV
       When he sways

حبي جماله فتنا

ḥubb-ī	ǧamāl-uh	fatan-nā
love-POSS.1SG	beauty-POSS.3SG.MASC	impress.PERV-1PL.O

my love – his beauty – impressed us,

امر ما بلحظة اسرنا

amr mā	bi-l-aḥẓuh	asar-nā
something	in-ART-moment	captivate.PERV-1PL.O

something in a moment captivated us.

Thomas Bauer (2014) suggests that such texts do not need to be read as metaphorical expressions of the love to god's creation, but as what they historically were: homoerotic poetry composed by men who, in the twelfth century, found it acceptable to have homosexual encounters and love affairs. Only much later, in the nineteenth and twentieth centuries, Bauer argues, the meanings of such poetic texts had to be disguised, as homoerotic narratives had become socially unacceptable. As a result, the extremely widespread and popular *muwaššah* was reanalysed as an example of courtly elite poetry, where women of noble descent were unattainable and therefore had to be linguistically heightened. The noble woman, popular explanations suggest, would be referred to in the masculine form in order to express the extraordinary powers she had. While the exquisite woman therefore would be referred to in a phrase such as *yataṯanna*, a more ordinary woman would be spoken or sung about using a phrase such as *tataṯanna* 'she swayed'. Bauer (p.c. 2019) suggests that this is basically a practice of colonial erasure, and while masculine constructions referring to women do occur elsewhere as expressions of respect and politeness (Aikhenvald 2016), in this space in-between, where we listen to music while we wait, different possibilities have to make sense.[3] A song with a history of centuries retains meaning and significance, as it remains shared by audiences in a rubber tarp tent who wait—for papers, jobs, and appointments, and who are exposed to imperial duress which shapes ideas about masculinity as well as poetry.

Months later, the Egyptian-Sudanese artist Amado Alfadni, in a conversation about cultural mobility, mentioned that *Lamma Bada* to him was one of

---

[3] Playing with ambiguity is a way to make language 'deep' in many African societies, as Kosrof (2007: 237–41) explains: 'This new language I create is linked with the Ethiopian literary tradition of "wax and gold" in which Ethiopian poets use a word in their poems that has a familiar meaning, the "wax." But the poets also intend a second, hidden meaning to the word, an unusual or unaccustomed association, which is the "gold." One purpose of this technique is to achieve maximum thought with minimum words, another is to produce double entendres. The technique provides mystery and challenge to the reader.'

the most obvious and ubiquitous expressions of Arab culture and heritage. Known to audiences across North Africa and the Middle East, the song belongs to a repertoire of classic music. To Alfadni, it was the insertion of آمان آمان *aman, aman* that characterizes almost all of the more recent interpretations that was foreign, strange. The expression denotes 'mercy', 'by the grace of god' in Turkish and is a resonance of musical and poetic practice during the era of the Ottoman Empire.

Language is deep in these love songs, which, much more than the advertisements and stickers and billboards usually studied in sociolinguistics as 'linguistic landscape', tell of the disruptions and cracks in the environments in which language is encountered. They are everywhere, and the walls and pavements that surround us seem to have been soaked by them much more than by the glue that is used to paste bilingual posters on shopfronts. They seem to be carried with them by traders and artists, tourists and migrants, and serve as easy access rituals for conversations and storytelling. Remembering a remark by Michael Taussig on such storytelling, however, lets me switch off my mobile music reservoir. In *Corn Wolf* (2015: 58), he writes about the wider implications of violence and migration:

> In thinking about storytelling as an outgrowth of place, it is helpful to remember Walter Benjamin's suggestion that the origin of storytelling lies in the encounter between the traveler and those who stay at home. He emphasizes the role played by the seafarer and the artisan as wandering journeyman, but in our day and age is it not the displaced person and illegal immigrant who assume that role? In which case, place assumes the status of a phantom limb.

The last sentence is not easy to read and bear. All our attempts to carry meaning from here to there, to translate and transmit, this quote suggests, in the end will fail us in the world and system in which we now live. Displacement and the state it implies—waiting—has ceased to bear the power in itself to accommodate others whom stories could be told to and space shared with. The storyteller is no longer a 'traveller' but an undocumented person, illegal and disturbing.

The contemporary German party songs and the medieval Andalusian love song have almost nothing in common—neither their audiences nor the cultural concepts underlying their respective lyrics seem to be connected in any way. Yet, disruption and waiting are contexts in which possible connections between different practices, texts, languages, and people become discernible:

fragments that can be reassembled in order to sustain constructions of home and heritage.

4 Sweets

Language, Aikhenvald et al. (this volume) argue, is meaningful and significant with respect to the society in which it is used, to an extent that its structure may reflect its speakers' social organization and cultural practices (also Dixon 2014; Lüpke and Storch 2013). Language in an environment where these are not present any longer, and where no other mooring for language and its speakers is provided—in the spaces in which different people spent time 'in-between', waiting to carry on—appears to reflect place and motion instead of practice and organization. Its peculiarities are a trace rather than structure (Szakolczai 2009) and the material from which it is made is deeply polysemic, never unequivocal. Yet, is this not what language appears to be much more often than an icon of organized and stable existences? Walter Benjamin, whom Taussig refers to in *Corn Wolf*, has pleaded for a different perspective on history, which also has significant consequences for how we look at language. In a famous passage in his last surviving text, Benjamin observes that the 'emergency state' in which we live is the norm and not the exception (Benjamin 2019 [1940]: 697):

Die Tradition der Unterdrückten belehrt uns darüber, daß der 'Ausnahmezustand', in dem wir leben, die Regel ist. Wir müssen zu einem Begriff der Geschichte kommen, der dem entspricht.

History, he argues, is catastrophe, not a telic process of bettering, and not stillness until something happens. From Benjamin's perspective, the twelfth-century love song would be rubble, re-used as a spoil, like the names for masks, and names in general, with their load of connotations. Those who sit around in the margins of a party space and wait for new opportunities, while others call them *Helmut*, lead lives that Stoler (2013) suggests are part of the *Imperial Debris*, colonial outfall that continues to shape the environments in which encounters between different people, distinguished by their languages, cultural practices, social organization and so on, continue to take place. Inequality and social injustice, marginalization and subordination, and not the way they are interesting or 'relevant' or 'worth exploring', determines the ways in which languages from the imperial periphery, such as African languages for example, are dealt with (Piller 2016; Lüpke and Storch 2013). It might therefore be helpful to move beyond the scopes of research on linguistic landscapes as outlined in fairly critical terms by Jaworski and Thurlow (2010: 1):

> [...] we are concerned here with the interplay between language, visual discourse, and the spatial practices and dimensions of culture, especially the textual mediation or discursive construction of place and the use of space as a semiotic resource in its own right. The broader context which we are interested in is the extent to which these mutual processes are in turn shaped by the economic and political reorderings of post-industrial or advanced capitalism, intense patterns of human mobility, the mediatization of social life [...], and transnational flows of information, ideas and ideologies [...].

What lies outside the visual regimes the authors refer to is yet part of 'landscape' that is experienced prominently by many speakers of marginalized languages, namely the neglected and understated places where people meet for some time until they are able to move on. If the emergency state Benjamin refers to is what people face much more than an existence shaped by continuity and order, the rubber tarp tent is indeed a good place to start from. Linguistic landscape there was not visual but aural, and humming a love song, we might want to move in the opposite direction of everybody else, backwards to where those whom we met on Mallorca might have come from at one point of their journey.

The old caravan routes that connect important places of trade, religion, and scholarship, such as Fez, Marrakech, Timbuktu, and Agadez, are still in use. Many of the old trading posts and resting places are ruined, but are still passed by large numbers of people. Coming from Senegal and other West African countries, travellers who are on pilgrimage or on the way to a better job or better life in Europe, move along the old routes and, like their forebears, get held up and are forced to wait. A wadi might be full of water so that it cannot be crossed for hours or even days, a border might be closed, a road blocked, weather stormy, local politics in crisis. The travellers of old walked or rode on horses, or perhaps camels, carrying loads, and must have relied quite often on the hospitality of those whose homelands they passed through. Others who travelled got held up as well, and the camp, the improvised resting place and the safe space provided for the break during the journey continue to play salient roles in tales about history. Many West African accounts of local history are indeed characterized by lengthy lists of toponyms: places the community's ancestors went through on their way from a mythological place of origin—often located in the Middle East or in Egypt and referred to as 'Kisra legend' (Adekunle 2004; Storch 2013) due to a legendary Persian king frequently named as founding hero—to their current settlement. An example is a text by Musa Tafida, who in the last decade of the twentieth century had written down what he considered important knowledge on the history of his village, Pindiga.[4] He wrote in Hausa, a language widespread in the region and closely connected to scholarship and religion, and not taboo to outsiders as is the language originally spoken by the firstcomers, namely Hone. His manuscript begins as follows:

Su Jukunawa sun fito ne daga Nyamal tare da Barebari. Don dama su Jukunawa dan na miji ne, su kuma Barebari 'dan mace ne. Suka zo suka zauna a Sudan daga Nyamal, sun yi kamar shekara (9) tara suna zaune a Sudan, sai suka tashi daga Sudan sai suka zo Gazarguno tare da Barebari watau a cikin kasar Borno, suka yi kamar shekara (3) uku, sai su Jukunawa suka tashi suka zo Tibati wato a gindin Dutsen Bima.

They, the Jukuns came from Yemen, together with the Kanuri people. [...] They came from Yemen and settled in the Sudan, where they remained for nine years together, until they left Sudan and came together with the Kanuri to Ngazargamo, this is to say to the country of Bornu, where they stayed for three years, until the Jukuns left and came to Tibati, this is the area of Dutsen Bima. (translated in Storch 2017: 204)

The many stations that are mentioned in such texts tell not only of the many encounters and bonds with other groups—which might resonate in the composition of multilingual repertoires, joking relationships or intermarriage practices—but also of a conceptualization of history as emergency state. Settlements were never safe and never static. Before long, there would be a conflict or famine, and whoever was defeated by the catastrophe would move on and seek a new, better settling ground elsewhere (Kopytoff 1987).

The accounts of current travellers along these roads equally tell about the ubiquitous experience of disruption, of moving from one place to another, always facing precarious conditions. Festus Badaseraye has recorded autobiographic narratives of Nigerian migrants, which provide illustrations of contemporary disruptive travel (Badaseraye ms.):

---

[4] Pindiga is located in Gombe State in Nigeria. A description of Hone, a Jukun language once spoken there, is provided in Storch (1999).

[…] Nigerians started rushing into Spain through Morroco, Algeria, Mali, Níger and Ceuta, l was so oportune to have plenty of garden to care for then, so I have to give Jobs to the new comers (people from Ghana, Nigeria, Mali, etc)

Yet, the autobiographical narratives are not only about places and routes; they also are about things—what one finds here and there, what one aims at, desires, and is denied (Badaseraye ms.):

I met a Nigerian pulling this very heavy wheel in a polygon, I stopped to appreciate his hard working and to ask him, how long has he been doing this for a living, he said he has been picking irons, woods, cables, etc for sale in Palma, and sometimes he found good used televiones, fans, fridges, micro-waves, etc, and do send these iterms to his country, to feed his family back home, and when I asked him, where is he from, he said, from a place that is not supposed to be called a country, (Nigeria) because, Nigeria government can not carter for his citizen, that Nigeria is not a country, that he lives better in Palma picking waste product than staying in Nigeria.

Lists of things that speak about the precarity of a person's life, such as lists of places speak about the contingency of everything in the world. And while some write this down, in order to bear witness, others weave their stories into the textures of places as they pass by. On the side of a road that connects the (closed) border between Algeria and Morocco with the Atlantic Ocean and with roads that link South and North, we sit and wait. A colleague wanted to look for a piano in order to play his music for us, and while he is searching for the instrument nobody is sure still exists, we have to wait. For some hours, we sit in front of a small shop in Ouarzazate and watch. On the other side of the road, two young men from Senegal are busy with brickwork. A young man from Nigeria passes by who sells postcards. Another man, again Senegalese, sells greeting cards, made of butterfly wings. He makes them himself he says, trying to earn money for his onward journey. Some people try for years to get ahead, waiting on the street or in prison for life to change, which is a context out of which a language of its own emerges: creative, imaginative, heteroglos-sic, and precious. The waiting spaces are the spaces that create secrecy and poetry, desire and lies (Smith 2019).

While travel anecdotes are exchanged, it is quiet around. An old man sleeps in his shop. In front of where we sit there is a sign that says *ISTANBUL* (see Figure 3). I wonder why and cross the street. A clothes shop. But a few shops

Figure 3 *ISTANBUL*

Figure 4 *LE SOUK* and *SUPER MARKET*

to the right, sweets are sold. *LE SOUK*, a bakery and pastry shop, the name a mixture of French and Arabic. We buy some biscuits and ask about their names. Next door, there is a supermarket with a signboard that advertises splendidness in three languages and scripts: English *SUPER MARKET*, Tamazight ⴰⵅⴰⵝ ⴰⵅⵜⵔⵔⵯⵓ *agdz akhatar* 'star trading', Arabic المتجر الممتاز *al-maġar al-mumtāz* 'the excellent store' (see Figure 4). On offer are *TOBACCOS FOODS DRINKS* for tourists on their way to the desert.

Joining the rest of the group for another hour of waiting, we try the sweets we purchased and talk about the connections between luxury (such as biscuits) and the language of desire (such as for adventure). In many communities in West Africa, it is important to bring a gift from a place one has visited or travelled to when one returns home: some mangoes, a loaf of bread, smoked fish. From here, we could bring sweets that bear names that encode desire and romantic love. They refer to the bodies of women, for example during her wedding night or in a love song:

(6) iṣbaʔ   al-ʕarūs   'finger of a bride'
     finger.SG.NOM   DEF-bride
     aṣābiʕ   Zaynab   'fingers of Zaynab'
     finger.PL.NOM   NAME
     kaʕb   al-ġazāl   'heel of a gazelle'
     heel.SG.NOM   DEF-gazelle

Looking at the *ISTANBUL* shop sign, I recall that Turkish sweets can be equally seductive in terms of how they are named, equating sweetness and women.

(7) kadin   budu   'woman's thighs'
     woman   ham.PL
     kiz   memesi   'maiden's bosoms'
     girl   bosom.PL
     dilber   dudaği   'a beauty's lips'
     beauty   lip

Such items, or the recipes after which they are made, as well as their names, or the concepts on which these are based, have been transmitted widely. They are present in the Mediterranean cuisine of the places where those who passed through the Saharan caravan routes, where we now wait, make a living by collecting garbage and carrying loads, and in globalized dishes such as lasagne

(Rodinson 2006). Such sweets are typically meant to be presented as gifts, luxury items that heighten the recipient in rituals of hospitality. The names for them work in similar ways, as they resonate the intimacy that presupposes such presents and make it conceivable that there is always the possibility that while one is stranded and lost somewhere, there still might be an invitation to join a feast. Even though there seems nothing but ruination inherent in the emergency state, Benjamin's thinking about endless disruption also bears in it the idea that only then one can be offered true hospitality. While the undisrupted state in which everything is done and set according to the law forces the foreigner to ask for hospitality in the language of the host, and is informed about the rules and laws he must obey as a guest in that same language (which Derrida describes as patriarchal and the first act of violence towards the foreigner), disruption and emergency place the host and the guest in a situation where they both have no home and therefore have to accommodate one another. Accordingly, Derrida (2016) asks whether we can only then be truly hospitable when we are foreign ourselves.

As if this state elicited some kind of blessing, the setting of the street in which nothing but waiting takes place is linguistically characterized by promises of the feast and of excellency, which are present in culinary discourse triggered by smell, shapes, and taste, in a barter trade of words where memories are shared and translations are offered. And while the banality of the supermarket with its global goods is only faintly masked by its multilingual advertisements, the deep meanings of luxury items made of almonds and sugar, the early modern roots of their ubiquity in the huge space 'in-between' that links (and not divides) Europe and Africa become discernible through the art of storytelling, among people who have been thrown together for a moment until it is time to move on.

5 A garden

In a world in which the emergency state is the normal state, what we might get to say and hear are murmured, whispered, yelled, shouted, or spoken pleas for help. What gets said and heard is language used in unpredictable ways, in unpredictable situations (Phipps 2007; Mietzner and Storch forthcoming). Seeking adventure, revelation, or salvage, people travel, migrate, and pilgrimage. At the places of rest, language is deeply integrated in culture and society, as a means of conveying what one has seen and experienced, of memory making, creating relations, and envisaging what might lay ahead, a view at the future.

As if language belied the fragility and precariousness of the camp and resting place, it is full of grand words—love, spirits, sweets. I wonder whether these words and topics are metaphors for the preciousness of the fragile relations that are shared, without whom travellers and pilgrims would perish. At the neglected and marginalized sites of resting and waiting, language is creative and opaque at the same time, not so much used to simply convey information but also to share sounds and embodied co-presences, as a tool for creating conviviality.

Yet, waiting is a situation where conviviality relies on help, and it is asking for assistance or hospitality that language in the emergency state normally might be used for. A reply to pleas for hospitality might be many things, I assume—fill in a form, provide a phone number, hand over some change. But additional to such bureaucratic or exculpating forms of quick aid, there are culturally integrated ways of offering hospitality that have been in place and use for a long time: gardens, meals, storytelling. A close view of the integration of language in social and cultural practices that take the emergency state seriously, requires a deeper look at those buzzwords that to no small extent shape sociolinguistic approaches to linguistic disruption and the mobilities of speakers. The term 'linguistic landscape', for example, offers much more insight into how language is inscribed into space when carefully historicized and dislodged from its Eurocentric perspective on language-as-literacy.

Alain Corbin, in his famous book on the *territoire du vide* (1988), suggests that the historical connections between the actual creation of a landscape and its imagination can be traced back to the transitional era that led from the Roman Republic to the Empire of Rome. Corbin reminds us of descriptions of mansions by the sea where hosts and their guests enjoyed times of leisure, which were devoted to the refreshment of the mind, self-discovery, and self-fulfilment. The Latin word *otium* here denotes a concept that vaguely translates into 'vacation'. The elites, for whom the *otium* was reserved, performed class and its privileges in an environment that was carefully landscaped in order to resemble idealized mythological settings. And here, the other meaning of *otium* comes into play: 'variety'. Surrounded by a bucolic yet built and arranged environment, one was listening to the sound of spring, birds singing, soft breeze in the trees, the waves rolling on the beach. Space organized in such a healing way was conceptualized as *locus amoenus*, a 'lovely place'.

Landscape, in other words, is not 'environment', but 'practice', in terms of being built and curated space, and in terms of being perceived as such. Such concepts play salient roles as well in the ways Persian, or Oriental gardens were conceived. The places where the exhausted pilgrims and travellers found peace remain in memory, and their ruined remains can be found everywhere near the sites discussed in the sections above, as in the case of the ruins of a walled garden in which a 'tree of paradise' was still growing: an ancient pomegranate tree with rosehip-sized fruit in the middle of the almost completely disappeared complex of the old Emir's palace near an impoverished village in northeastern Nigeria, years ago.

In the *Encyclopaedia Iranica* (Eilers 2011) the following entry tells more about these sites:

باغ

Bāḡ, the Middle and New Persian word for "garden," as also the Sogdian βāγ, strictly meant "piece" or "patch of land," corresponding to the Gathic Avestan neuter noun *bāga-* "share," "lot" (*Y.* 51.1; see Ch. Bartholomae, *Altiranisches Wörterbuch*, Strasburg, 1904, col. 952) and to the Old Indian masculine noun *bhāgá* "share," "possession," "lot," which appears in Kauṭilya's *Arthaśāstra* with the similar connotation of a share in landed properties. [...] The old word for "garden" *paridaiza-* (Old Persian **paridayda-*), literally "walled" (whence *pardēz*, Greek *ho parádeisos* "park for animals," "paradise," Arabic *ferdaws*) survives in the New Persian *pālīz* "vegetable garden," "melon bed," though today this most often denotes an unenclosed patch.

The etymological connection of 'plot', 'land ownership', 'paradise', and 'melon bed' is first of all beautiful. The Persian gardens, which were the models for the gardens of India, the Oriental, Moorish, Andalusian, and medieval European gardens, exhibited, in addition to pomegranate trees, almond trees and oranges, along with many other beautiful plants that either smelled pleasant or tasted good, or both. The architectural design of these gardens based on the principle of the چهار باغ *čahār-bāḡ*, which is structured by canals. In such gardens, not only are the individual plants, which often have healing properties, of particular importance, but also the components of the entire space. The light of the sun, the shade of the trees, the coolness of the ground, the kiosks, and the springs reflect the order of an ideal world, its essence, its perfect condition. Gardens of this kind were used for rest and spiritual gathering, leisure and hospitality, providing shelter from the dust and noise of the city and street. An anthropopomorphic tap in such a garden is shown in Figure 5.

The fountains, which constantly splash with the help of elaborate engineering, serve another purpose, namely the design of segregated spaces in which intimate dialogue and quiet retreat are possible without violating social

Figure 5 Anthropomorphic tap in a Moorish garden

conventions. Those who are chatting near the water are not out of the sight of others, but are certainly out of their audience. What is discussed at the edge of the spring, mixes with the gurgling sounds of the water and becomes incomprehensible, although it remains audible.

The central placement of the fountain creates a stage that appears to be visible from all sides, but in a completely sensible way prevents a good auditory understanding of what is presented there. This site is a place of rest without the obligation to cleverly throw in a repartee, a clever question, an assessment. Time passes and lapses, what is said is said, and we can rest in silence or speaking, as we like, and concentrate on the voices and resonances within.

The invitation to rest and cool off in the garden relieves the guest of the task and burden of translation. The spring in the middle of the garden or the fountain in the courtyard in the *riad* thus fulfil something that is not possible beyond this *locus amoenus*: it frees the guest from the burdens of language, and yet allows him to remain in the company of others. This architecturally embedded speechlessness is the deepest form of integration that language might be given: allowing for a conversation without presupposing understanding.

6 Conclusion

Waiting and the reflection on disruption result in a gaze at language beyond the categories that are otherwise considered meaningful. There, a linguistic style or a particular terminology do not fit into where they are thrown and where they suddenly co-exist with other equally unfitting language—ghosts, poetry, luxury, silence at a roadside. Whatever does not seem to fit together—feast and street, medieval poetry and non-place, hospitality and opacity—acquires meaning and substance in settings where nothing remains but storytelling, reflection, and rest. The different languages and tales brought together where I sat in order to listen, watch, and wait offered a different gaze at language, which became simply hospitable, inclusive, and generous. Associative and boundary-crossing thought helped to pass time, deal with bland spaces, and appreciate the diverse and incomplete in language. It helped to integrate stories and narratives about what different people had left behind at different places, and what was intended to be brought along to where they hoped to go. Adeline Masquelier, in her work (2019, 2020) on the *fada*, youth clubs in Niger where unemployed young people—mostly men—while away time, drink tea, and talk, demonstrates that waiting is not only a practice that binds together places where people have been, but also utopian places. Boredom, in Masquelier's work, is where creativity, the making of futures and healing of the scars of disappointment and desperation take place. The incompleteness of tales and epistemological discourse, the jumping from here to there, crossing boundaries between languages or between talk and silence there, as well as on the roadside, serve as means to integrate, for a limited period of time, different people, cultures, histories, and knowledges. Flaherty and his colleagues (2020) suggest the term 'temporal agency' for such practices. And temporal agency in language is achieved in liminal settings, under ambiguous conditions, where the order of things gets briefly, just for a moment perhaps, interrupted. Multilingualism (a difficult term in this context) here means the capacity to use a large variety of diverse communicative strategies, in order to create conviviality and hospitality, without necessarily being forced to use these strategies in a certain 'correct' way; no truncated repertoire at work here, but openness and intuition. The valuing of incompleteness as a precondition for conviviality has been recently explored by

Nyamnjoh (2017) as a means of constructing society in Frontier Africa (also Kopytoff 1987): as we are never complete without our neighbour and cannot attain humanity without sharing, the processes that are sustained and enhanced by and in unprecedented situations, are crucial for the creation of community. The fragments brought together in the settings of waiting and disruption described here all have the power to turn into something on which a home or homeland can be built.

References

Adenkule, Julius O. 2004. *Politics and society in Nigeria's middle belt*. Trenton, NJ/ Asmara: Africa World Press.

Aikhenvald, Alexandra Y. 2016. *How gender shapes the world*. Oxford: Oxford University Press.

Badaseraye, Festus. 2018. *African Journey – A memoir*. The Mouth, special issue 1.

Badaseraye, Festus. n.d. Autobiographical texts by Nigerian migrants in Mallorca. Ms.

Bauer, Thomas. 2014. 'Male-male love in classical Arabic poetry', in E. L. McCallum and Mikko Tuhkanen (eds), *The Cambridge history of gay and lesbian literature*. Cambridge: Cambridge University Press, 107–24.

Benjamin, Walter. 2019 [1940]. 'Über den Begriff der Geschichte'. *Gesammelte Schriften* 1.2. Berlin: Suhrkamp, 691–704.

Block, David. 2014. *Social class in applied linguistics*. Oxford/New York: Routledge.

Corbin, Alain. 1988. *Le territoire du vide. L'Occident et le plaisir du rivage 1750–1840*. Paris: Flammarion.

Derrida, Jacques. 2016. *Von der Gastfreundschaft*. Vienna: Passagen.

Diawara, Manthia. 2010. *One world in relation*. Third World Newsreel.

Dixon, R. M. W. 2014. 'The non-visible marker in Dyirbal', in Alexandra Y. Aikhenvald and R. M. W. Dixon (eds), *The grammar of knowledge*. Oxford: Oxford University Press, 171–89.

Eilers, Wilhelm. 2011. 'Bagh'. *Encyclopaedia Iranica* Vol. III, Fasc. 4, 392–93. <http://www.iranicaonline.org/articles/bag-i>.

Faraclas, Nicholas (ed.). 2012. *Agency in the emergence of Creole languages*. Amsterdam: John Benjamins.

Flaherty, Michael G., Lotte Meinert, and Anne Line Dalsgård (eds). 2020. *Time work. Studies of temporal agency*. New York: Berghahn.

Gabalier, Andreas. 2015. *Hula Palu*. Universal.

Genesis, Marita. 2018. 'Archäologie der Angst. Apotropäische Praktiken auf den Richtstätten des Mittelalters und der Neuzeit als Zeichen von Aberglauben'. *Mitteilungen der Deutschen Gesellschaft für Archäologie des Mittelalters und der Neuzeit* 31: 123–34.

Ginzburg, Carlo 1990 [1976]. *The cheese and the worms: The cosmos of a sixteenth century miller*. Baltimore: Johns Hopkins University Press.

Ginzburg, Carlo. 2005 [1989]. *Hexensabbat*. Berlin: Wagenbach.

Glissant, Édouard. 1996 [1981]. *Caribbean discourse*. Charlottesville/London: University Press of Virginia.

Glissant, Édouard. 2010 [1990]. *Poetics of relation*. Ann Arbor: University of Michigan Press.

Goldschmidt, Georges Arthur. 2016. *Heidegger et la langue allemande*. Paris: CNRS.

Greenblatt, S. 2010. 'Cultural mobility. An introduction', in S. Greenblatt et al. *Cultural Mobility. A Manifesto*. Cambridge: Cambridge University Press, 1–20.

Groschwitz, Helmut. 2008. *Mondzeiten*. Münster: Waxmann.

Hoffmann-Krayer, Eduard and Hanns Bächthold-Stäubli. 1935/36. *Handwörterbuch des deutschen Aberglaubens*, vol. 7. Berlin/Leipzig: De Gruyter.

Jaworksi, Adam and Crispin Thurlow. 2010. 'Introducing semiotic landscapes', in Adam Jaworski and Crispin Thurlow (eds), *Semiotic landscapes*. London/New York: Continuum, 1–40.

Jones, Alan and Richard Hitchcock (eds). 1991. *Studies on the muwaššah and the kharja*. Oxford: Ithaca Press.

Kopytoff, Igor (ed.). 1987. *The African frontier: The reproduction of traditional African society*. Bloomington: Indiana University Press.

Kosrof, Wosene Worke. 2007. 'The color of words', in M. Nooter Roberts, E. Harney, A. Purpura, and C. Mullen Kreamer (eds), *Inscribing meaning: Writing and graphic systems in African art*. Los Angeles: Smithsonian, 237–41.

Kremer, Peter. 2003. *Wo das Grauen lauert*. Düren: Pekade.

Lüpke, Friederike and Anne Storch. 2013. *Repertoires and choices in African languages*. Berlin: Mouton De Gruyter.

Masquelier, Adeline. 2019. *Fada. Boredom and belonging in Niger*. Chicago: University of Chicago Press.

Masquelier, Adeline. 2020. 'The work of waiting: Boredom, teatime, and future-making in Niger', in Michael G. Flaherty, Lotte Meinert, and Anne Line Dalsgård (eds), *Time work. Studies of temporal agency*. New York: Berghahn, 175–92.

Mbembe, Achille. 2017. *Critique of Black reason*. Durham, NC: Duke.

Mietzner, Angelika and Anne Storch. 2021 *Language and tourism in East Africa: A ruinous system*. Bristol: Channel View.

Nyamnjoh, Francis B. 2017. 'Incompleteness: Frontier Africa and the currency of conviviality'. *Journal of Asian and African Studies* 52 (3): 253–70.

Phipps, Alison. 2007. *Learning the arts of survival. Languaging, Tourism, Life.* Clevedon: Channel.

Piller, Ingrid. 2016. *Linguistic diversity and social justice.* Oxford: Oxford University Press.

Rodinson, Maxime. 2006. 'Venice, the spice trade and eastern influences on European cooking', in Maxime Rodinson, A. J. Arberry, and Charles Perry (eds), *Medieval Arab cookery.* Totnes: Prospect, 199–216.

Rötgens, Michael, Hartmut Weßling, and Peter Wackel. 2018. *I love Mallorca.* Xtreme Sound.

Seebach, Helmut. 2002. *Odenwälder Brauchtum: Mit Fotografien aus dem Nachlaß von Heinrich Winter.* Weinheim: Diesbach.

Smith, M. A. 2019. *Senegal abroad.* Madison: University of Wisconsin Press.

Stoler, Ann Laura. 2013. 'Introduction. "The rot remains": from ruins to ruination', in Ann Laura Stoler (ed.), *Imperial Debris.* Durham, NC: Duke, 1–37.

Storch, Anne. 1999. *Das Hone und seine Stellung im Zentral-Jukunoid.* Cologne: Köppe.

Storch, Anne. 2013. 'How the West was won: Ways of making history in Hone (Jukun, Nigeria)'. *Frankfurter Afrikanistische Blätter* 18: 185–205.

Storch, Anne. 2017. 'Emotional edgelands', in Anne Storch (ed.), *Consensus and dissent: Negotiating emotion in the public space.* Amsterdam: John Benjamins, 193–212.

Storch, Anne. 2020. 'Die Prekarität der Anderen'. *Wiener Linguistische Gazette* 85: 1–21.

Storch, Anne and Nico Nassenstein. 2020. 'Balamane: variations on a noisy ground', pp. 23–51 of *Kontradiktorische Diskurse und Macht im Widerspruch,* edited by Warnke, Ingo H, Hornidge, Anna-Katharina, Schattenberg, Susanne. Berlin: Springer Verlag.

Szakolczai, Arpad. 2009. 'Liminality and experience: Structuring transitory situations and transformative events'. *International Political Anthropology* 2 (1): 141–72.

Tarkovsky, Andrei. 1983. *Nostalghia.* Rome: Gaumont.

Taussig, Michael. 2015. *The Corn Wolf.* Chicago: University of Chicago Press.

Turner, Victor. 1969: *The ritual process: Structure and antistructure.* New York: PAJ.

Wing, Betsy. 2010. 'Translator's introduction', in Édouard Glissant (ed.), *Poetics of relation.* Ann Arbor: University of Michigan Press, xi–xx.

Wodak, Ruth. 2015. *The politics of fear.* London: Sage.

Zwartjes, Otto. 1997. *Love songs from al-Andalus: History, structure, and meaning of the Kharja.* Leiden/New York: Brill.

Index of authors

Index of languages, language families, and linguistic areas

Index of subjects

.